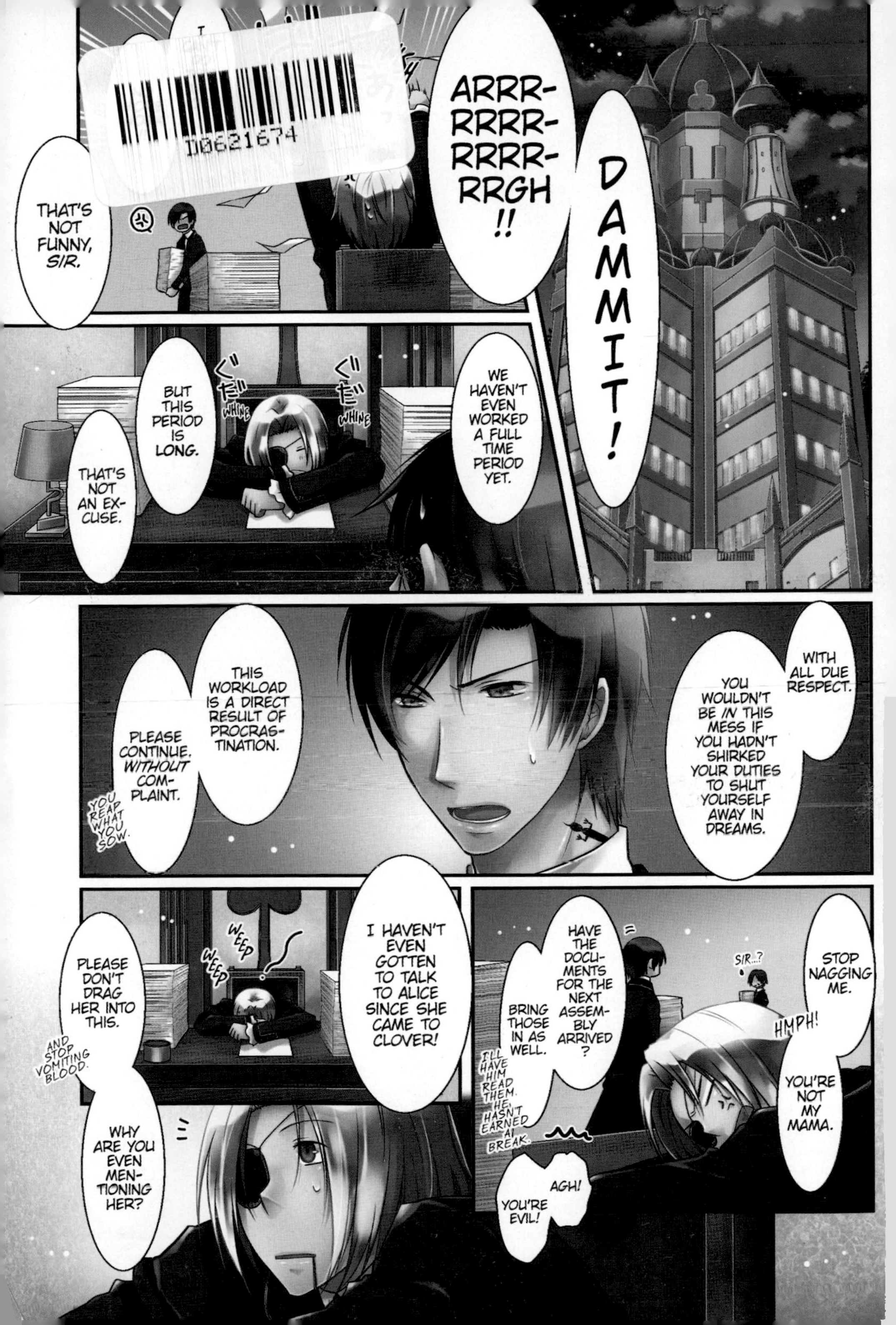
DAMMIT!
ARRRRRRRRRRRRGH!!
THAT'S NOT FUNNY, SIR.
WE HAVEN'T EVEN WORKED A FULL TIME PERIOD YET.
ぐだ WHINE
ぐだ WHINE
BUT THIS PERIOD IS LONG.
THAT'S NOT AN EXCUSE.
WITH ALL DUE RESPECT.
YOU WOULDN'T BE IN THIS MESS IF YOU HADN'T SHIRKED YOUR DUTIES TO SHUT YOURSELF AWAY IN DREAMS.
THIS WORKLOAD IS A DIRECT RESULT OF PROCRASTINATION.
PLEASE CONTINUE. WITHOUT COMPLAINT.
YOU REAP WHAT YOU SOW.
STOP NAGGING ME.
SIR...?
HMPH!
YOU'RE NOT MY MAMA.
HAVE THE DOCUMENTS FOR THE NEXT ASSEMBLY ARRIVED?
BRING THOSE IN AS WELL.
I'LL HAVE HIM READ THEM. HE HASN'T EARNED A BREAK.
AGH!
YOU'RE EVIL!
I HAVEN'T EVEN GOTTEN TO TALK TO ALICE SINCE SHE CAME TO CLOVER!
WEEP
WEEP
PLEASE DON'T DRAG HER INTO THIS.
AND STOP VOMITING BLOOD.
WHY ARE YOU EVEN MENTIONING HER?

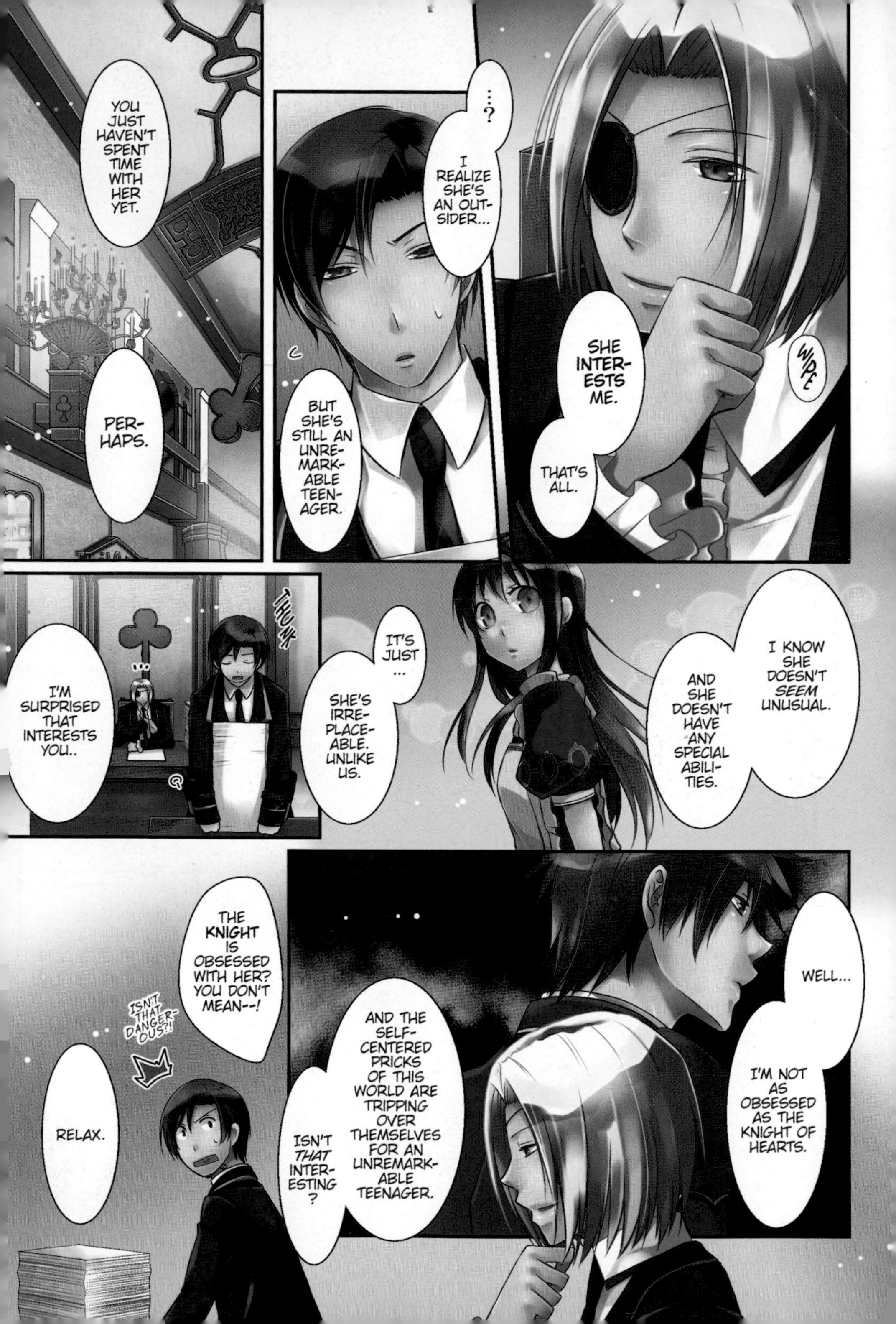
WIPE
SHE INTERESTS ME.
THAT'S ALL.
...?
I REALIZE SHE'S AN OUTSIDER...
BUT SHE'S STILL AN UNREMARKABLE TEENAGER.
YOU JUST HAVEN'T SPENT TIME WITH HER YET.
PERHAPS.
I KNOW SHE DOESN'T *SEEM* UNUSUAL.
AND SHE DOESN'T HAVE ANY SPECIAL ABILITIES.
IT'S JUST...
SHE'S IRREPLACEABLE. UNLIKE US.
THUNK
...
I'M SURPRISED THAT INTERESTS YOU..
WELL...
I'M NOT AS OBSESSED AS THE KNIGHT OF HEARTS.
THE **KNIGHT** IS OBSESSED WITH HER? YOU DON'T MEAN--!
ISN'T THAT DANGEROUS?!
AND THE SELF-CENTERED PRICKS OF THIS WORLD ARE TRIPPING OVER THEMSELVES FOR AN UNREMARKABLE TEENAGER.
ISN'T *THAT* INTERESTING?
RELAX.

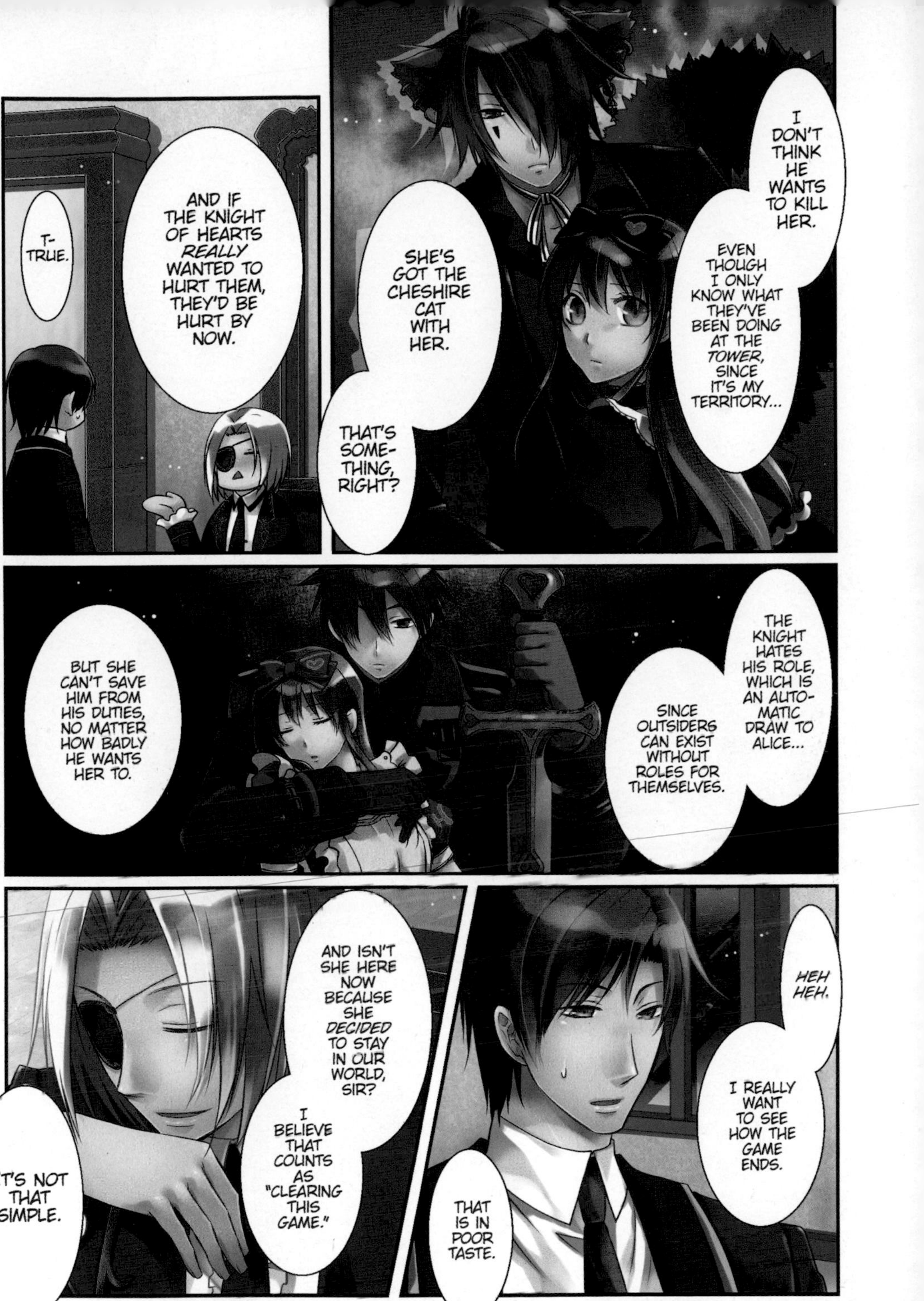
I DON'T THINK HE WANTS TO KILL HER.
EVEN THOUGH I ONLY KNOW WHAT THEY'VE BEEN DOING AT THE *TOWER*, SINCE IT'S MY TERRITORY...
SHE'S GOT THE CHESHIRE CAT WITH HER.
THAT'S SOME-THING, RIGHT?
AND IF THE KNIGHT OF HEARTS *REALLY* WANTED TO HURT THEM, THEY'D BE HURT BY NOW.
T-TRUE.
THE KNIGHT HATES HIS ROLE, WHICH IS AN AUTO-MATIC DRAW TO ALICE...
SINCE OUTSIDERS CAN EXIST WITHOUT ROLES FOR THEMSELVES.
BUT SHE CAN'T SAVE HIM FROM HIS DUTIES, NO MATTER HOW BADLY HE WANTS HER TO.
HEH HEH.
I REALLY WANT TO SEE HOW THE GAME ENDS.
THAT IS IN POOR TASTE.
AND ISN'T SHE HERE NOW BECAUSE SHE *DECIDED* TO STAY IN OUR WORLD, SIR?
I BELIEVE THAT COUNTS AS "CLEARING THIS GAME."
IT'S NOT THAT SIMPLE.

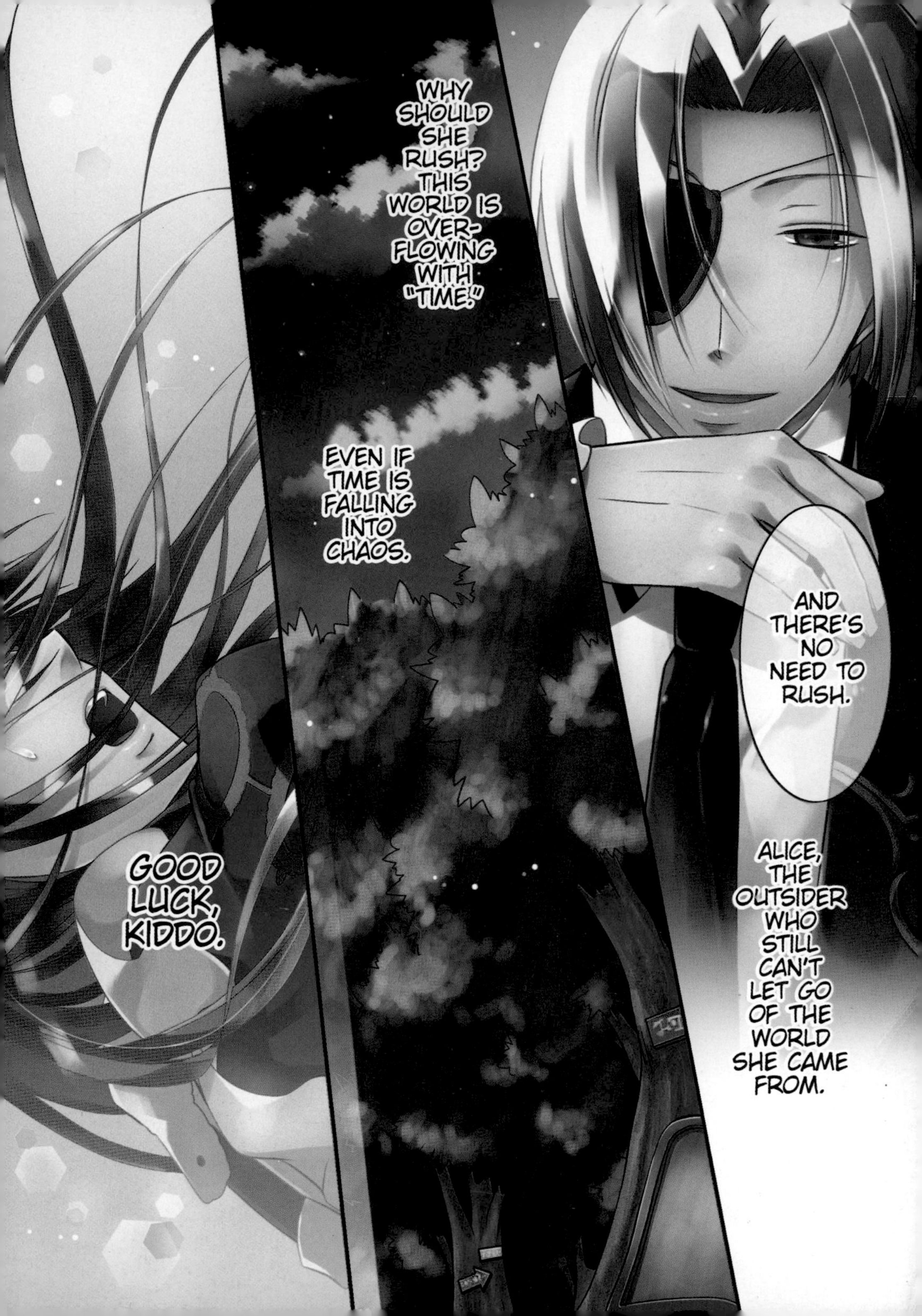
AND THERE'S NO NEED TO RUSH.
ALICE, THE OUTSIDER WHO STILL CAN'T LET GO OF THE WORLD SHE CAME FROM.
WHY SHOULD SHE RUSH? THIS WORLD IS OVER-FLOWING WITH "TIME."
EVEN IF TIME IS FALLING INTO CHAOS.
GOOD LUCK, KIDDO.

Alice in the Country of Clover
~Cheshire Cat Waltz~ 3

Mamenosuke Fujimaru

藤丸 豆ノ介

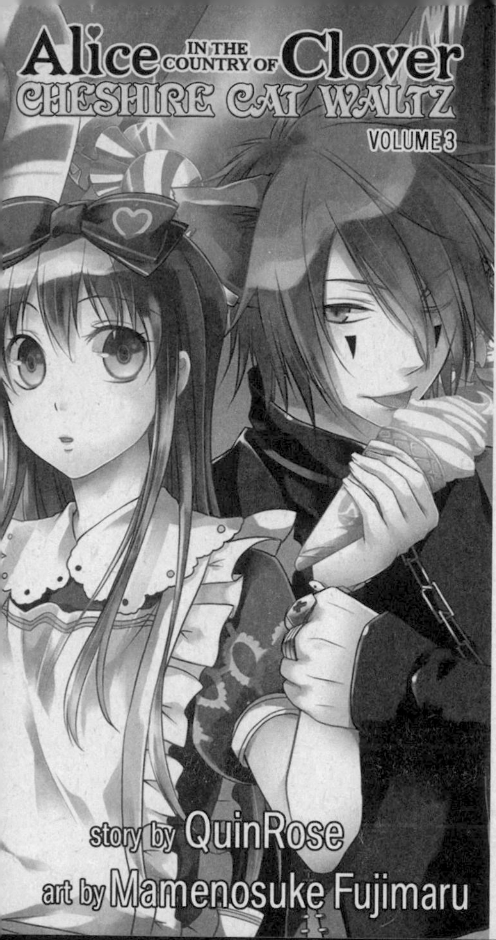
Alice IN THE COUNTRY OF Clover
CHESHIRE CAT WALTZ
VOLUME 3
story by QuinRose
art by Mamenosuke Fujimaru

STAFF CREDITS

translation Angela Liu
adaptation Lianne Sentar
lettering Roland Amago
layout Bambi Eloriaga-Amago
cover design Nicky Lim
copy editor Shanti Whitesides
editor Adam Arnold

publisher Jason DeAngelis
Seven Seas Entertainment

ALICE IN THE COUNTRY OF CLOVER: CHESHIRE CAT WALTZ VOL. 3

First published in Japan in 2010 by ICHIJINSHA Inc., Tokyo.
English translation rights arranged with ICHIJINSHA Inc., Tokyo, Japan.

ISBN: 978-1-935934-93-6

Printed in Canada

First Printing: November 2012

10 9 8 7 6 5 4 3

READING DIRECTIONS

This book reads from ***right to left***, Japanese style. If this is your first time reading manga, you start reading from the top right panel on each page and take it from there. If you get lost, just follow the numbered diagram here. It may seem backwards at first, but you'll get the hang of it! Have fun!!

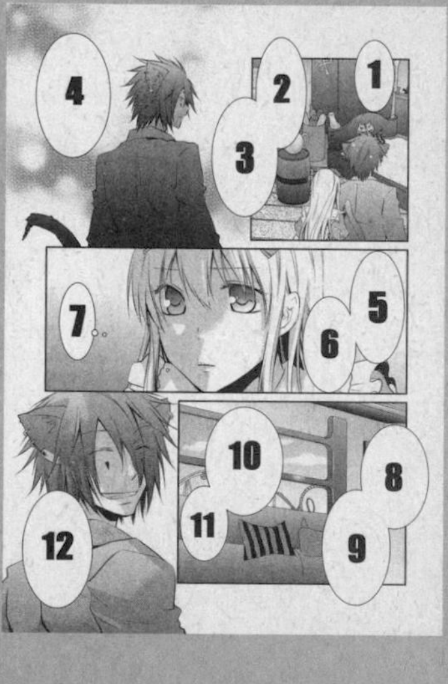
1
2
3
4
5
6
7
8
9
10
11
12

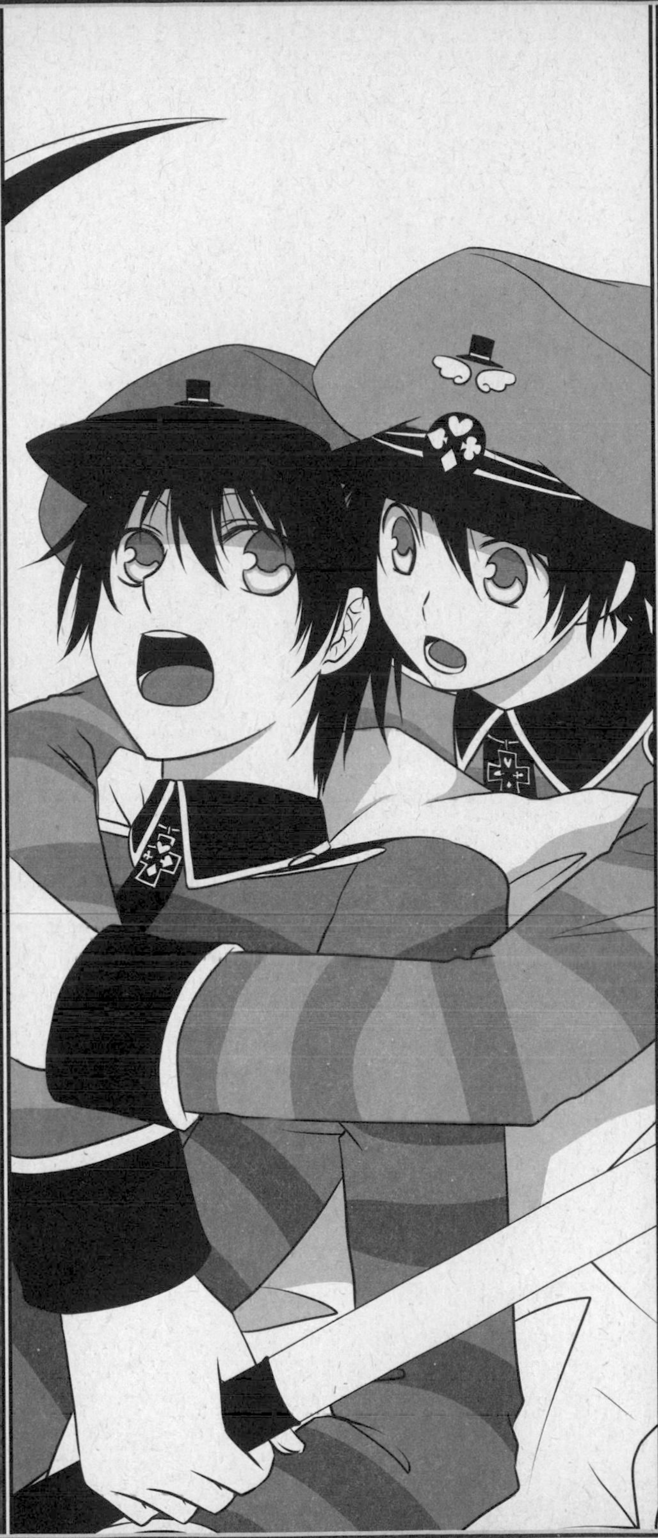

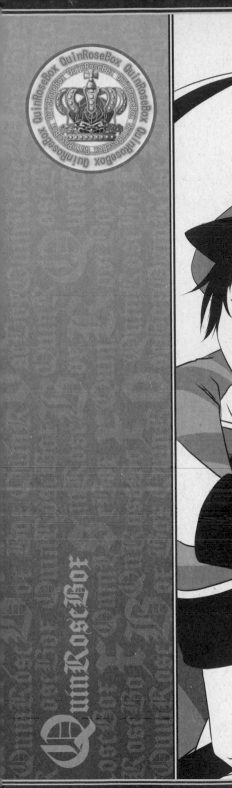

Alice in the Country of Clover
クローバーの国の
アリス
~Wonderful Wonder World~

- STORY -

In *Alice in the Country of Clover*, the game starts with Alice having not fallen in love, but still deciding to stay in Wonderland.

She's acquainted with all the characters from the previous game, *Alice in the Country of Hearts*.

Since love would now start from a place of friendship rather than passion with a new stranger, she can experience a different type of romance from that in the previous game. Her dynamic with the characters is different through this friendship—characters can't always be forceful with her, and in many ways it's more comfortable to grow intimate. The relationships *between* the Ones With Duties have also become more of a factor.

In this game, the story focuses on the mafia. Alice attends the suited meetings (forcefully) and gets involved in various gunfights (forcefully), among other things.

Land fluctuations, sea creatures in the forest, and whispering doors--it's a game more fantastic and more eerie than the first.

Will our everywoman Alice be able to have a romantic relationship in a world devoid of common sense?

Alice in the Country of Clover
Character Information

Elliot March
VA: Tsuguo Mogami

Blood's right-hand man has a criminal past... and a temperamental present. But he's not as bad as he used to be, so that's something. Joining Blood has been good(?) for him.

Blood Dupre
VA: Katsuyuki Konishi

The head of the mafia Hatter Family, Blood is a cunning yet moody puppet-master. Alice now has the pleasure of having him for a landlord.

Alice Liddell
VA: Rie Kugimiya

A normal girl with a bit of a chip on her shoulder. Deciding to stay in the Wonderland she was carried to, she's adapted to her strange new lifestyle.

Vivaldi
VA: Yuuko Kaida

The beautiful Queen of Hearts has an unrivaled temper—which is really saying something in Wonderland. Although a picture-perfect Mad Queen, she cares for Alice as if Alice were her little sister...or a very interesting plaything.

Tweedle Dum
VA: Jun Fukuyama

The second "Bloody Twin" is equally cute and equally scary. In *Clover*, Dum can also turn into an adult.

Tweedle Dee
VA: Jun Fukuyama

One of the "Bloody Twin" gatekeepers of the Hatter territory, Dee can be cute when he's not being terrifying. In *Clover*, he sometimes turns into an adult.

Boris Airay
VA: Noriaki Sugiyama

This riddle-loving cat has a signature smirk—and in *Clover*, a new toy. One of his favorite pastimes is giving the Sleepy Mouse a hard time.

Ace
VA: Daisuke Hirakawa

The unlucky knight of Hearts was a former subordinate of Vivaldi and is perpetually lost. Even though he's depressed to be separated from his friend and boss Julius, he stays positive and tries to overcome it with a smile. He seems like a classic nice guy... or is he?

Peter White
VA: Kouki Miyata

The Prime Minister of Heart Castle—who has rabbit ears growing out of his head—invited (kidnapped) Alice to Wonderland. He loves Alice and hates everything else. His cruel, irrational actions are disturbing, but he acts like a completely different person (rabbit?) when in the throes of his love for Alice.

Gray Ringmarc
VA: Kazuya Nakai

Nightmare's subordinate in *Clover*. He used to have strong social ambition and considered assassinating Nightmare... but since Nightmare was such a useless boss, Gray couldn't help but feel sorry for him and ended up a dedicated assistant. He's a sound thinker with a strong work ethic. He's also highly skilled with his blades, rivaling even Ace.

Nightmare Gottschalk
VA: Tomokazu Sugita

A sickly nightmare who hates the hospital and needles. He has the power to read people's thoughts and enter dreams. Even though he likes to shut himself away in dreams, Gray drags him out to sulk from time to time. He technically holds a high position and has many subordinates, but since he can't even take care of his own self, he leaves most things to Gray.

Pierce Villiers
VA: Souichirou Hoshi

New to *Clover*, Pierce is an insomniac mouse who drinks too much coffee. He loves Nightmare (who can help him sleep) and hates Boris (who terrifies him). He dislikes Blood and Vivaldi for discarding coffee in favor of tea. He likes Elliot and Peter well enough, since rabbits aren't natural predators of mice.

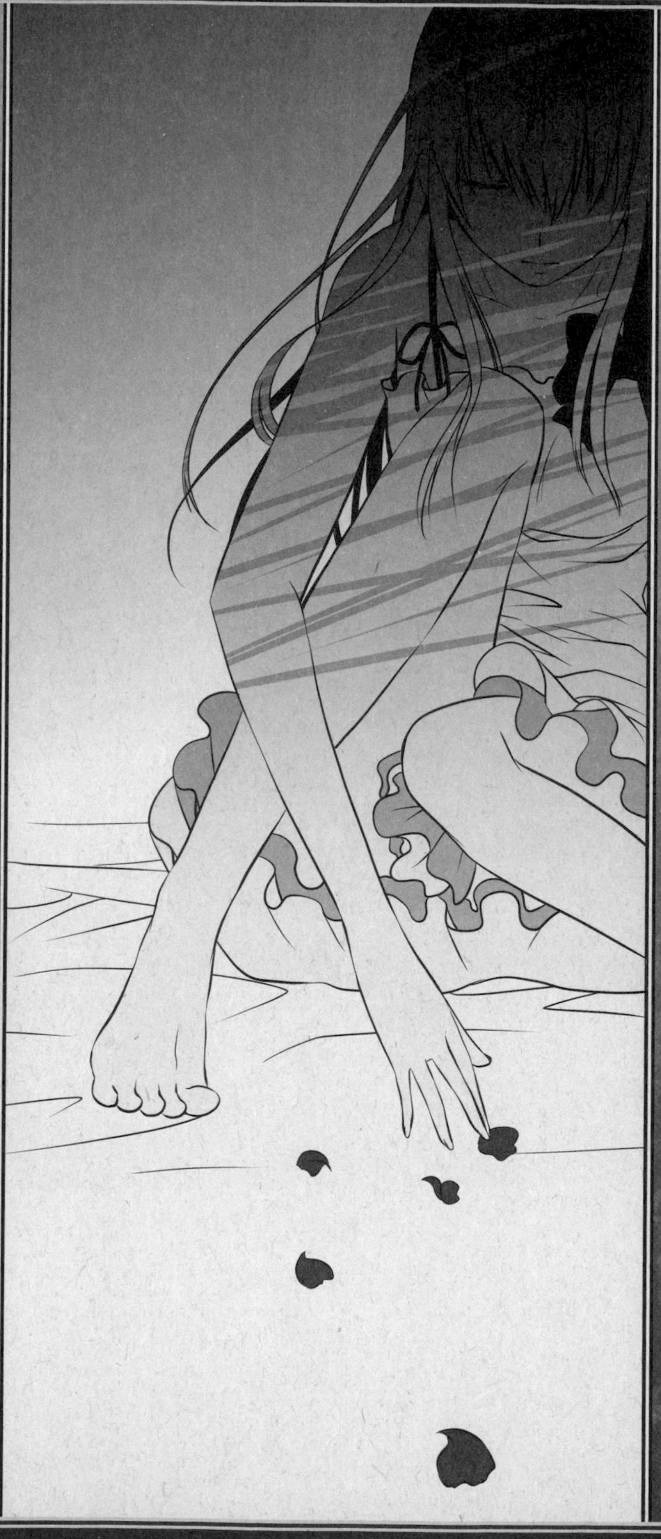

QuinRoseBox

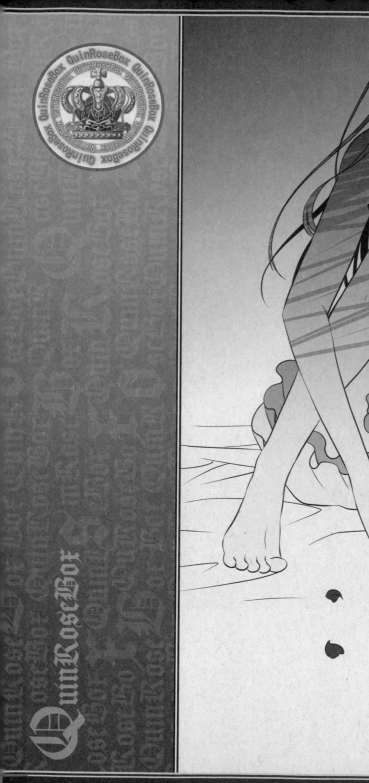

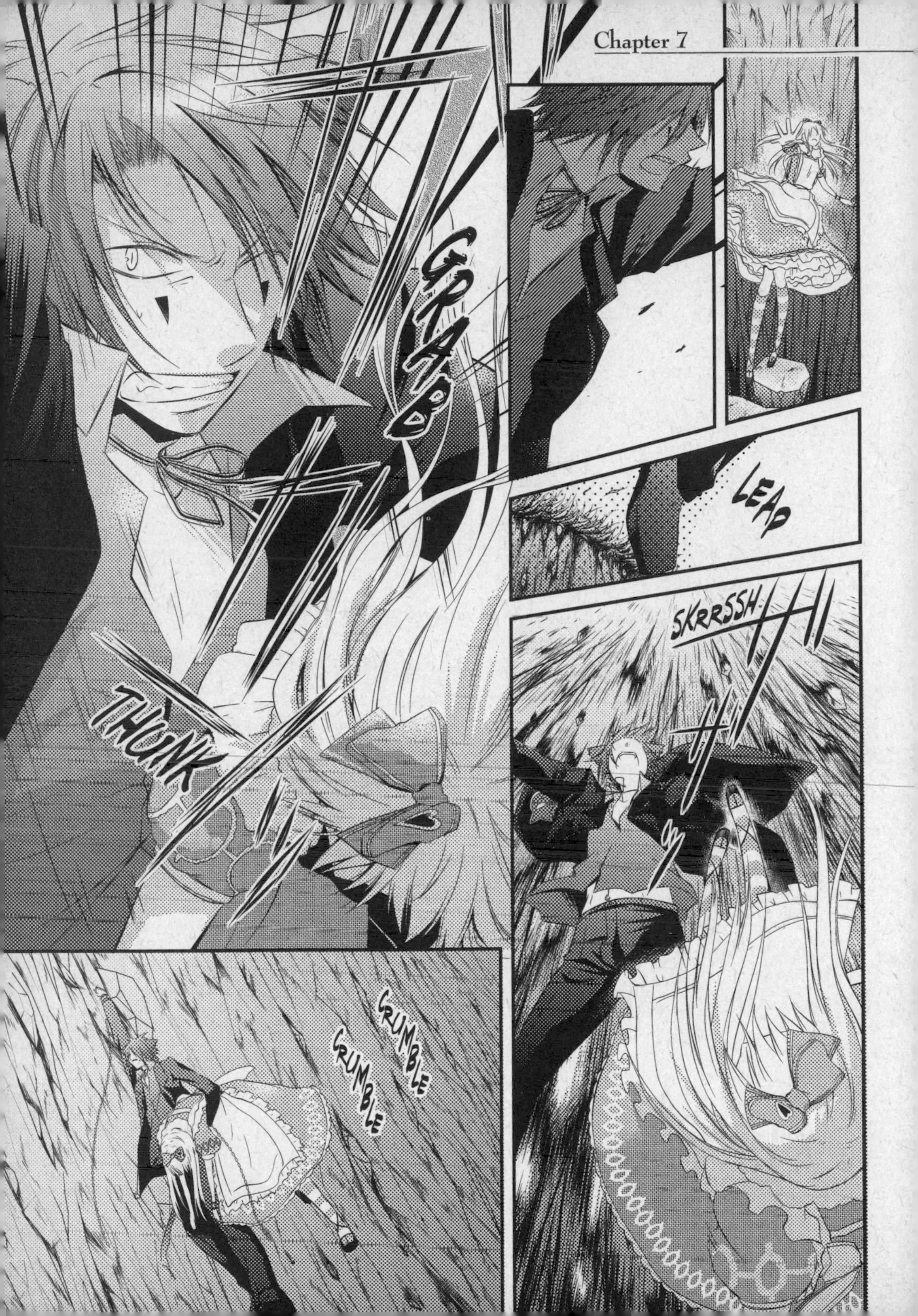
LEAP
SKRRSSH
GRABB
THUNK
CRUMBLE
CRUMBLE

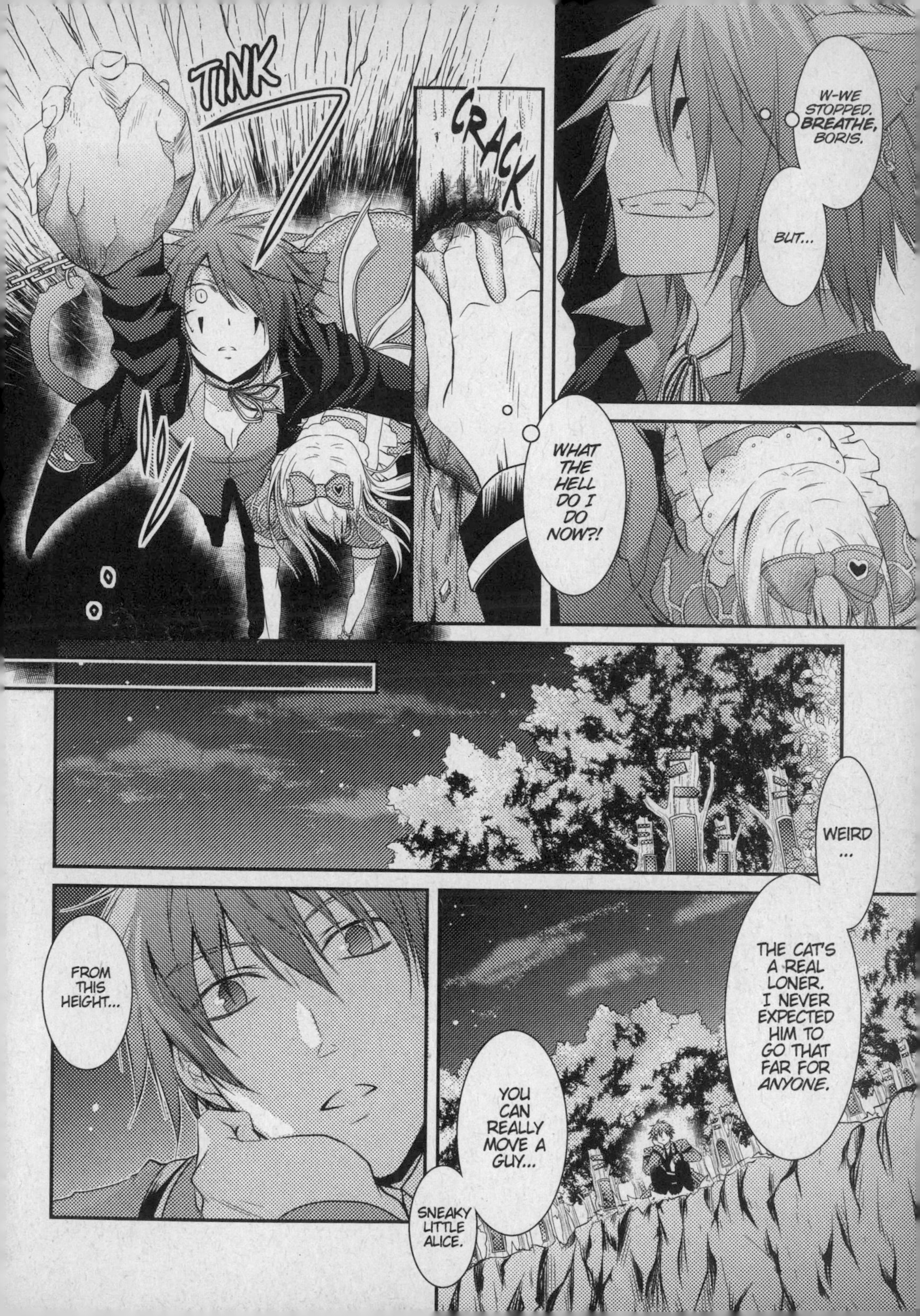
W-WE STOPPED. BREATHE, BORIS.
BUT...
WHAT THE HELL DO I DO NOW?!
CRACK
TINK
WEIRD...
THE CAT'S A REAL LONER. I NEVER EXPECTED HIM TO GO THAT FAR FOR ANYONE.
YOU CAN REALLY MOVE A GUY...
SNEAKY LITTLE ALICE.
FROM THIS HEIGHT...

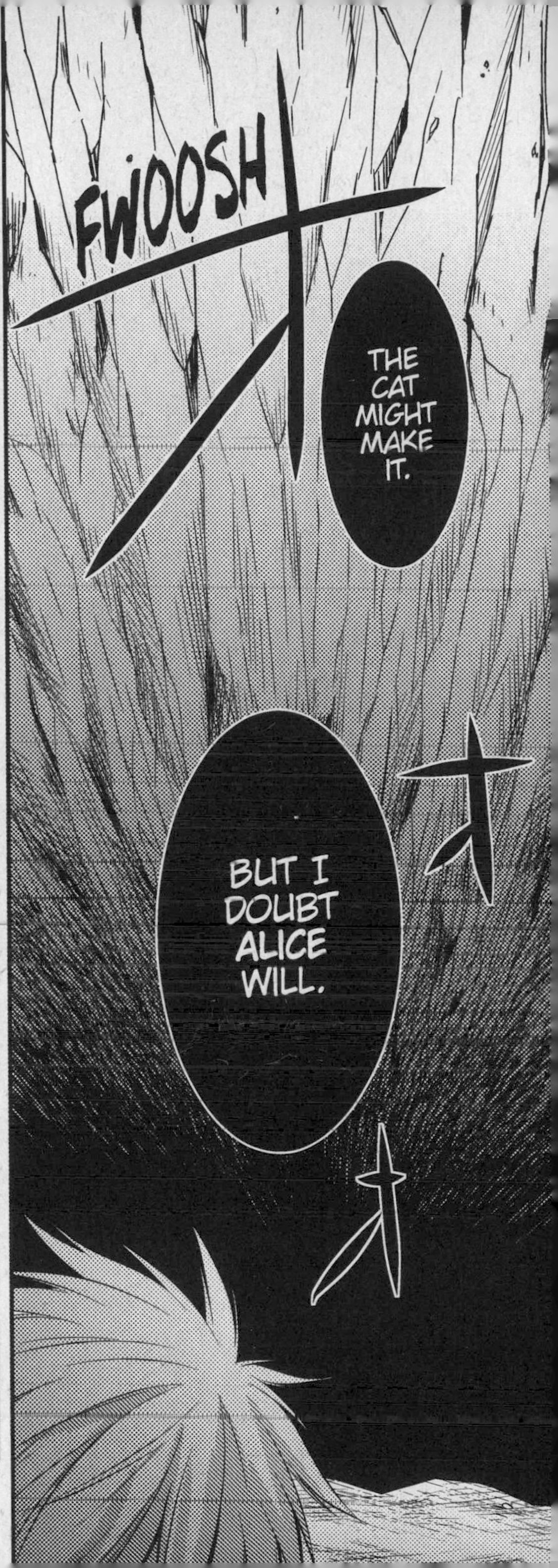
FWOOSH
THE CAT MIGHT MAKE IT.
BUT I DOUBT ALICE WILL.

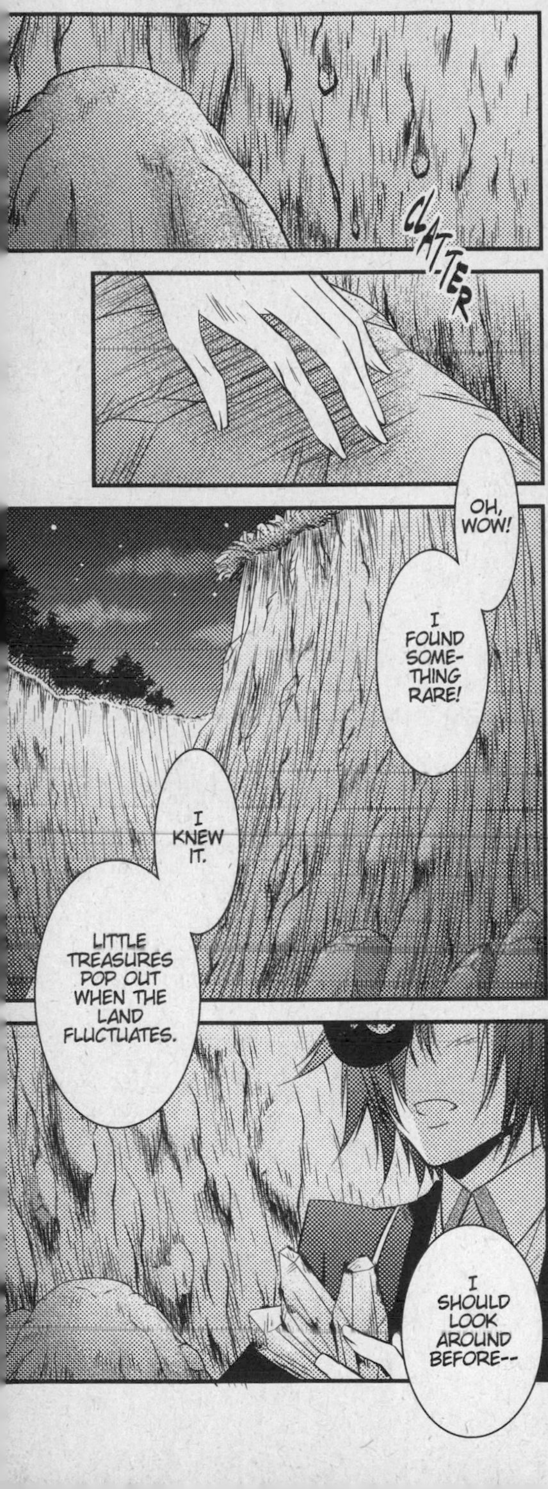
CLAT-TER
OH, WOW!
I FOUND SOME-THING RARE!
I KNEW IT.
LITTLE TREASURES POP OUT WHEN THE LAND FLUCTUATES.
I SHOULD LOOK AROUND BEFORE--

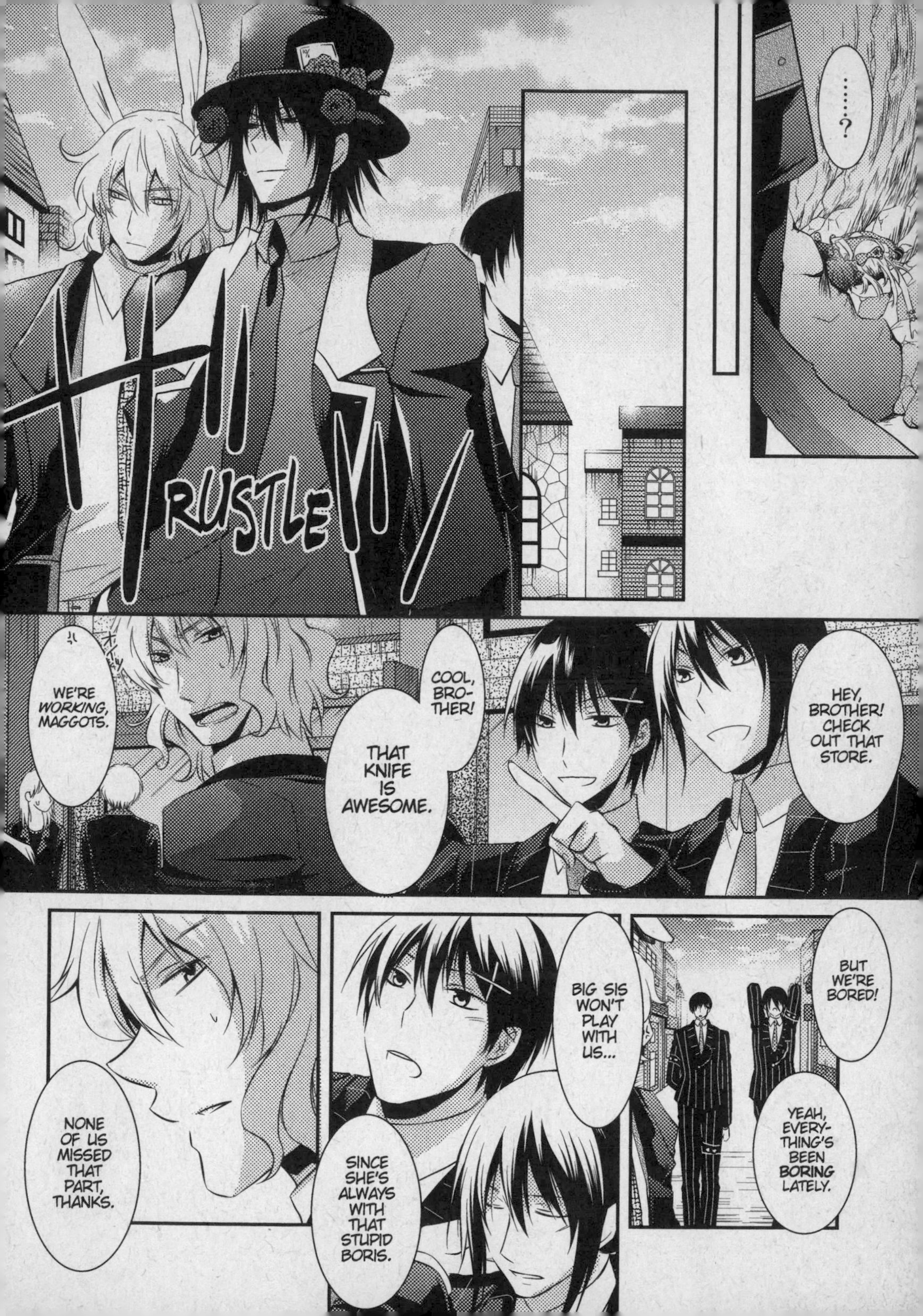
……?
RUSTLE
HEY, BROTHER! CHECK OUT THAT STORE.
COOL, BROTHER!
THAT KNIFE IS AWESOME.
WE'RE WORKING, MAGGOTS.
BUT WE'RE BORED!
YEAH, EVERY-THING'S BEEN BORING LATELY.
BIG SIS WON'T PLAY WITH US...
SINCE SHE'S ALWAYS WITH THAT STUPID BORIS.
NONE OF US MISSED THAT PART, THANKS.

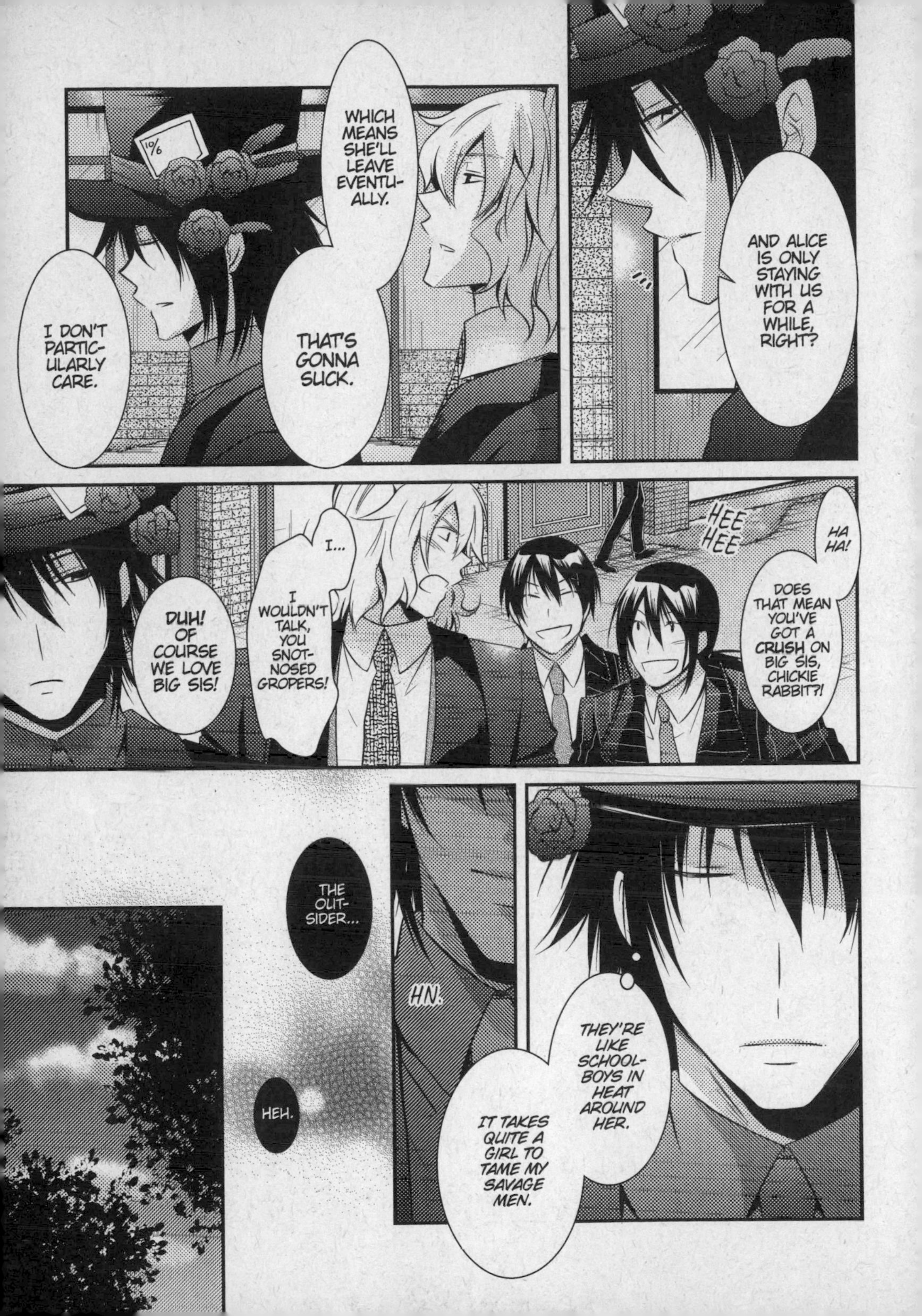
...
AND ALICE IS ONLY STAYING WITH US FOR A WHILE, RIGHT?
WHICH MEANS SHE'LL LEAVE EVENTU-ALLY.
THAT'S GONNA SUCK.
I DON'T PARTIC-ULARLY CARE.
HA HA!
HEE HEE
DOES THAT MEAN YOU'VE GOT A CRUSH ON BIG SIS, CHICKIE RABBIT?!
I...
I WOULDN'T TALK, YOU SNOT-NOSED GROPERS!
DUH! OF COURSE WE LOVE BIG SIS!
HN.
THEY'RE LIKE SCHOOL-BOYS IN HEAT AROUND HER.
IT TAKES QUITE A GIRL TO TAME MY SAVAGE MEN.
THE OUT-SIDER...
HEH.

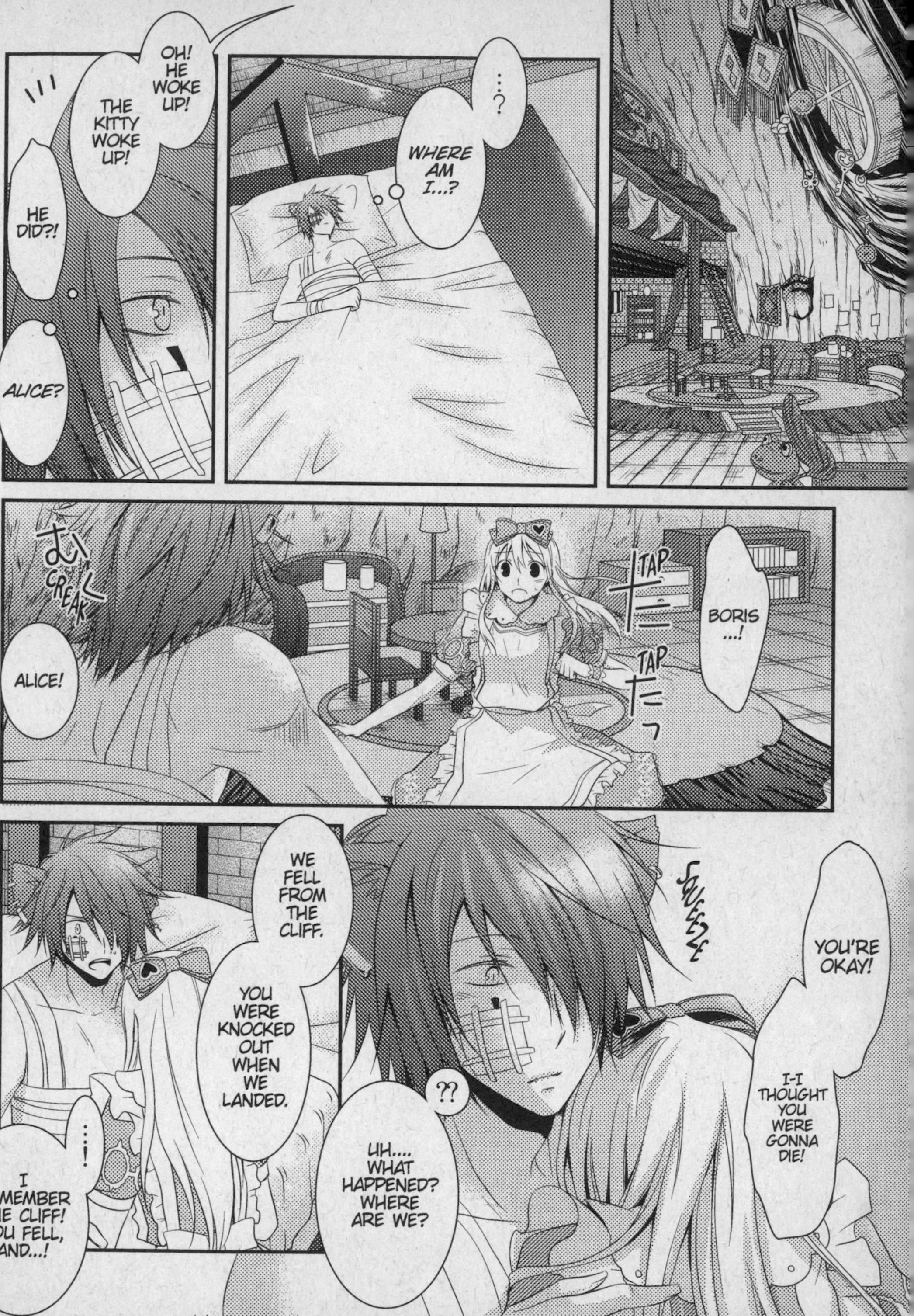
...?
WHERE AM I...?
OH! HE WOKE UP! THE KITTY WOKE UP!
HE DID?!
ALICE?
BORIS ...!
TAP
TAP
CREAK
ALICE!
YOU'RE OKAY!
SQUEEZE
I-I THOUGHT YOU WERE GONNA DIE!
??
UH.... WHAT HAPPENED? WHERE ARE WE?
WE FELL FROM THE CLIFF.
YOU WERE KNOCKED OUT WHEN WE LANDED.
...!
I REMEMBER THE CLIFF! YOU FELL, AND...!

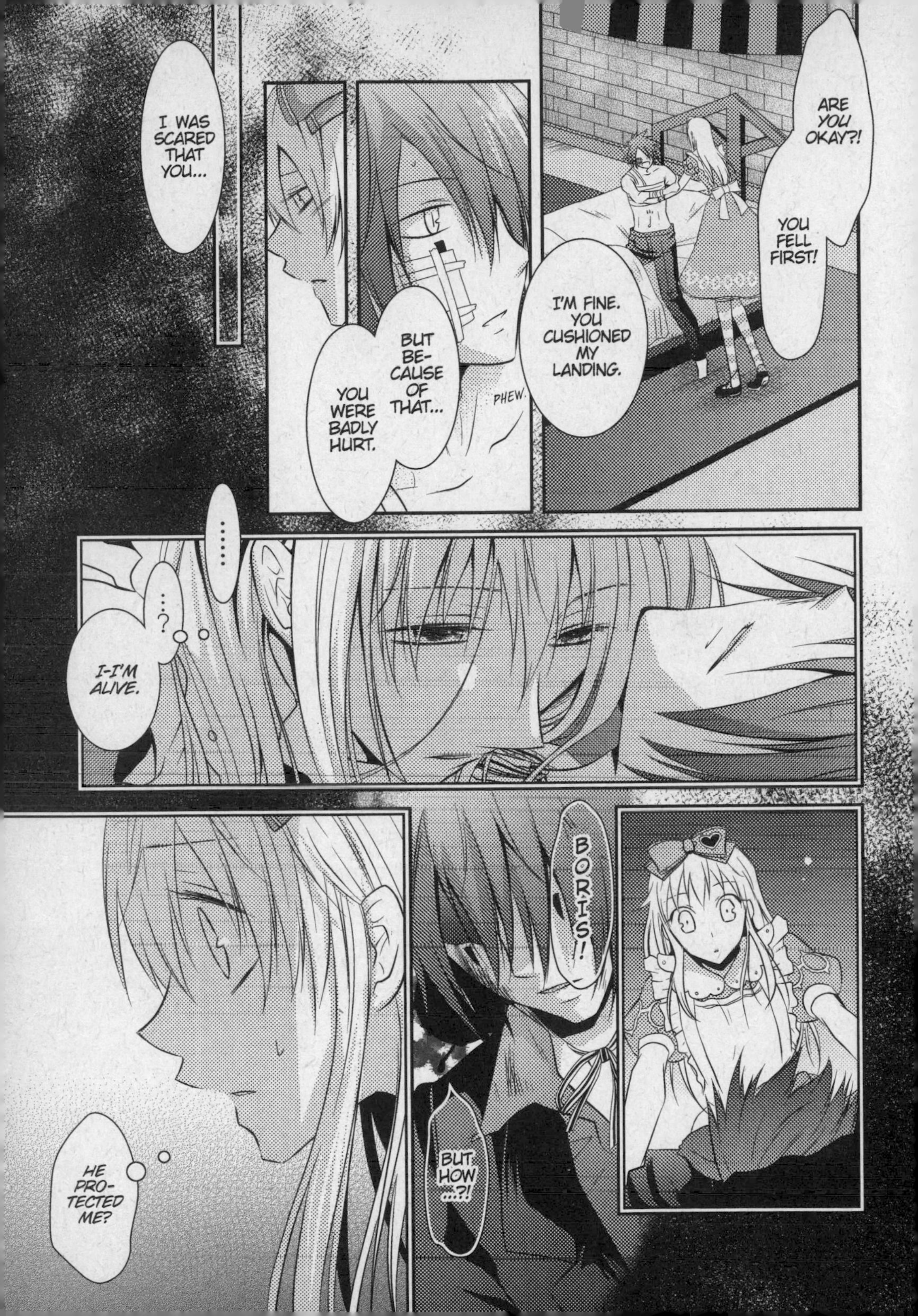
ARE YOU OKAY?!
YOU FELL FIRST!
I'M FINE. YOU CUSHIONED MY LANDING.
PHEW.
BUT BE-CAUSE OF THAT...
YOU WERE BADLY HURT.
I WAS SCARED THAT YOU...
......
...?
I-I'M ALIVE.
BORIS!
BUT. HOW ...?!
HE PRO-TECTED ME?

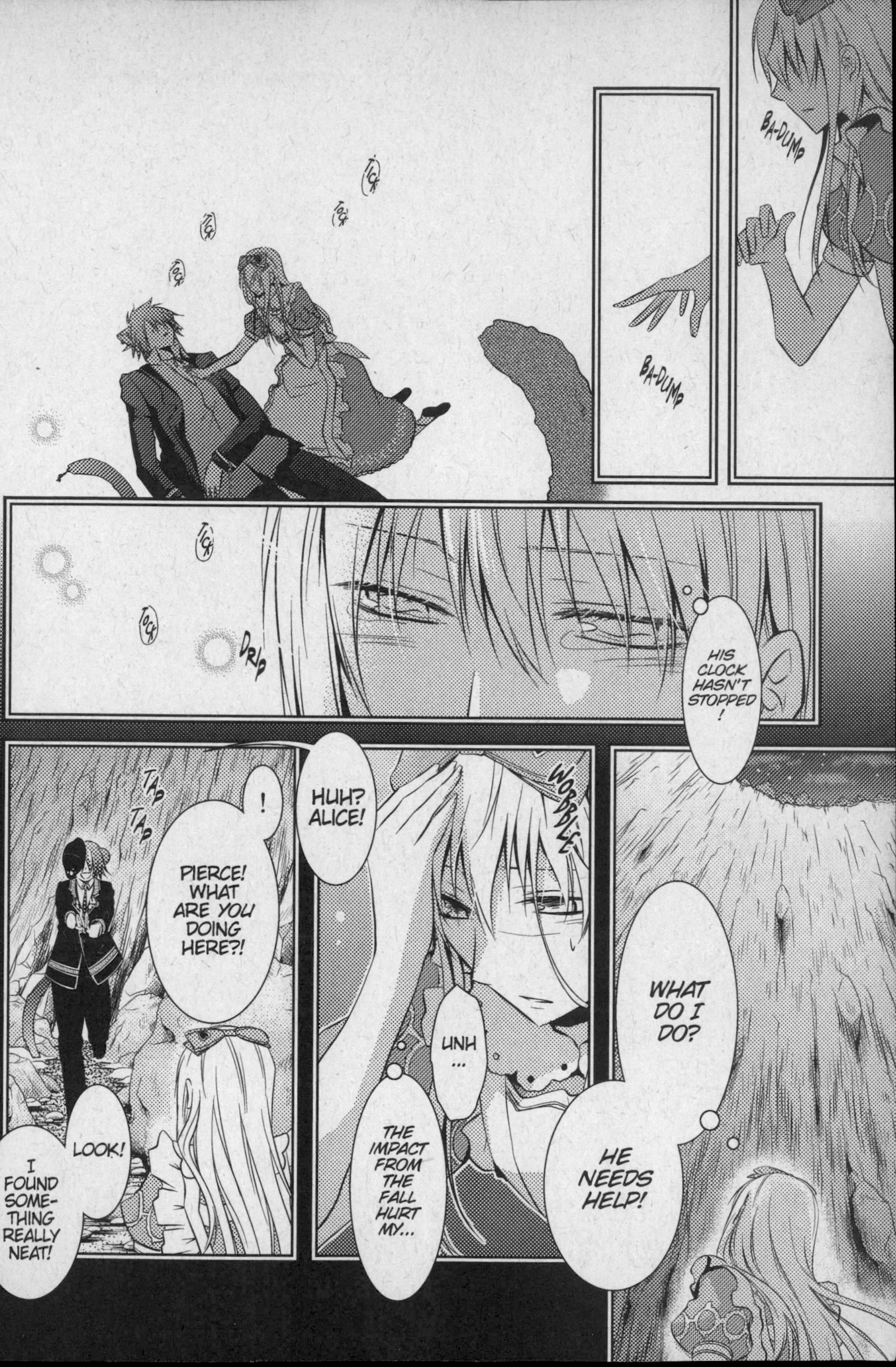
BA-DUMP
BA-DUMP
TICK
TOCK
TICK
TOCK
TICK
TOCK
DRIP
HIS CLOCK HASN'T STOPPED!
WHAT DO I DO?
HE NEEDS HELP!
WOBBLE
UNH...
THE IMPACT FROM THE FALL HURT MY...
HUH? ALICE!
!
PIERCE! WHAT ARE YOU DOING HERE?!
TAP TAP
LOOK!
I FOUND SOME-THING REALLY NEAT!

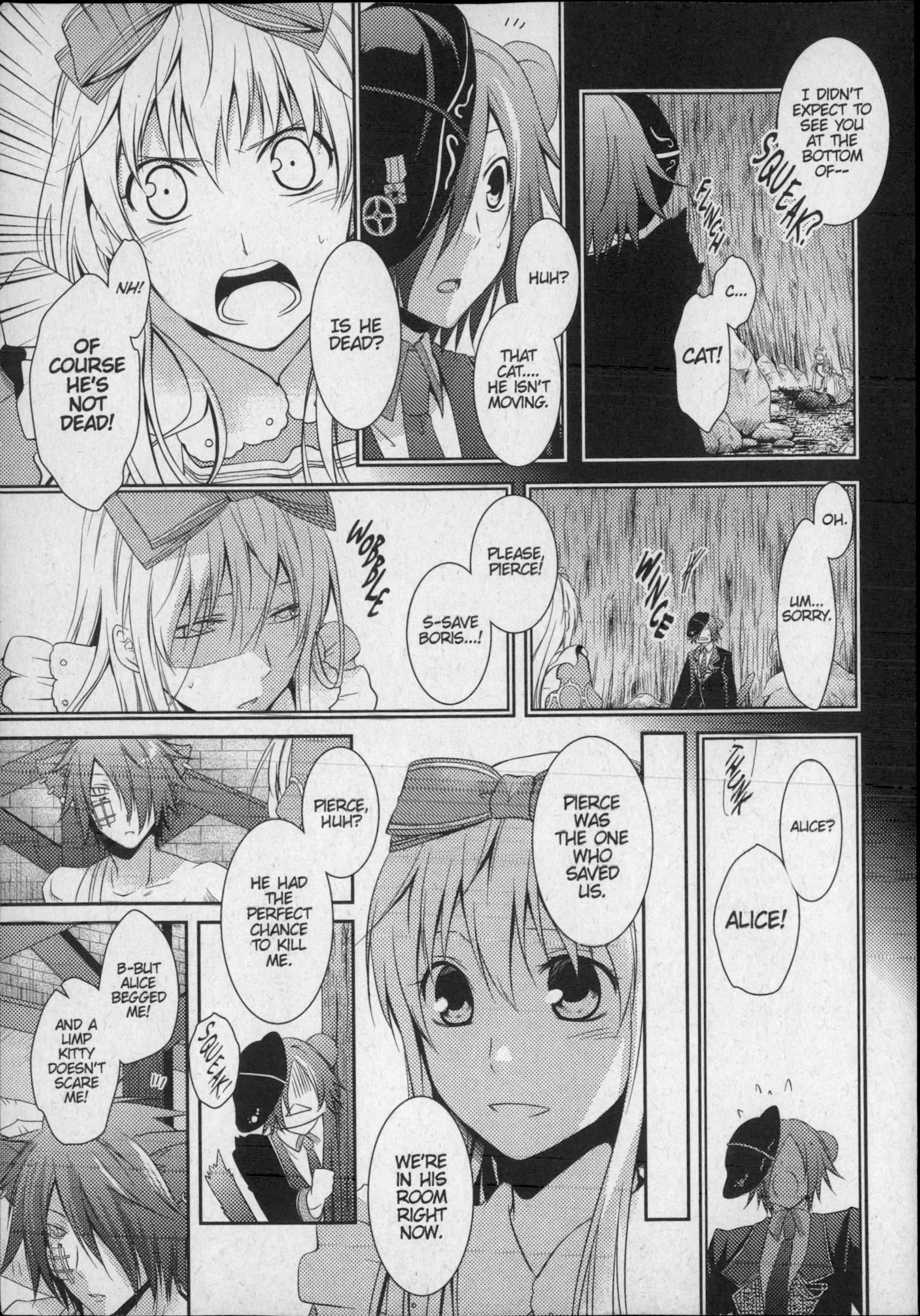
I DIDN'T EXPECT TO SEE YOU AT THE BOTTOM OF--
SQUEAK!?
FLINCH
C...
CAT!
HUH?
THAT CAT.... HE ISN'T MOVING.
IS HE DEAD?
NH!
OF COURSE HE'S NOT DEAD!
OH.
UM... SORRY.
WINCE
PLEASE, PIERCE!
S-SAVE BORIS...!
WOBBLE
THUNK
ALICE?
ALICE!
PIERCE WAS THE ONE WHO SAVED US.
WE'RE IN HIS ROOM RIGHT NOW.
PIERCE, HUH?
HE HAD THE PERFECT CHANCE TO KILL ME.
B-BUT ALICE BEGGED ME!
SQUEAK!
AND A LIMP KITTY DOESN'T SCARE ME!

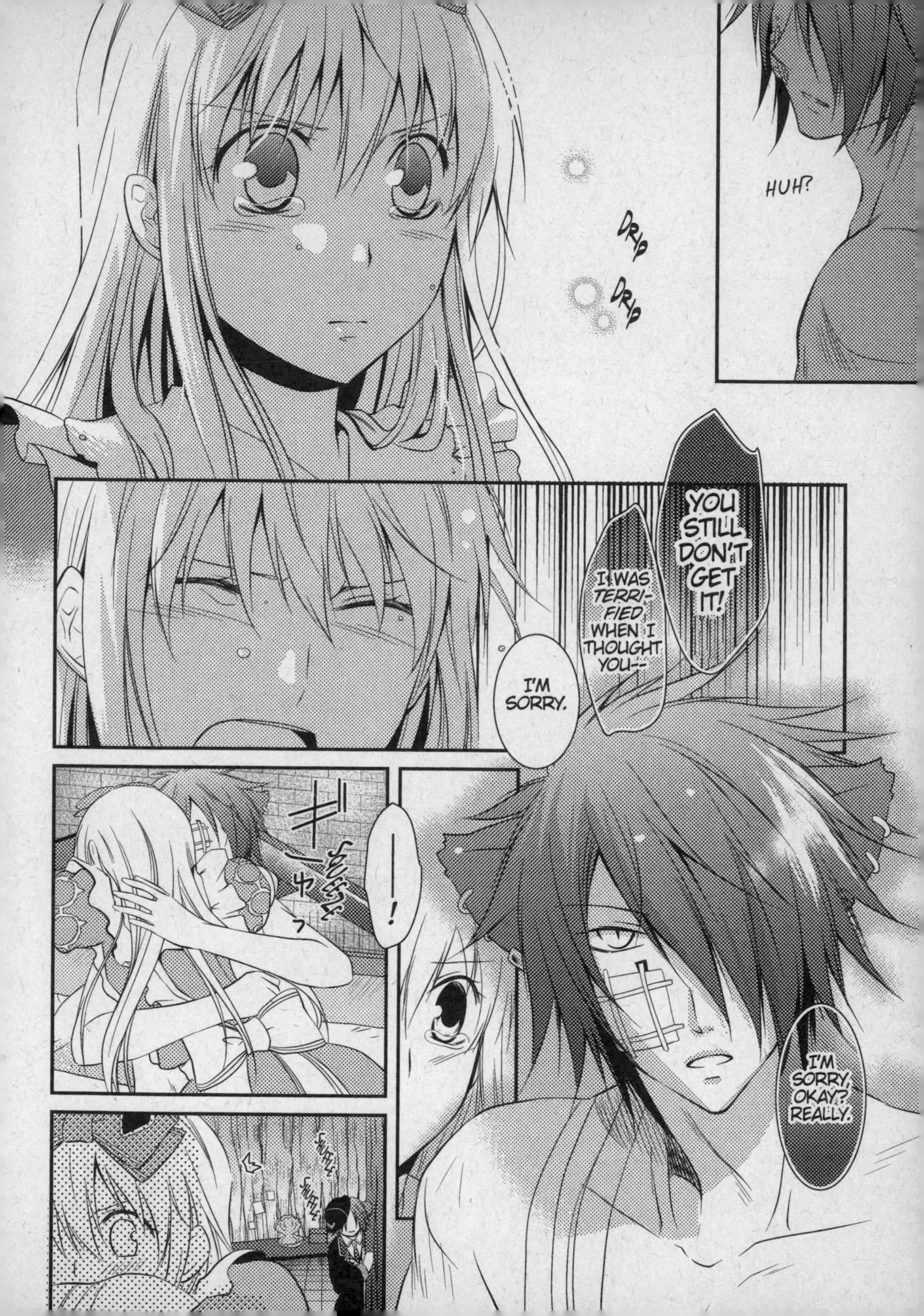
HUH?
DRIP
DRIP
YOU STILL DON'T GET IT!
I WAS TERRI-FIED WHEN I THOUGHT YOU--
I'M SORRY.
I'M SORRY, OKAY? REALLY.
!
SQUEEZE
SHUFFLE
SHUFFLE

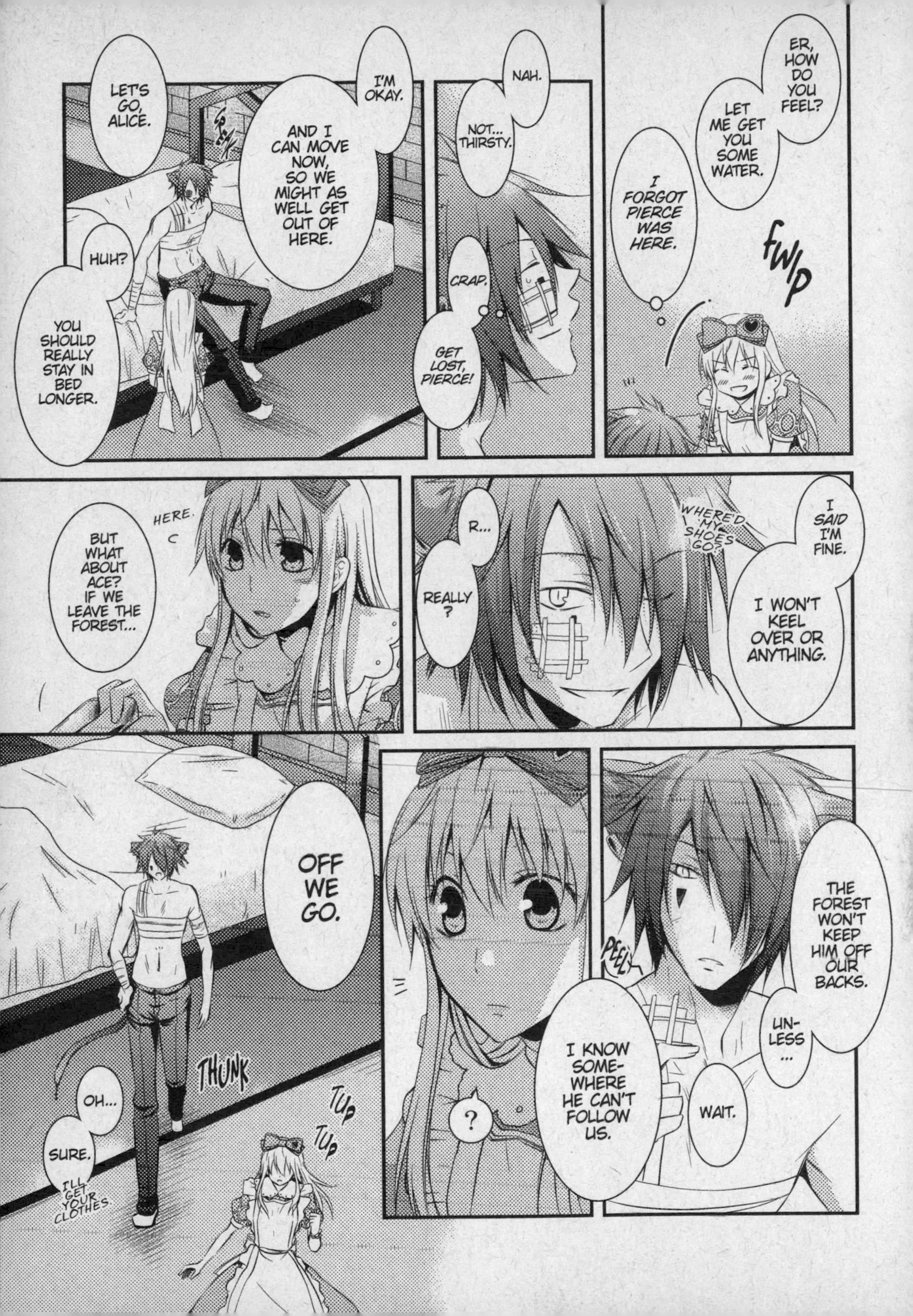
ER, HOW DO YOU FEEL?
LET ME GET YOU SOME WATER.
FWIP
I FORGOT PIERCE WAS HERE.
NAH.
NOT... THIRSTY.
CRAP.
GET LOST, PIERCE!
I'M OKAY.
AND I CAN MOVE NOW, SO WE MIGHT AS WELL GET OUT OF HERE.
LET'S GO, ALICE.
HUH?
YOU SHOULD REALLY STAY IN BED LONGER.
I SAID I'M FINE.
I WON'T KEEL OVER OR ANYTHING.
WHERE'D MY SHOES GO?
R...
REALLY?
HERE.
BUT WHAT ABOUT ACE? IF WE LEAVE THE FOREST...
THE FOREST WON'T KEEP HIM OFF OUR BACKS.
UN-LESS...
PEEL
WAIT.
I KNOW SOME-WHERE HE CAN'T FOLLOW US.
?
OFF WE GO.
THUNK
OH...
TUP TUP
SURE.
I'LL GET YOUR CLOTHES.

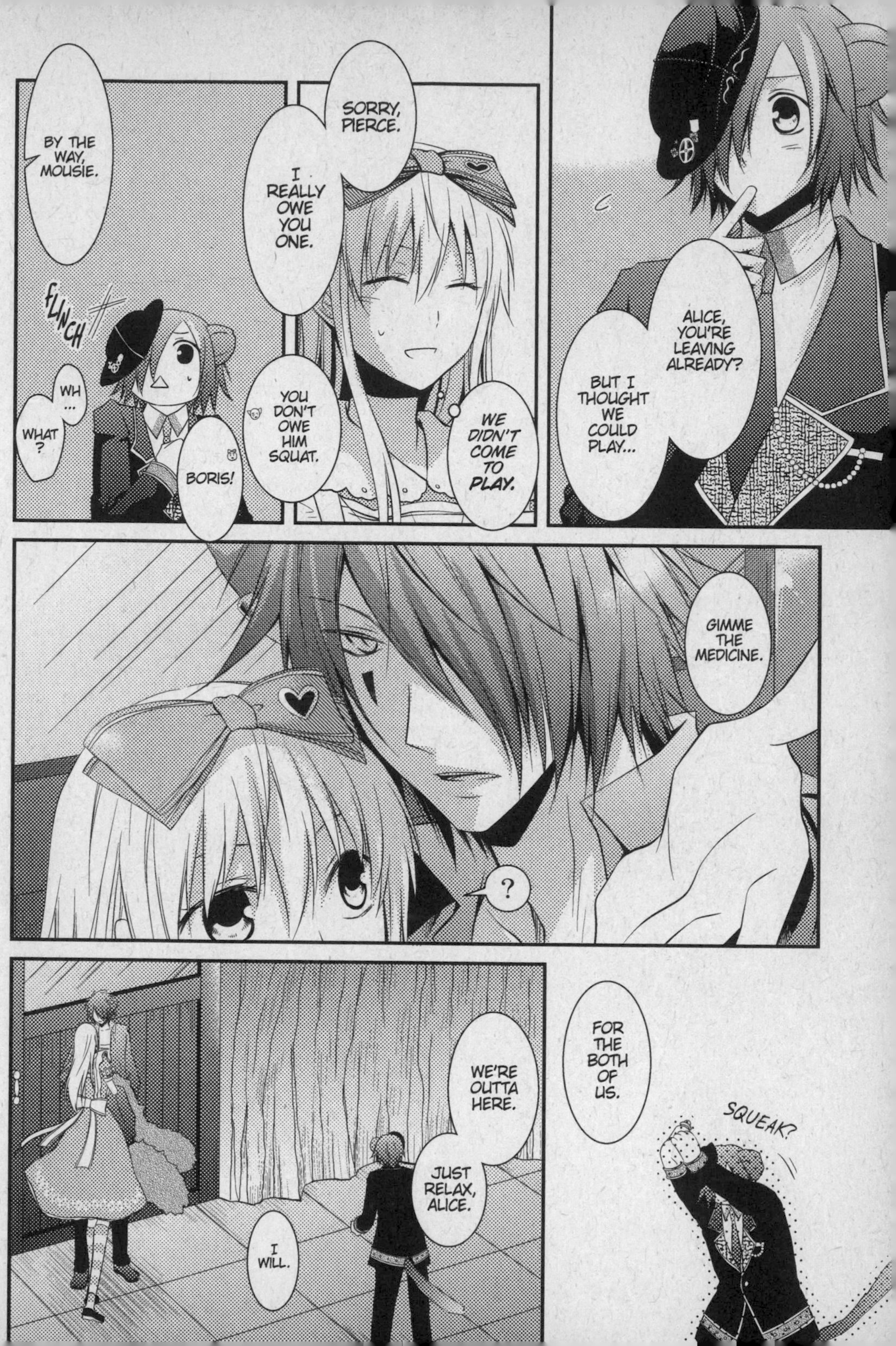
ALICE, YOU'RE LEAVING ALREADY?
BUT I THOUGHT WE COULD PLAY...
SORRY, PIERCE.
I REALLY OWE YOU ONE.
WE DIDN'T COME TO PLAY.
YOU DON'T OWE HIM SQUAT.
BY THE WAY, MOUSIE.
FLINCH
BORIS!
WH... WHAT?
GIMME THE MEDICINE.
?
FOR THE BOTH OF US.
SQUEAK?
WE'RE OUTTA HERE.
JUST RELAX, ALICE.
I WILL.

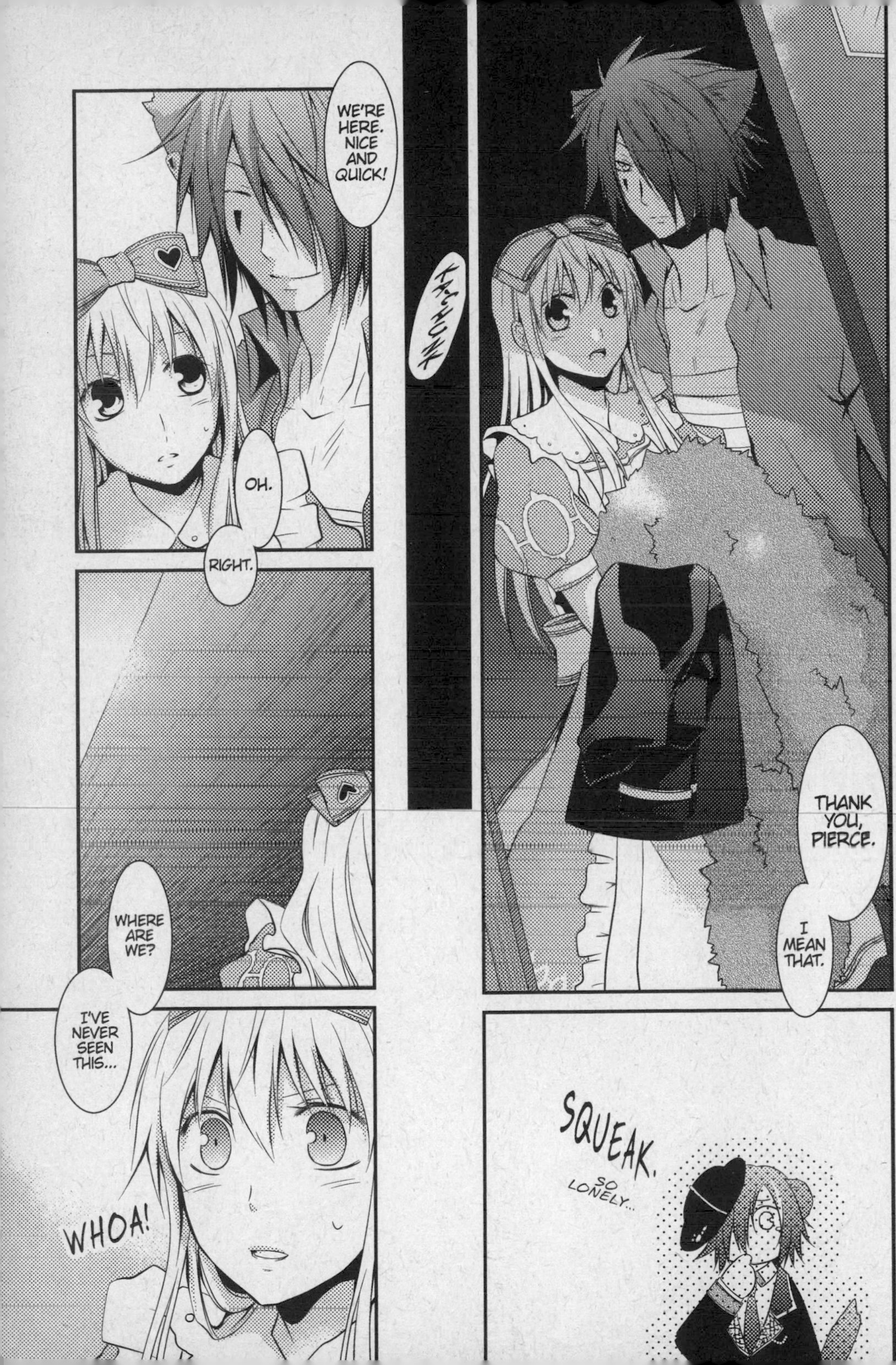
THANK YOU, PIERCE.
I MEAN THAT.
WE'RE HERE. NICE AND QUICK!
KACHUNK
OH.
RIGHT.
WHERE ARE WE?
SQUEAK.
SO LONELY...
I'VE NEVER SEEN THIS...
WHOA!

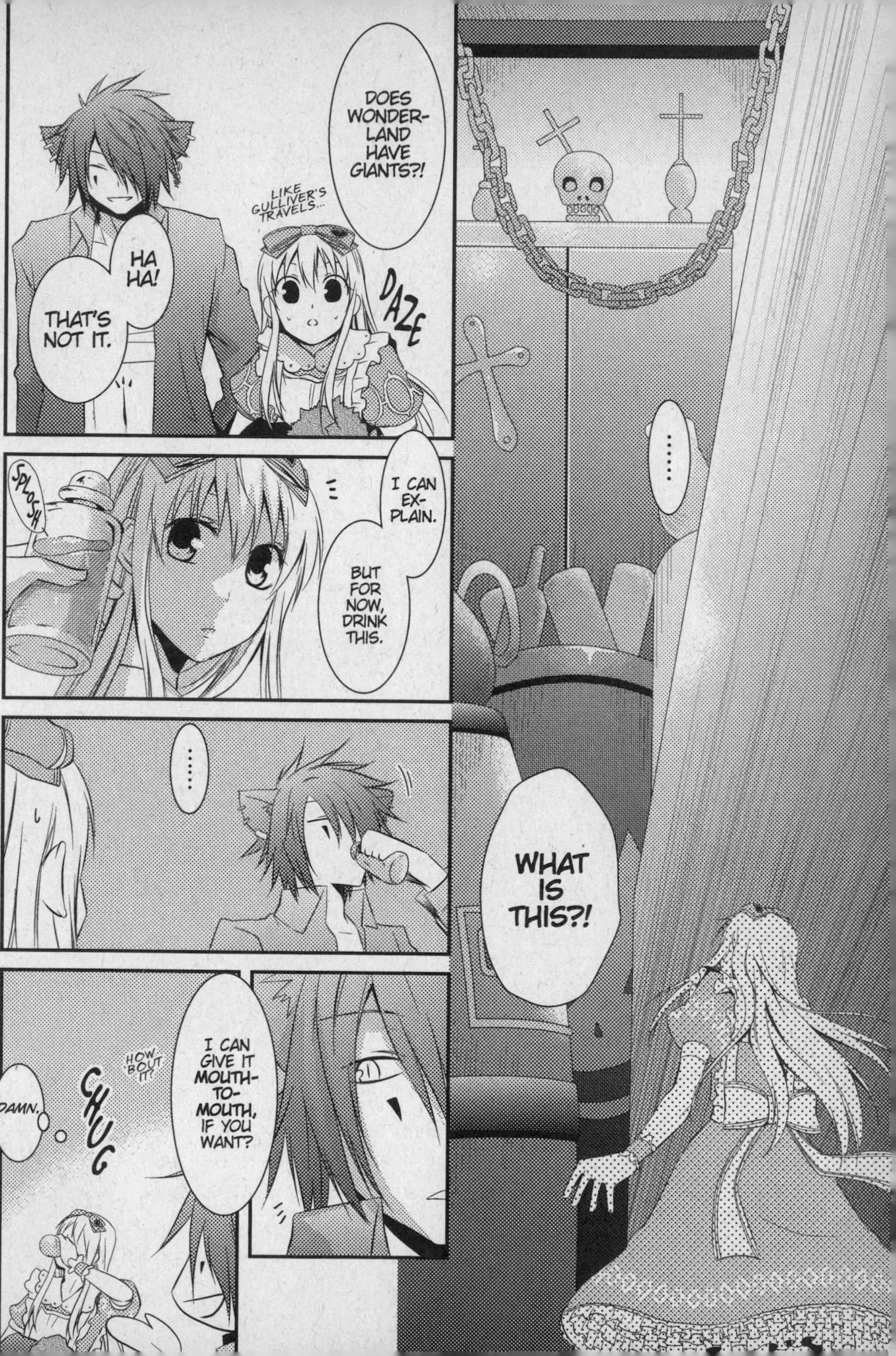
......
WHAT IS THIS?!
DOES WONDER-LAND HAVE GIANTS?!
LIKE GULLIVER'S TRAVELS...
DAZE
HA HA!
THAT'S NOT IT.
I CAN EX-PLAIN.
BUT FOR NOW, DRINK THIS.
SPLOSH
......
I CAN GIVE IT MOUTH-TO-MOUTH, IF YOU WANT?
HOW 'BOUT IT?
CHUG
DAMN.

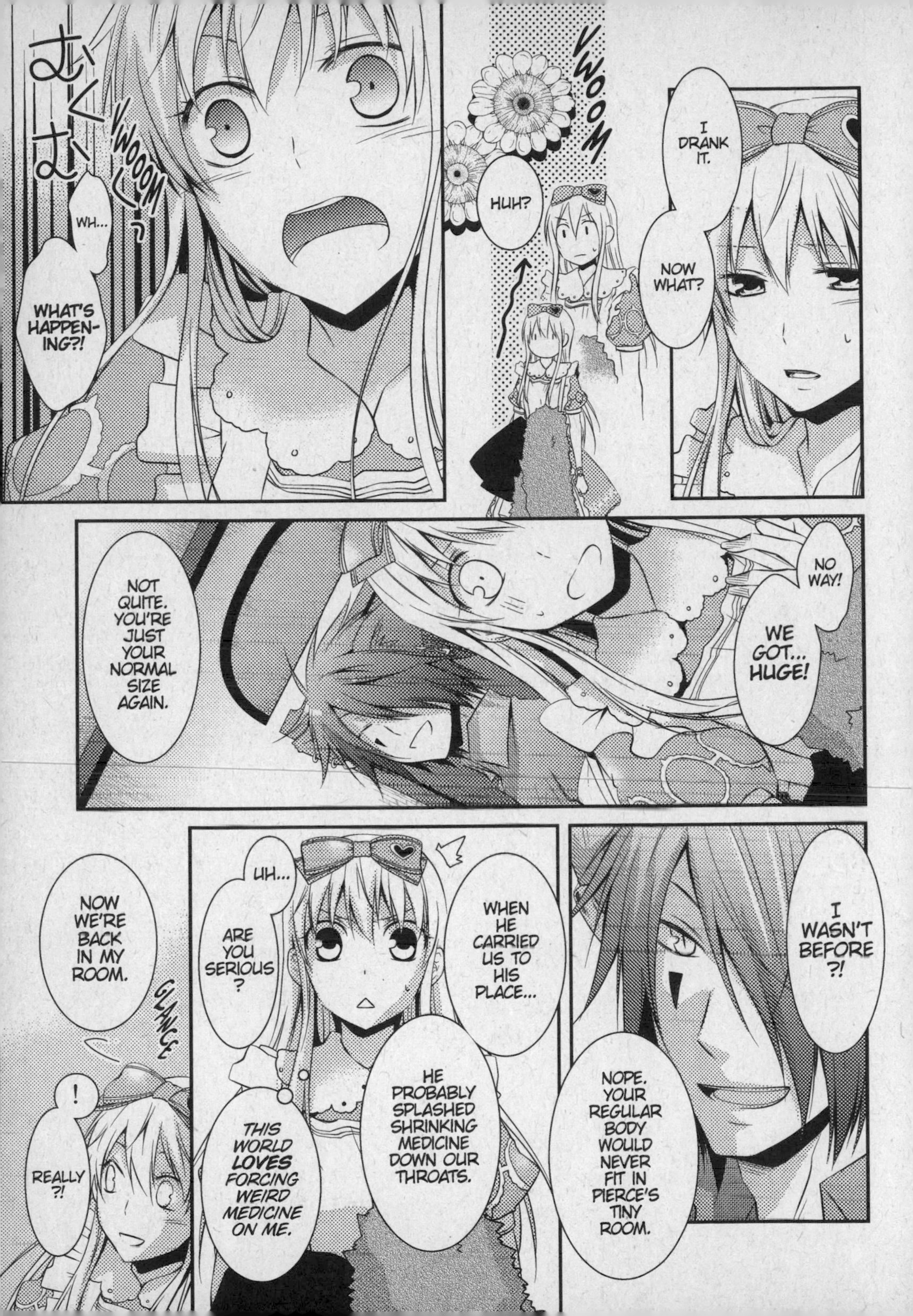
I DRANK IT.
NOW WHAT?
VWOOM
HUH?
むくむくっ
VWOOM
WH...
WHAT'S HAPPENING?!
NO WAY!
WE GOT... HUGE!
NOT QUITE. YOU'RE JUST YOUR NORMAL SIZE AGAIN.
I WASN'T BEFORE?!
NOPE. YOUR REGULAR BODY WOULD NEVER FIT IN PIERCE'S TINY ROOM.
WHEN HE CARRIED US TO HIS PLACE...
HE PROBABLY SPLASHED SHRINKING MEDICINE DOWN OUR THROATS.
UH...
ARE YOU SERIOUS?
THIS WORLD LOVES FORCING WEIRD MEDICINE ON ME.
NOW WE'RE BACK IN MY ROOM.
GLANCE
!
REALLY?!

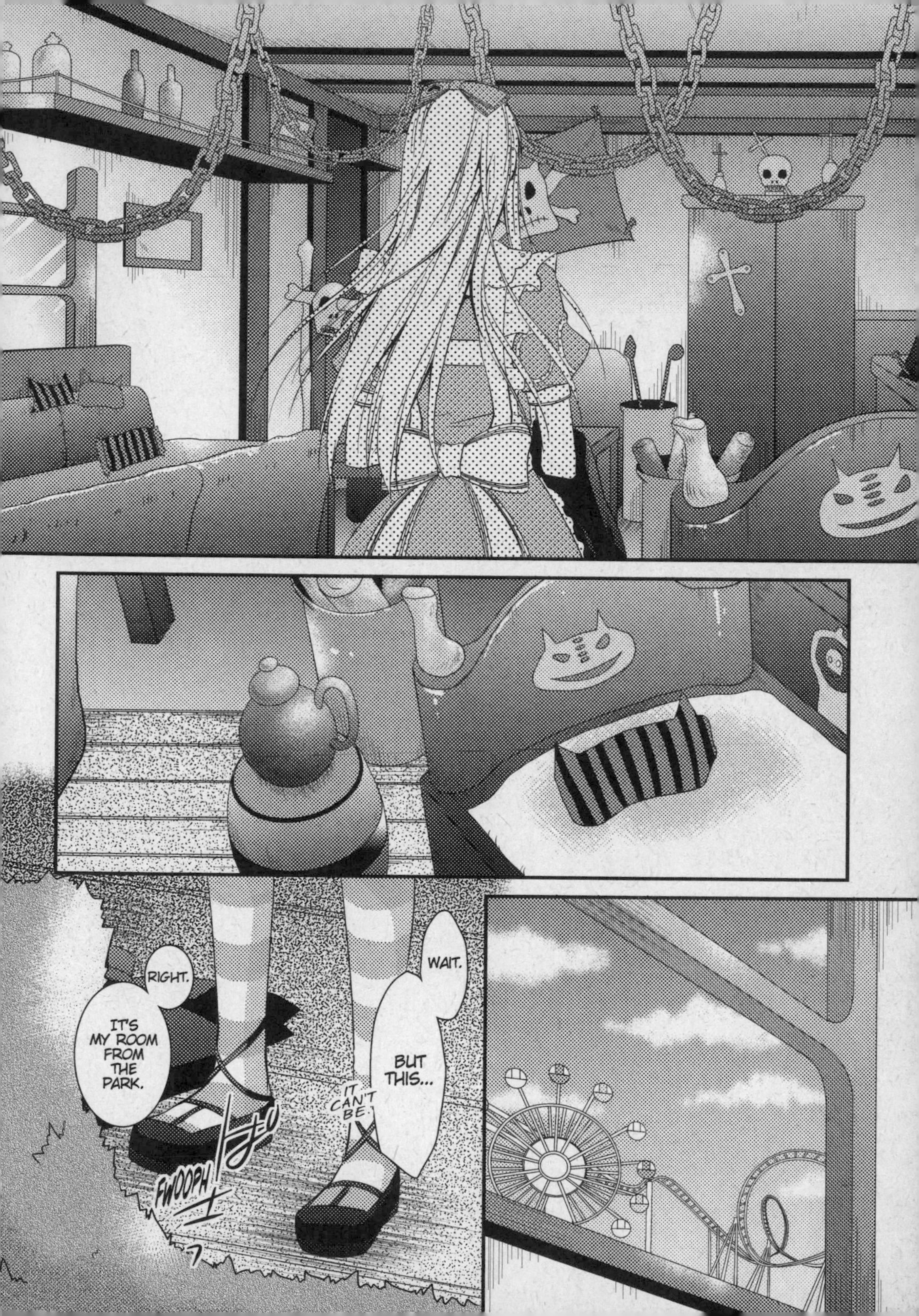
WAIT.
BUT THIS...
IT CAN'T BE.
RIGHT.
IT'S MY ROOM FROM THE PARK.
FWOOPH

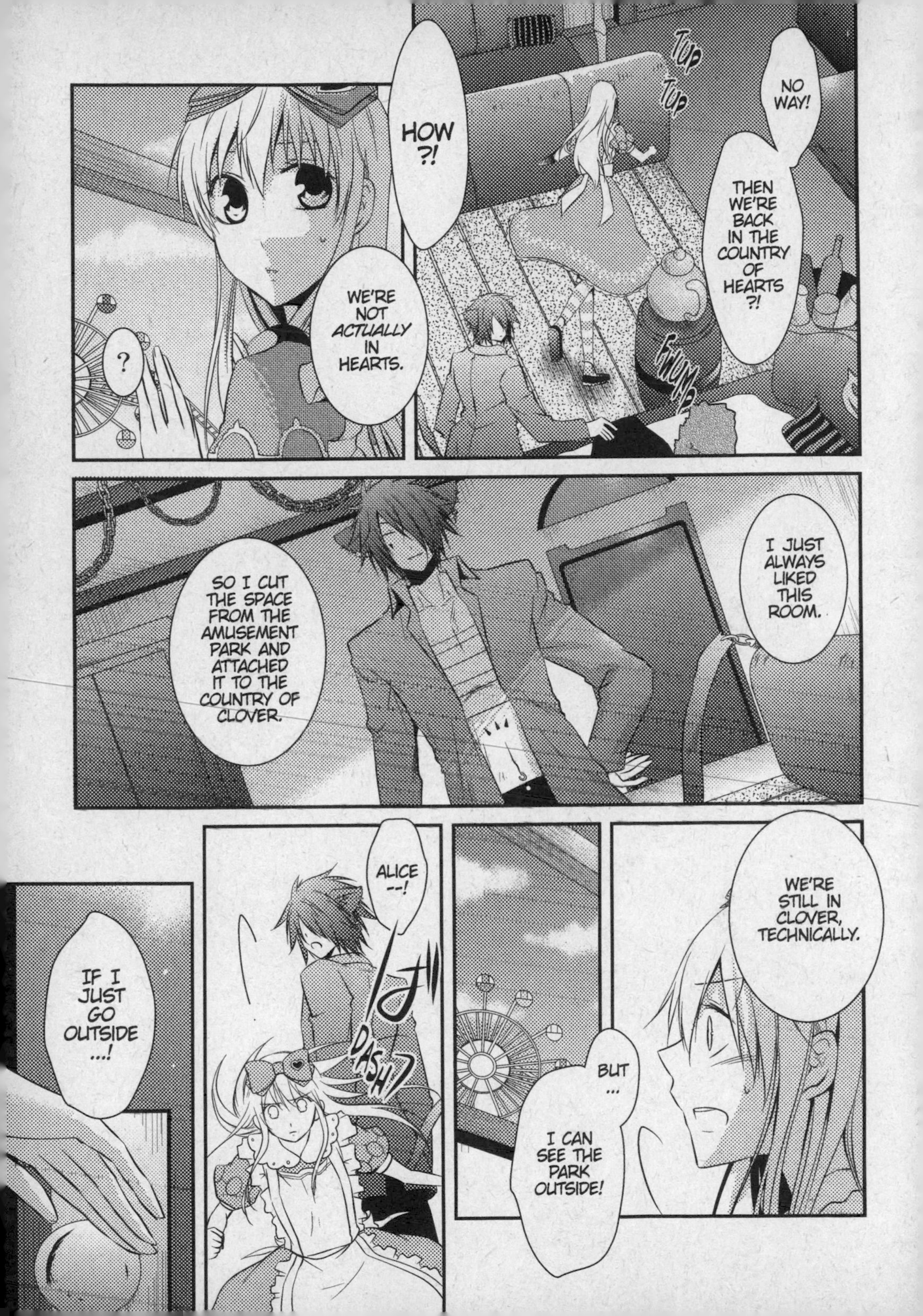
Tup Tup
NO WAY!
THEN WE'RE BACK IN THE COUNTRY OF HEARTS?!
Frump
WE'RE NOT ACTUALLY IN HEARTS.
HOW?!
?
I JUST ALWAYS LIKED THIS ROOM.
SO I CUT THE SPACE FROM THE AMUSEMENT PARK AND ATTACHED IT TO THE COUNTRY OF CLOVER.
WE'RE STILL IN CLOVER, TECHNICALLY.
BUT...
I CAN SEE THE PARK OUTSIDE!
ALICE--!
DASH
IF I JUST GO OUTSIDE...!

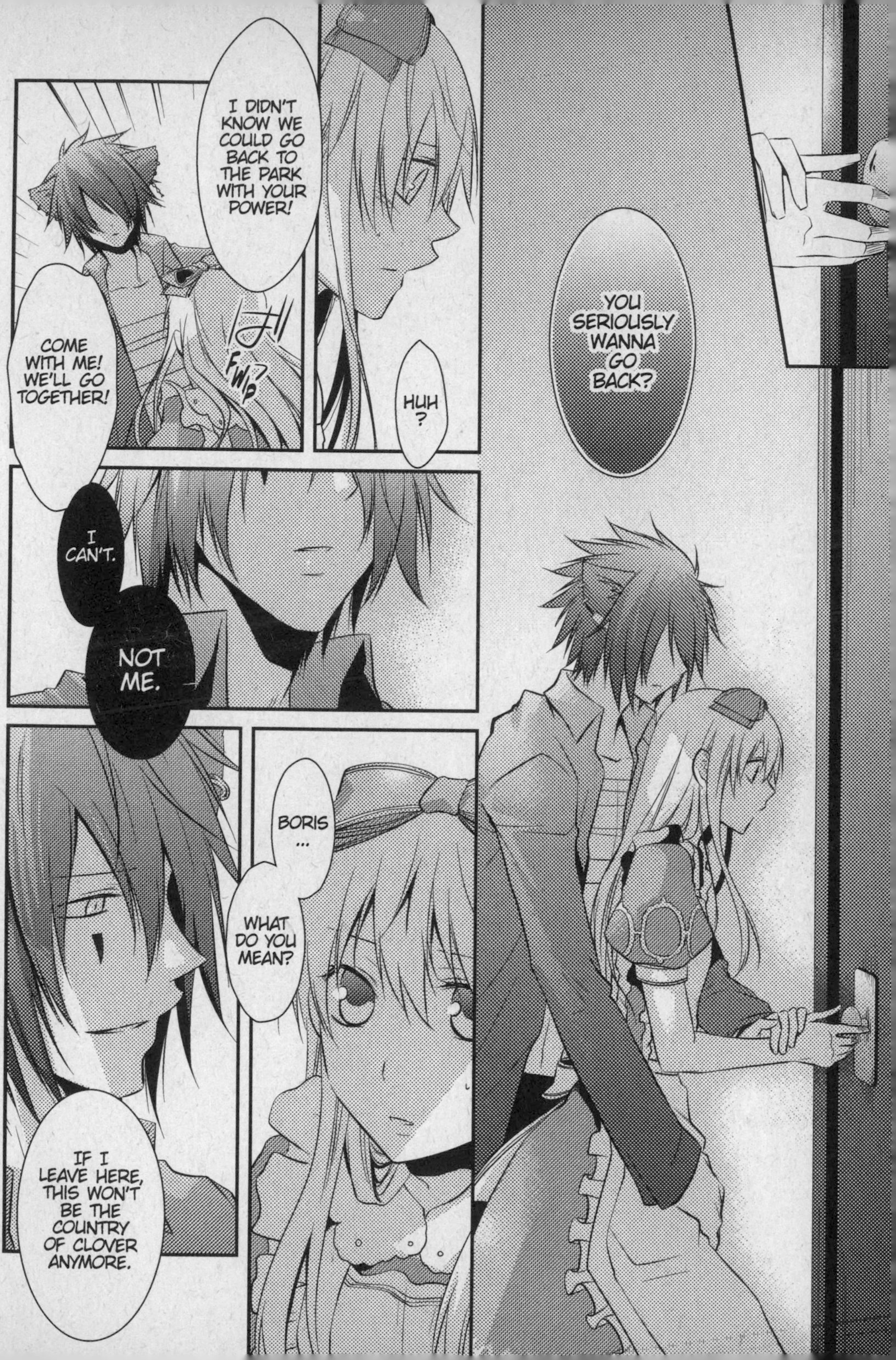
YOU SERIOUSLY WANNA GO BACK?
I DIDN'T KNOW WE COULD GO BACK TO THE PARK WITH YOUR POWER!
HUH?
COME WITH ME! WE'LL GO TOGETHER!
FWIP
I CAN'T.
NOT ME.
BORIS...
WHAT DO YOU MEAN?
IF I LEAVE HERE, THIS WON'T BE THE COUNTRY OF CLOVER ANYMORE.

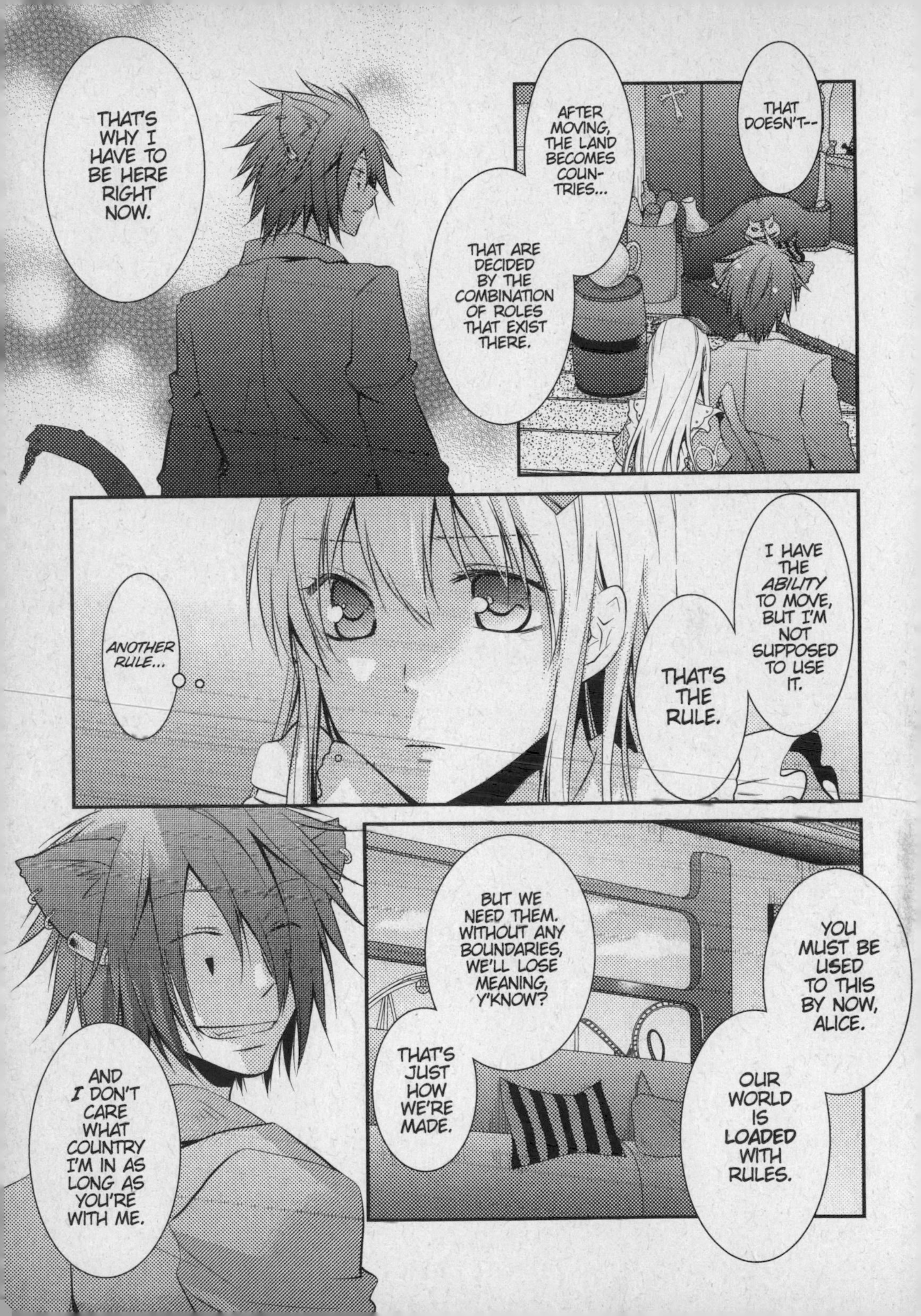
THAT DOESN'T--
AFTER MOVING, THE LAND BECOMES COUN-TRIES...
THAT ARE DECIDED BY THE COMBINATION OF ROLES THAT EXIST THERE.
THAT'S WHY I HAVE TO BE HERE RIGHT NOW.
I HAVE THE *ABILITY* TO MOVE, BUT I'M NOT SUPPOSED TO USE IT.
THAT'S THE RULE.
ANOTHER RULE...
YOU MUST BE USED TO THIS BY NOW, ALICE.
OUR WORLD IS LOADED WITH RULES.
BUT WE NEED THEM. WITHOUT ANY BOUNDARIES, WE'LL LOSE MEANING, Y'KNOW?
THAT'S JUST HOW WE'RE MADE.
AND *I* DON'T CARE WHAT COUNTRY I'M IN AS LONG AS YOU'RE WITH ME.

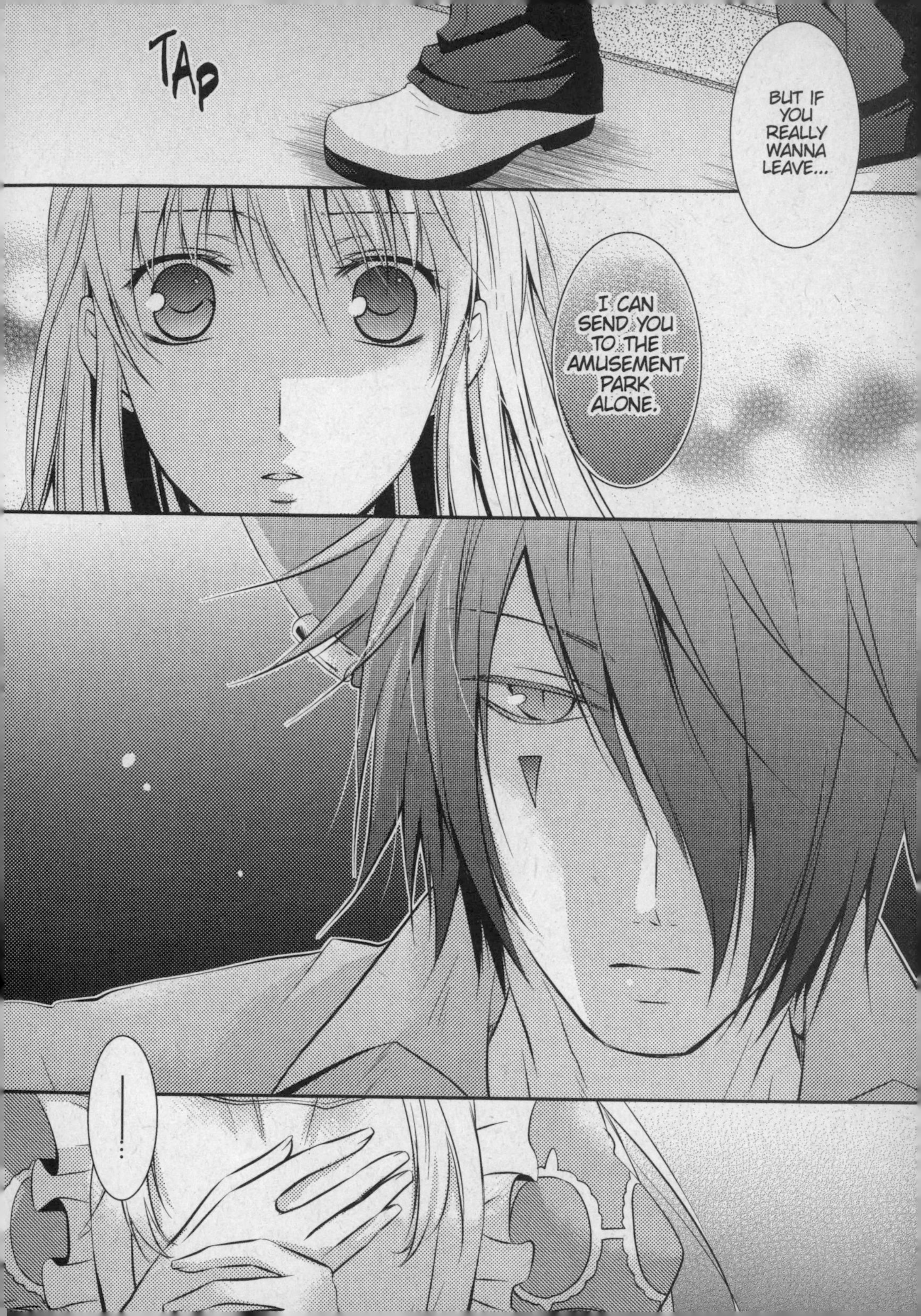
BUT IF YOU REALLY WANNA LEAVE...
TAP
I CAN SEND YOU TO THE AMUSEMENT PARK ALONE.
...!

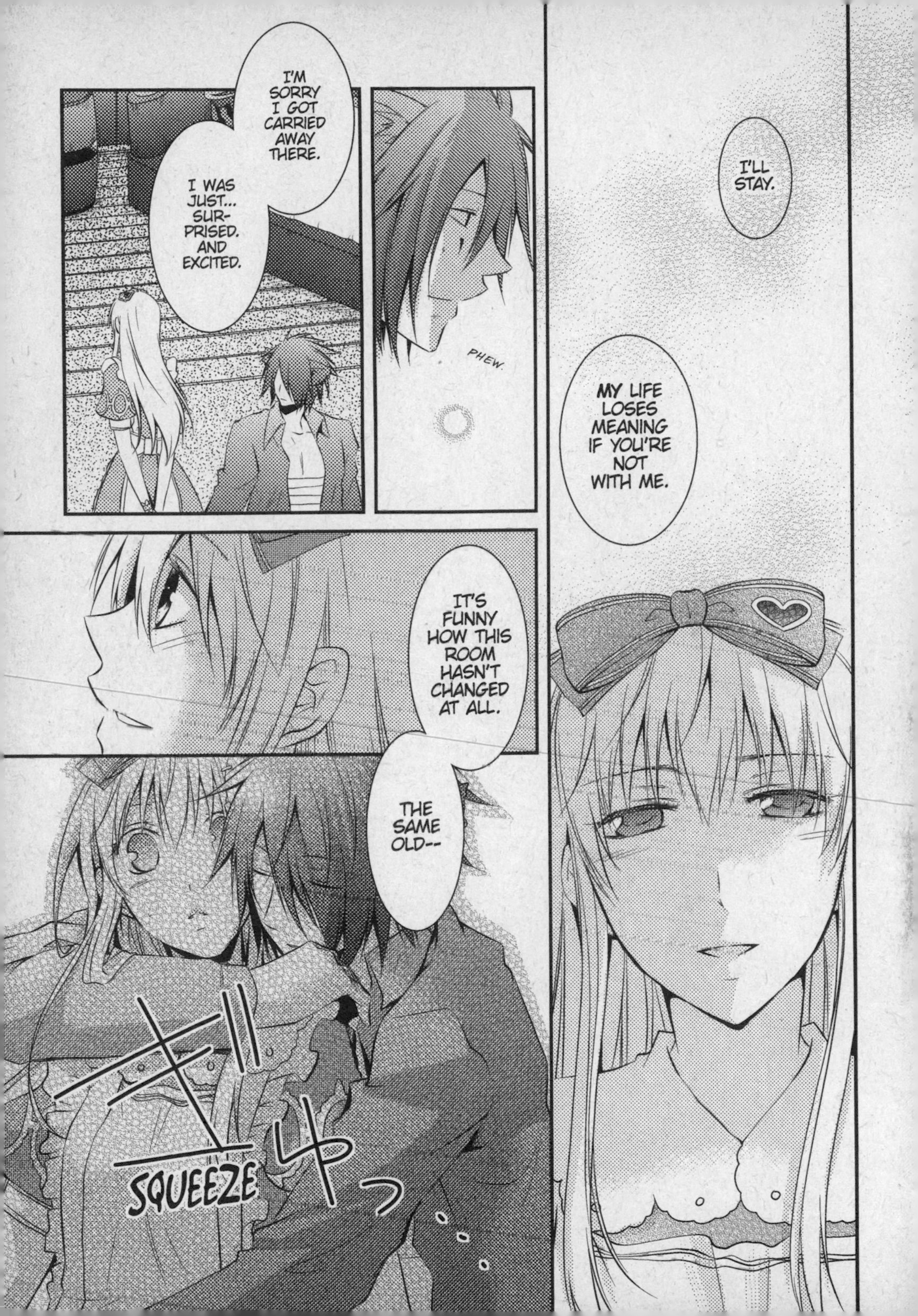
I'LL STAY.
MY LIFE LOSES MEANING IF YOU'RE NOT WITH ME.
I'M SORRY I GOT CARRIED AWAY THERE.
PHEW.
I WAS JUST... SUR-PRISED. AND EXCITED.
IT'S FUNNY HOW THIS ROOM HASN'T CHANGED AT ALL.
THE SAME OLD--
SQUEEZE

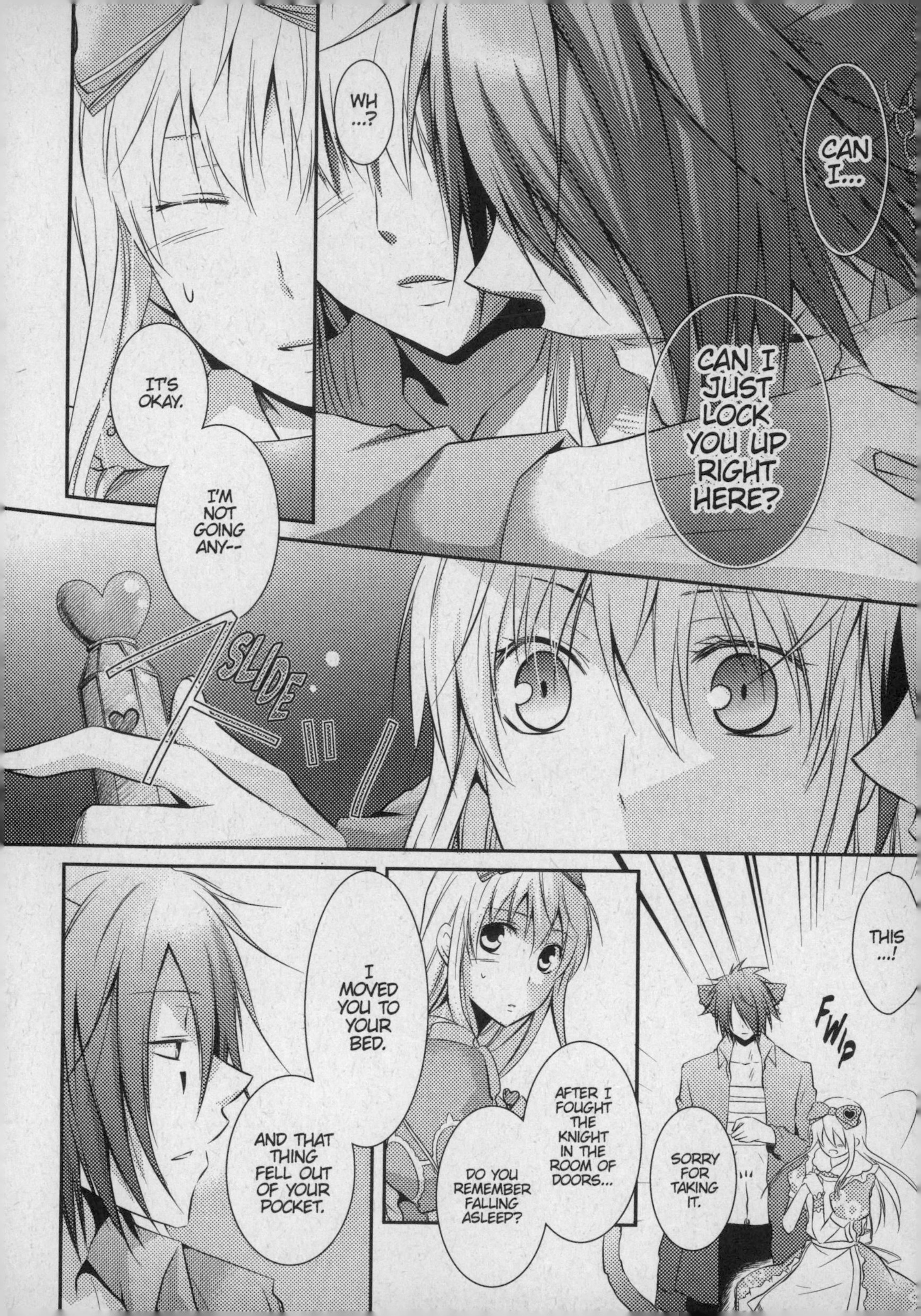
CAN I...
CAN I JUST LOCK YOU UP RIGHT HERE?
WH...?
IT'S OKAY.
I'M NOT GOING ANY--
SLIDE
THIS...!
FWIP
SORRY FOR TAKING IT.
AFTER I FOUGHT THE KNIGHT IN THE ROOM OF DOORS...
DO YOU REMEMBER FALLING ASLEEP?
I MOVED YOU TO YOUR BED.
AND THAT THING FELL OUT OF YOUR POCKET.

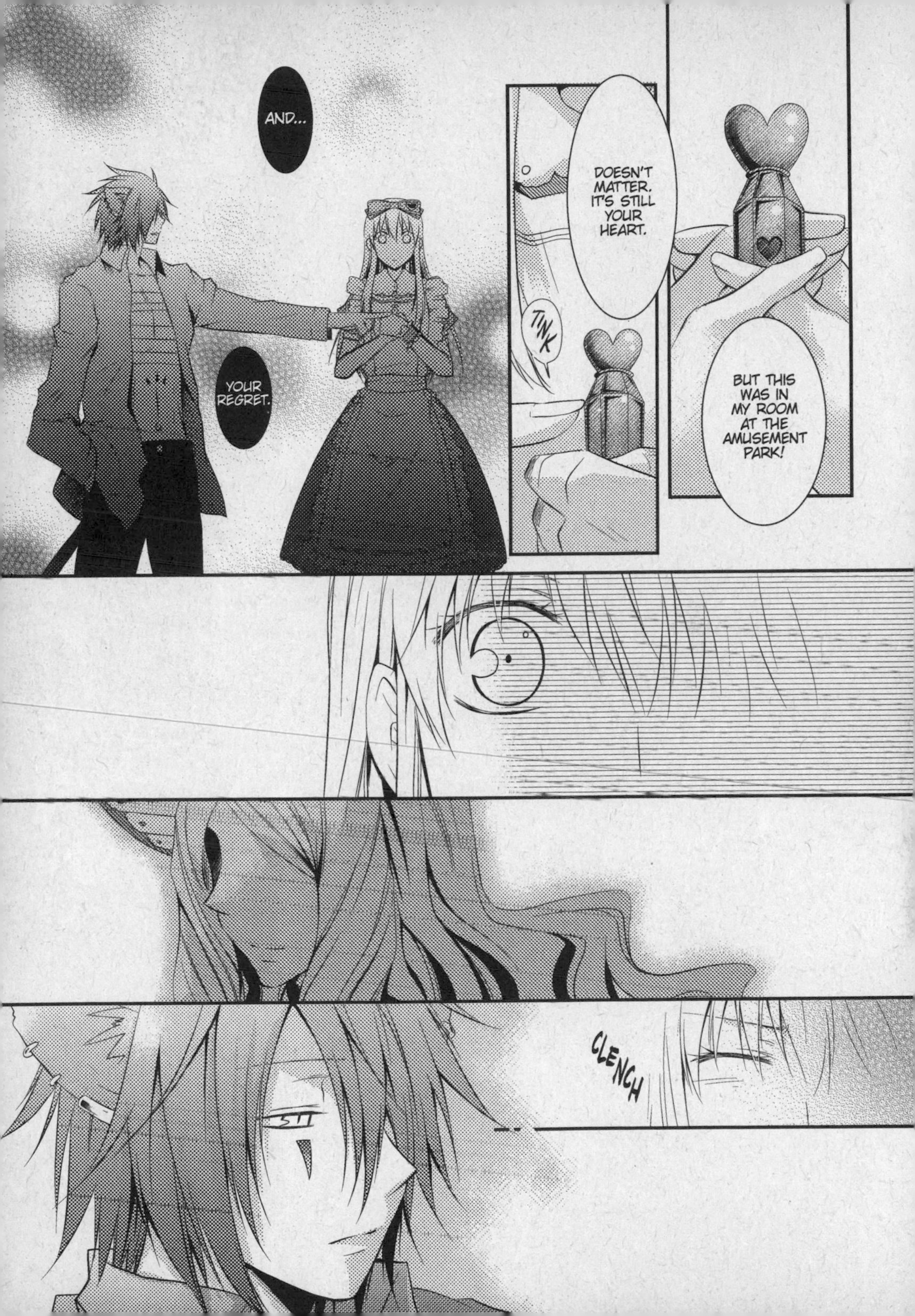
BUT THIS WAS IN MY ROOM AT THE AMUSEMENT PARK!
DOESN'T MATTER. IT'S STILL YOUR HEART.
TINK
AND...
YOUR REGRET.
CLENCH

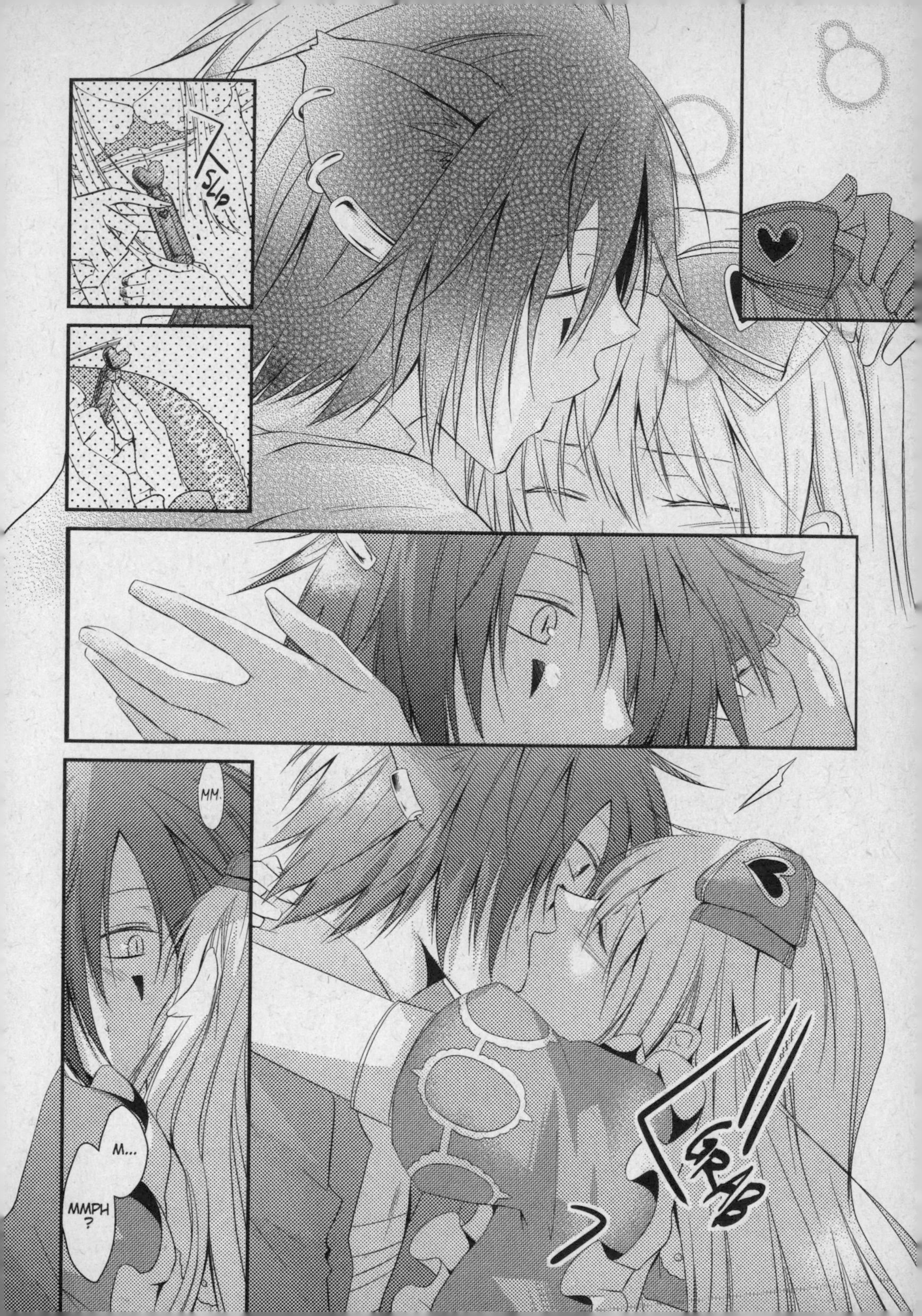
SLIP
MM.
GRAB
M...
MMPH ?

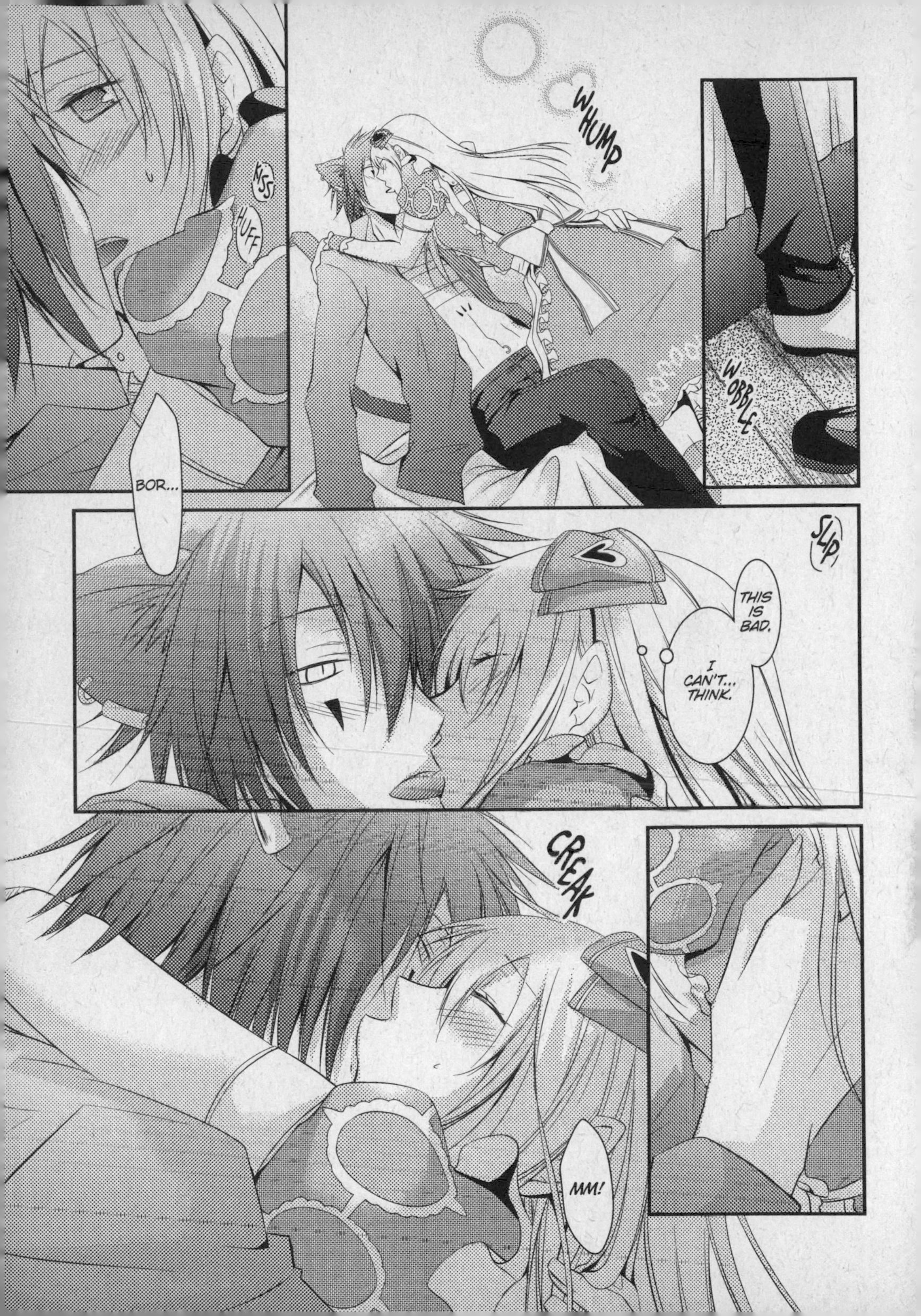
WOBBLE
WHUMP
KISS
HUFF
BOR...
SLIP
THIS IS BAD.
I CAN'T... THINK.
CREAK
MM!

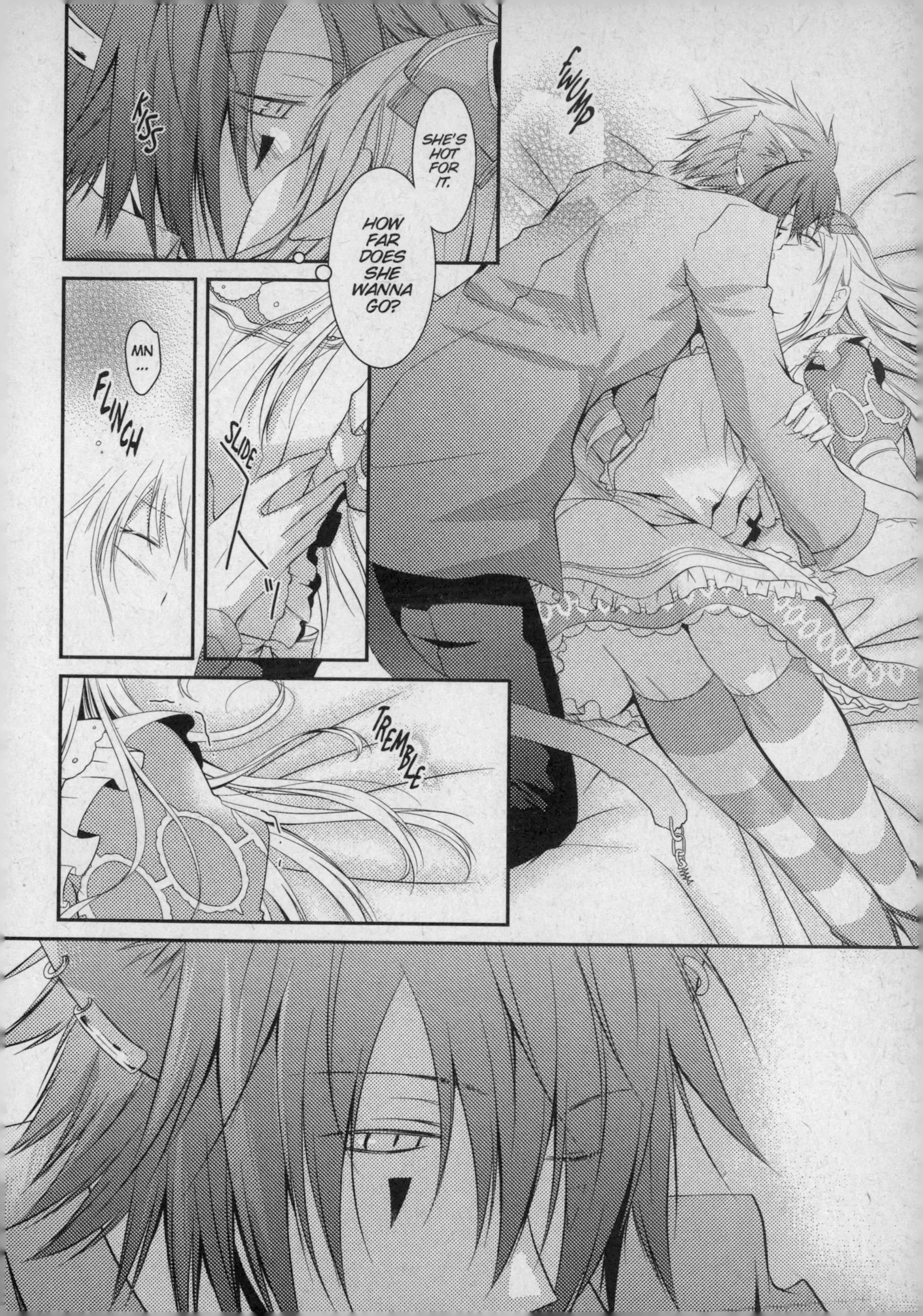
FWUMP
KISS
SHE'S HOT FOR IT.
HOW FAR DOES SHE WANNA GO?
SLIDE
MN...
FLINCH
TREMBLE

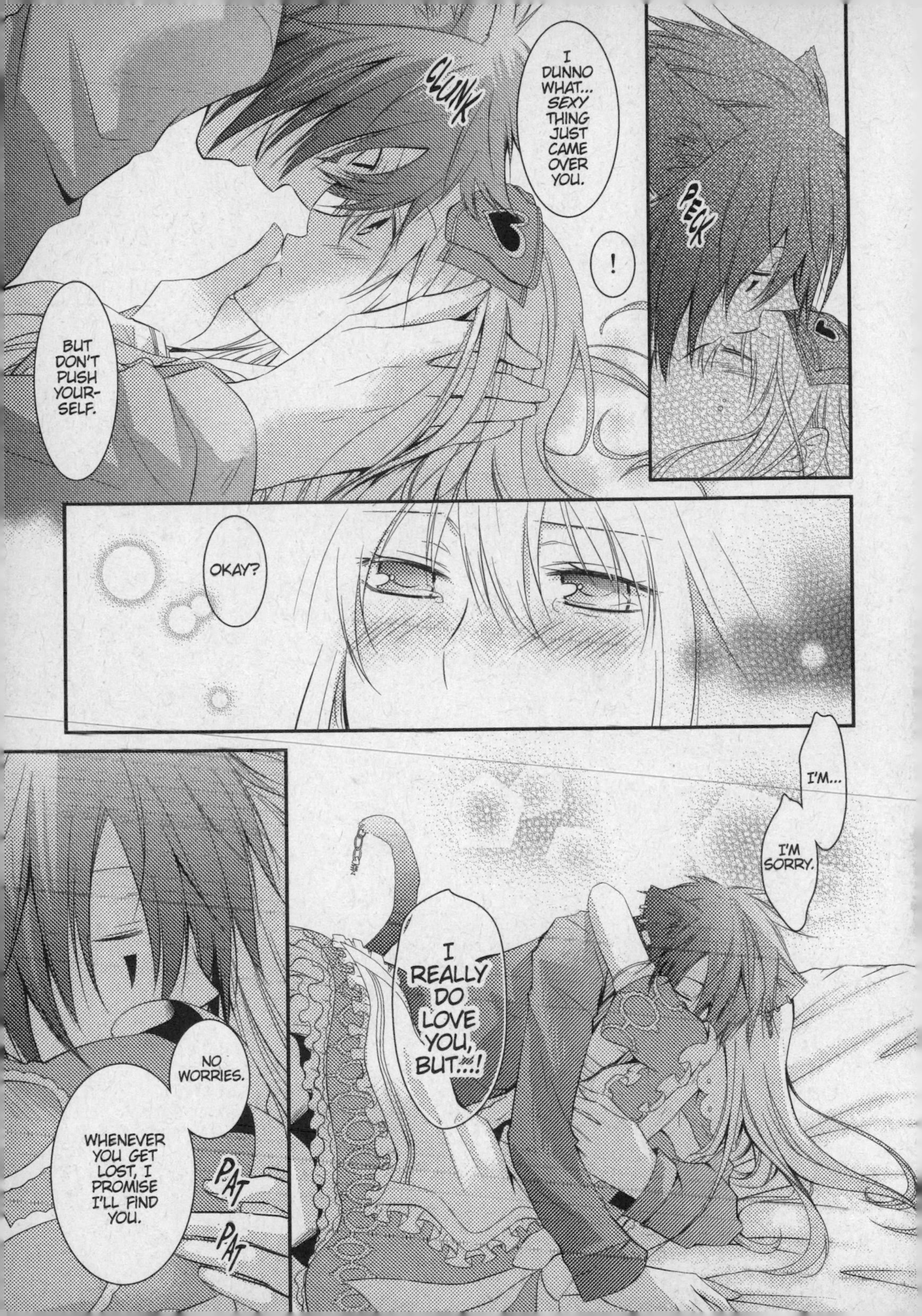
PECK
I DUNNO WHAT... SEXY THING JUST CAME OVER YOU.
CLUNK
!
BUT DON'T PUSH YOURSELF.
OKAY?
I'M...
I'M SORRY.
I REALLY DO LOVE YOU, BUT...!
NO WORRIES.
WHENEVER YOU GET LOST, I PROMISE I'LL FIND YOU.
PAT
PAT

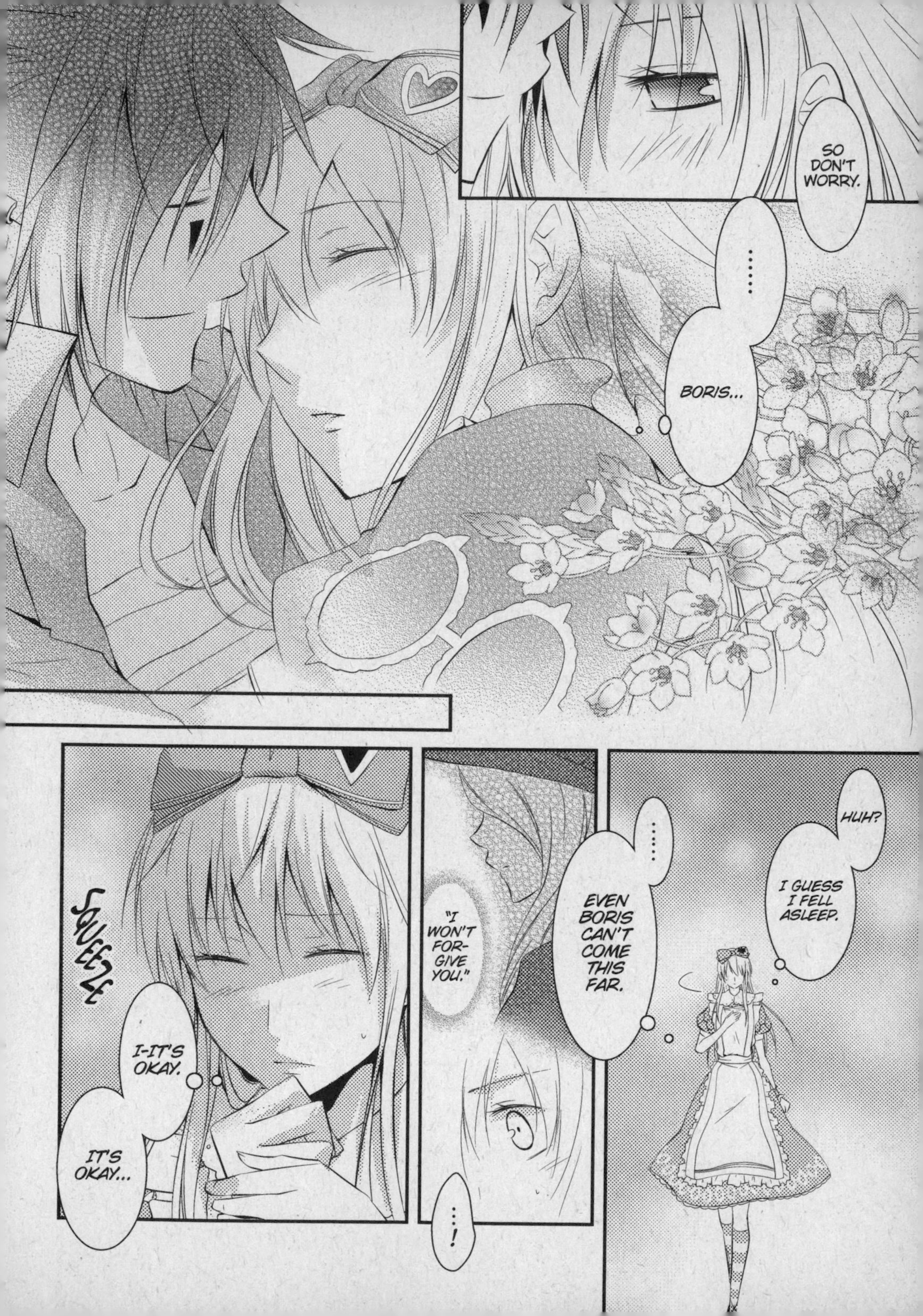
SO DON'T WORRY.
......
BORIS...
HUH?
I GUESS I FELL ASLEEP.
......
EVEN BORIS CAN'T COME THIS FAR.
"I WON'T FOR-GIVE YOU."
...!
SQUEEZE
I-IT'S OKAY.
IT'S OKAY...

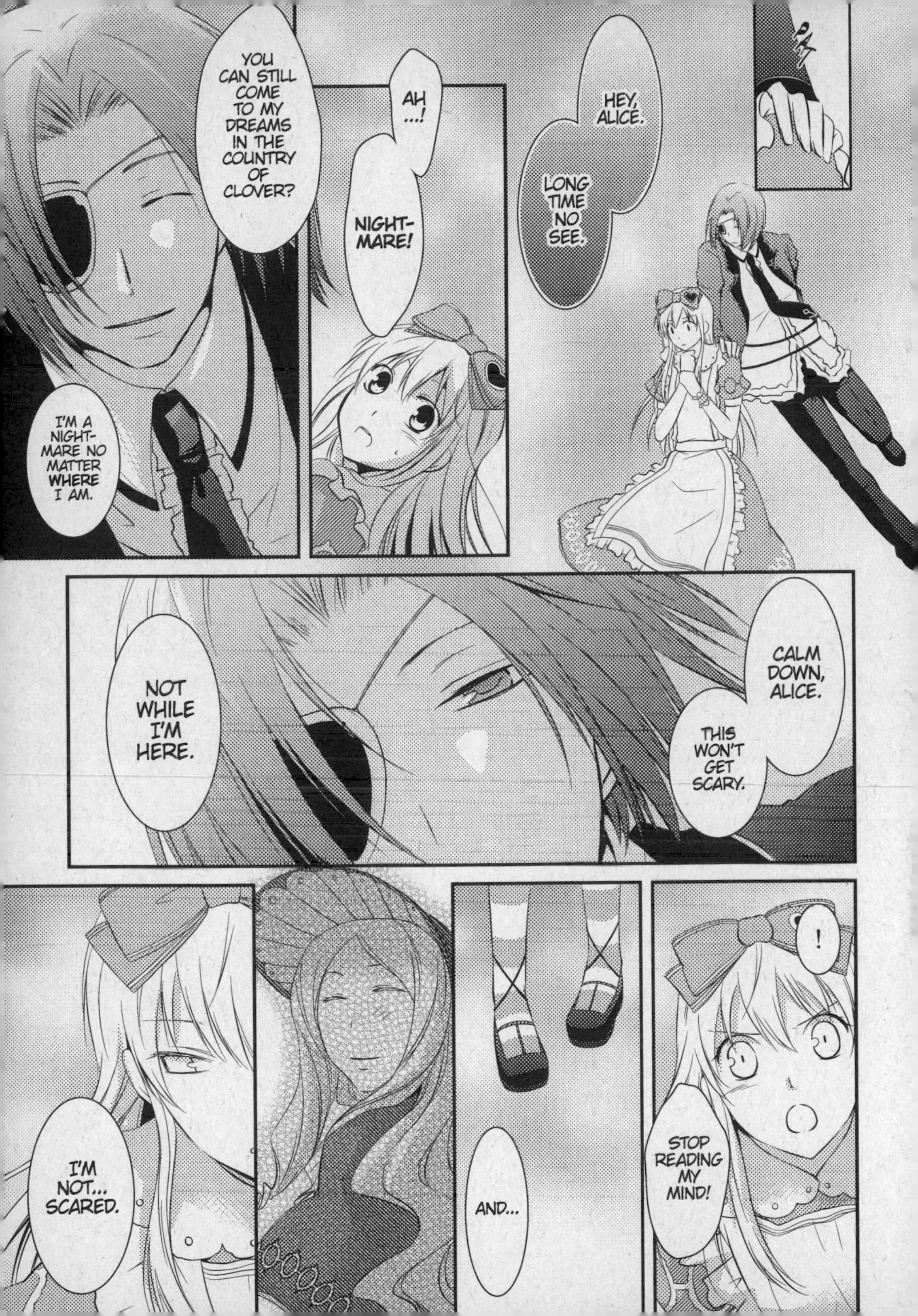
PAT
HEY, ALICE.
LONG TIME NO SEE.
AH ...!
NIGHT-MARE!
YOU CAN STILL COME TO MY DREAMS IN THE COUNTRY OF CLOVER?
I'M A NIGHT-MARE NO MATTER WHERE I AM.
CALM DOWN, ALICE.
THIS WON'T GET SCARY.
NOT WHILE I'M HERE.
!
STOP READING MY MIND!
AND...
I'M NOT... SCARED.

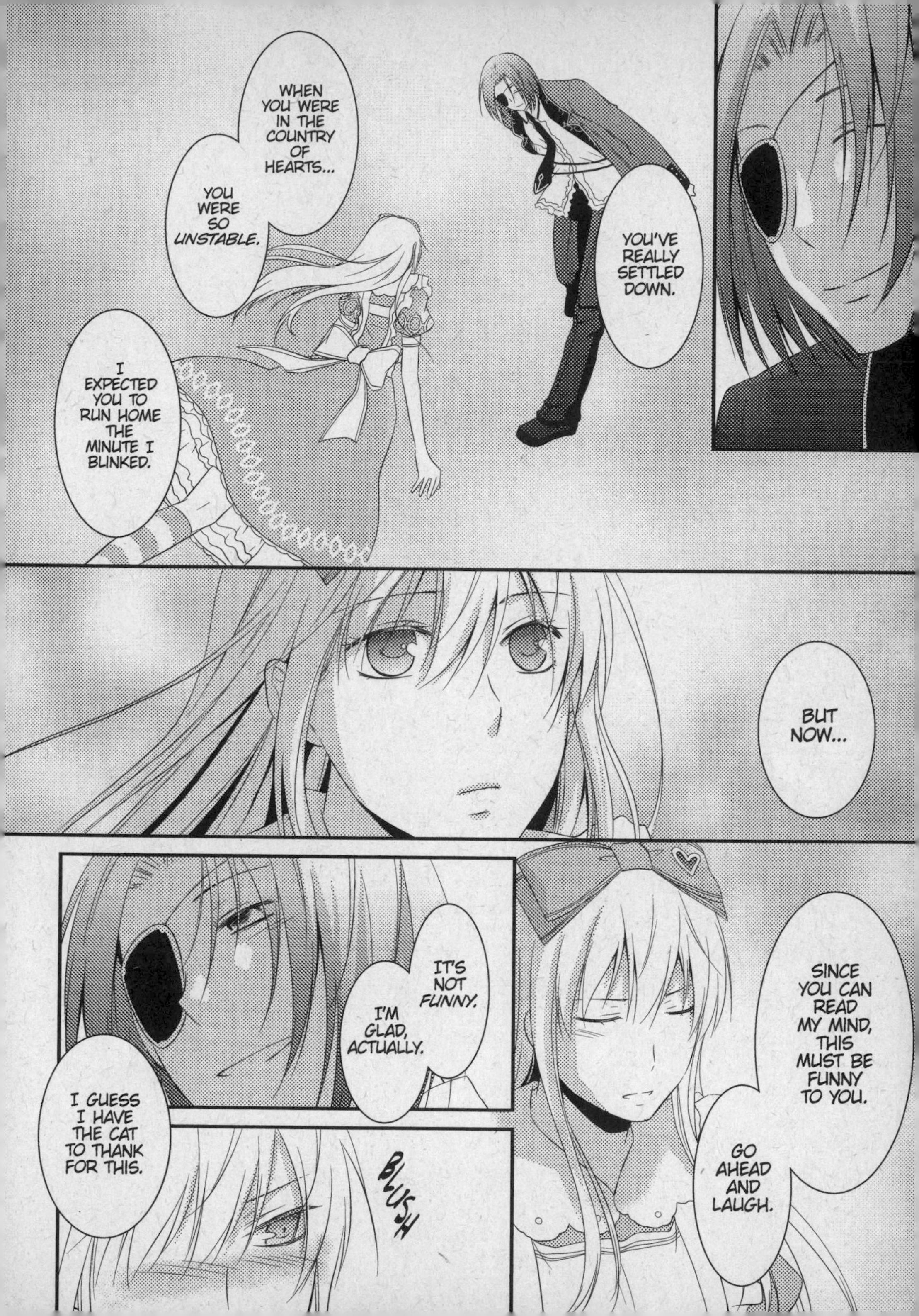
YOU'VE REALLY SETTLED DOWN.
WHEN YOU WERE IN THE COUNTRY OF HEARTS...
YOU WERE SO *UNSTABLE.*
I EXPECTED YOU TO RUN HOME THE MINUTE I BLINKED.
BUT NOW...
SINCE YOU CAN READ MY MIND, THIS MUST BE FUNNY TO YOU.
GO AHEAD AND LAUGH.
IT'S NOT *FUNNY.*
I'M GLAD, ACTUALLY.
I GUESS I HAVE THE CAT TO THANK FOR THIS.
BLUSH

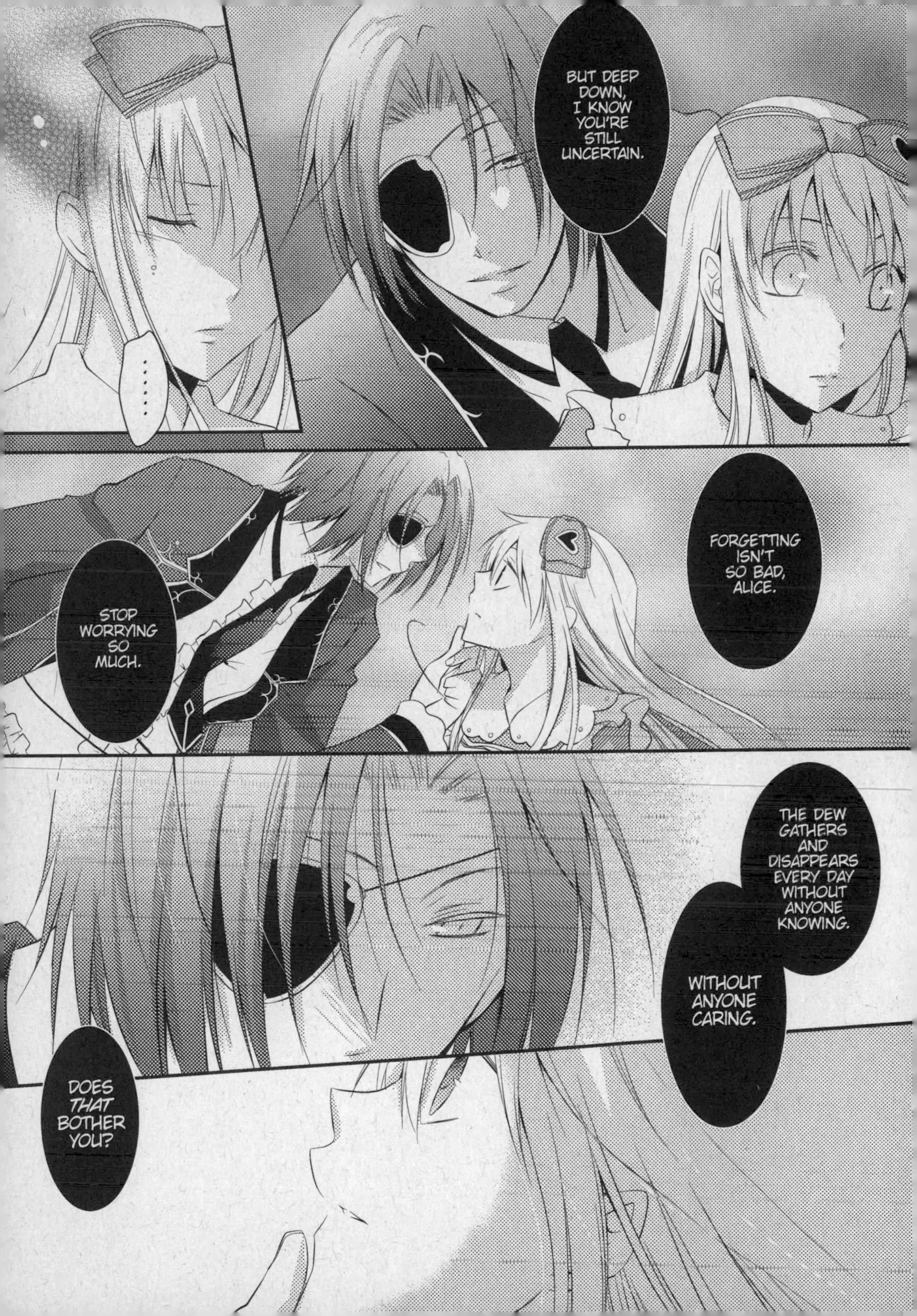
BUT DEEP DOWN, I KNOW YOU'RE STILL UNCERTAIN.
......
FORGETTING ISN'T SO BAD, ALICE.
STOP WORRYING SO MUCH.
THE DEW GATHERS AND DISAPPEARS EVERY DAY WITHOUT ANYONE KNOWING.
WITHOUT ANYONE CARING.
DOES *THAT* BOTHER YOU?

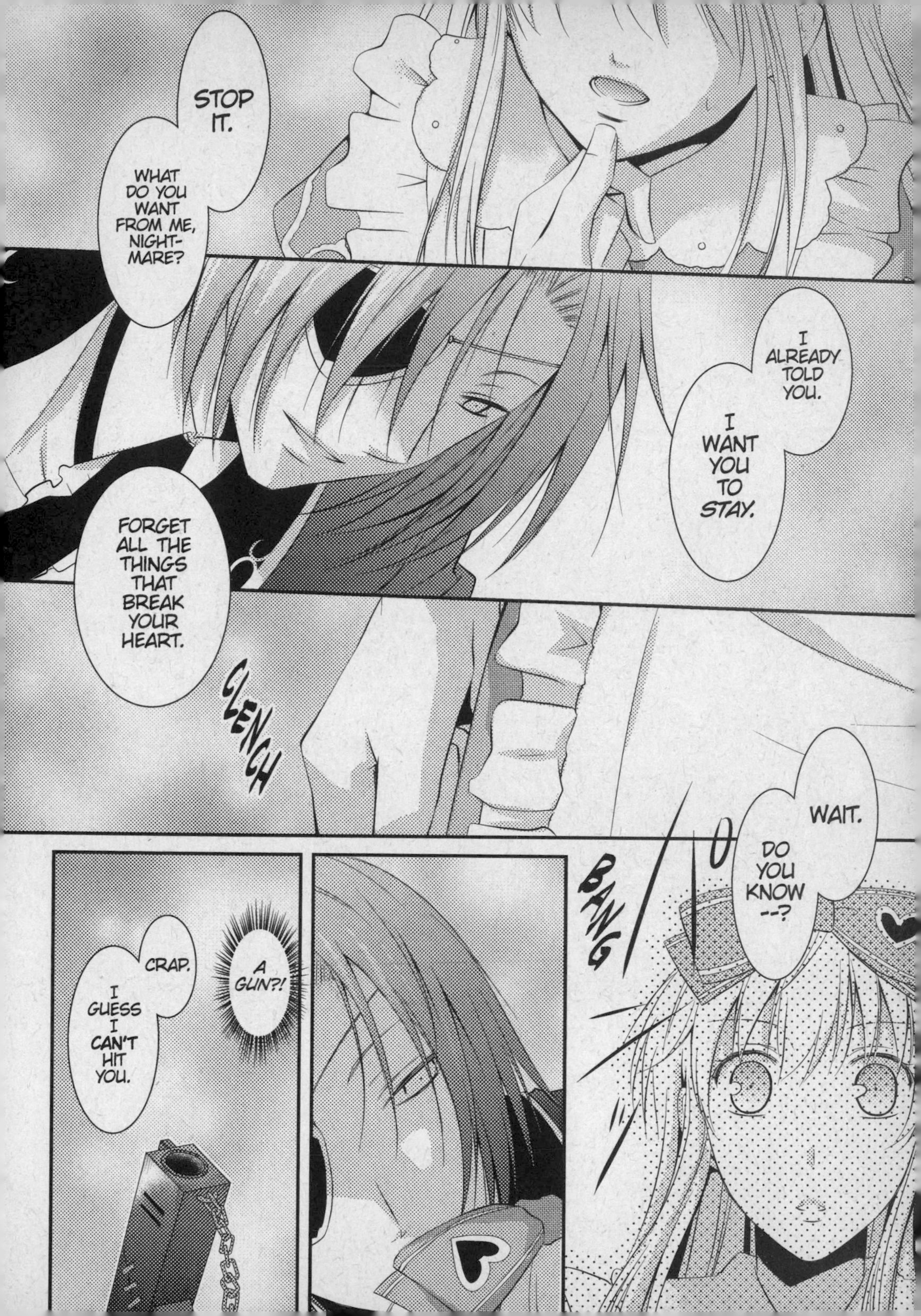
STOP IT.
WHAT DO YOU WANT FROM ME, NIGHTMARE?
I ALREADY TOLD YOU.
I WANT YOU TO STAY.
FORGET ALL THE THINGS THAT BREAK YOUR HEART.
CLENCH
WAIT.
DO YOU KNOW --?
BANG
A GUN?!
CRAP.
I GUESS I CAN'T HIT YOU.

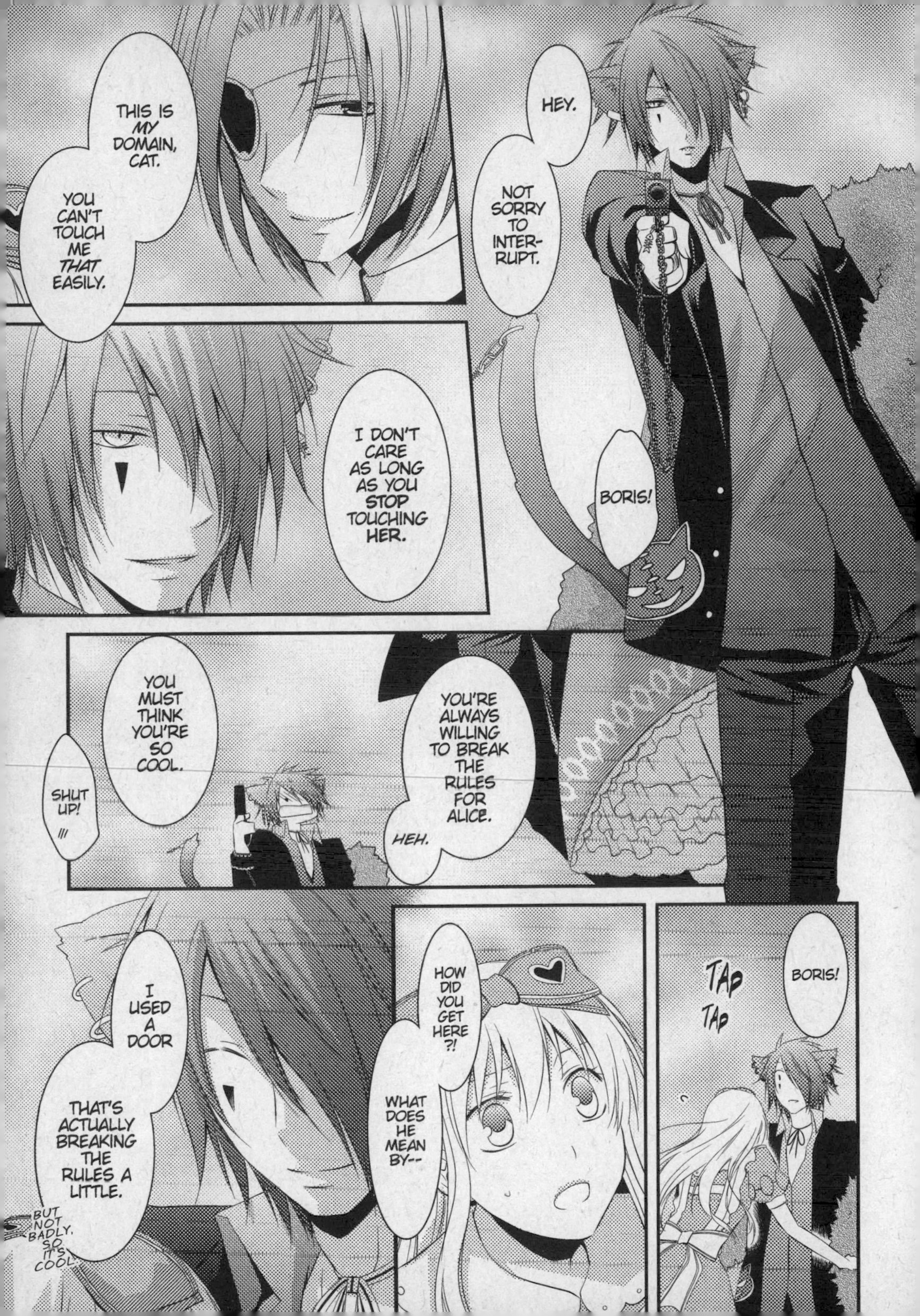
HEY.
NOT SORRY TO INTERRUPT.
BORIS!
THIS IS *MY* DOMAIN, CAT.
YOU CAN'T TOUCH ME *THAT* EASILY.
I DON'T CARE AS LONG AS YOU STOP TOUCHING HER.
YOU'RE ALWAYS WILLING TO BREAK THE RULES FOR ALICE.
HEH.
YOU MUST THINK YOU'RE SO COOL.
SHUT UP!
///
TAP
TAP
BORIS!
HOW DID YOU GET HERE?!
WHAT DOES HE MEAN BY--
I USED A DOOR
THAT'S ACTUALLY BREAKING THE RULES A LITTLE.
BUT NOT BADLY. SO IT'S COOL.

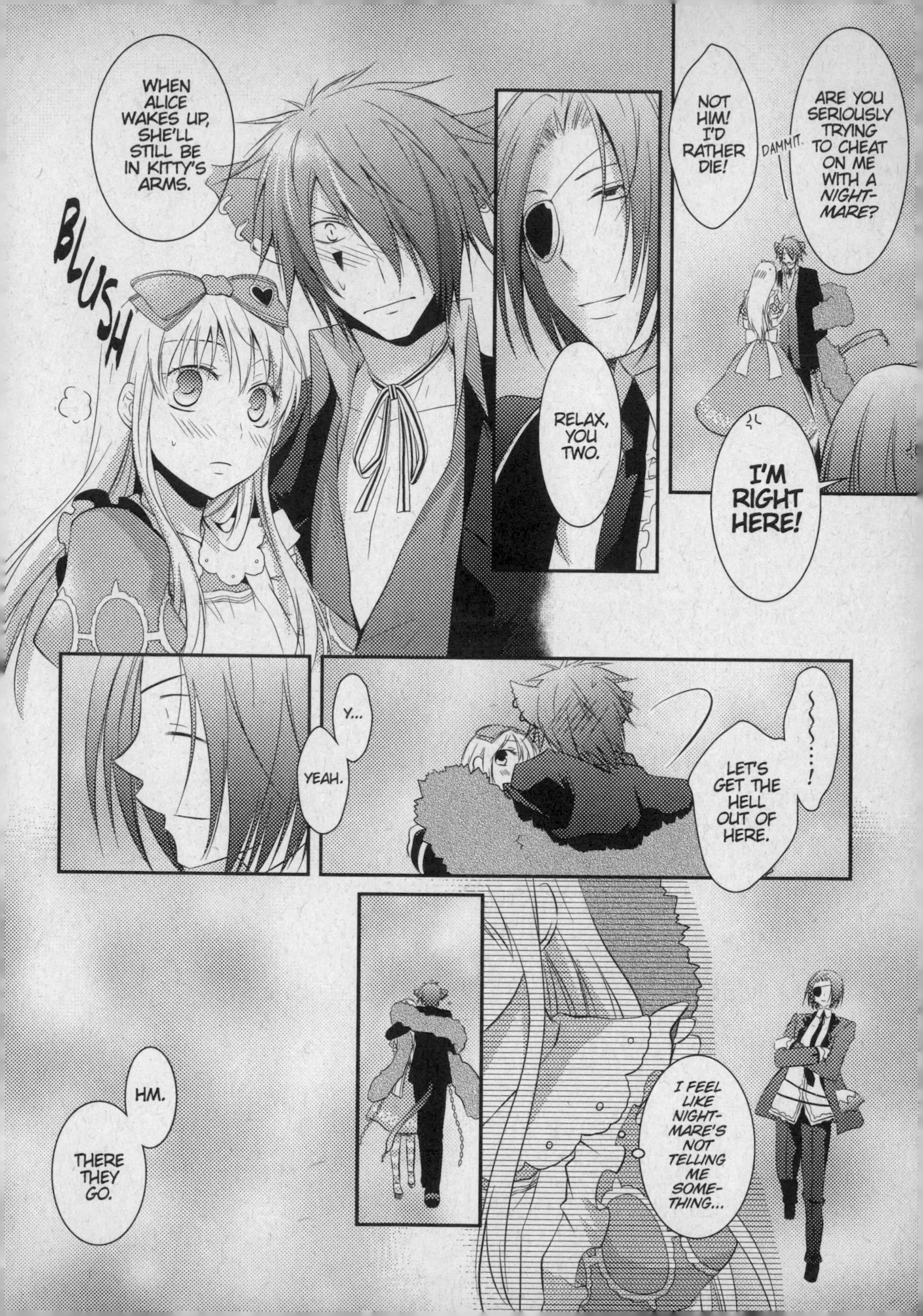
ARE YOU SERIOUSLY TRYING TO CHEAT ON ME WITH A *NIGHTMARE?*
DAMMIT.
NOT HIM! I'D RATHER DIE!
I'M RIGHT HERE!
RELAX, YOU TWO.
WHEN ALICE WAKES UP, SHE'LL STILL BE IN KITTY'S ARMS.
BLUSH
......!
LET'S GET THE HELL OUT OF HERE.
Y...
YEAH.
I FEEL LIKE NIGHTMARE'S NOT TELLING ME SOMETHING...
HM.
THERE THEY GO.

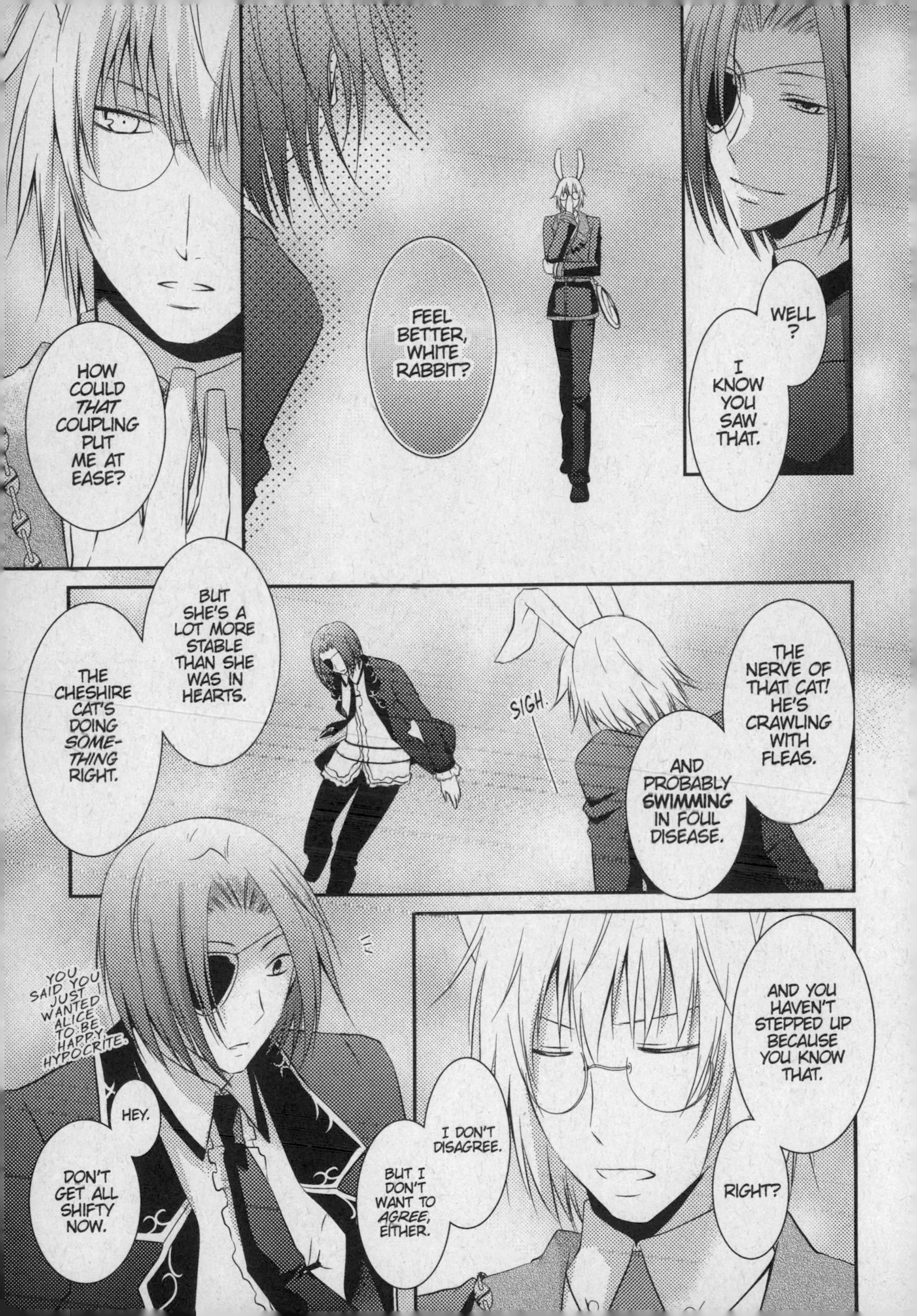
WELL?
I KNOW YOU SAW THAT.
FEEL BETTER, WHITE RABBIT?
HOW COULD THAT COUPLING PUT ME AT EASE?
THE NERVE OF THAT CAT! HE'S CRAWLING WITH FLEAS.
AND PROBABLY SWIMMING IN FOUL DISEASE.
SIGH.
BUT SHE'S A LOT MORE STABLE THAN SHE WAS IN HEARTS.
THE CHESHIRE CAT'S DOING SOMETHING RIGHT.
AND YOU HAVEN'T STEPPED UP BECAUSE YOU KNOW THAT.
RIGHT?
I DON'T DISAGREE.
BUT I DON'T WANT TO AGREE, EITHER.
YOU SAID YOU JUST WANTED ALICE TO BE HAPPY, HYPOCRITE.
HEY.
DON'T GET ALL SHIFTY NOW.

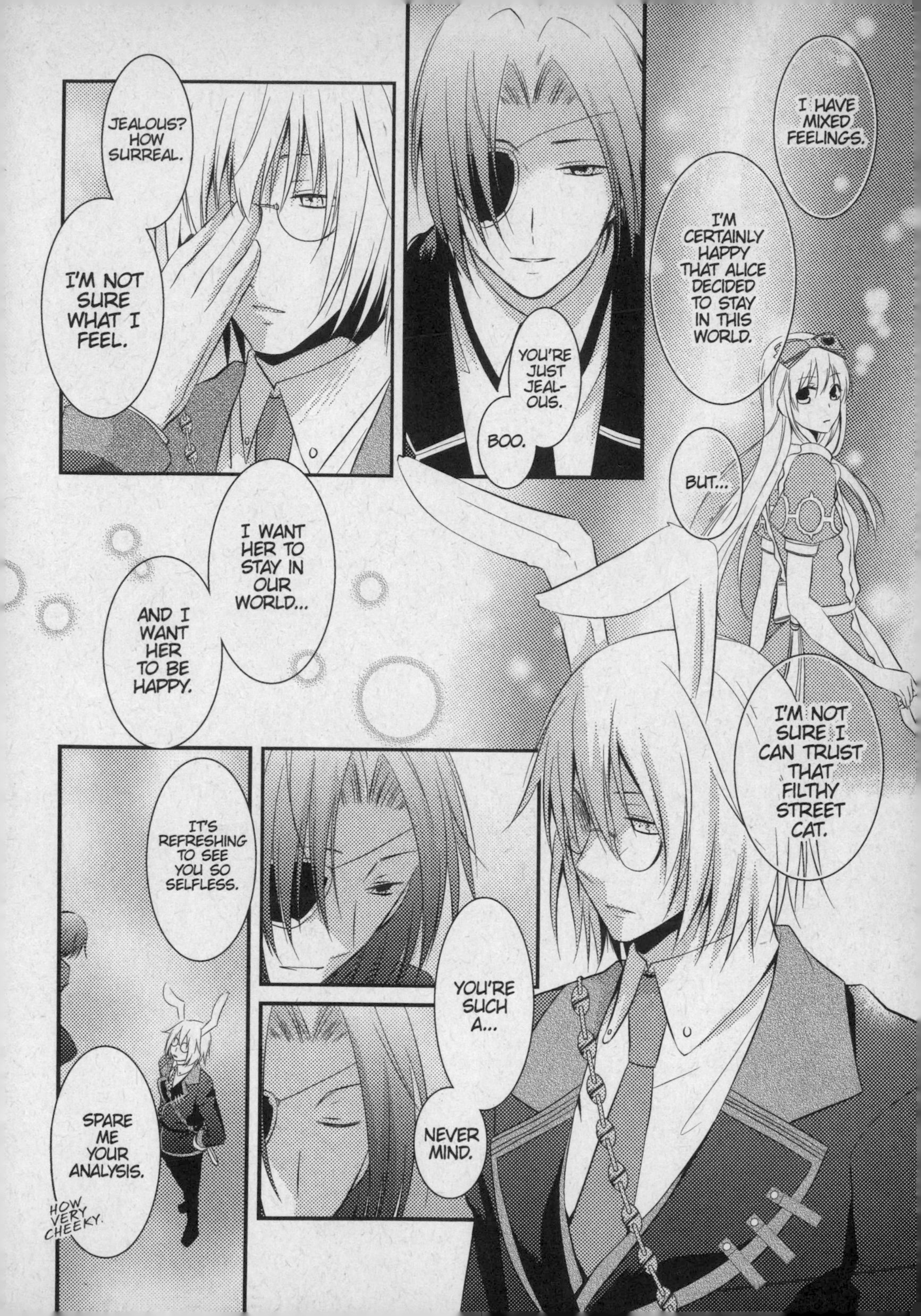
I HAVE MIXED FEELINGS.
I'M CERTAINLY HAPPY THAT ALICE DECIDED TO STAY IN THIS WORLD.
YOU'RE JUST JEAL-OUS.
BOO.
JEALOUS? HOW SURREAL.
I'M NOT SURE WHAT I FEEL.
BUT...
I'M NOT SURE I CAN TRUST THAT FILTHY STREET CAT.
I WANT HER TO STAY IN OUR WORLD...
AND I WANT HER TO BE HAPPY.
IT'S REFRESHING TO SEE YOU SO SELFLESS.
YOU'RE SUCH A...
NEVER MIND.
SPARE ME YOUR ANALYSIS.
HOW VERY CHEEKY.

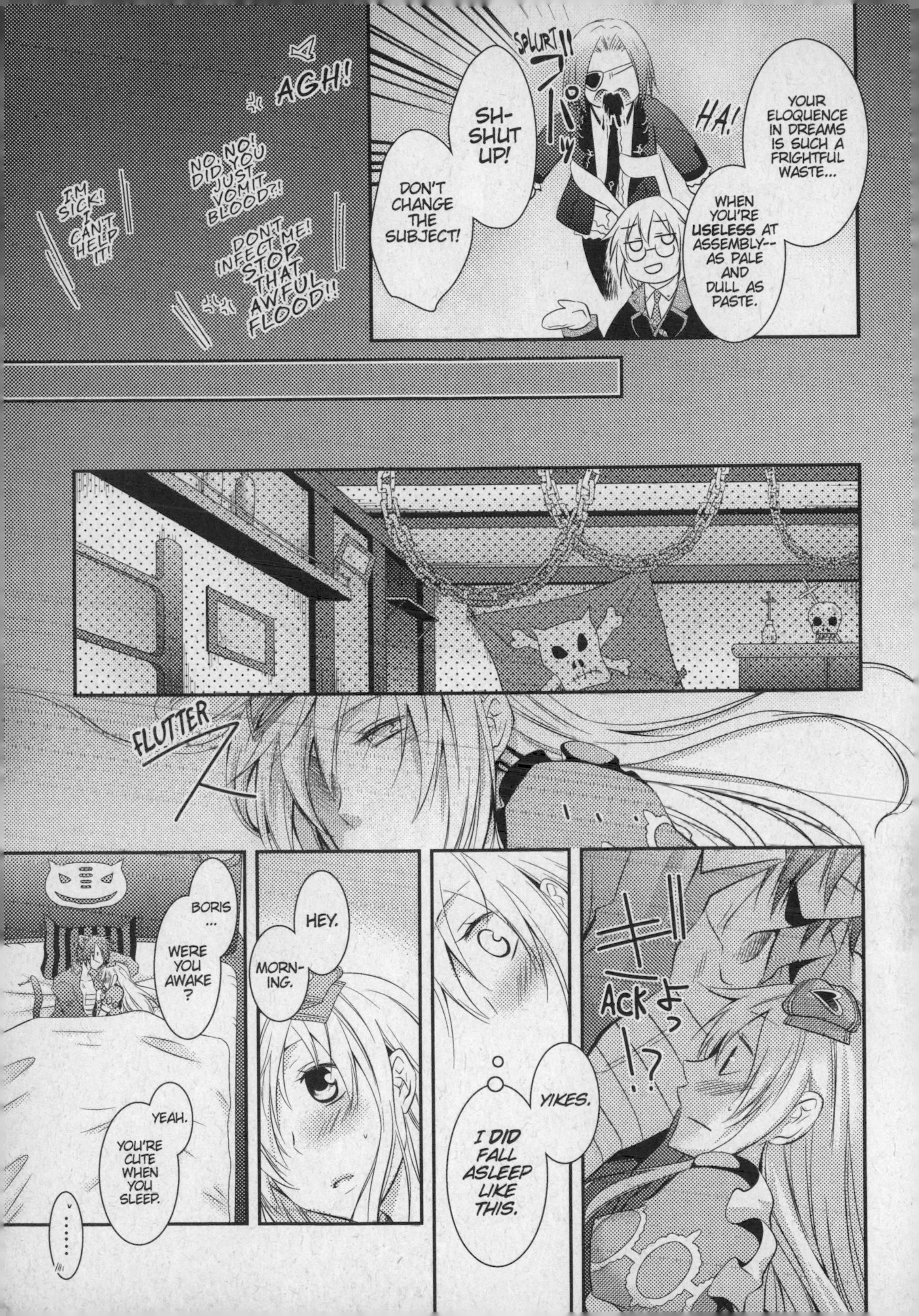

YOUR ELOQUENCE IN DREAMS IS SUCH A FRIGHTFUL WASTE...
WHEN YOU'RE USELESS AT ASSEMBLY-- AS PALE AND DULL AS PASTE.
HA!
SPLURT!!
SH-SHUT UP!
DON'T CHANGE THE SUBJECT!
AGH!
NO NO! DID YOU JUST VOMIT BLOOD?!
DON'T INFECT ME! STOP THAT AWFUL FLOOD!!
I'M SICK! I CAN'T HELP IT!
FLUTTER
...
ACK!?
YIKES.
I DID FALL ASLEEP LIKE THIS.
HEY.
MORN-ING.
BORIS ... WERE YOU AWAKE?
YEAH.
YOU'RE CUTE WHEN YOU SLEEP.
......

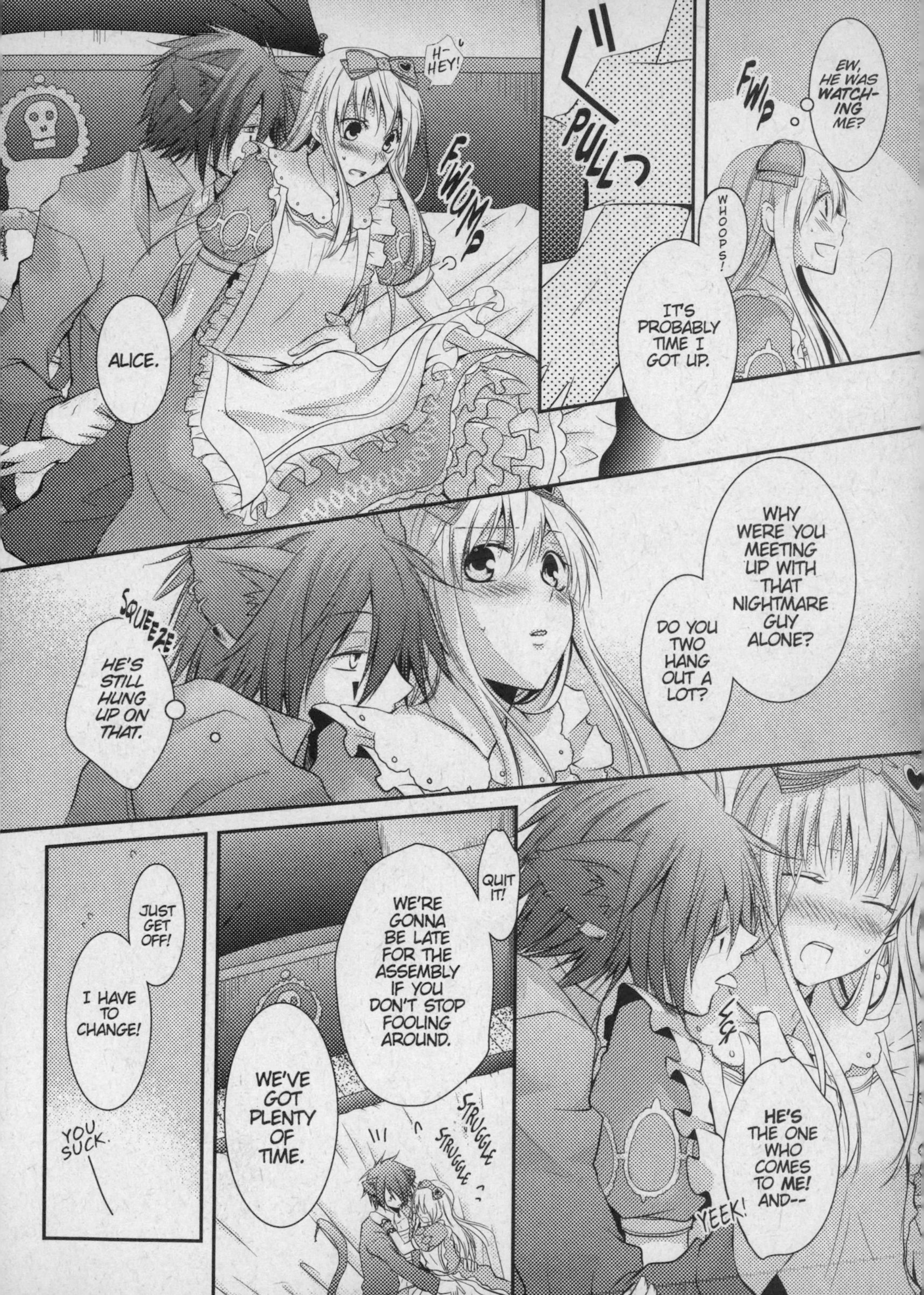
EW, HE WAS WATCHING ME?
FWIP
WHOOPS!
IT'S PROBABLY TIME I GOT UP.
PULL
H-HEY!
FWUMP
ALICE.
WHY WERE YOU MEETING UP WITH THAT NIGHTMARE GUY ALONE?
DO YOU TWO HANG OUT A LOT?
SQUEEZE
HE'S STILL HUNG UP ON THAT.
QUIT IT!
LICK
HE'S THE ONE WHO COMES TO ME! AND--
YEEK!
WE'RE GONNA BE LATE FOR THE ASSEMBLY IF YOU DON'T STOP FOOLING AROUND.
WE'VE GOT PLENTY OF TIME.
STRUGGLE
STRUGGLE
JUST GET OFF!
I HAVE TO CHANGE!
YOU SUCK.

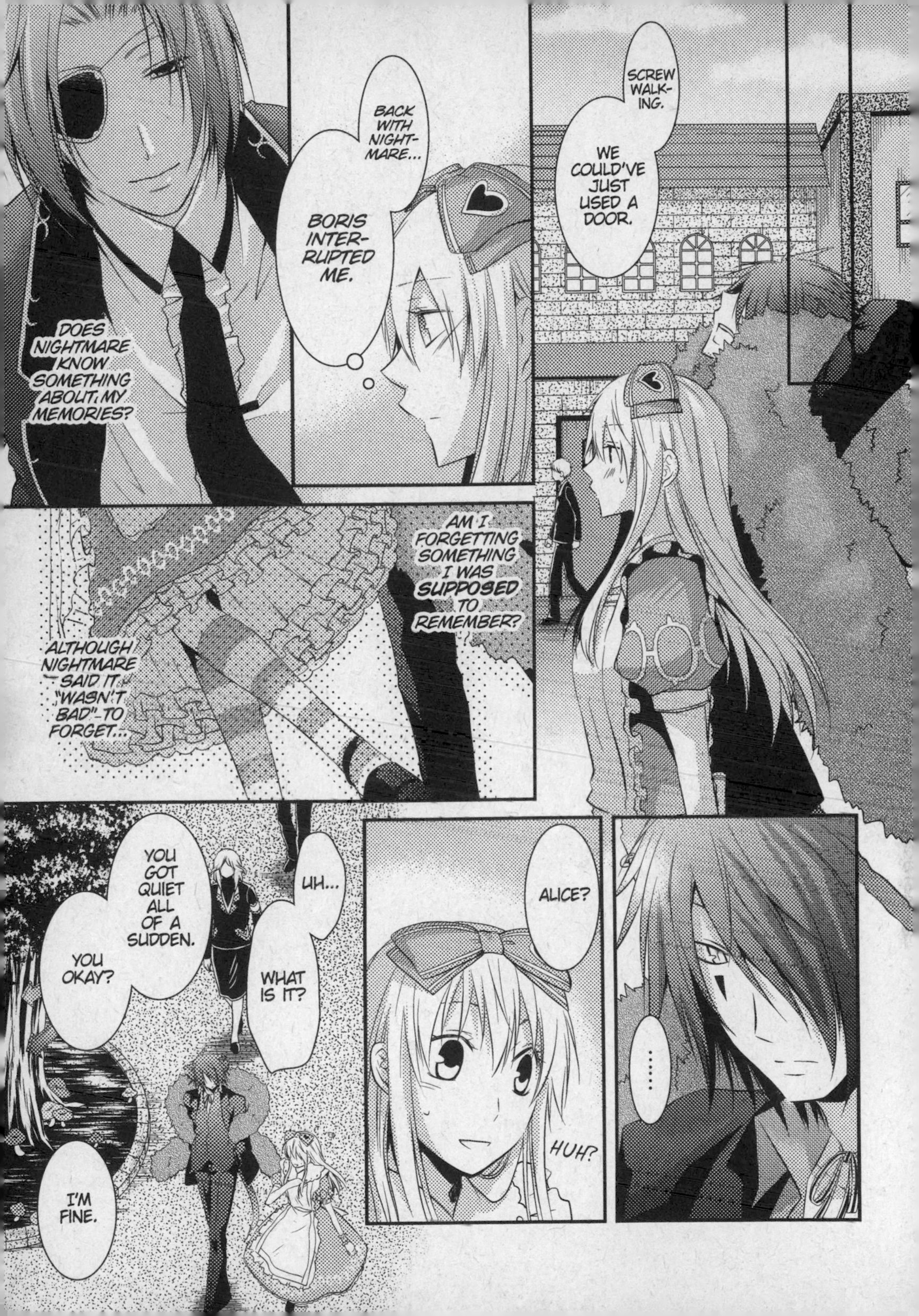
SCREW WALKING.
WE COULD'VE JUST USED A DOOR.
BACK WITH NIGHTMARE...
BORIS INTERRUPTED ME.
DOES NIGHTMARE KNOW SOMETHING ABOUT MY MEMORIES?
AM I FORGETTING SOMETHING I WAS SUPPOSED TO REMEMBER?
ALTHOUGH NIGHTMARE SAID IT "WASN'T BAD" TO FORGET...
......
ALICE?
HUH?
UH...
WHAT IS IT?
YOU GOT QUIET ALL OF A SUDDEN.
YOU OKAY?
I'M FINE.

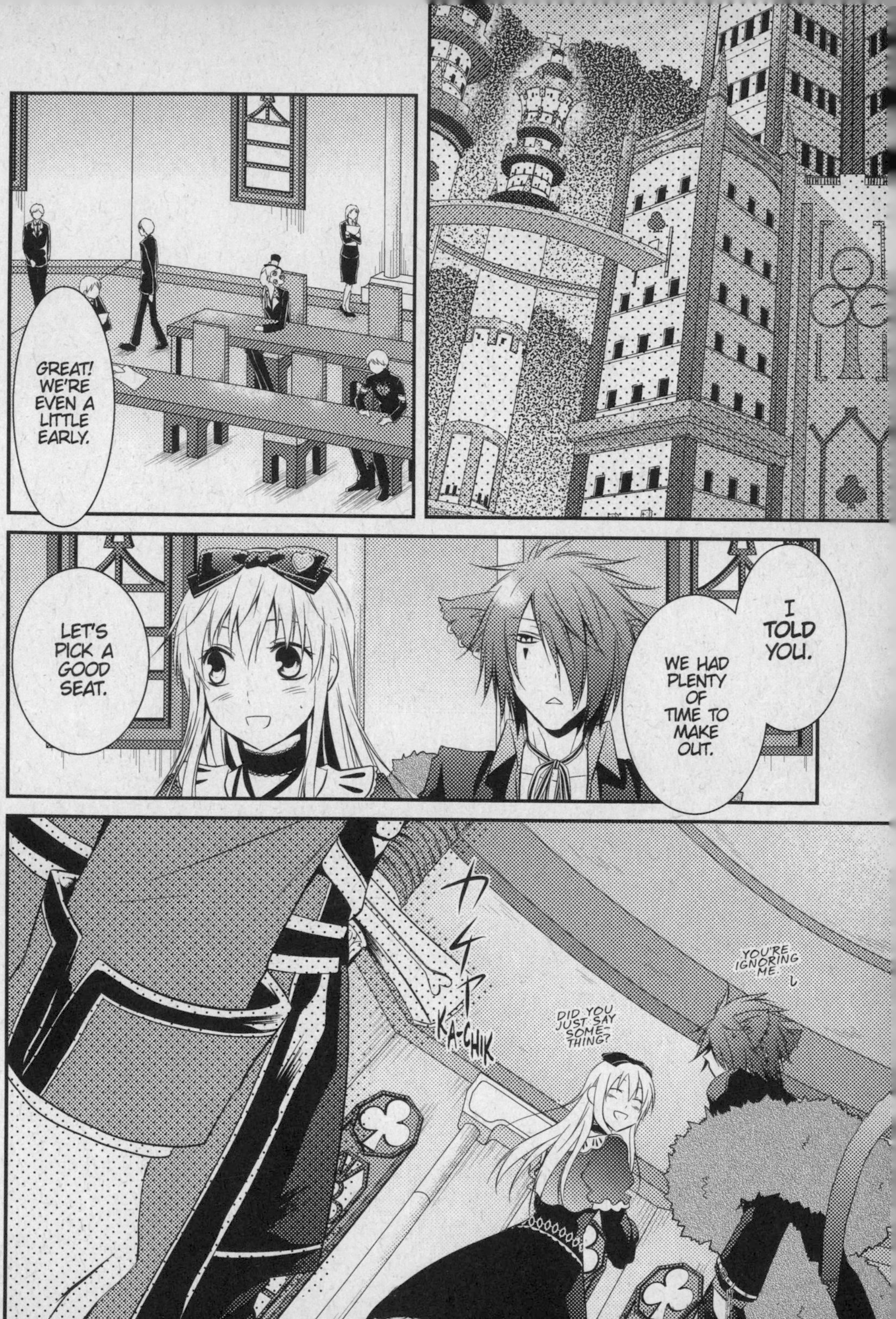
GREAT! WE'RE EVEN A LITTLE EARLY.
I TOLD YOU.
WE HAD PLENTY OF TIME TO MAKE OUT.
LET'S PICK A GOOD SEAT.
YOU'RE IGNORING ME.
DID YOU JUST SAY SOME-THING?
KA-CHIK

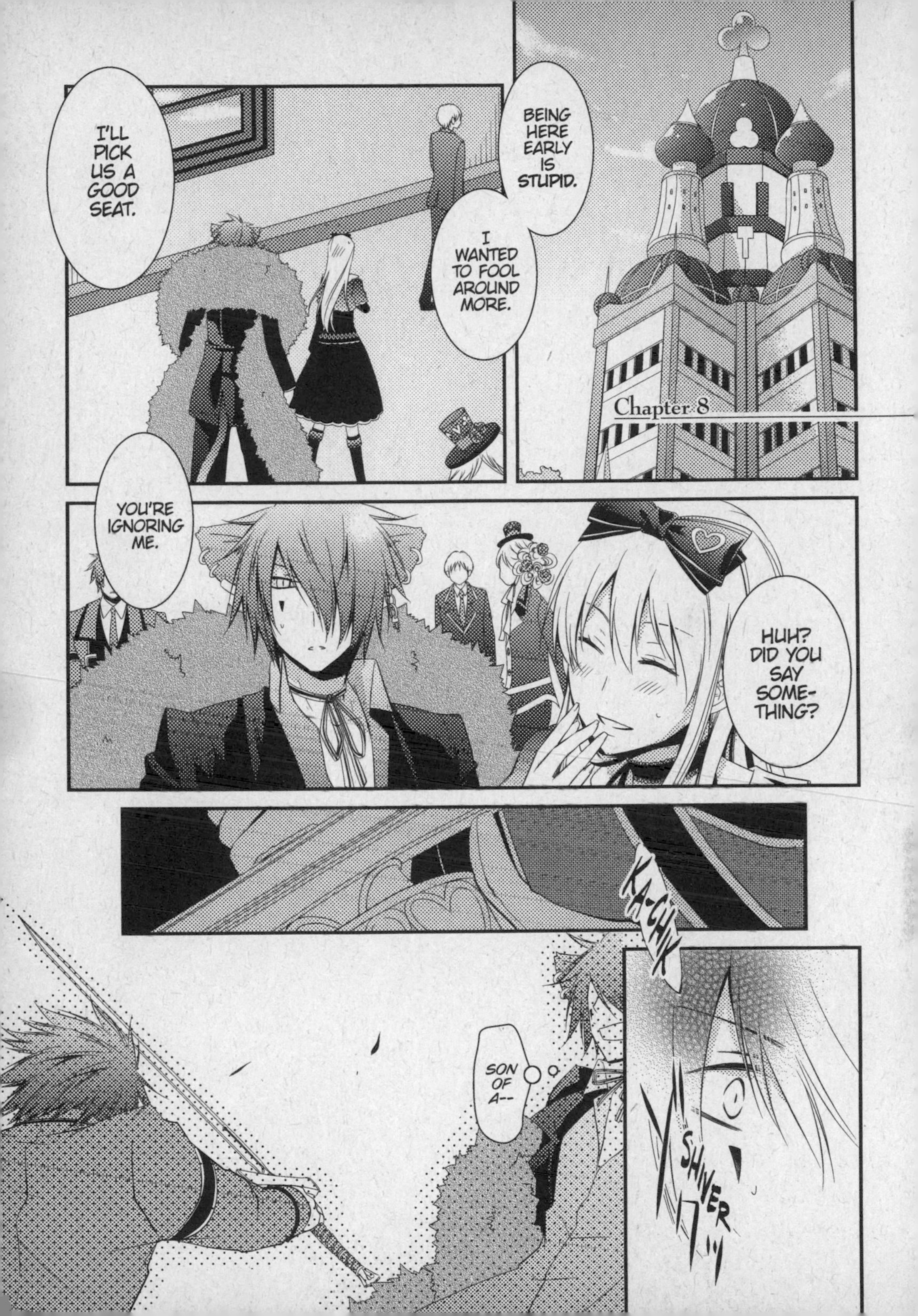
Chapter 8
BEING HERE EARLY IS STUPID.
I WANTED TO FOOL AROUND MORE.
I'LL PICK US A GOOD SEAT.
YOU'RE IGNORING ME.
HUH? DID YOU SAY SOME-THING?
KA-CHIK
SHIVER
SON OF A--

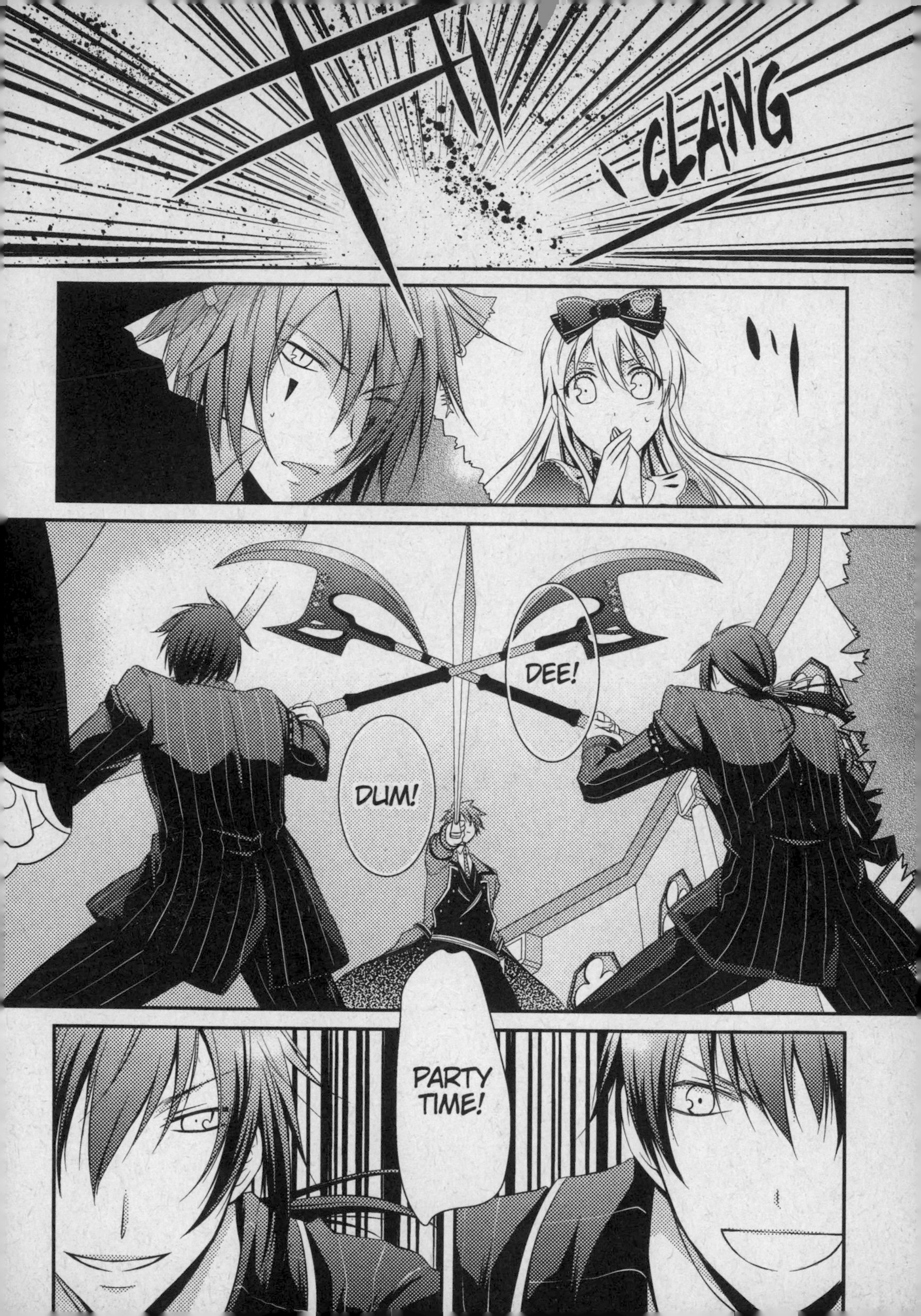
CLANG
DEE!
DUM!
PARTY TIME!

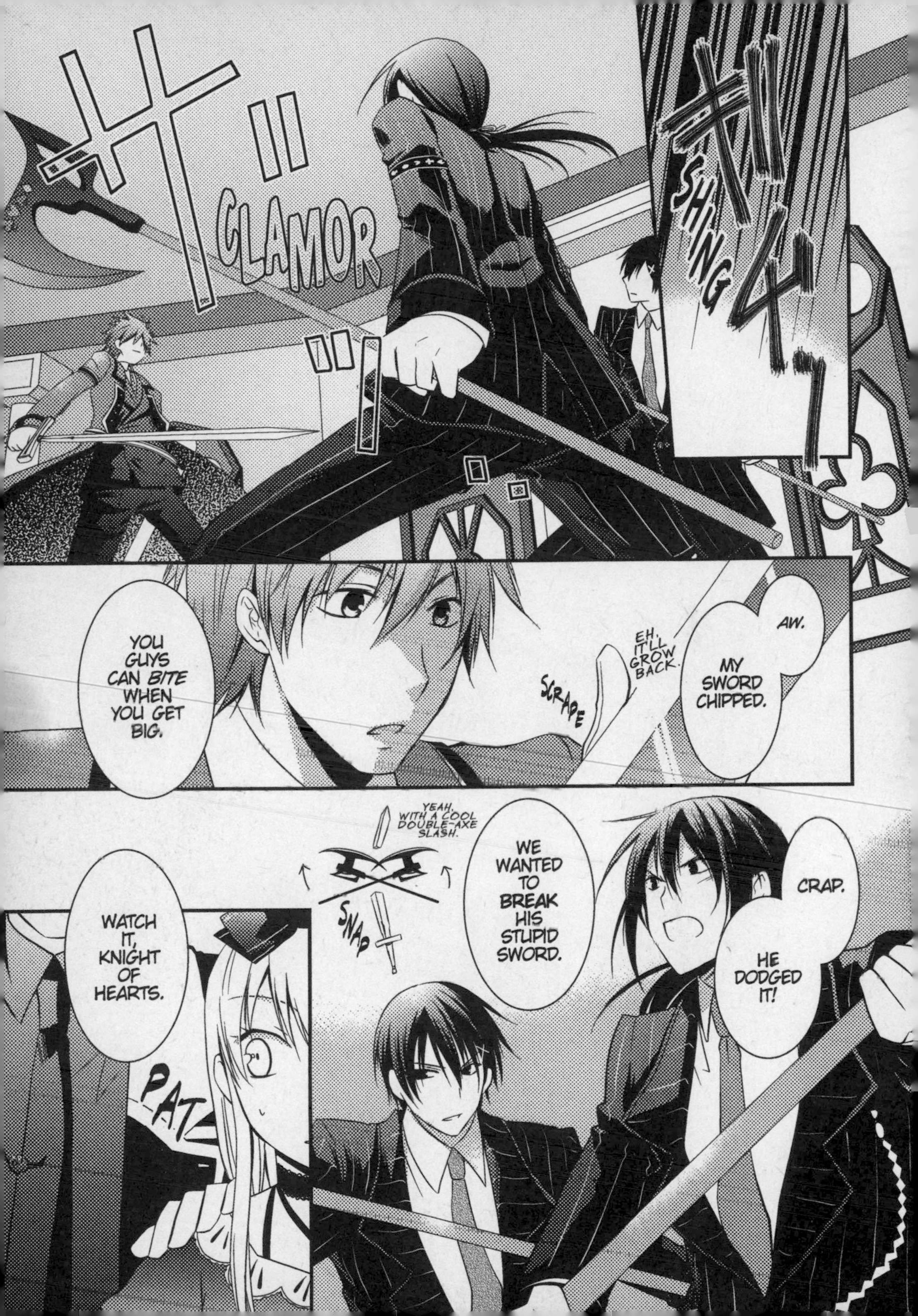
SHING
CLAMOR
AW.
MY SWORD CHIPPED.
EH, IT'LL GROW BACK.
SCRAPE
YOU GUYS CAN *BITE* WHEN YOU GET BIG.
CRAP.
HE DODGED IT!
WE WANTED TO BREAK HIS STUPID SWORD.
YEAH, WITH A COOL DOUBLE-AXE SLASH.
SNAP
WATCH IT, KNIGHT OF HEARTS.
PAT

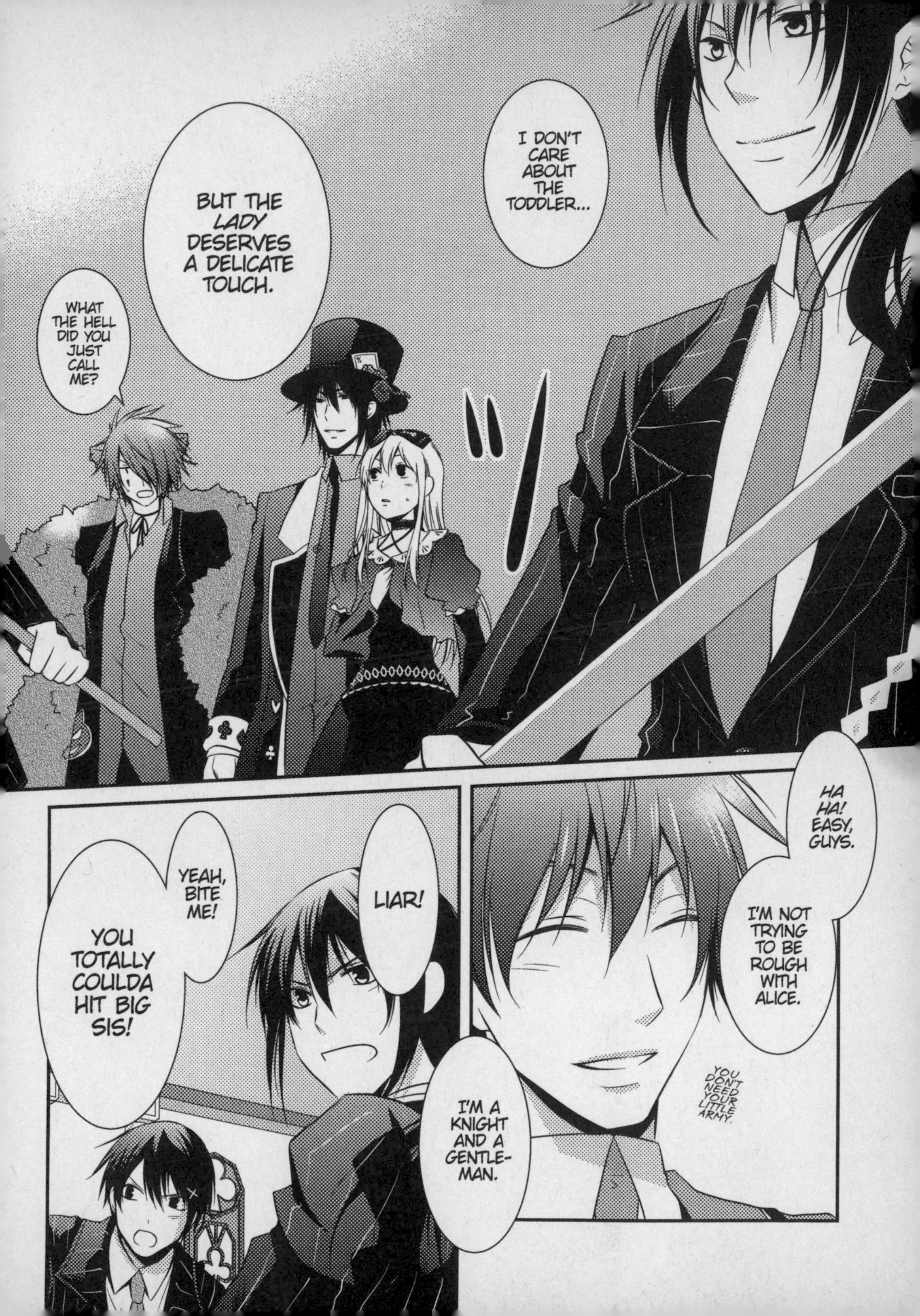
I DON'T CARE ABOUT THE TODDLER...
BUT THE *LADY* DESERVES A DELICATE TOUCH.
!!
WHAT THE HELL DID YOU JUST CALL ME?
HA HA! EASY, GUYS.
I'M NOT TRYING TO BE ROUGH WITH ALICE.
YOU DON'T NEED YOUR LITTLE ARMY.
I'M A KNIGHT AND A GENTLE-MAN.
LIAR!
YEAH, BITE ME!
YOU TOTALLY COULDA HIT BIG SIS!

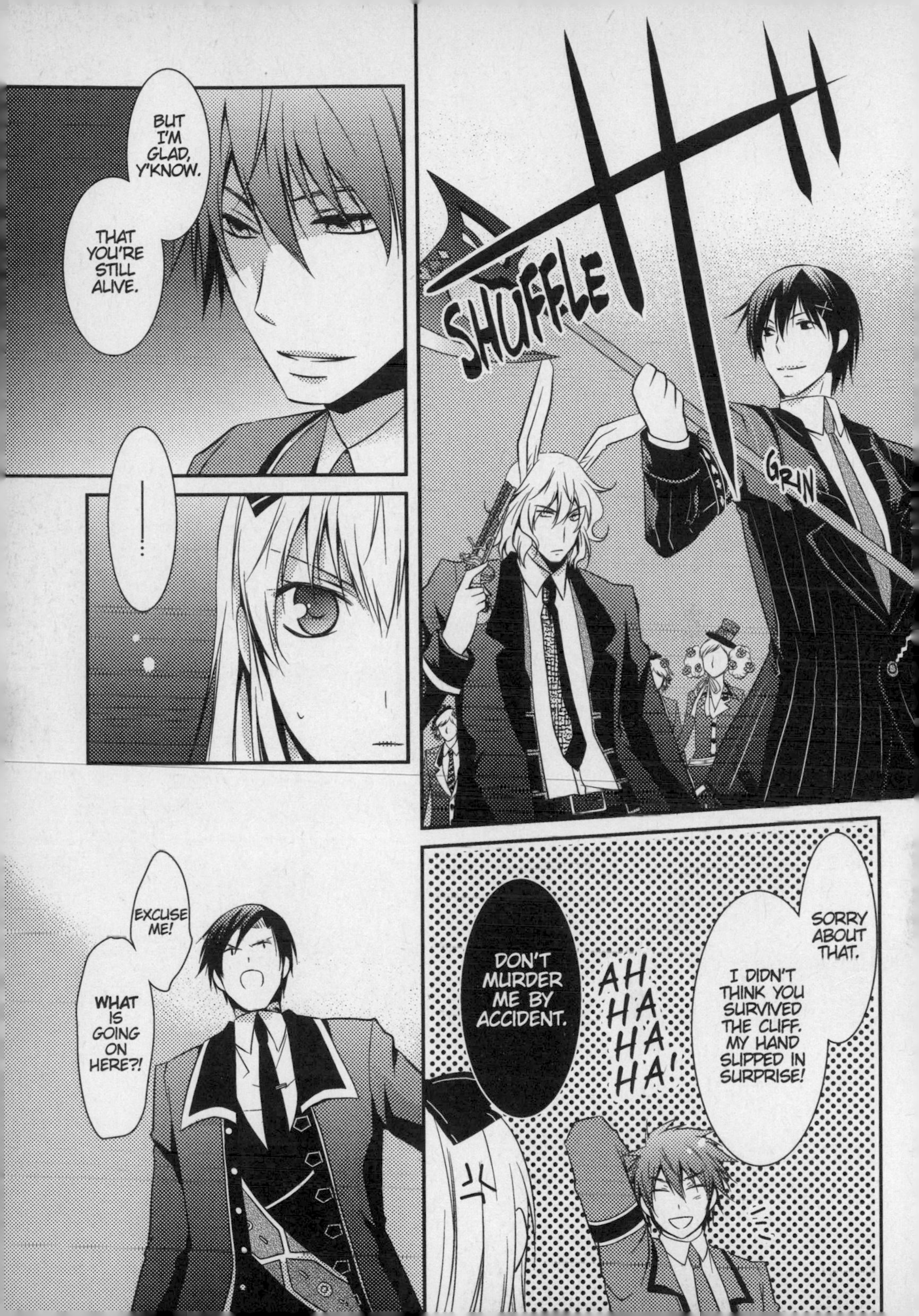
SHUFFLE
GRIN
BUT I'M GLAD, Y'KNOW.
THAT YOU'RE STILL ALIVE.
—!
SORRY ABOUT THAT.
I DIDN'T THINK YOU SURVIVED THE CLIFF. MY HAND SLIPPED IN SURPRISE!
AH HA HA HA HA!
DON'T MURDER ME BY ACCIDENT.
EXCUSE ME!
WHAT IS GOING ON HERE?!

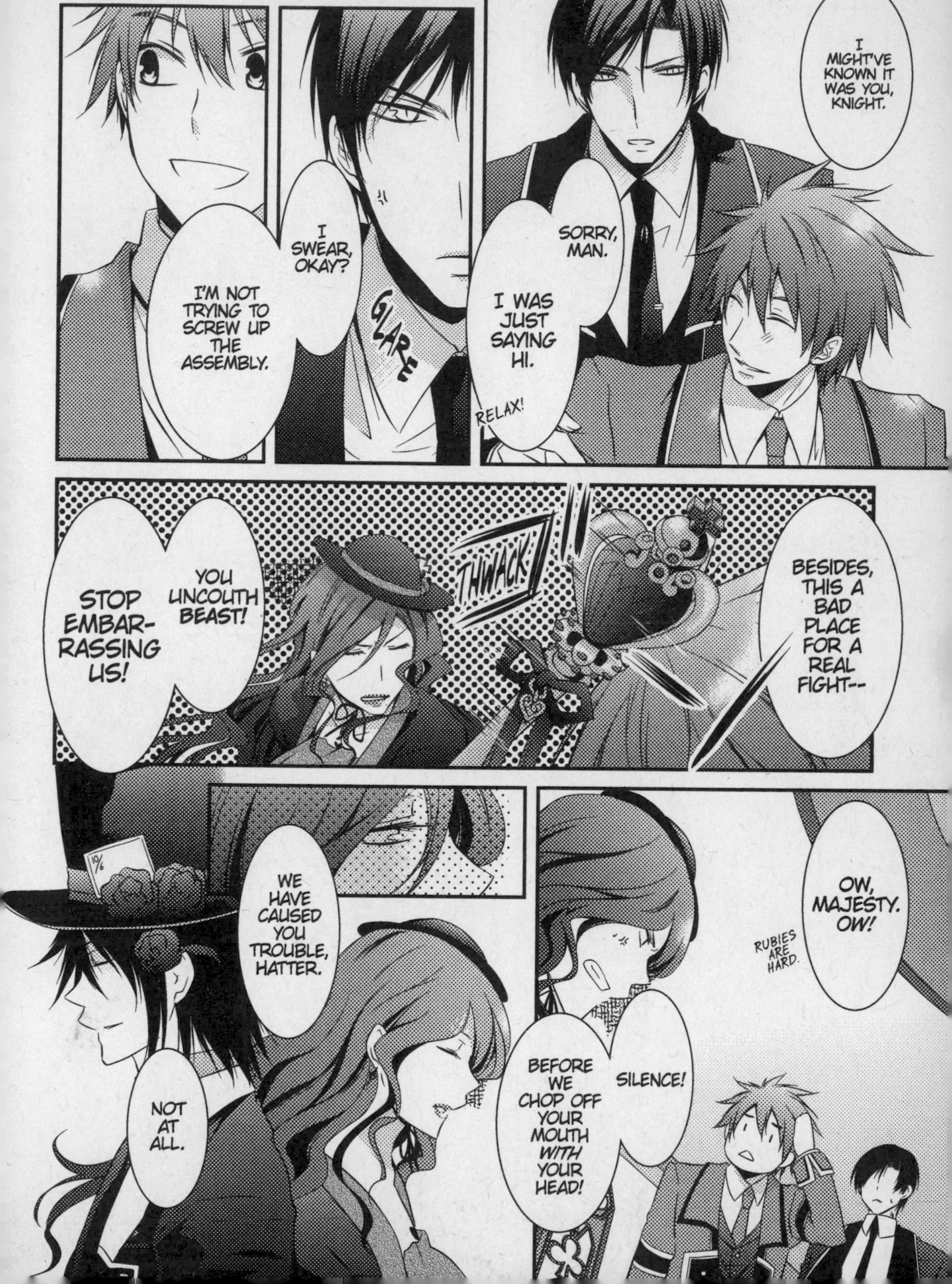
I MIGHT'VE KNOWN IT WAS YOU, KNIGHT.
SORRY, MAN.
I WAS JUST SAYING HI.
RELAX!
I SWEAR, OKAY?
GLARE
I'M NOT TRYING TO SCREW UP THE ASSEMBLY.
BESIDES, THIS A BAD PLACE FOR A REAL FIGHT--
THWACK
YOU UNCOUTH BEAST!
STOP EMBAR-RASSING US!
OW, MAJESTY. OW!
RUBIES ARE HARD.
SILENCE!
BEFORE WE CHOP OFF YOUR MOUTH *WITH* YOUR HEAD!
WE HAVE CAUSED YOU TROUBLE, HATTER.
NOT AT ALL.

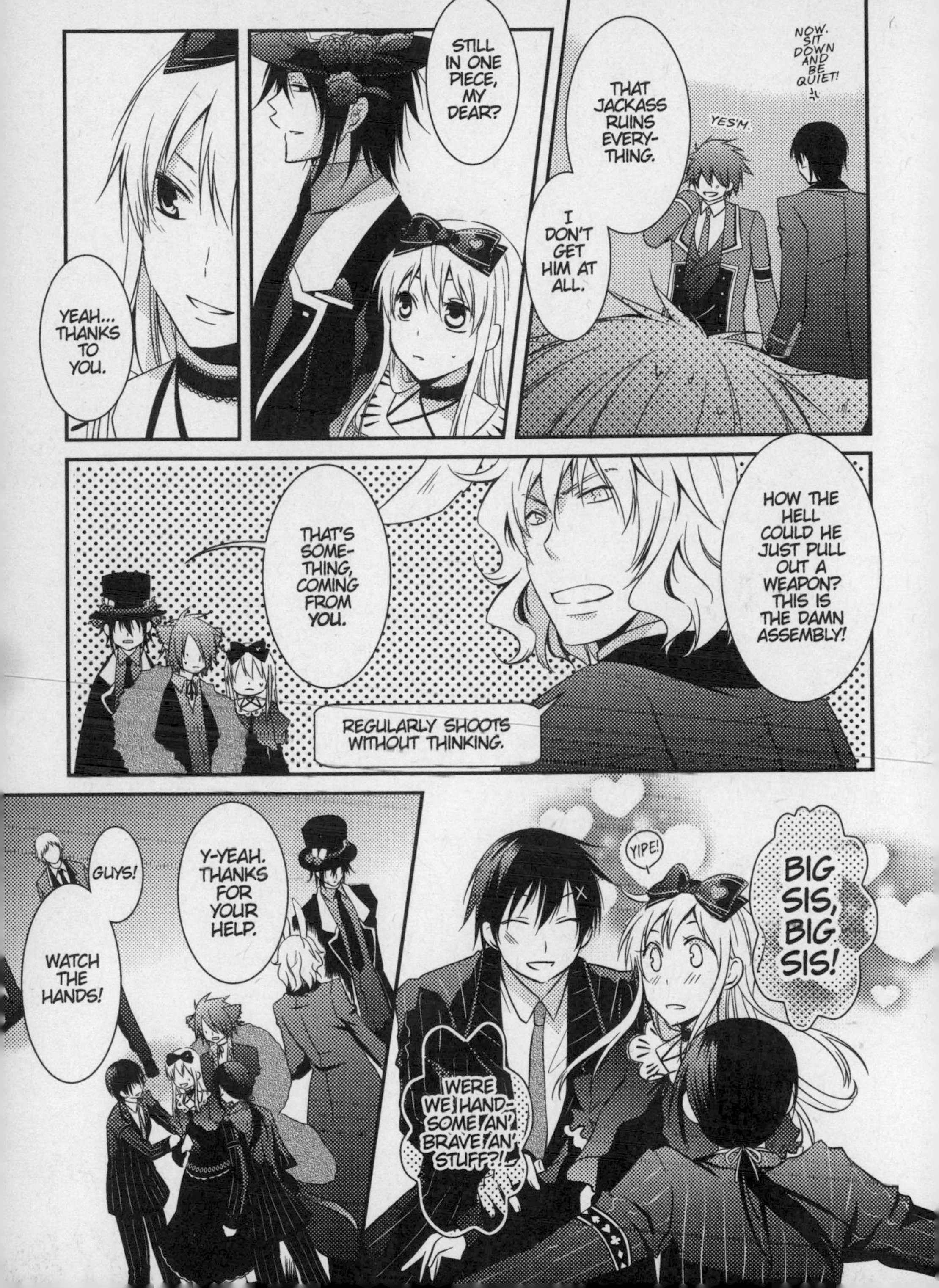
NOW. SIT DOWN AND BE QUIET!
YES'M.
THAT JACKASS RUINS EVERYTHING.
I DON'T GET HIM AT ALL.
STILL IN ONE PIECE, MY DEAR?
YEAH... THANKS TO YOU.
HOW THE HELL COULD HE JUST PULL OUT A WEAPON? THIS IS THE DAMN ASSEMBLY!
THAT'S SOME-THING, COMING FROM YOU.
REGULARLY SHOOTS WITHOUT THINKING.
BIG SIS, BIG SIS!
YIPE!
WERE WE HAND-SOME AN' BRAVE AN' STUFF?!
Y-YEAH. THANKS FOR YOUR HELP.
GUYS!
WATCH THE HANDS!

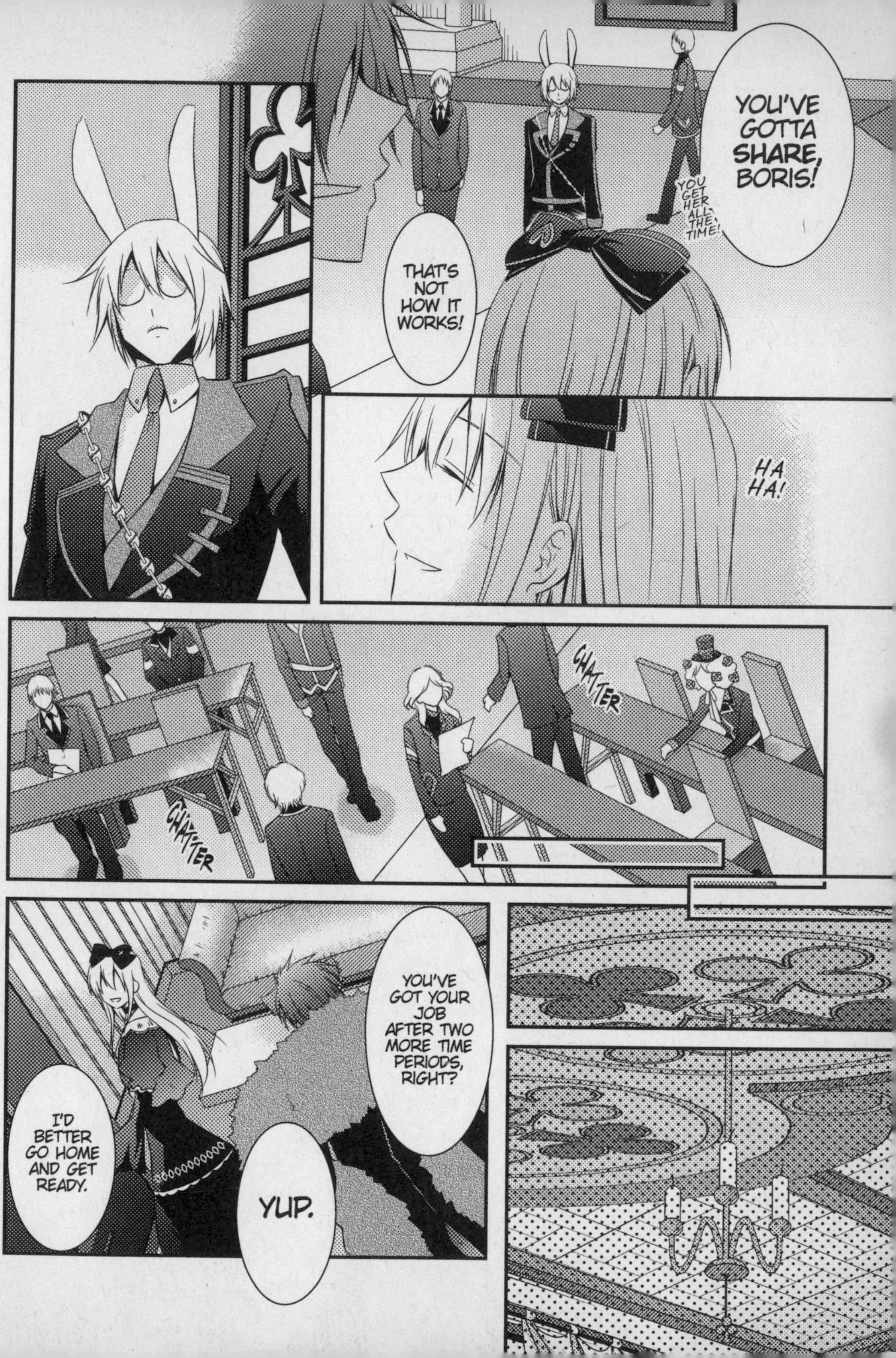

YOU'VE GOTTA SHARE, BORIS!
YOU GET HER ALL THE TIME!
THAT'S NOT HOW IT WORKS!
HA HA!
CHATTER
CHATTER
YOU'VE GOT YOUR JOB AFTER TWO MORE TIME PERIODS, RIGHT?
I'D BETTER GO HOME AND GET READY.
YUP.

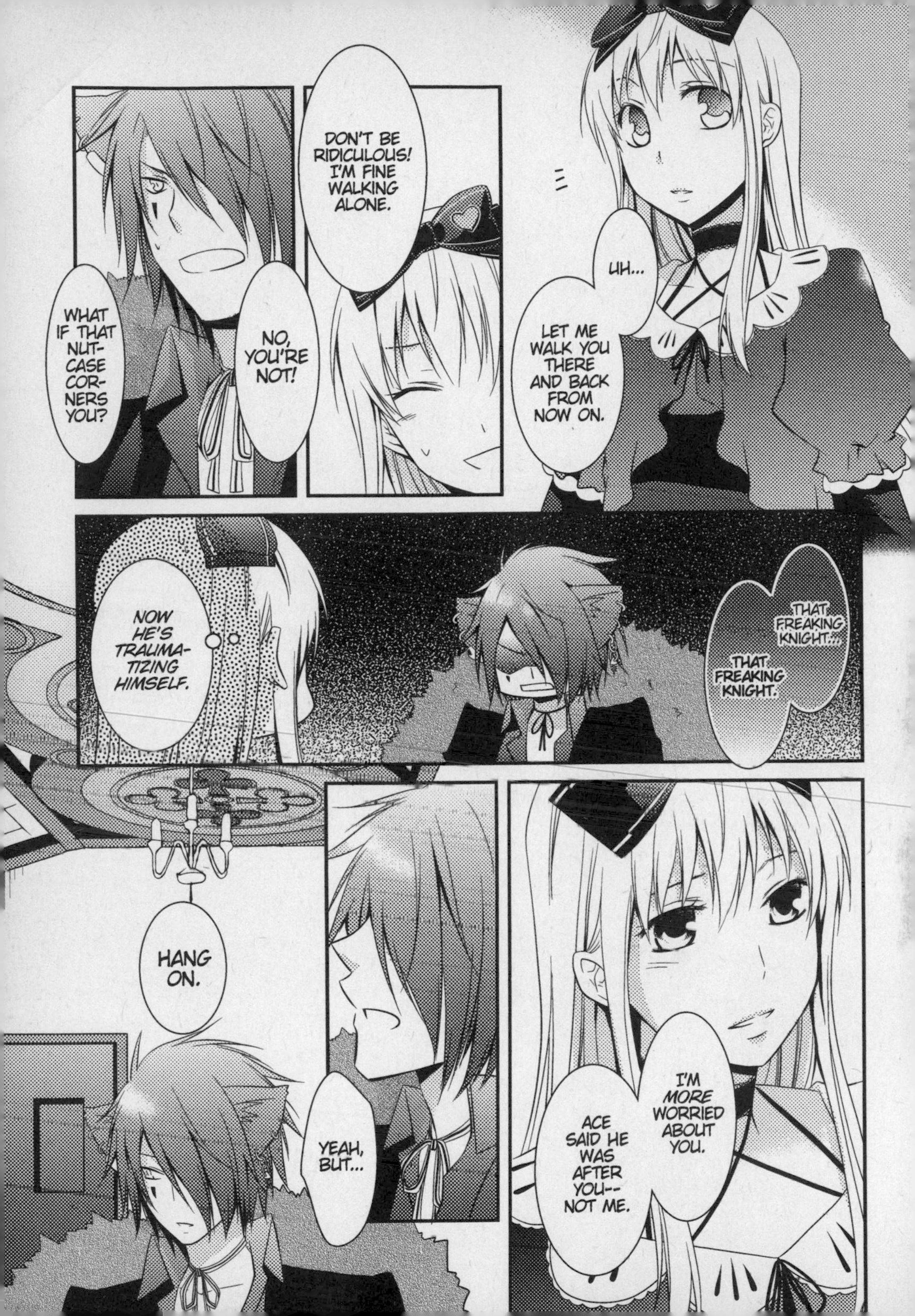
UH...
LET ME WALK YOU THERE AND BACK FROM NOW ON.
DON'T BE RIDICULOUS! I'M FINE WALKING ALONE.
NO, YOU'RE NOT!
WHAT IF THAT NUT-CASE COR-NERS YOU?
THAT FREAKING KNIGHT...
THAT FREAKING KNIGHT.
NOW HE'S TRAUMA-TIZING HIMSELF.
I'M MORE WORRIED ABOUT YOU.
ACE SAID HE WAS AFTER YOU-- NOT ME.
HANG ON.
YEAH, BUT...

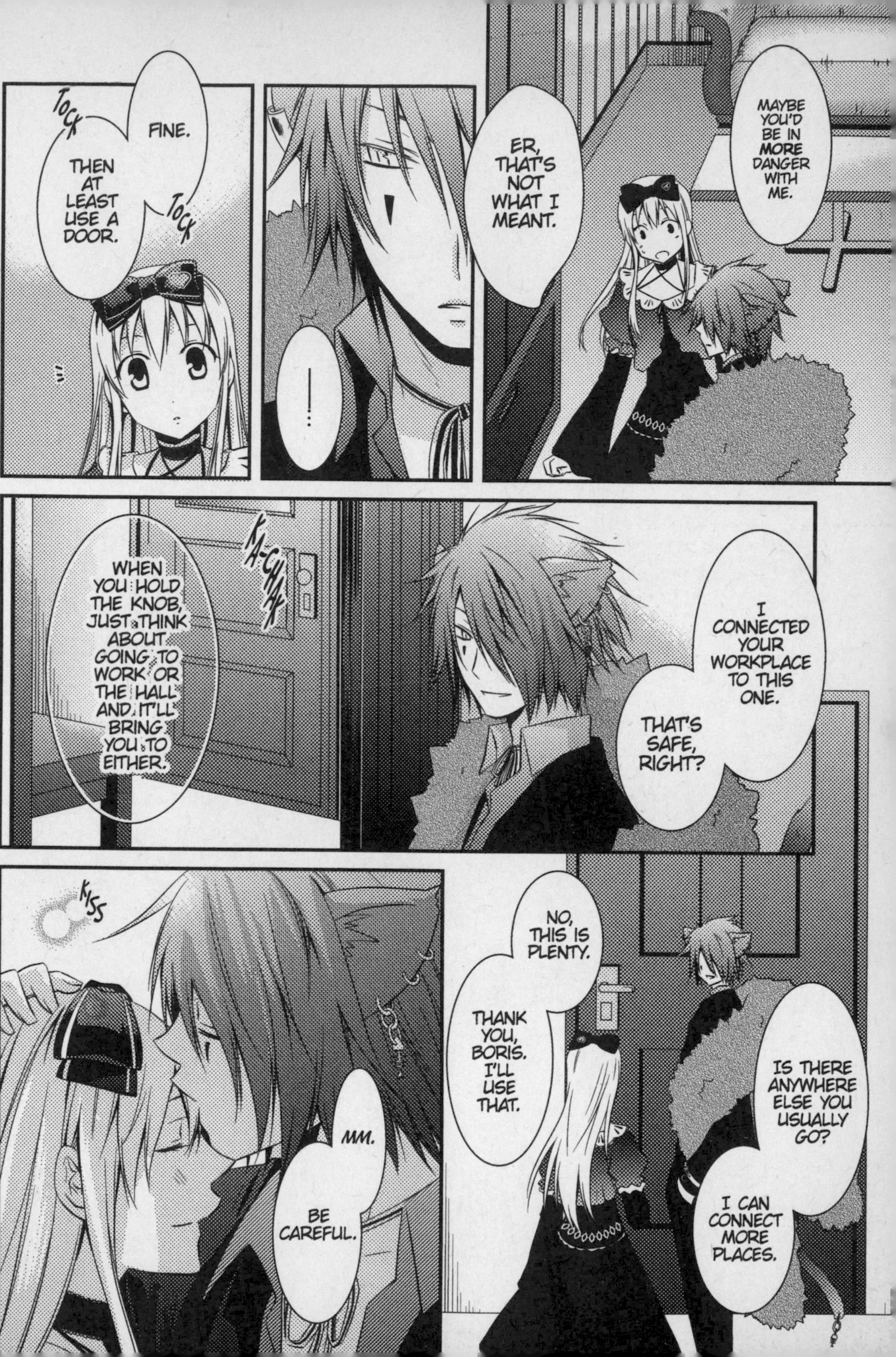
MAYBE YOU'D BE IN MORE DANGER WITH ME.
ER, THAT'S NOT WHAT I MEANT.
...!
TOCK
TOCK
FINE.
THEN AT LEAST USE A DOOR.
...
I CONNECTED YOUR WORKPLACE TO THIS ONE.
THAT'S SAFE, RIGHT?
KA-CHAK
WHEN YOU HOLD THE KNOB, JUST THINK ABOUT GOING TO WORK OR THE HALL AND IT'LL BRING YOU TO EITHER.
IS THERE ANYWHERE ELSE YOU USUALLY GO?
I CAN CONNECT MORE PLACES.
NO, THIS IS PLENTY.
THANK YOU, BORIS. I'LL USE THAT.
KISS
MM.
BE CAREFUL.

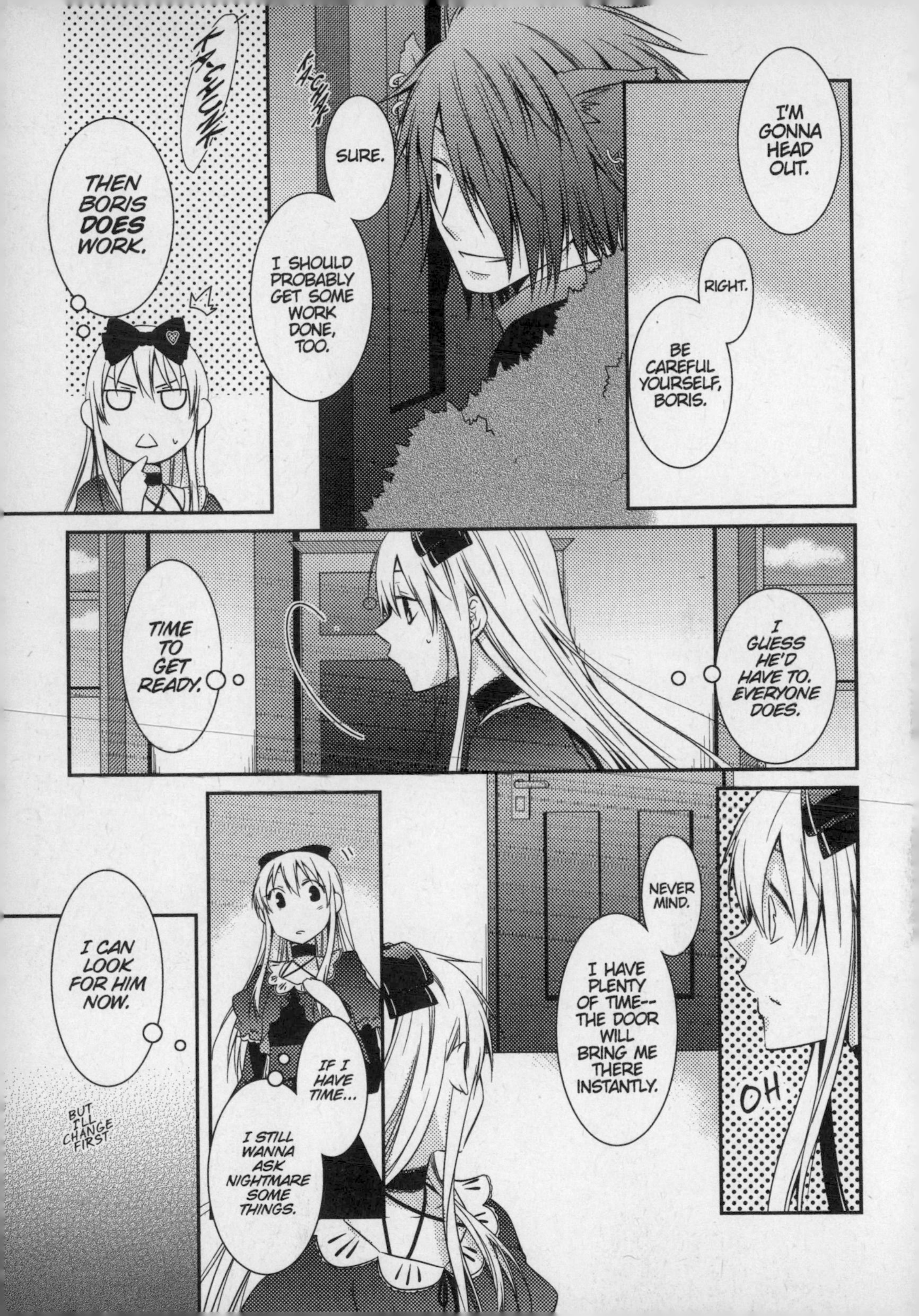
I'M GONNA HEAD OUT.
RIGHT.
BE CAREFUL YOURSELF, BORIS.
KA-CHAK
SURE.
I SHOULD PROBABLY GET SOME WORK DONE, TOO.
KA-CHUNK
THEN BORIS DOES WORK.
I GUESS HE'D HAVE TO. EVERYONE DOES.
TIME TO GET READY.
OH
NEVER MIND.
I HAVE PLENTY OF TIME-- THE DOOR WILL BRING ME THERE INSTANTLY.
IF I HAVE TIME...
I STILL WANNA ASK NIGHTMARE SOME THINGS.
I CAN LOOK FOR HIM NOW.
BUT I'LL CHANGE FIRST

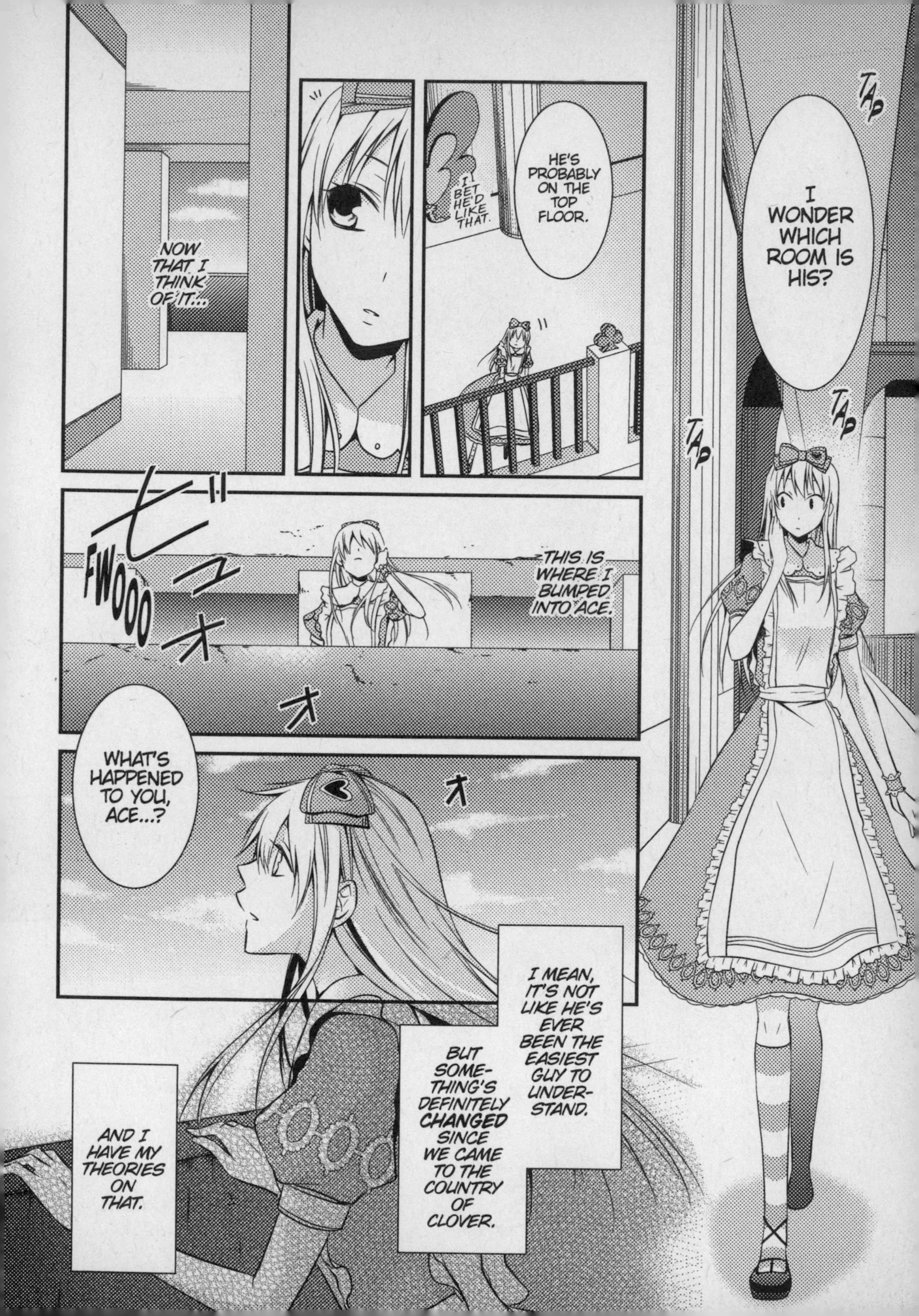
TAP
I WONDER WHICH ROOM IS HIS?
TAP
TAP
HE'S PROBABLY ON THE TOP FLOOR.
I BET HE'D LIKE THAT.
NOW THAT I THINK OF IT...
THIS IS WHERE I BUMPED INTO ACE.
FWOOO
WHAT'S HAPPENED TO YOU, ACE...?
I MEAN, IT'S NOT LIKE HE'S EVER BEEN THE EASIEST GUY TO UNDER-STAND.
BUT SOME-THING'S DEFINITELY CHANGED SINCE WE CAME TO THE COUNTRY OF CLOVER.
AND I HAVE MY THEORIES ON THAT.

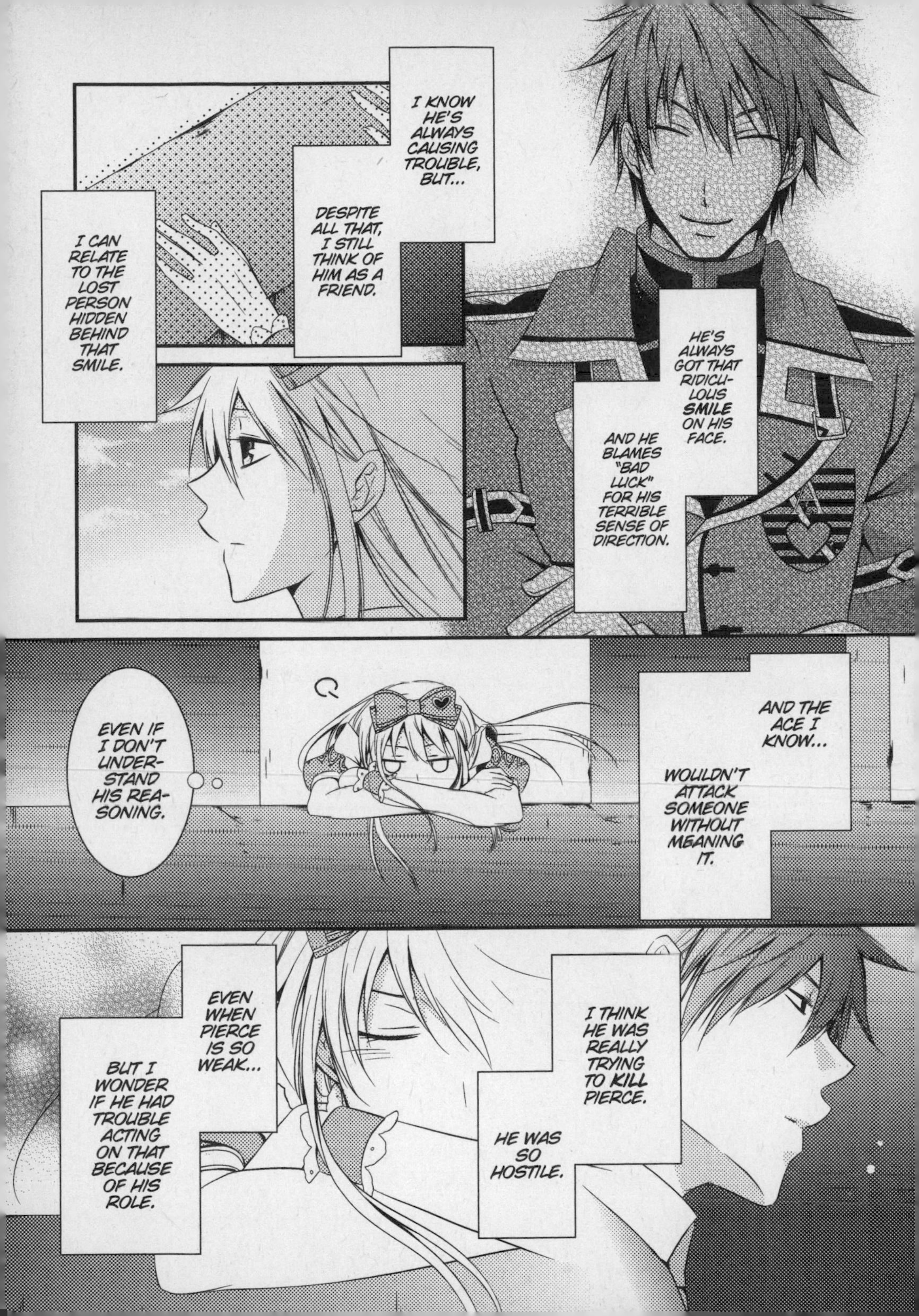
HE'S ALWAYS GOT THAT RIDICULOUS SMILE ON HIS FACE.
AND HE BLAMES "BAD LUCK" FOR HIS TERRIBLE SENSE OF DIRECTION.
I KNOW HE'S ALWAYS CAUSING TROUBLE, BUT...
DESPITE ALL THAT, I STILL THINK OF HIM AS A FRIEND.
I CAN RELATE TO THE LOST PERSON HIDDEN BEHIND THAT SMILE.
AND THE ACE I KNOW...
WOULDN'T ATTACK SOMEONE WITHOUT MEANING IT.
EVEN IF I DON'T UNDERSTAND HIS REASONING.
I THINK HE WAS REALLY TRYING TO KILL PIERCE.
HE WAS SO HOSTILE.
EVEN WHEN PIERCE IS SO WEAK...
BUT I WONDER IF HE HAD TROUBLE ACTING ON THAT BECAUSE OF HIS ROLE.

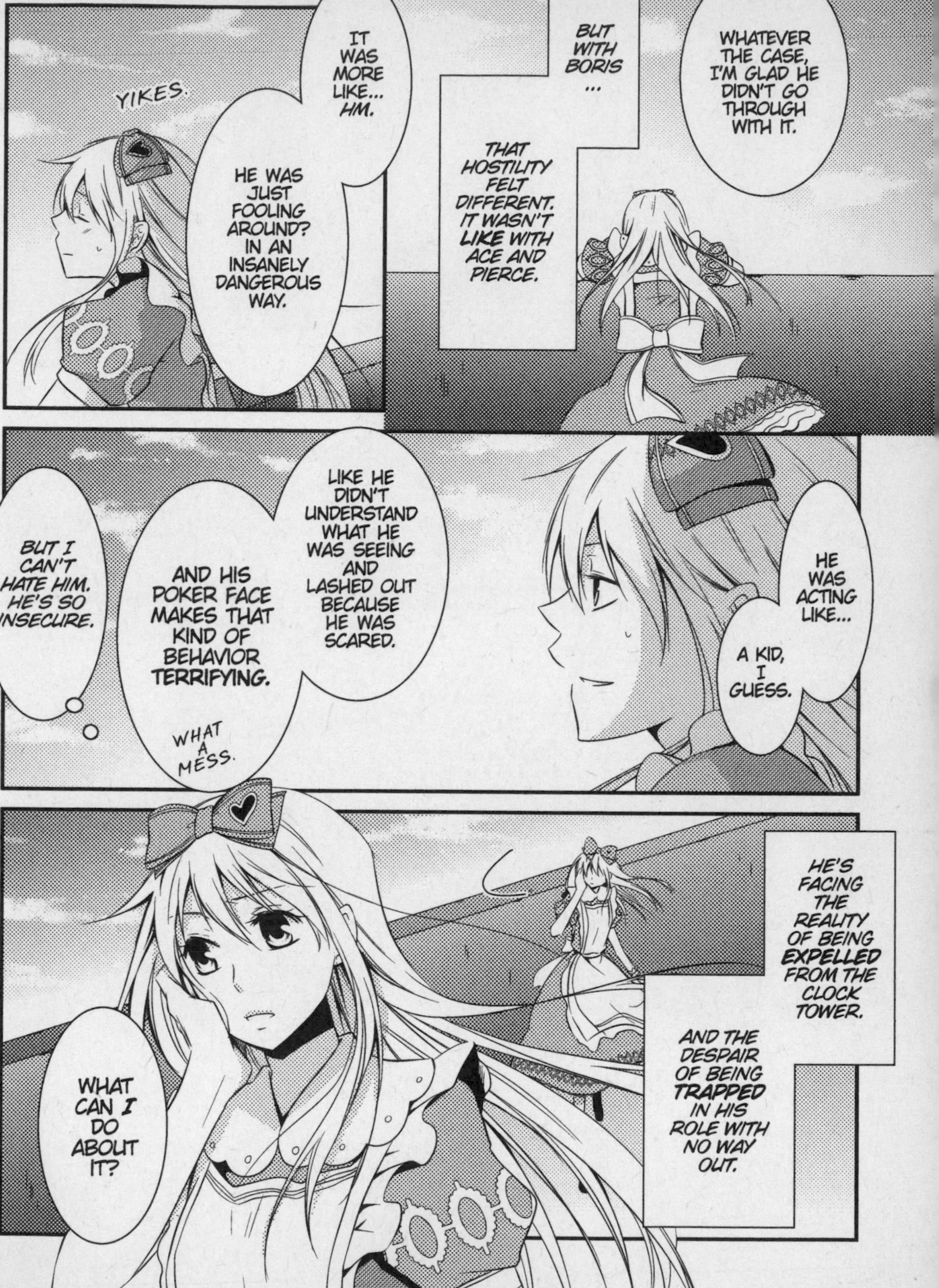
WHATEVER THE CASE, I'M GLAD HE DIDN'T GO THROUGH WITH IT.
BUT WITH BORIS ...
THAT HOSTILITY FELT DIFFERENT. IT WASN'T LIKE WITH ACE AND PIERCE.
IT WAS MORE LIKE... HM.
HE WAS JUST FOOLING AROUND? IN AN INSANELY DANGEROUS WAY.
YIKES.
HE WAS ACTING LIKE...
A KID, I GUESS.
LIKE HE DIDN'T UNDERSTAND WHAT HE WAS SEEING AND LASHED OUT BECAUSE HE WAS SCARED.
AND HIS POKER FACE MAKES THAT KIND OF BEHAVIOR TERRIFYING.
WHAT A MESS.
BUT I CAN'T HATE HIM. HE'S SO INSECURE.
HE'S FACING THE REALITY OF BEING EXPELLED FROM THE CLOCK TOWER.
AND THE DESPAIR OF BEING TRAPPED IN HIS ROLE WITH NO WAY OUT.
WHAT CAN I DO ABOUT IT?

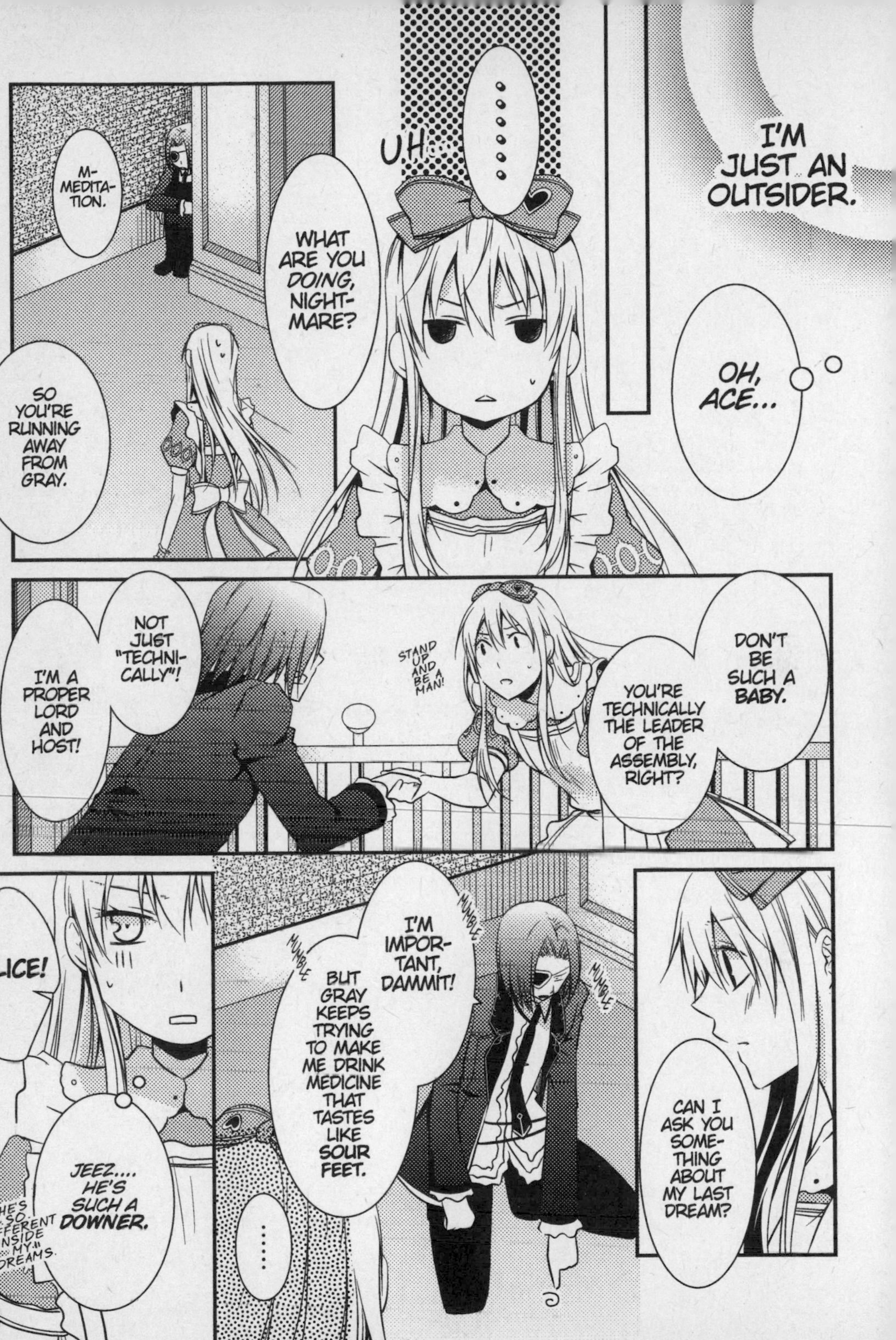
I'M JUST AN OUTSIDER.
OH, ACE...
......
UH...
WHAT ARE YOU DOING, NIGHTMARE?
M-MEDITATION.
SO YOU'RE RUNNING AWAY FROM GRAY.
DON'T BE SUCH A BABY.
YOU'RE TECHNICALLY THE LEADER OF THE ASSEMBLY, RIGHT?
STAND UP AND BE A MAN!
NOT JUST "TECHNICALLY"!
I'M A PROPER LORD AND HOST!
CAN I ASK YOU SOMETHING ABOUT MY LAST DREAM?
MUMBLE
MUMBLE
I'M IMPORTANT, DAMMIT!
MUMBLE
BUT GRAY KEEPS TRYING TO MAKE ME DRINK MEDICINE THAT TASTES LIKE SOUR FEET.
......
ALICE!
JEEZ.... HE'S SUCH A DOWNER.
HE'S SO DIFFERENT INSIDE MY DREAMS.

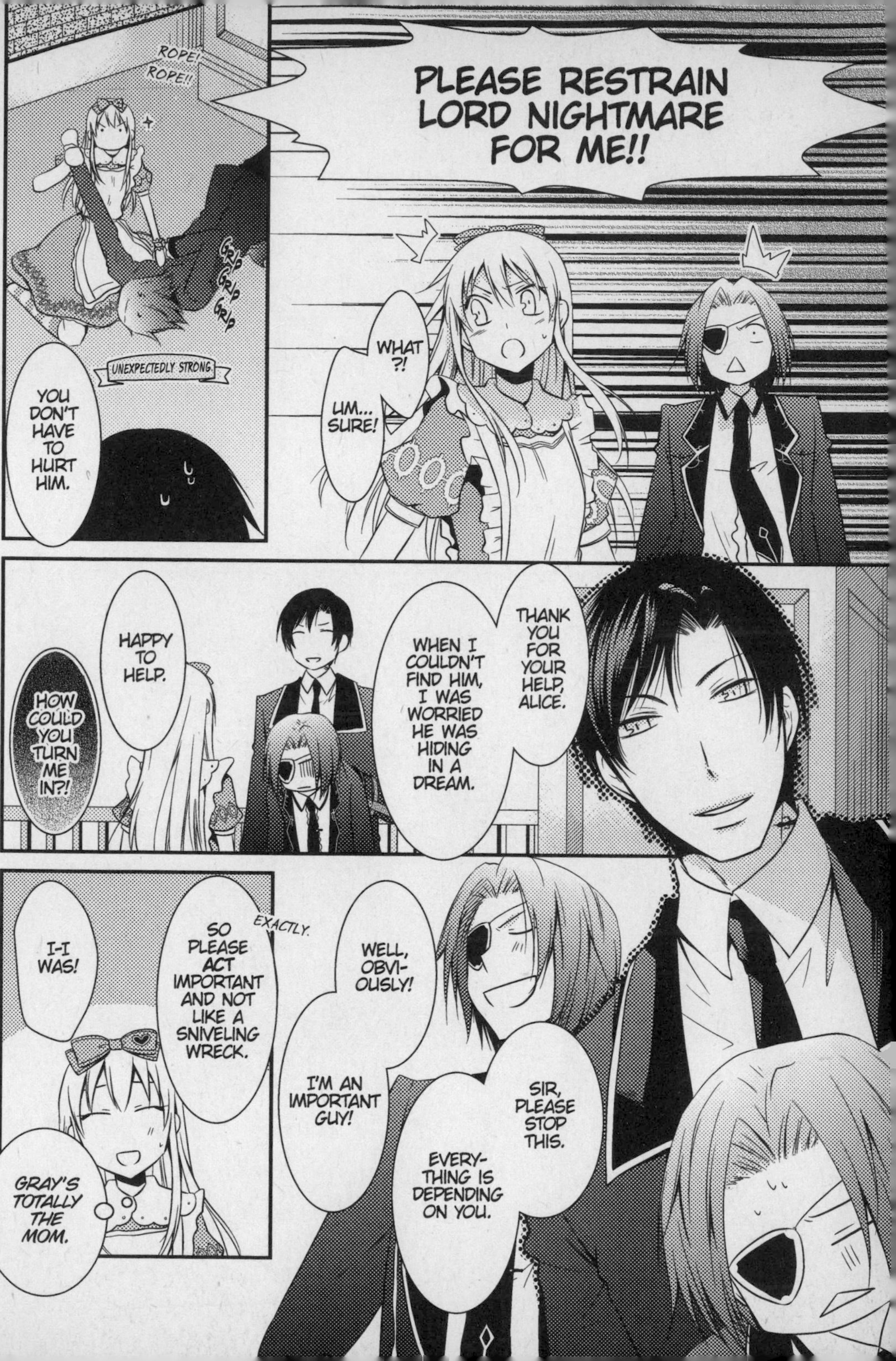
PLEASE RESTRAIN LORD NIGHTMARE FOR ME!!
WHAT?!
UM... SURE!
ROPE! ROPE!!
GRIP GRIP GRIP
UNEXPECTEDLY STRONG.
YOU DON'T HAVE TO HURT HIM.
THANK YOU FOR YOUR HELP, ALICE.
WHEN I COULDN'T FIND HIM, I WAS WORRIED HE WAS HIDING IN A DREAM.
HAPPY TO HELP.
HOW COULD YOU TURN ME IN?!
SIR, PLEASE STOP THIS.
EVERYTHING IS DEPENDING ON YOU.
WELL, OBVIOUSLY!
I'M AN IMPORTANT GUY!
EXACTLY.
SO PLEASE ACT IMPORTANT AND NOT LIKE A SNIVELING WRECK.
I-I WAS!
GRAY'S TOTALLY THE MOM.

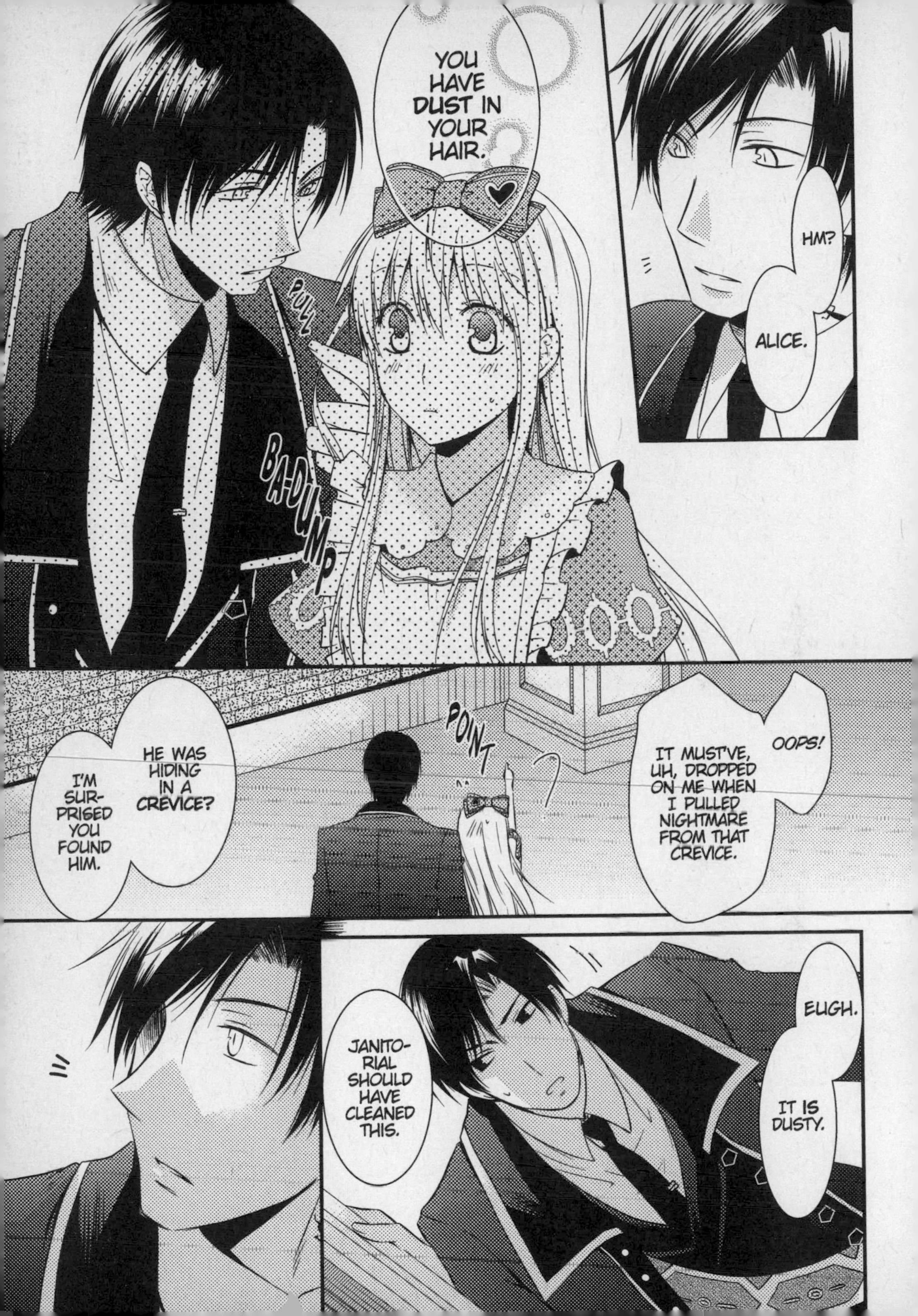
HM?
ALICE.
YOU HAVE DUST IN YOUR HAIR.
PULL
BA-DUMP
OOPS!
IT MUST'VE, UH, DROPPED ON ME WHEN I PULLED NIGHTMARE FROM THAT CREVICE.
POINT
HE WAS HIDING IN A CREVICE?
I'M SUR-PRISED YOU FOUND HIM.
EUGH.
IT IS DUSTY.
JANITO-RIAL SHOULD HAVE CLEANED THIS.

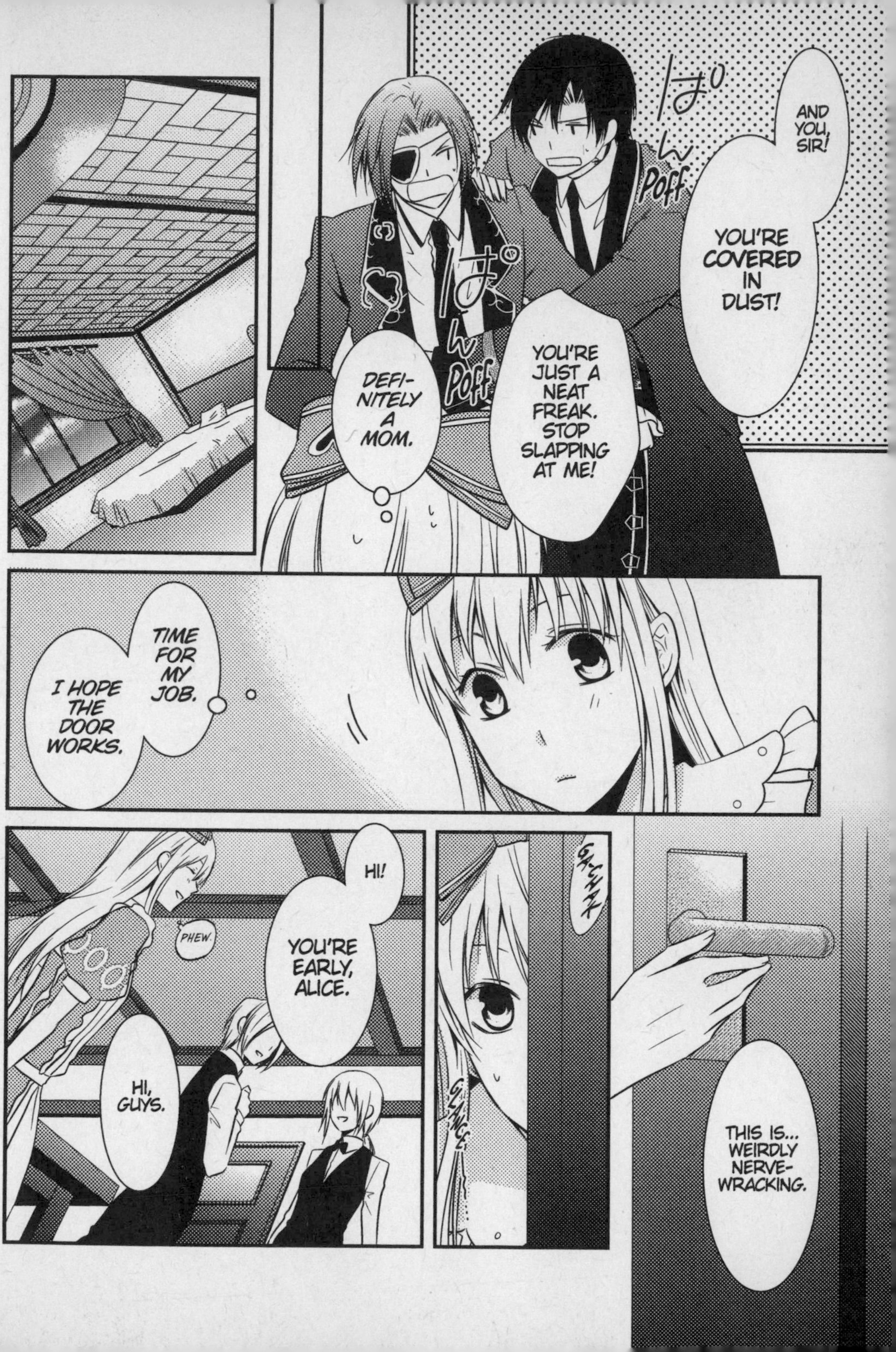
ぱん
Poff
AND YOU, SIR!
YOU'RE COVERED IN DUST!
YOU'RE JUST A NEAT FREAK. STOP SLAPPING AT ME!
ぱん
Poff
DEFI-NITELY A MOM.
TIME FOR MY JOB.
I HOPE THE DOOR WORKS.
GA-CHAK
THIS IS... WEIRDLY NERVE-WRACKING.
GLANCE
HI!
YOU'RE EARLY, ALICE.
PHEW.
HI, GUYS.

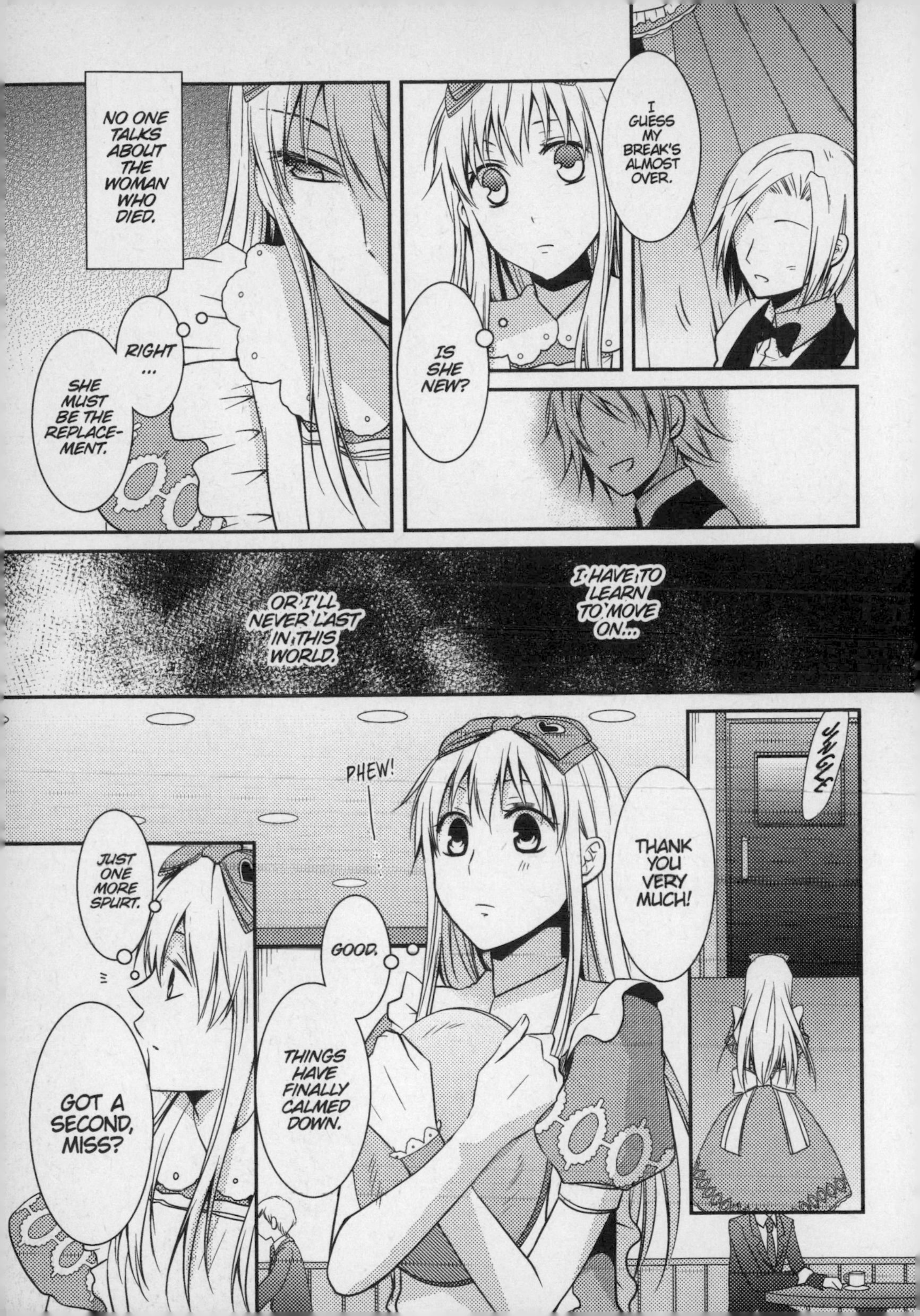
I GUESS MY BREAK'S ALMOST OVER.
IS SHE NEW?
NO ONE TALKS ABOUT THE WOMAN WHO DIED.
RIGHT ...
SHE MUST BE THE REPLACEMENT.
I HAVE TO LEARN TO MOVE ON...
OR I'LL NEVER LAST IN THIS WORLD.
JINGLE
THANK YOU VERY MUCH!
PHEW!
GOOD.
THINGS HAVE FINALLY CALMED DOWN.
JUST ONE MORE SPURT.
GOT A SECOND, MISS?

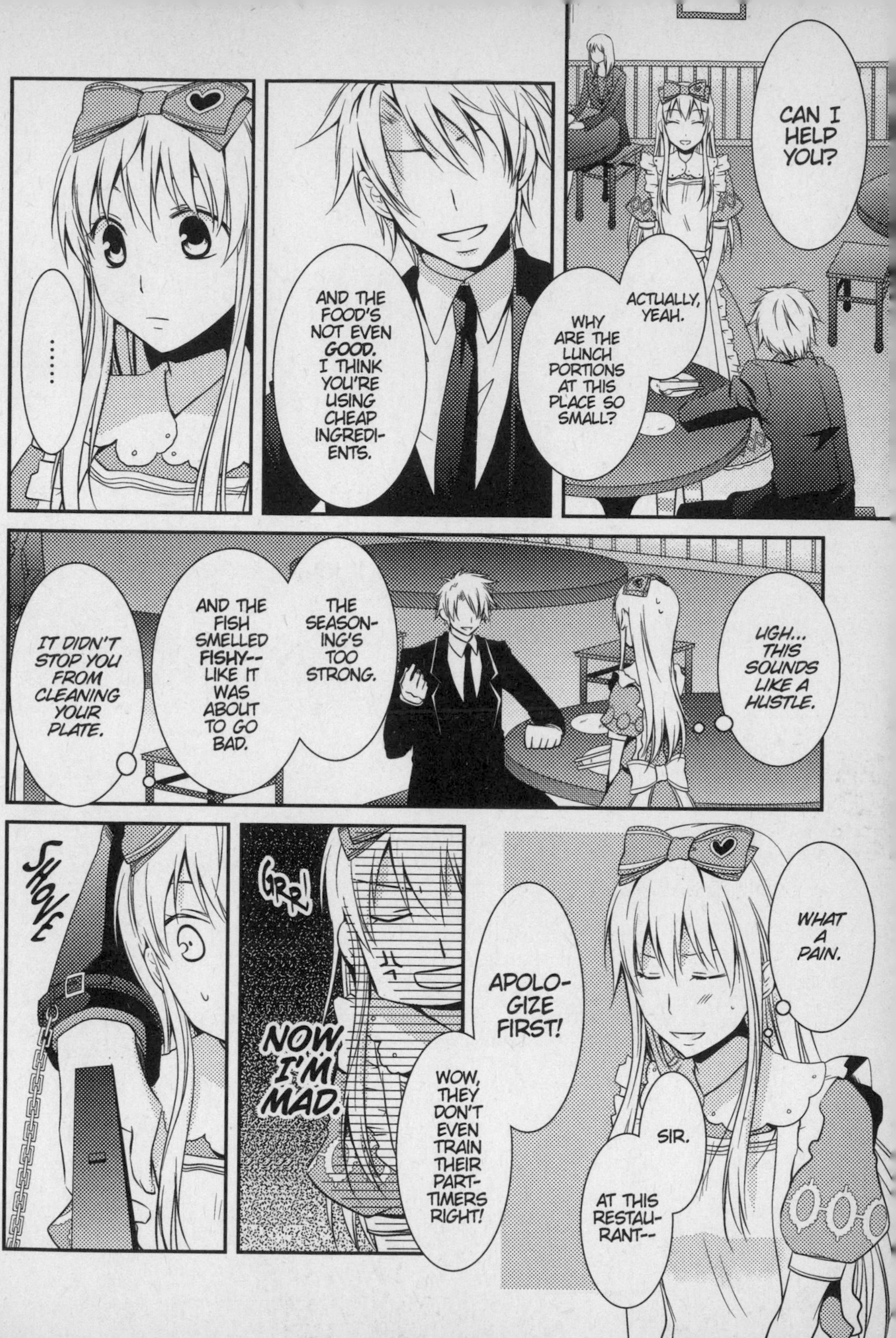

CAN I HELP YOU?
ACTUALLY, YEAH.
WHY ARE THE LUNCH PORTIONS AT THIS PLACE SO SMALL?
AND THE FOOD'S NOT EVEN GOOD. I THINK YOU'RE USING CHEAP INGREDI-ENTS.
......
UGH... THIS SOUNDS LIKE A HUSTLE.
THE SEASON-ING'S TOO STRONG.
AND THE FISH SMELLED FISHY-- LIKE IT WAS ABOUT TO GO BAD.
IT DIDN'T STOP YOU FROM CLEANING YOUR PLATE.
WHAT A PAIN.
SIR.
AT THIS RESTAU-RANT--
APOLO-GIZE FIRST!
WOW, THEY DON'T EVEN TRAIN THEIR PART-TIMERS RIGHT!
GRR!
NOW I'M MAD.
SHOVE

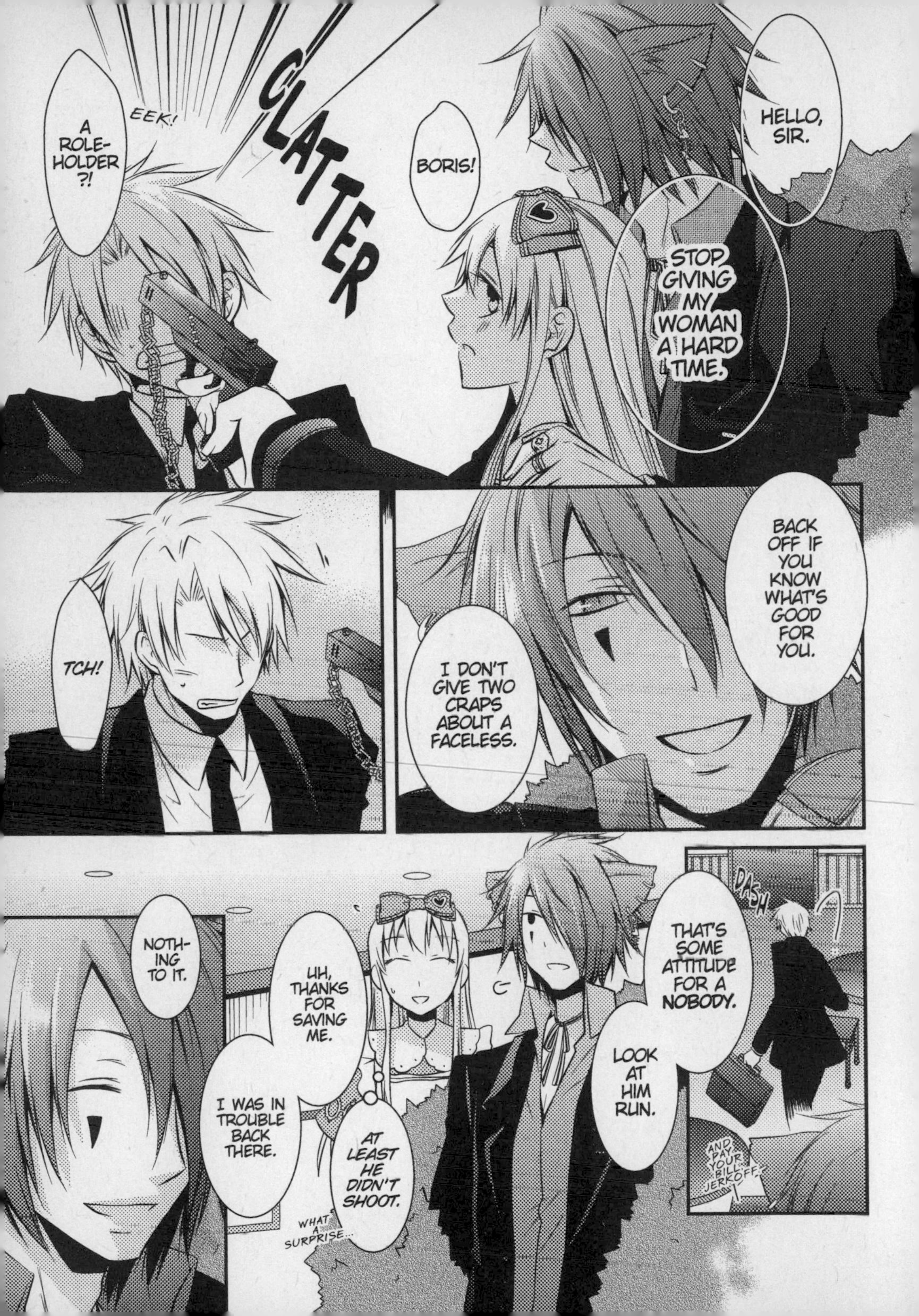
HELLO, SIR.
STOP GIVING MY WOMAN A HARD TIME.
BORIS!
CLATTER
EEK!
A ROLE-HOLDER?!
BACK OFF IF YOU KNOW WHAT'S GOOD FOR YOU.
I DON'T GIVE TWO CRAPS ABOUT A FACELESS.
TCH!
DASH
AND PAY YOUR BILL, JERKOFF!
THAT'S SOME ATTITUDE FOR A NOBODY.
LOOK AT HIM RUN.
AT LEAST HE DIDN'T SHOOT.
WHAT A SURPRISE...
UH, THANKS FOR SAVING ME.
I WAS IN TROUBLE BACK THERE.
NOTH-ING TO IT.

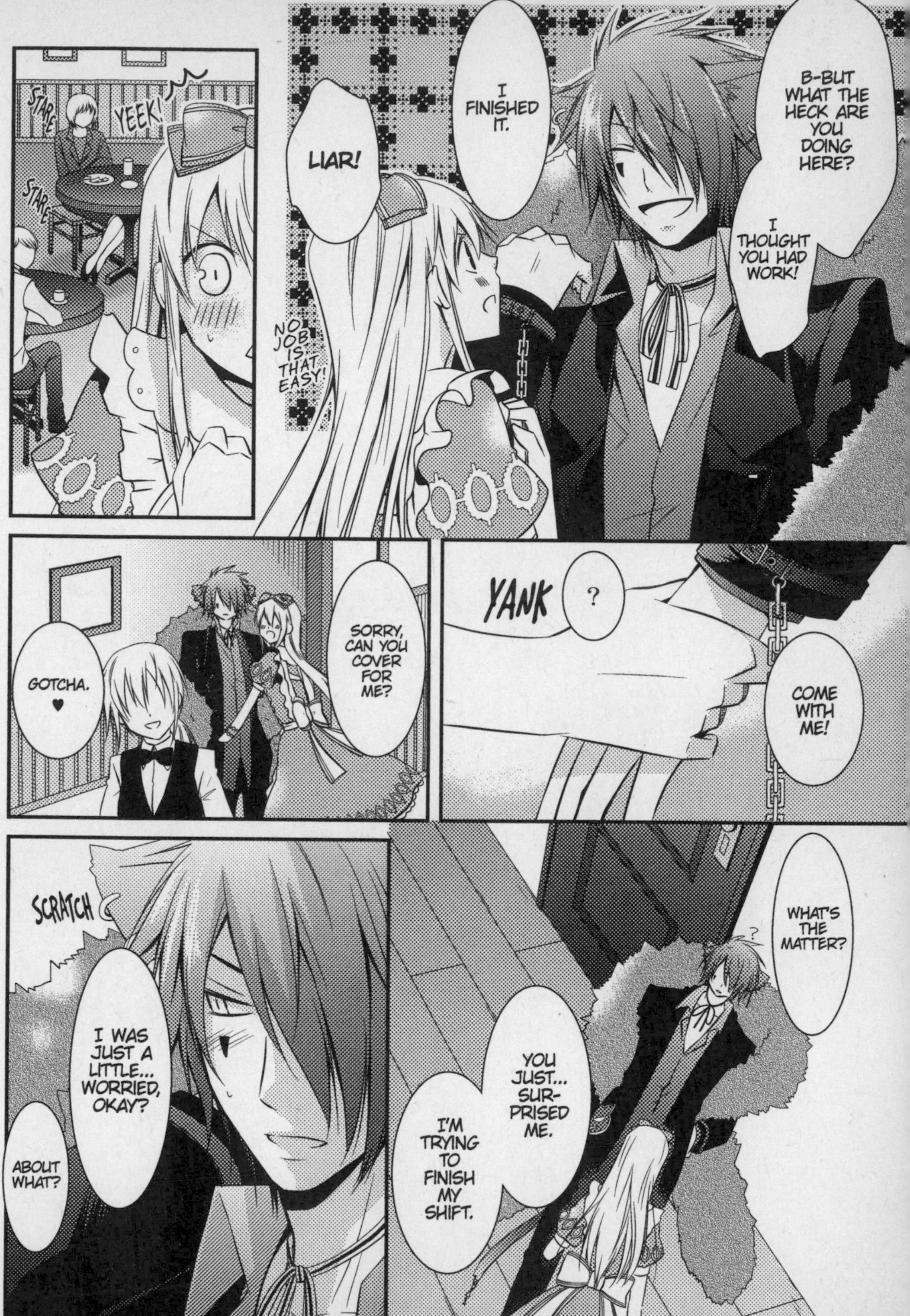
B-BUT WHAT THE HECK ARE YOU DOING HERE?
I THOUGHT YOU HAD WORK!
I FINISHED IT.
LIAR!
NO JOB IS THAT EASY!
YEEK!
STARE
STARE
YANK
?
COME WITH ME!
SORRY, CAN YOU COVER FOR ME?
GOTCHA. ♥
WHAT'S THE MATTER?
YOU JUST... SURPRISED ME.
I'M TRYING TO FINISH MY SHIFT.
SCRATCH
I WAS JUST A LITTLE... WORRIED, OKAY?
ABOUT WHAT?

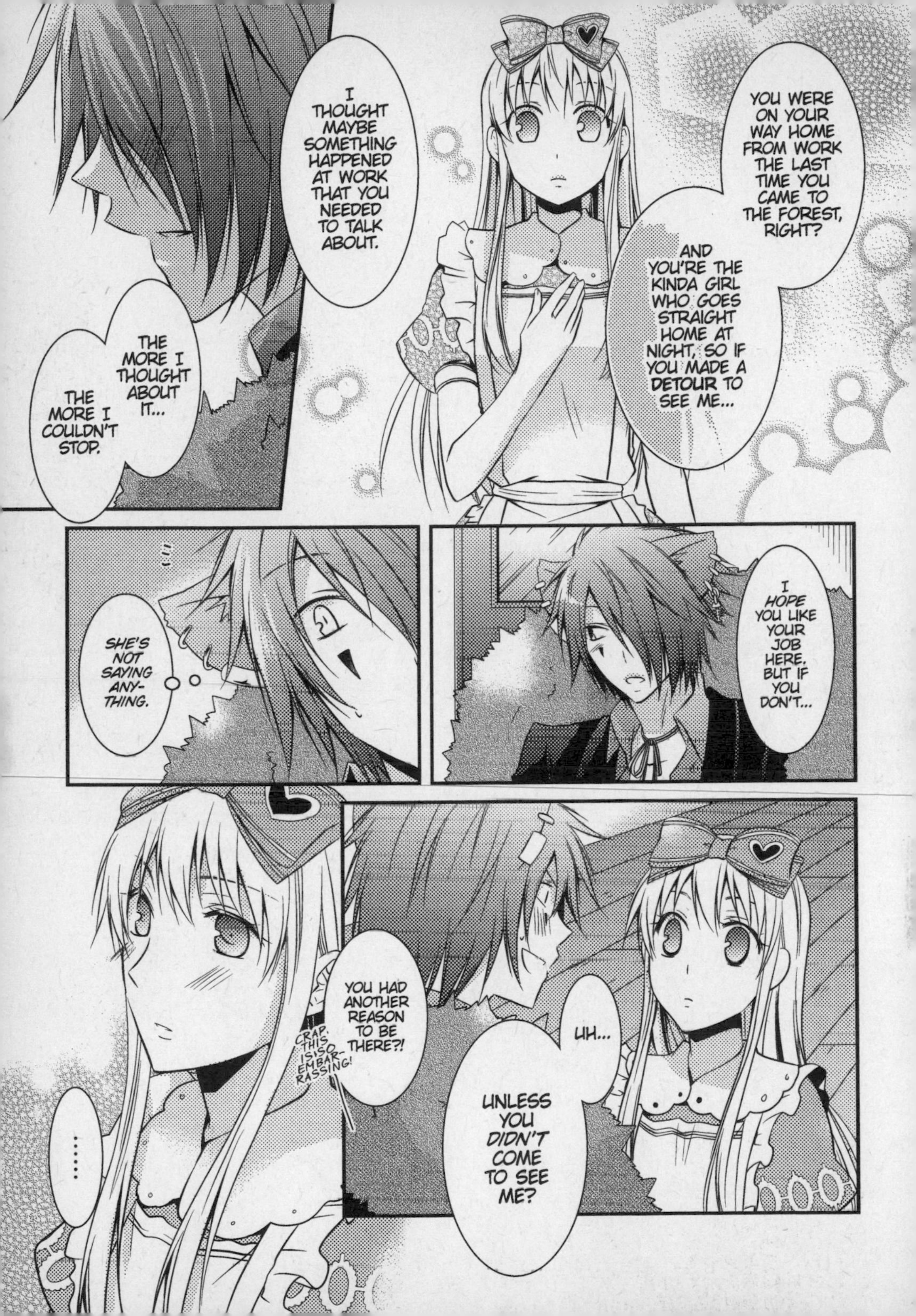
YOU WERE ON YOUR WAY HOME FROM WORK THE LAST TIME YOU CAME TO THE FOREST, RIGHT?
AND YOU'RE THE KINDA GIRL WHO GOES STRAIGHT HOME AT NIGHT, SO IF YOU MADE A DETOUR TO SEE ME...
I THOUGHT MAYBE SOMETHING HAPPENED AT WORK THAT YOU NEEDED TO TALK ABOUT.
THE MORE I THOUGHT ABOUT IT...
THE MORE I COULDN'T STOP.
I *HOPE* YOU LIKE YOUR JOB HERE. BUT IF YOU DON'T...
!!
SHE'S NOT SAYING ANY-THING.
UH...
UNLESS YOU *DIDN'T* COME TO SEE ME?
YOU HAD ANOTHER REASON TO BE THERE?!
CRAP. THIS IS SO EMBAR-RASSING!
......

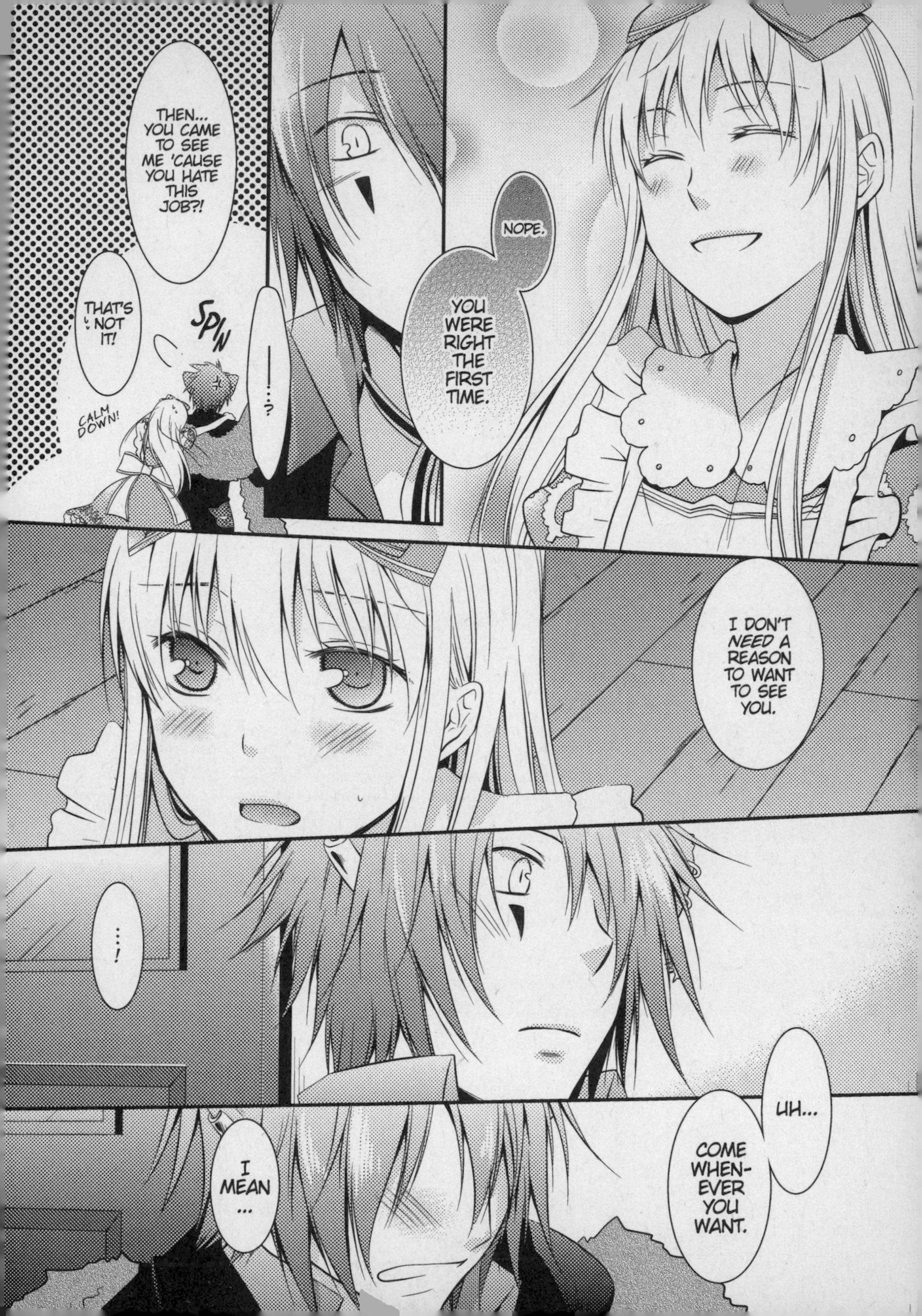
NOPE.
YOU WERE RIGHT THE FIRST TIME.
......?
THEN... YOU CAME TO SEE ME 'CAUSE YOU HATE THIS JOB?!
THAT'S NOT IT!
SPIN
CALM DOWN!
I DON'T NEED A REASON TO WANT TO SEE YOU.
...!
UH...
COME WHEN-EVER YOU WANT.
I MEAN...

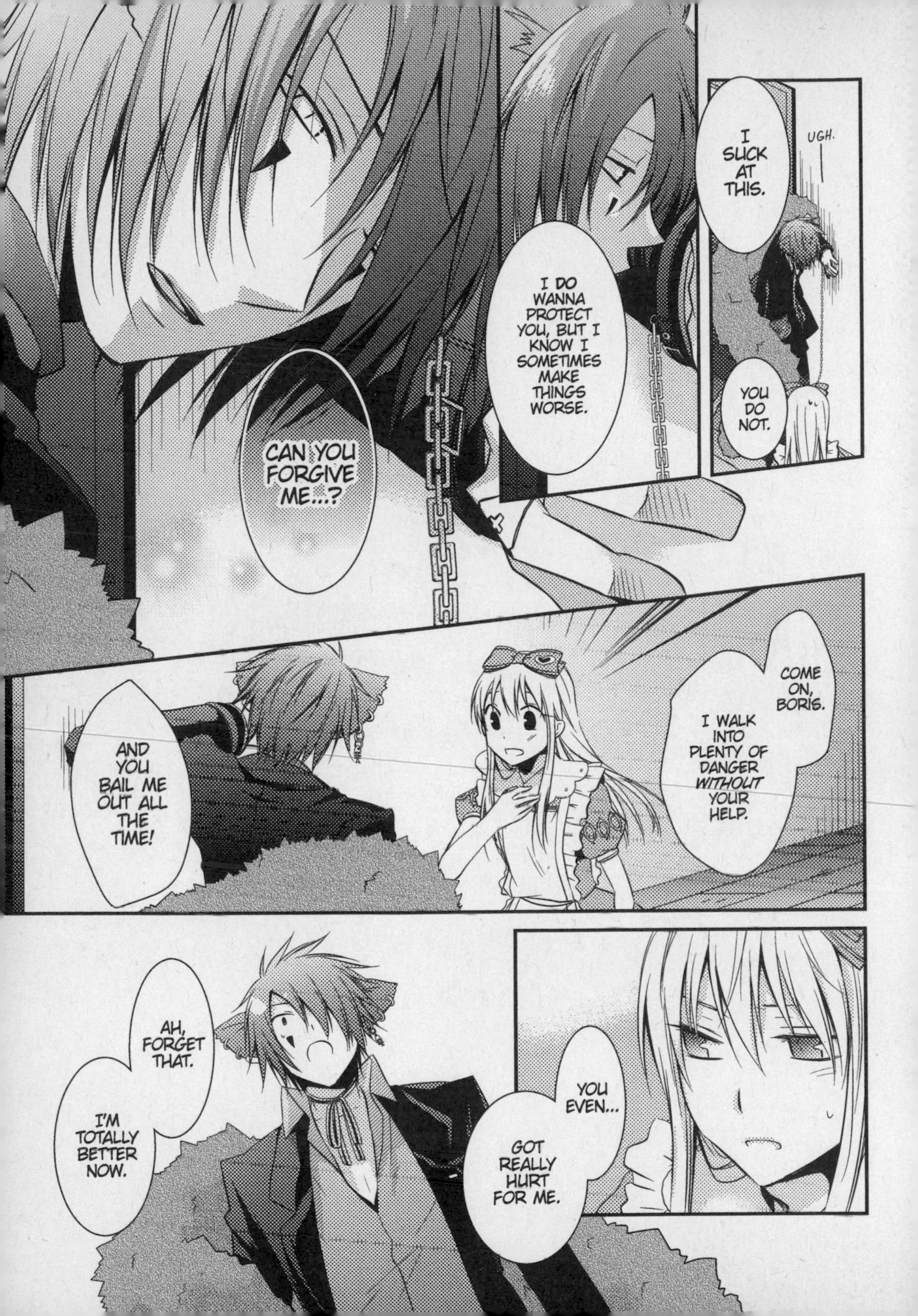
UGH.
I SUCK AT THIS.
YOU DO NOT.
I DO WANNA PROTECT YOU, BUT I KNOW I SOMETIMES MAKE THINGS WORSE.
CAN YOU FORGIVE ME...?
COME ON, BORIS.
I WALK INTO PLENTY OF DANGER *WITHOUT* YOUR HELP.
AND YOU BAIL ME OUT ALL THE TIME!
YOU EVEN...
GOT REALLY HURT FOR ME.
AH, FORGET THAT.
I'M TOTALLY BETTER NOW.

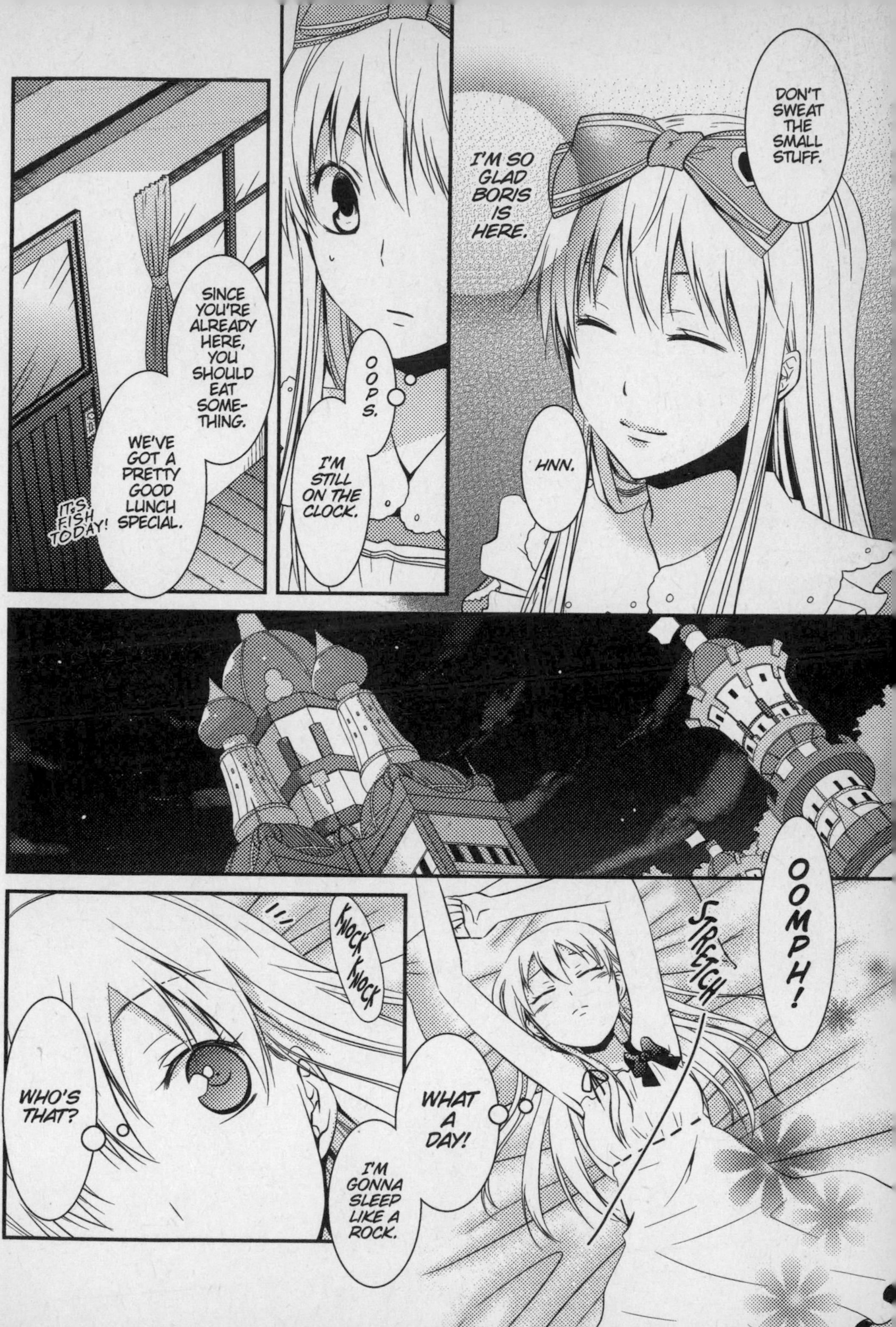
DON'T SWEAT THE SMALL STUFF.
I'M SO GLAD BORIS IS HERE.
HNN.
OOPS.
I'M STILL ON THE CLOCK.
SINCE YOU'RE ALREADY HERE, YOU SHOULD EAT SOME-THING.
WE'VE GOT A PRETTY GOOD LUNCH SPECIAL.
IT'S FISH TODAY!
OOMPH!
STRETCH
WHAT A DAY!
I'M GONNA SLEEP LIKE A ROCK.
KNOCK KNOCK
!!
WHO'S THAT?

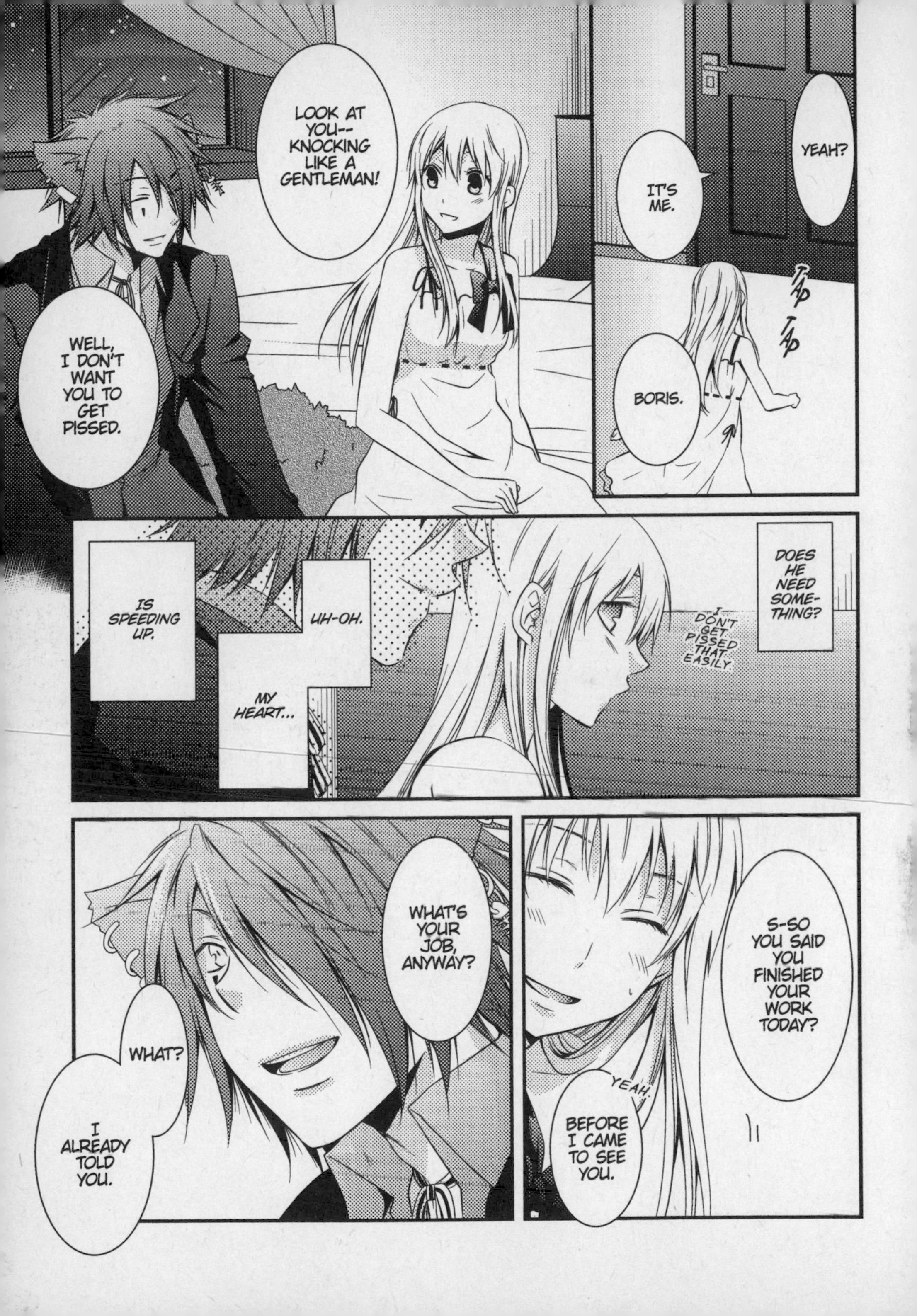
YEAH?
IT'S ME.
TAP TAP
BORIS.
LOOK AT YOU-- KNOCKING LIKE A GENTLEMAN!
WELL, I DON'T WANT YOU TO GET PISSED.
DOES HE NEED SOMETHING?
I DON'T GET PISSED THAT EASILY.
UH-OH.
MY HEART...
IS SPEEDING UP.
S-SO YOU SAID YOU FINISHED YOUR WORK TODAY?
YEAH.
BEFORE I CAME TO SEE YOU.
WHAT'S YOUR JOB, ANYWAY?
WHAT?
I ALREADY TOLD YOU.

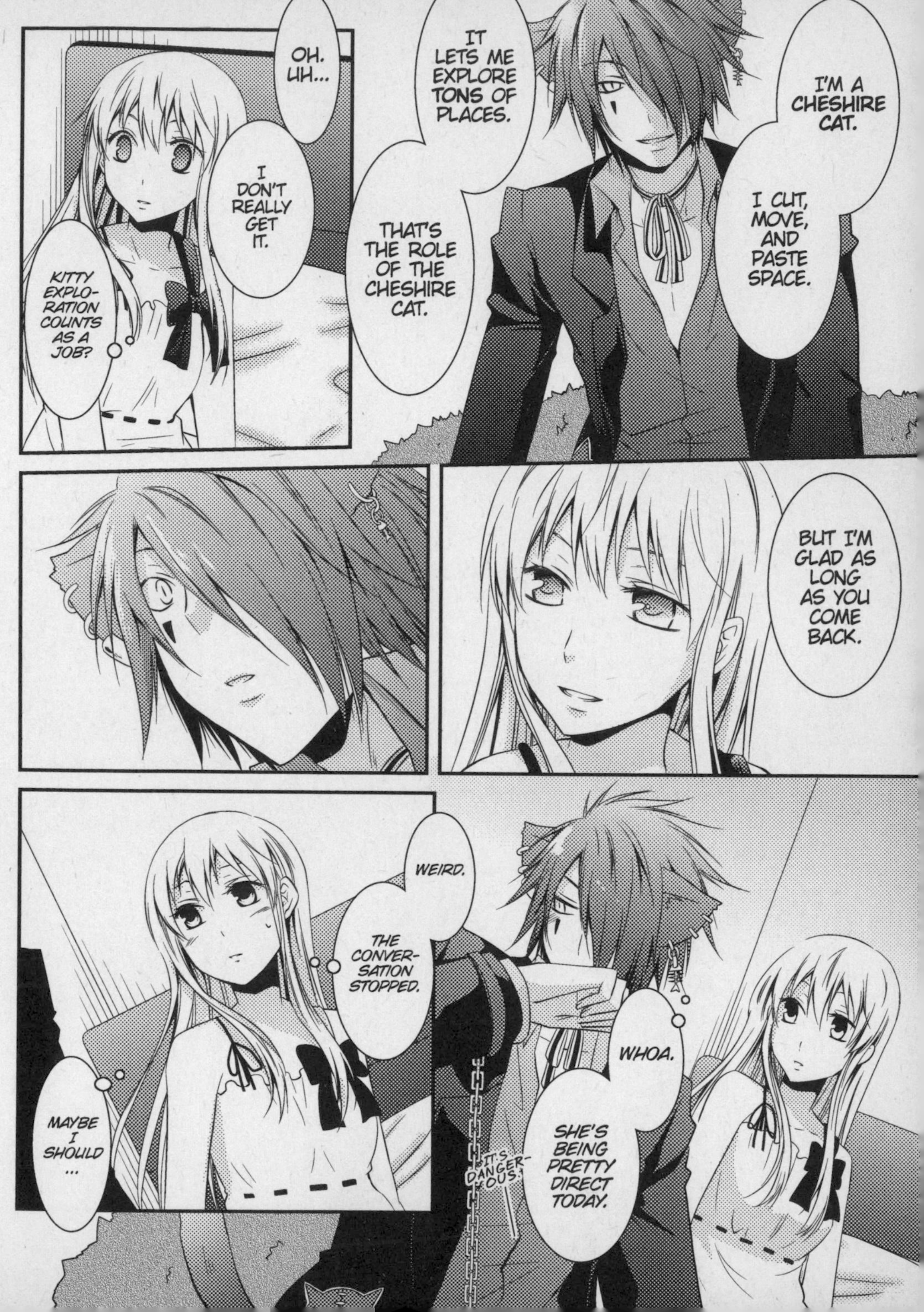
I'M A CHESHIRE CAT.
I CUT, MOVE, AND PASTE SPACE.
IT LETS ME EXPLORE TONS OF PLACES.
THAT'S THE ROLE OF THE CHESHIRE CAT.
OH. UH...
I DON'T REALLY GET IT.
KITTY EXPLORATION COUNTS AS A JOB?
BUT I'M GLAD AS LONG AS YOU COME BACK.
WHOA.
SHE'S BEING PRETTY DIRECT TODAY.
IT'S DANGER-OUS.
WEIRD.
THE CONVER-SATION STOPPED.
MAYBE I SHOULD ...

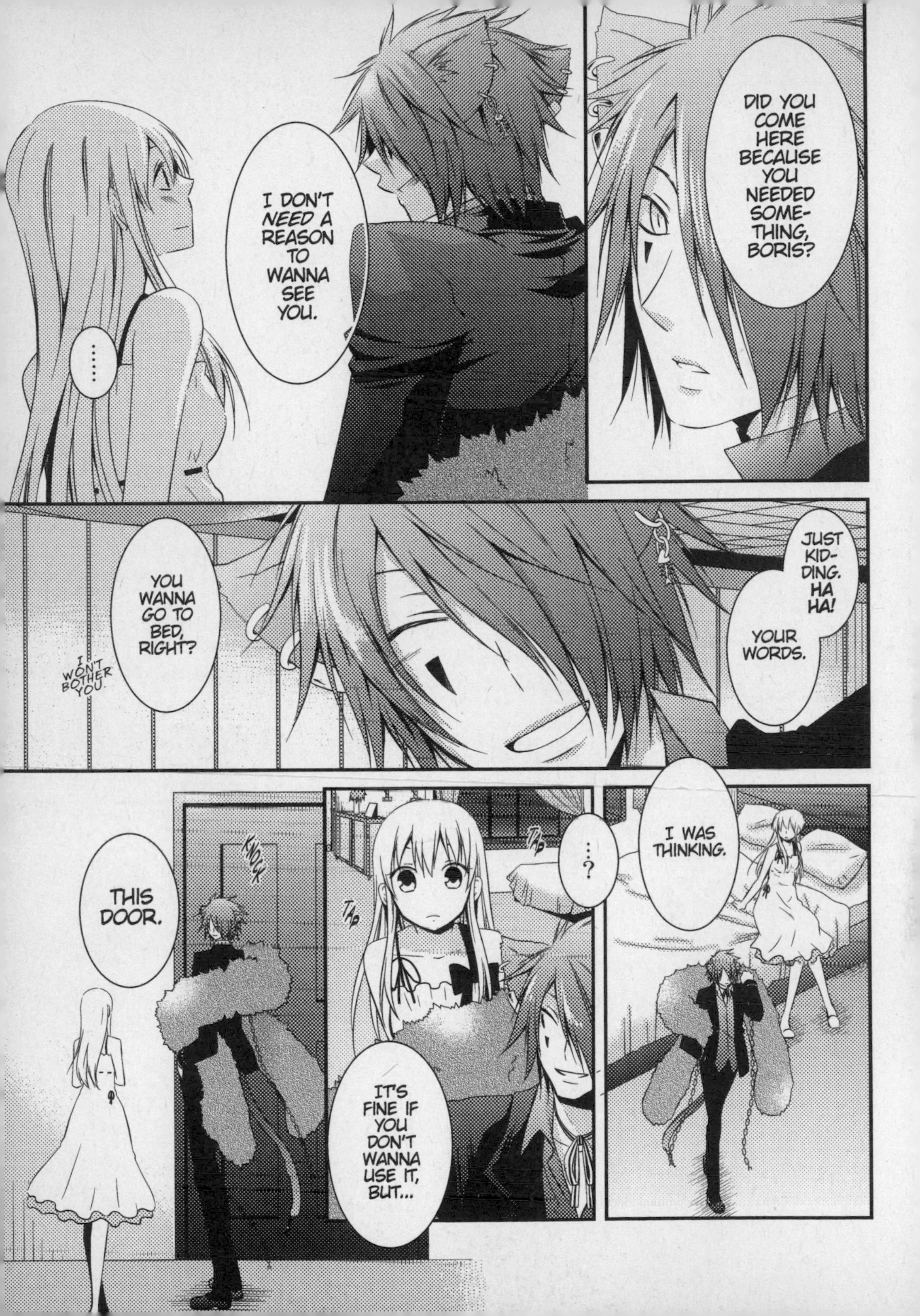
DID YOU COME HERE BECAUSE YOU NEEDED SOME-THING, BORIS?
I DON'T NEED A REASON TO WANNA SEE YOU.
......
JUST KID-DING. HA HA!
YOUR WORDS.
YOU WANNA GO TO BED, RIGHT?
I WON'T BOTHER YOU.
I WAS THINKING.
...?
TAP
TAP
IT'S FINE IF YOU DON'T WANNA USE IT, BUT...
KNOCK
THIS DOOR.
...

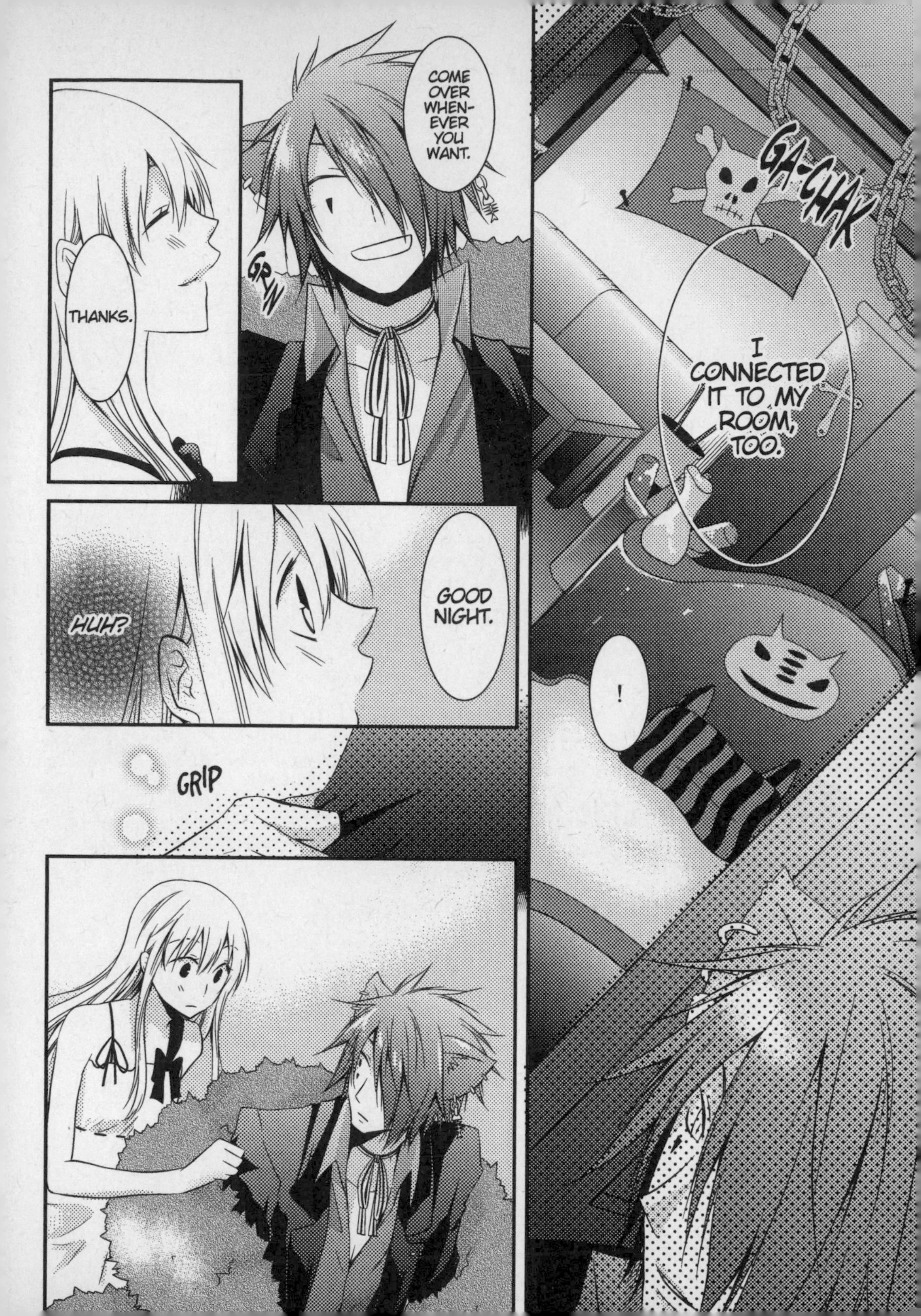
GA-CHAK
I CONNECTED IT TO MY ROOM, TOO.
!
COME OVER WHEN-EVER YOU WANT.
GRIN
THANKS.
GOOD NIGHT.
HUH?
GRIP

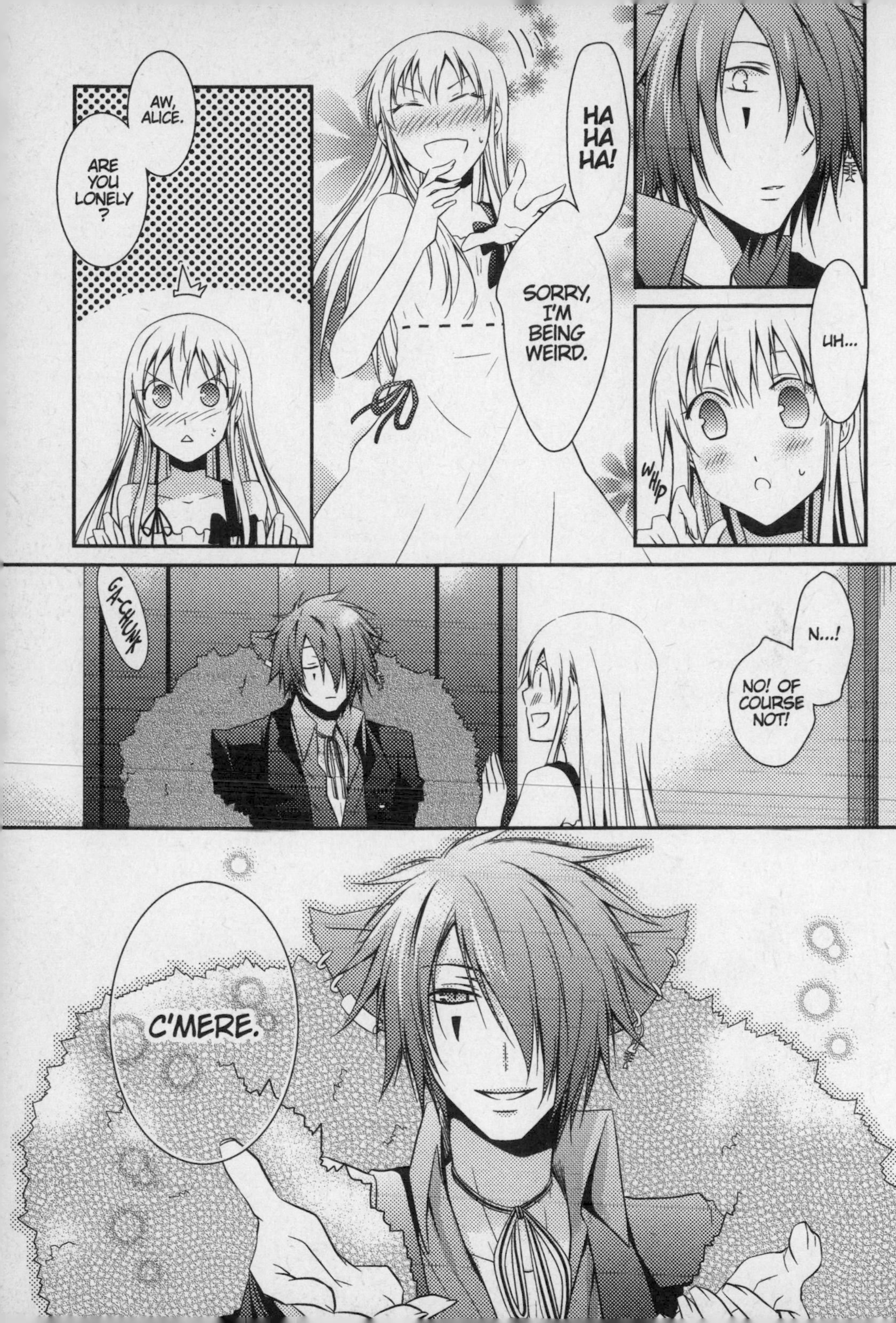
UH...
WHIP
HA HA HA!
SORRY, I'M BEING WEIRD.
AW, ALICE.
ARE YOU LONELY?
N...!
NO! OF COURSE NOT!
GA-CHUNK
C'MERE.

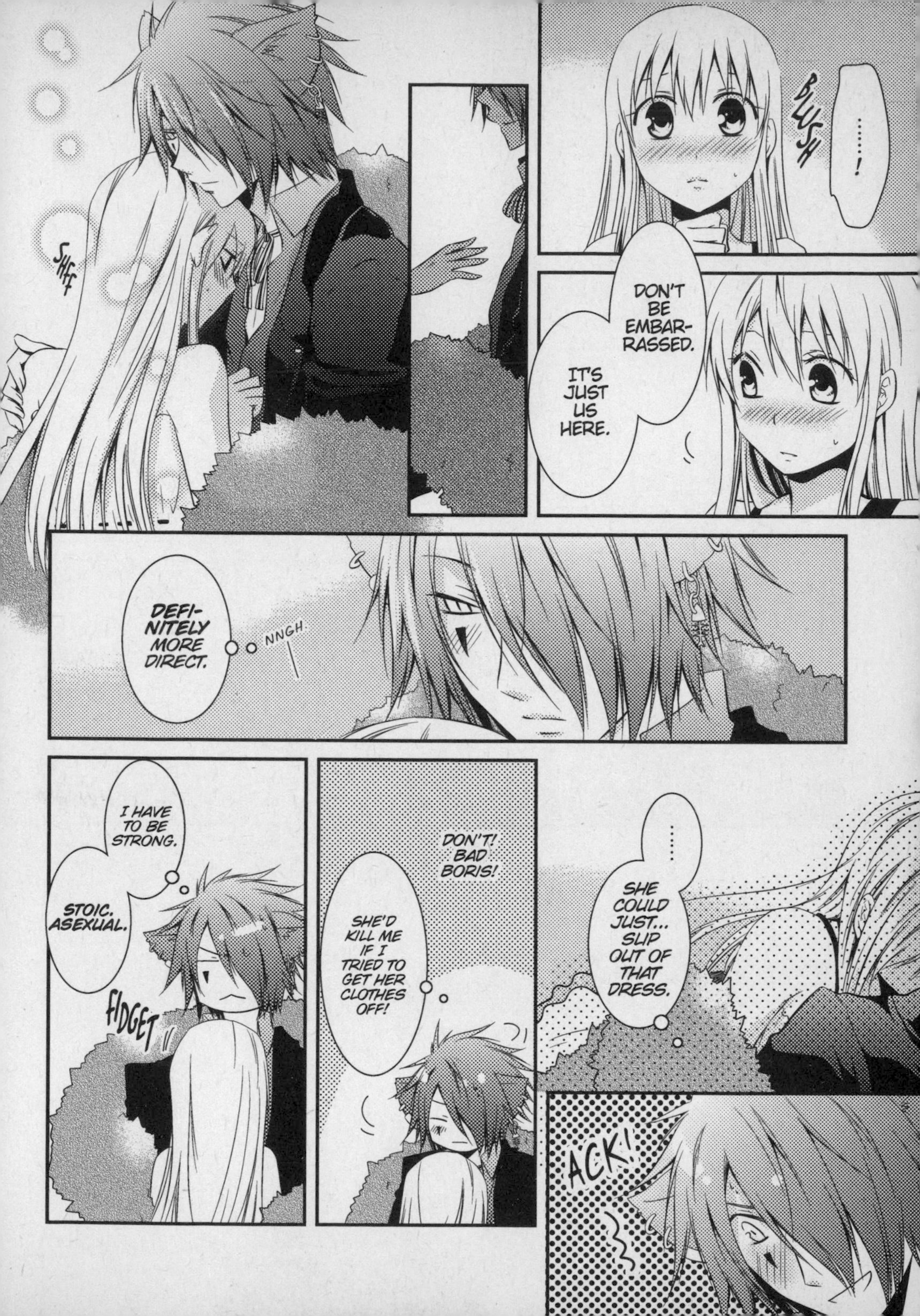
BLUSH
......!
DON'T BE EMBARRASSED.
IT'S JUST US HERE.
SHFF
NNGH.
DEFINITELY MORE DIRECT.
......
SHE COULD JUST... SLIP OUT OF THAT DRESS.
ACK!
DON'T! BAD BORIS!
SHE'D KILL ME IF I TRIED TO GET HER CLOTHES OFF!
I HAVE TO BE STRONG.
STOIC. ASEXUAL.
FIDGET

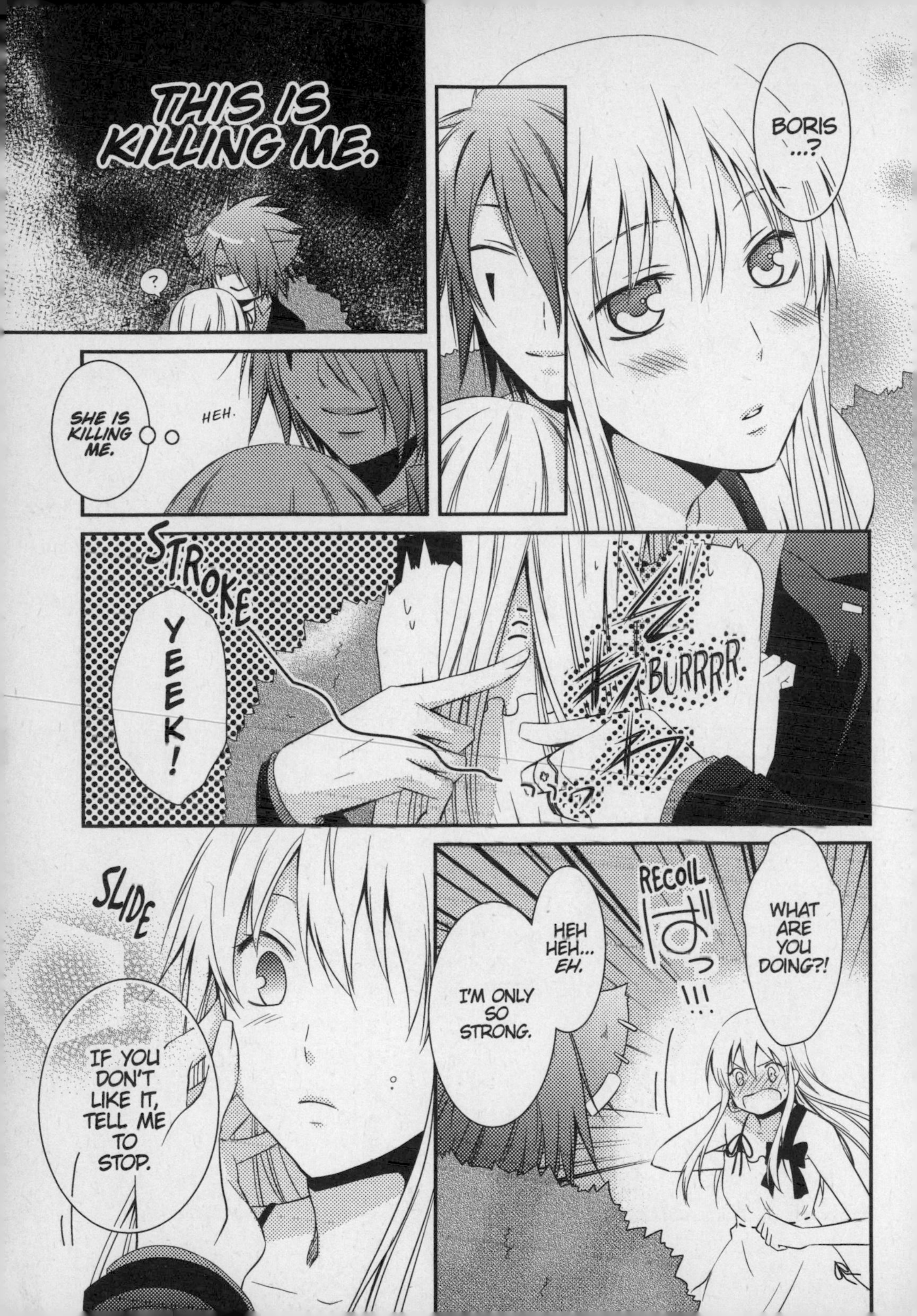
BORIS ...?
THIS IS KILLING ME.
?
SHE IS KILLING ME.
HEH.
BURRRR
STROKE
YEEK!
WHAT ARE YOU DOING?!
RECOIL
HEH HEH... EH.
I'M ONLY SO STRONG.
SLIDE
IF YOU DON'T LIKE IT, TELL ME TO STOP.

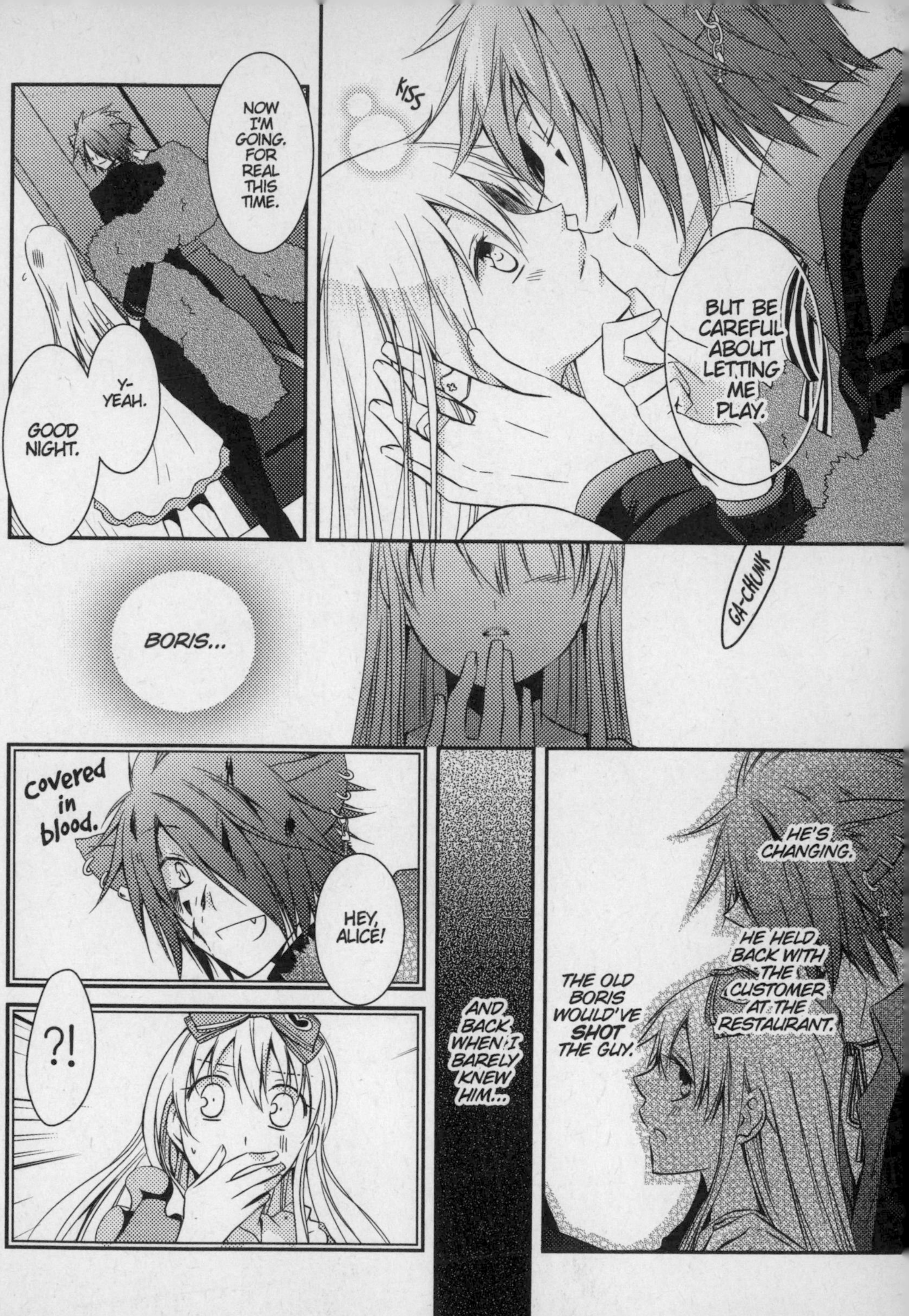
KISS
BUT BE CAREFUL ABOUT LETTING ME PLAY.
NOW I'M GOING. FOR REAL THIS TIME.
Y-YEAH.
GOOD NIGHT.
GA-CHUNK
BORIS...
HE'S CHANGING.
HE HELD BACK WITH THE CUSTOMER AT THE RESTAURANT.
THE OLD BORIS WOULD'VE SHOT THE GUY.
AND BACK WHEN I BARELY KNEW HIM...
covered in blood.
HEY, ALICE!
?!

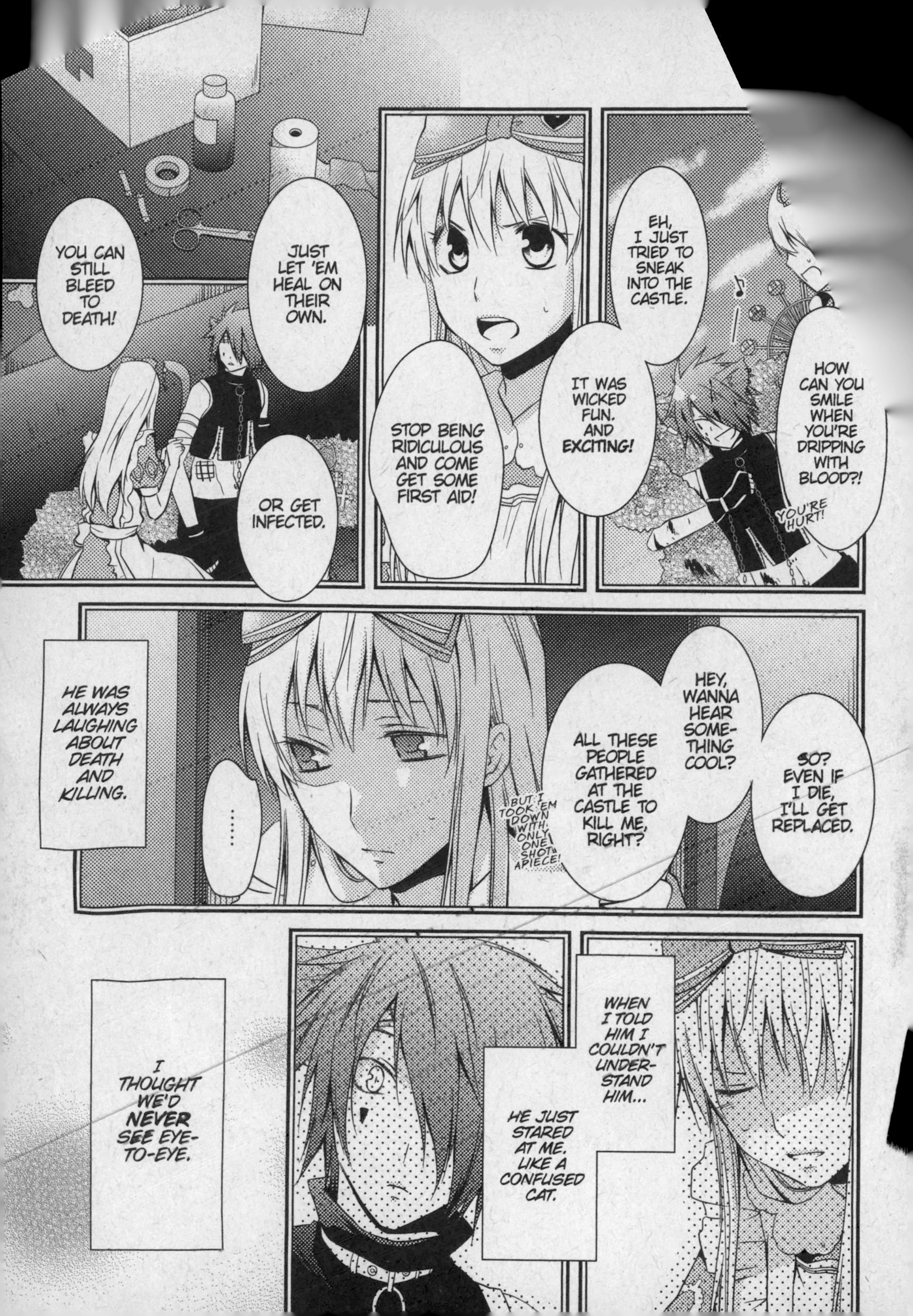
YOU'RE HURT!
HOW CAN YOU SMILE WHEN YOU'RE DRIPPING WITH BLOOD?!
EH, I JUST TRIED TO SNEAK INTO THE CASTLE.
IT WAS WICKED FUN. AND EXCITING!
STOP BEING RIDICULOUS AND COME GET SOME FIRST AID!
JUST LET 'EM HEAL ON THEIR OWN.
YOU CAN STILL BLEED TO DEATH!
OR GET INFECTED.
SO? EVEN IF I DIE, I'LL GET REPLACED.
HEY, WANNA HEAR SOME-THING COOL?
ALL THESE PEOPLE GATHERED AT THE CASTLE TO KILL ME, RIGHT?
BUT I TOOK 'EM DOWN WITH ONLY ONE SHOT APIECE!
......
HE WAS ALWAYS LAUGHING ABOUT DEATH AND KILLING.
WHEN I TOLD HIM I COULDN'T UNDER-STAND HIM...
HE JUST STARED AT ME. LIKE A CONFUSED CAT.
I THOUGHT WE'D NEVER SEE EYE-TO-EYE.

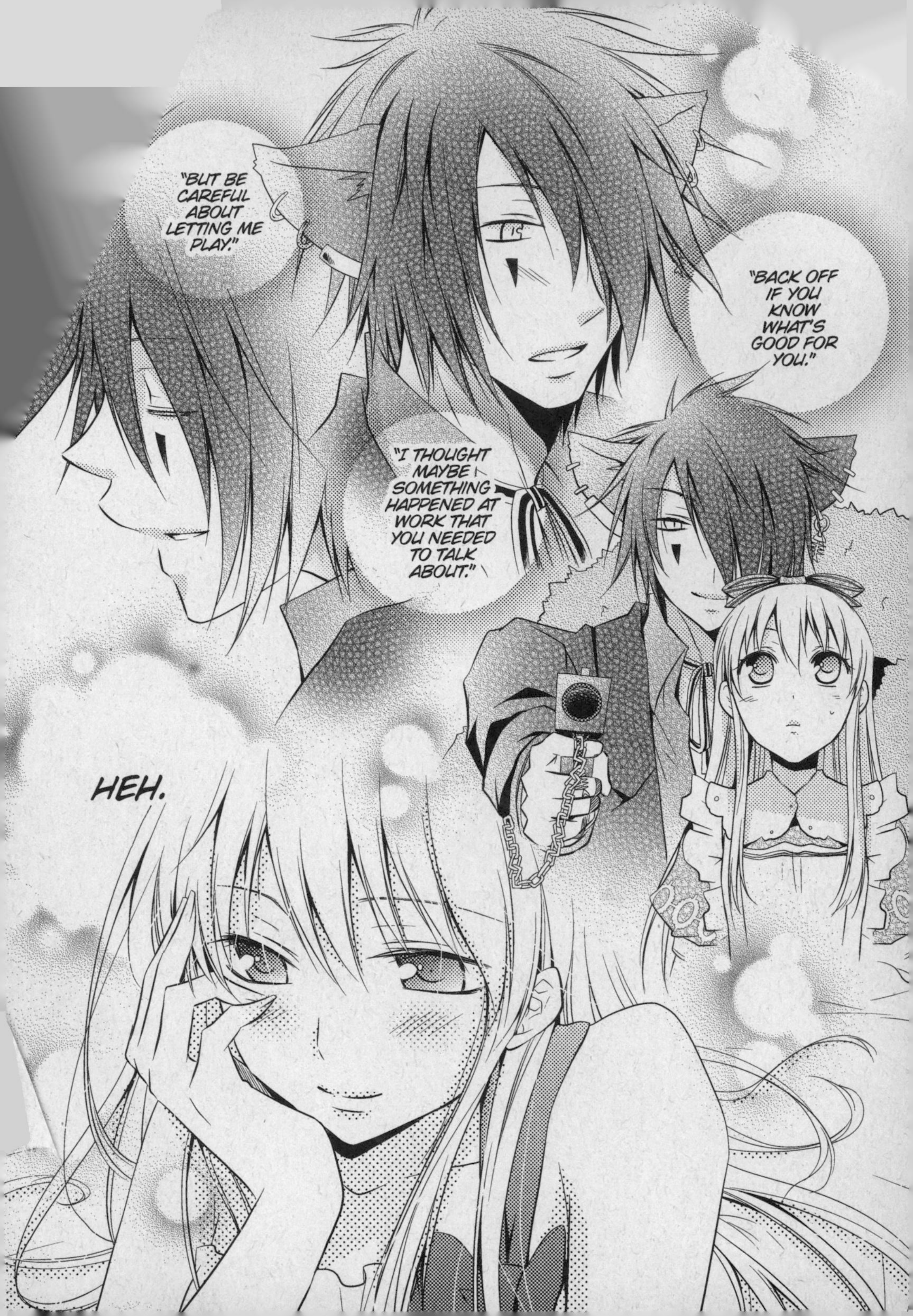
"BACK OFF IF YOU KNOW WHAT'S GOOD FOR YOU."
"BUT BE CAREFUL ABOUT LETTING ME PLAY."
"I THOUGHT MAYBE SOMETHING HAPPENED AT WORK THAT YOU NEEDED TO TALK ABOUT."
HEH.

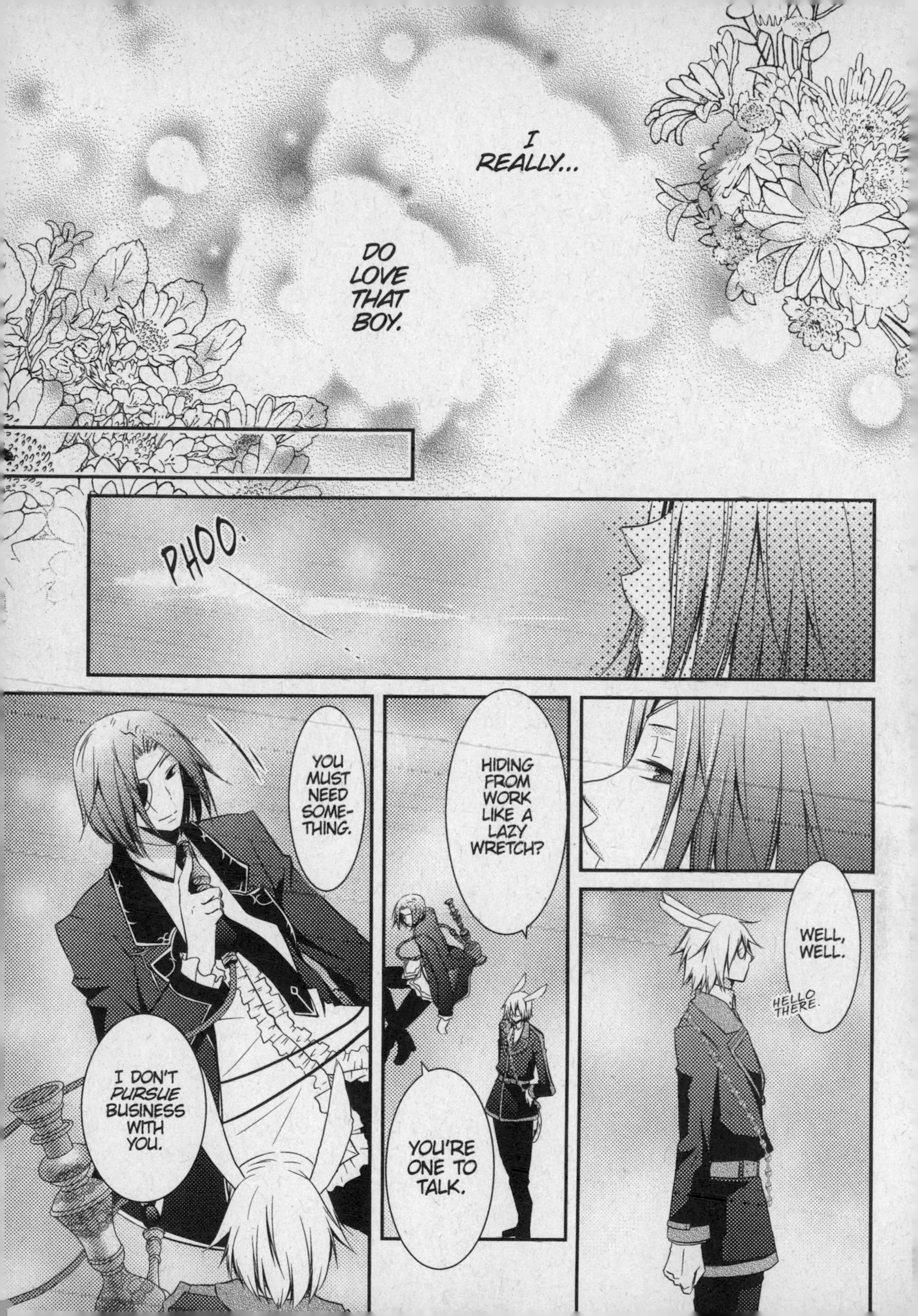
I REALLY...
DO LOVE THAT BOY.
PHOO.
WELL, WELL.
HELLO THERE.
HIDING FROM WORK LIKE A LAZY WRETCH?
YOU'RE ONE TO TALK.
YOU MUST NEED SOMETHING.
I DON'T *PURSUE* BUSINESS WITH YOU.

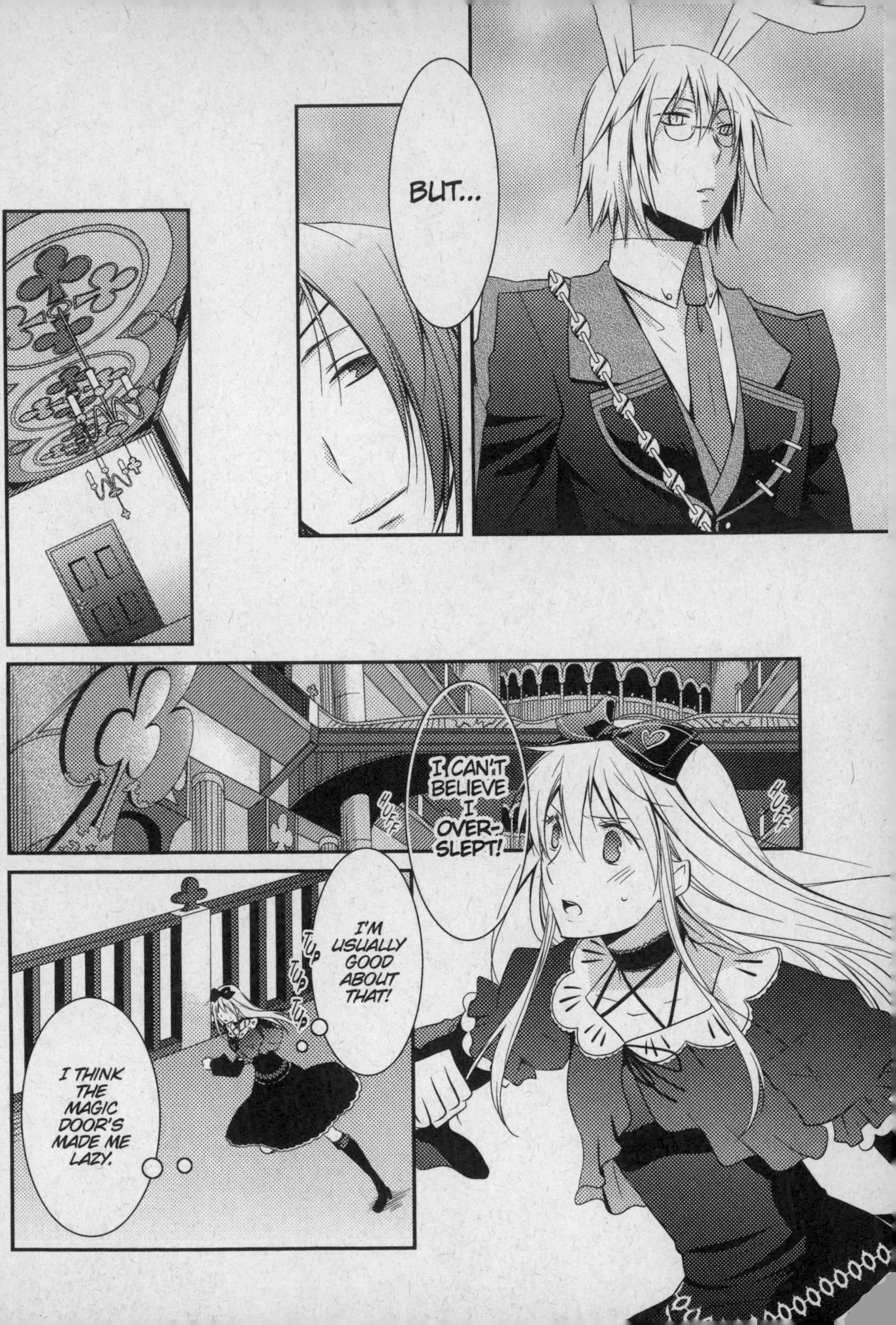
BUT...
HUFF
HUFF
I CAN'T BELIEVE I OVER-SLEPT!
I'M USUALLY GOOD ABOUT THAT!
TUP TUP TUP TUP
I THINK THE MAGIC DOOR'S MADE ME LAZY.

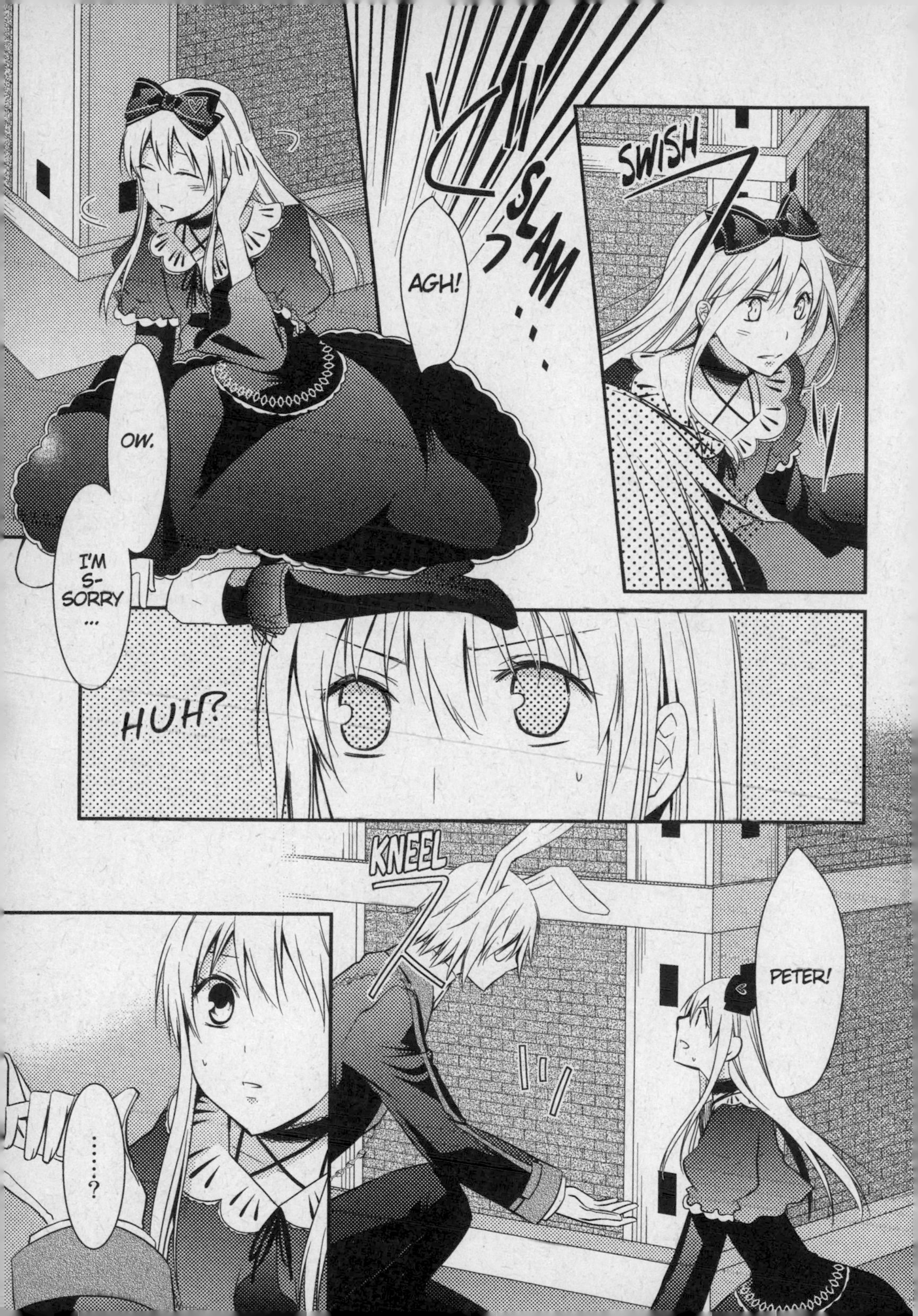
SWISH
SLAM...
AGH!
OW.
I'M S-SORRY...
HUH?
KNEEL
PETER!
......?

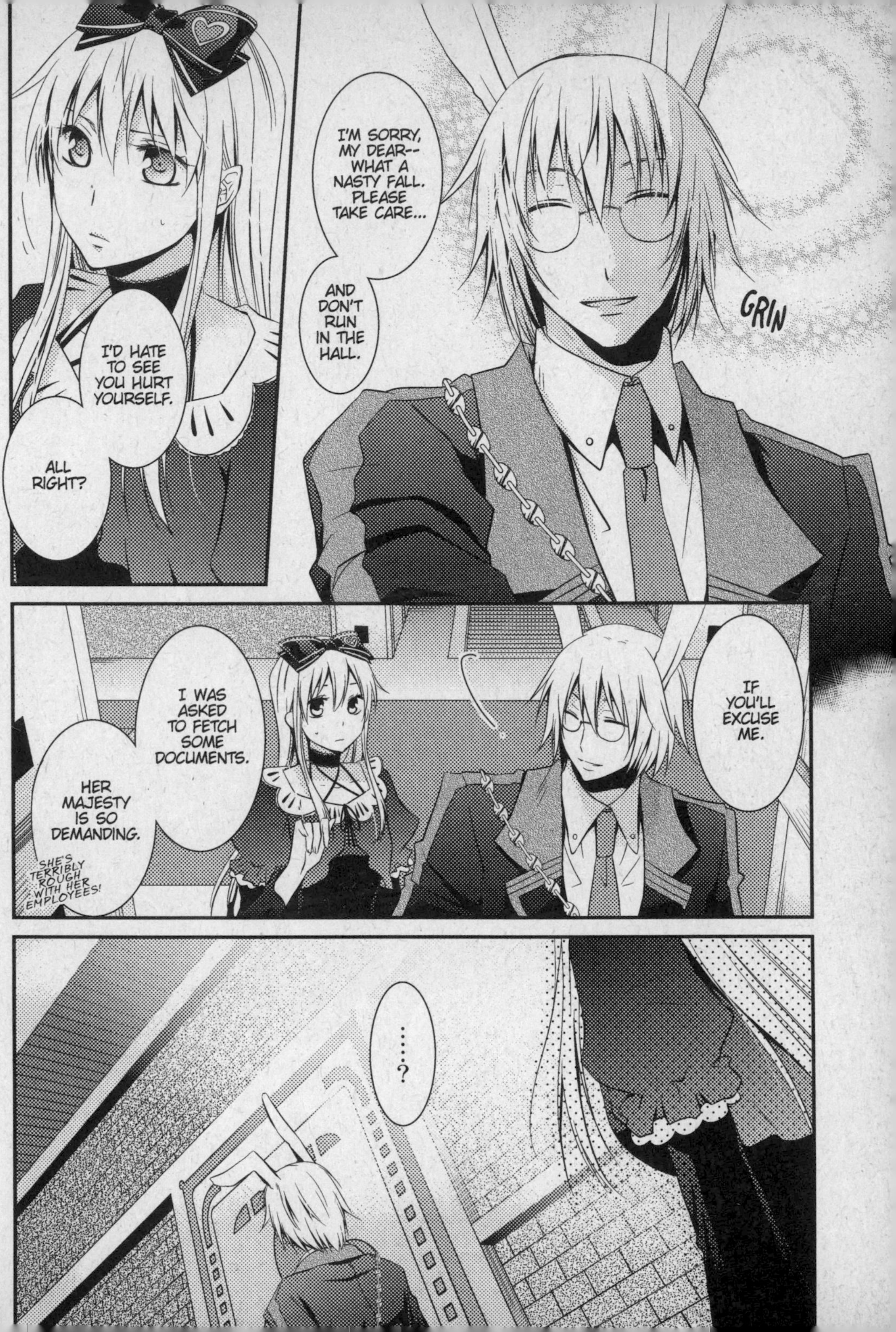
I'M SORRY, MY DEAR-- WHAT A NASTY FALL. PLEASE TAKE CARE...
AND DON'T RUN IN THE HALL.
GRIN
I'D HATE TO SEE YOU HURT YOURSELF.
ALL RIGHT?
IF YOU'LL EXCUSE ME.
I WAS ASKED TO FETCH SOME DOCUMENTS.
HER MAJESTY IS SO DEMANDING.
SHE'S TERRIBLY ROUGH WITH HER EMPLOYEES!
.....?

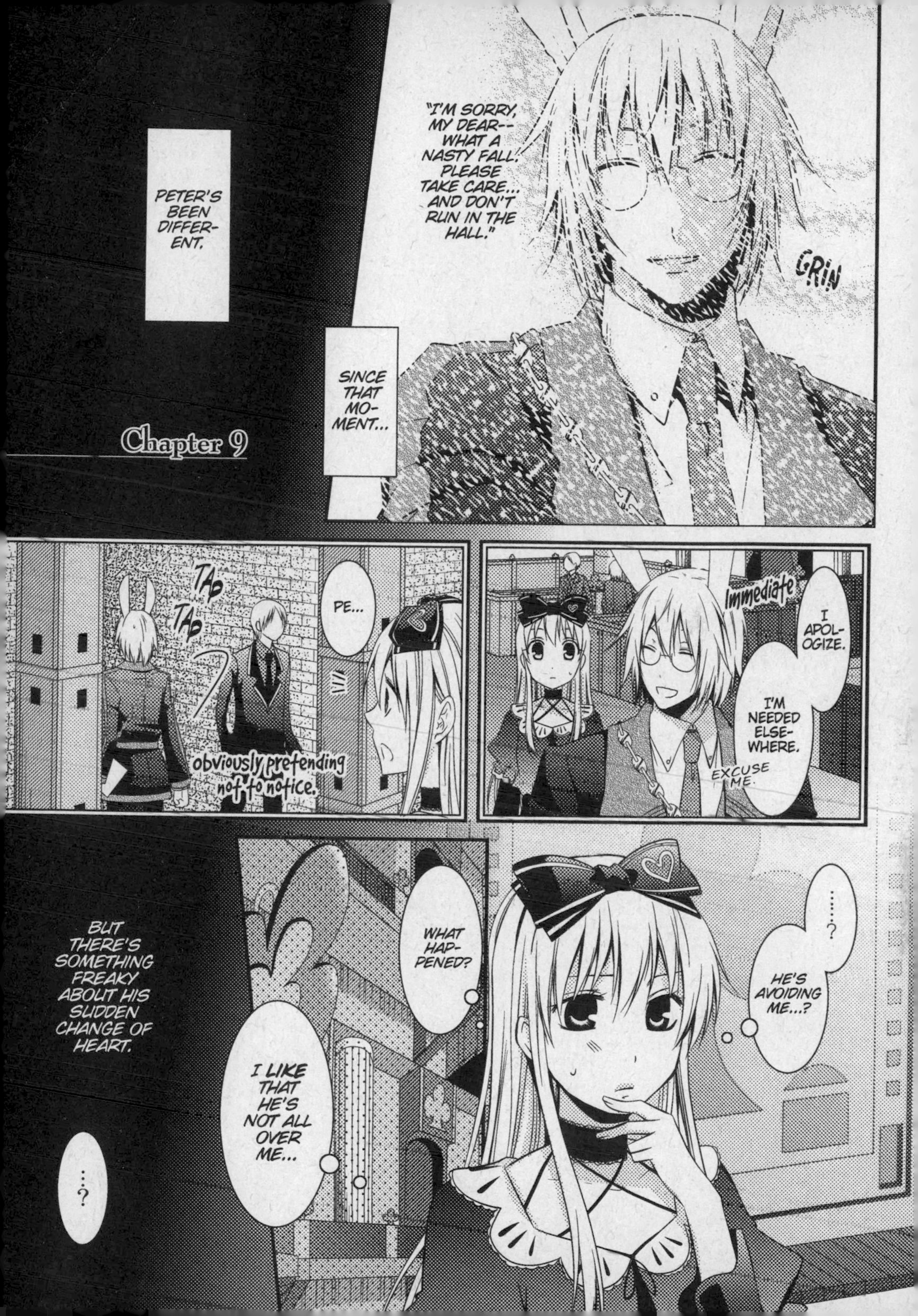
"I'M SORRY, MY DEAR--WHAT A NASTY FALL. PLEASE TAKE CARE... AND DON'T RUN IN THE HALL."
GRIN
PETER'S BEEN DIFFER-ENT.
SINCE THAT MO-MENT...
Chapter 9
Immediate
I APOLO-GIZE.
I'M NEEDED ELSE-WHERE.
EXCUSE ME.
PE...
TAP TAP
obviously pretending not to notice.
......?
HE'S AVOIDING ME...?
WHAT HAP-PENED?
I LIKE THAT HE'S NOT ALL OVER ME...
BUT THERE'S SOMETHING FREAKY ABOUT HIS SUDDEN CHANGE OF HEART.
...?

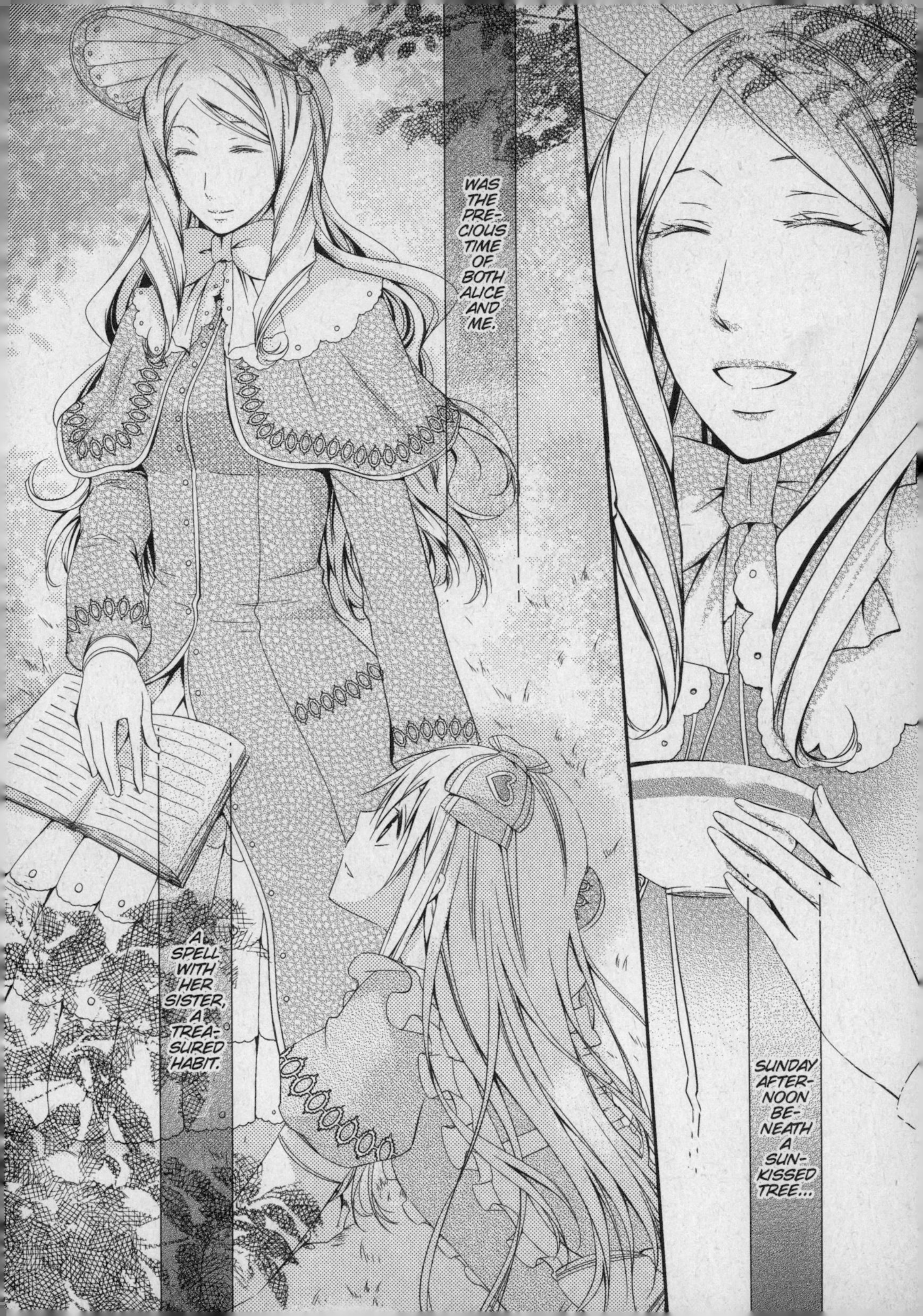
SUNDAY AFTER-NOON BE-NEATH A SUN-KISSED TREE...
WAS THE PRE-CIOUS TIME OF BOTH ALICE AND ME.
A SPELL WITH HER SISTER, A TREA-SURED HABIT.

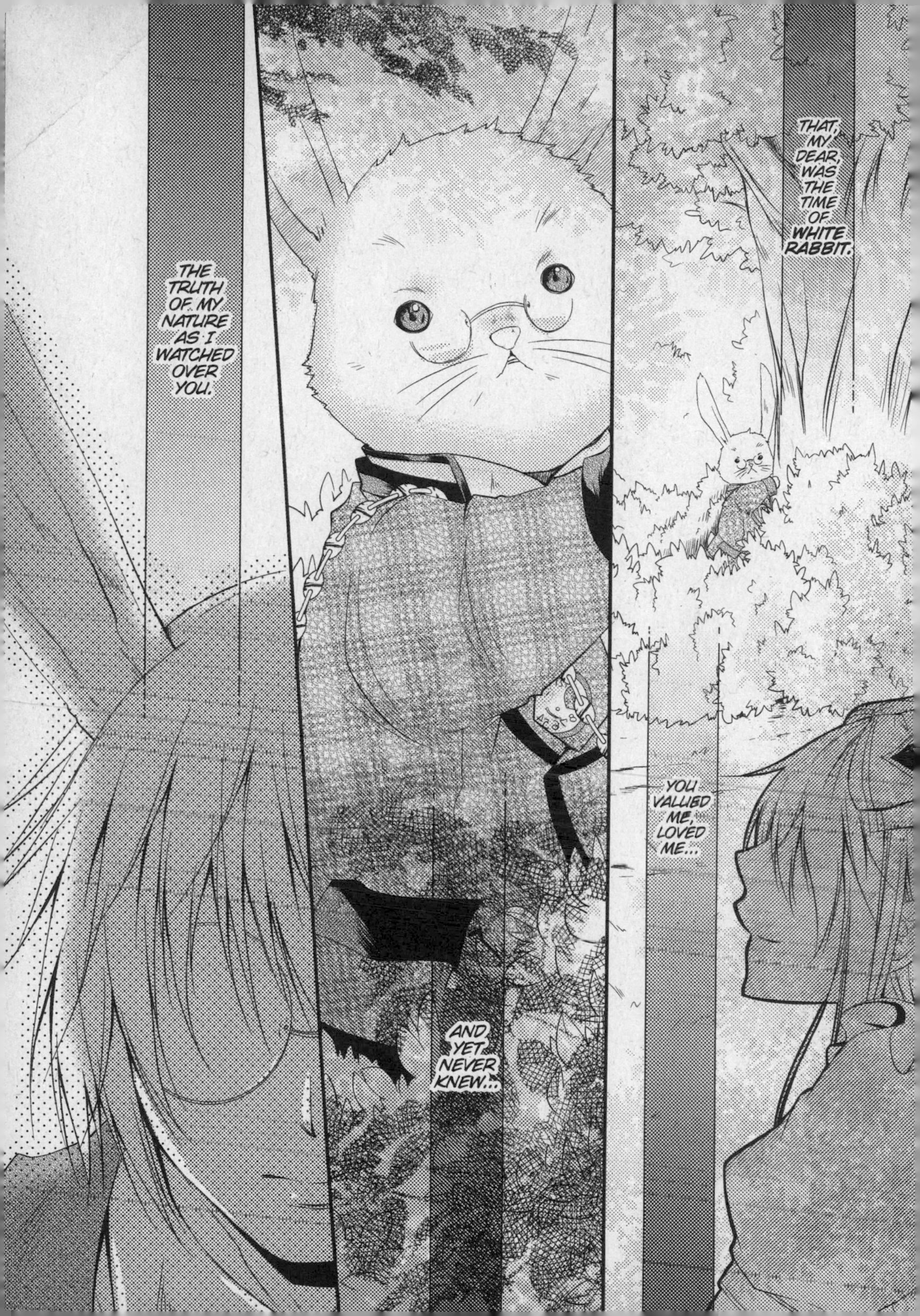
THAT, MY DEAR, WAS THE TIME OF WHITE RABBIT.
YOU VALUED ME, LOVED ME...
AND YET NEVER KNEW...
THE TRUTH OF MY NATURE AS I WATCHED OVER YOU.

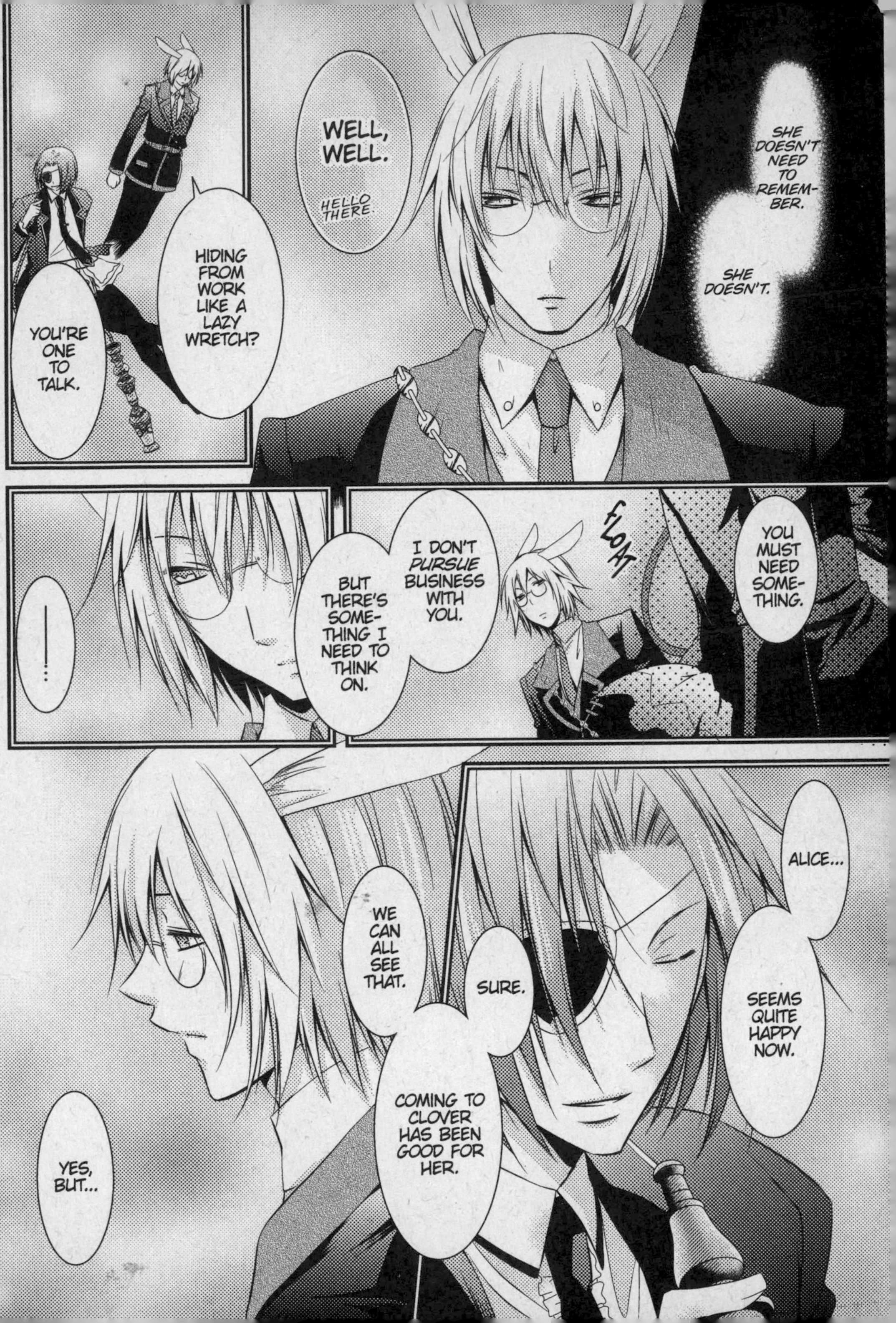
SHE DOESN'T NEED TO REMEMBER.
SHE DOESN'T.
WELL, WELL.
HELLO THERE.
HIDING FROM WORK LIKE A LAZY WRETCH?
YOU'RE ONE TO TALK.
FLOAT
YOU MUST NEED SOMETHING.
I DON'T *PURSUE* BUSINESS WITH YOU.
BUT THERE'S SOMETHING I NEED TO THINK ON.
......!
ALICE...
SEEMS QUITE HAPPY NOW.
SURE.
WE CAN ALL SEE THAT.
COMING TO CLOVER HAS BEEN GOOD FOR HER.
YES, BUT...

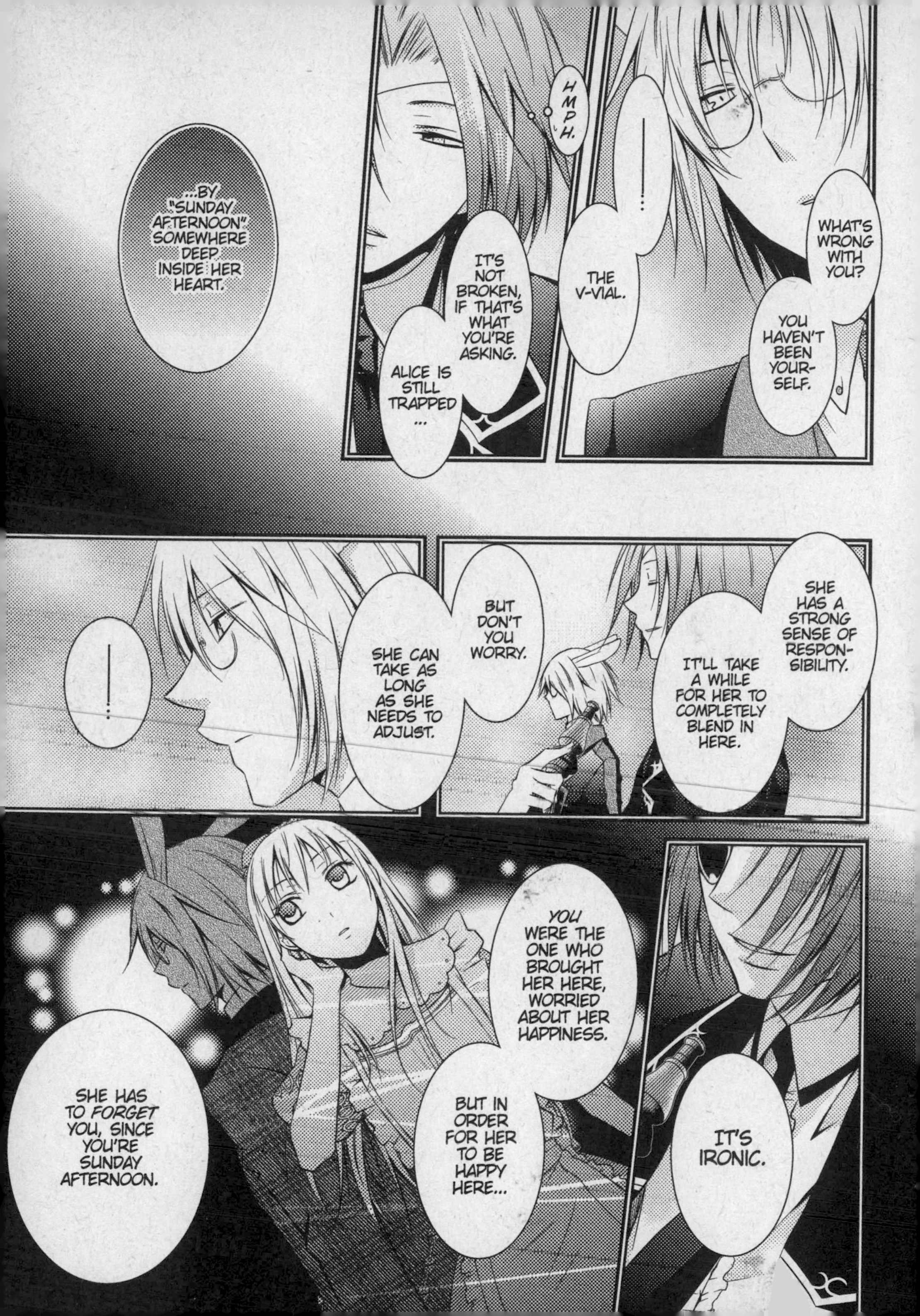
WHAT'S WRONG WITH YOU?
YOU HAVEN'T BEEN YOUR-SELF.
...
THE V-VIAL.
HMPH.
IT'S NOT BROKEN, IF THAT'S WHAT YOU'RE ASKING.
ALICE IS STILL TRAPPED ...
...BY "SUNDAY AFTERNOON" SOMEWHERE DEEP INSIDE HER HEART.
SHE HAS A STRONG SENSE OF RESPON-SIBILITY.
IT'LL TAKE A WHILE FOR HER TO COMPLETELY BLEND IN HERE.
BUT DON'T YOU WORRY.
SHE CAN TAKE AS LONG AS SHE NEEDS TO ADJUST.
!
IT'S IRONIC.
YOU WERE THE ONE WHO BROUGHT HER HERE, WORRIED ABOUT HER HAPPINESS.
BUT IN ORDER FOR HER TO BE HAPPY HERE...
SHE HAS TO *FORGET* YOU, SINCE YOU'RE SUNDAY AFTERNOON.

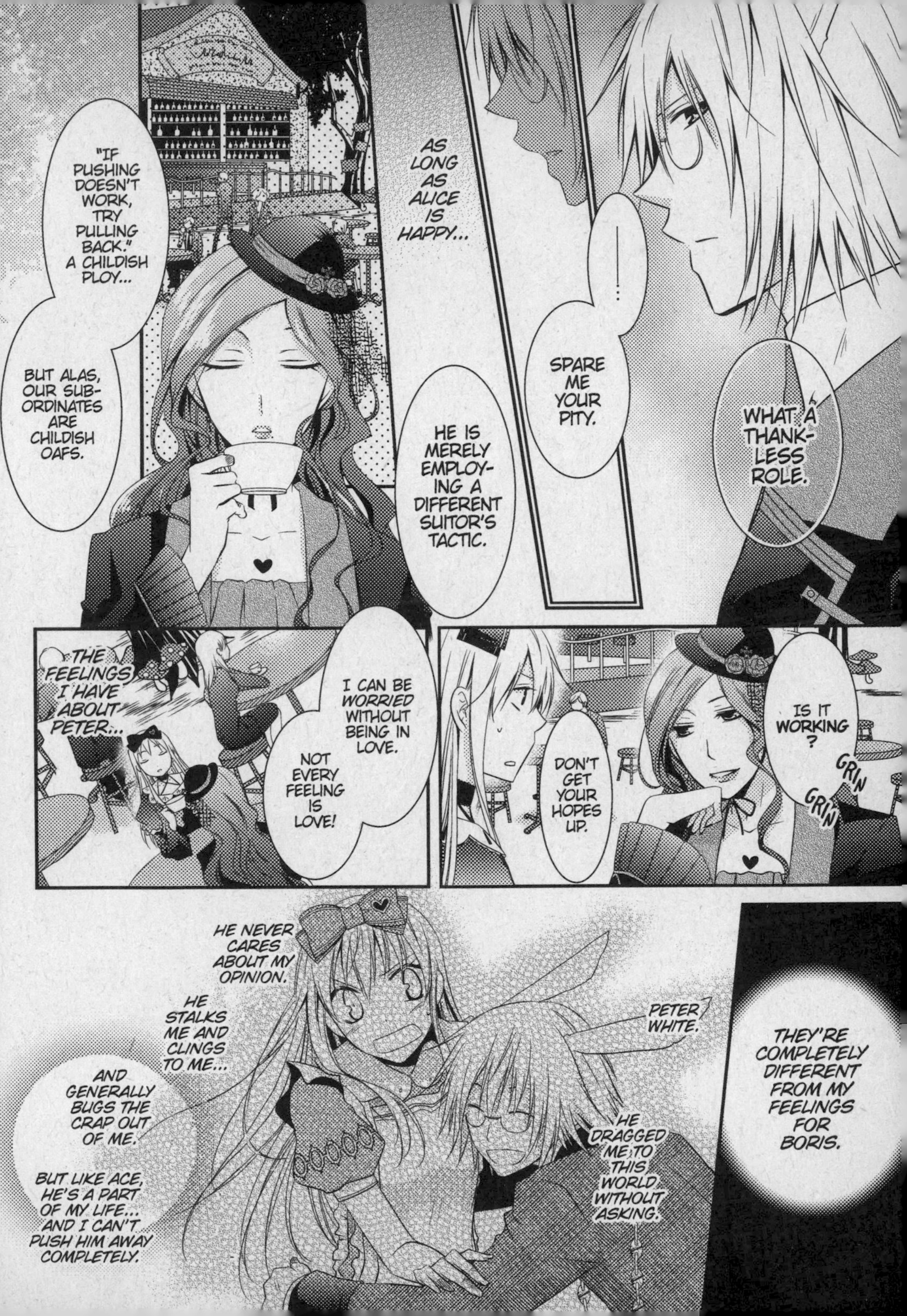
......
WHAT A THANKLESS ROLE.
SPARE ME YOUR PITY.
AS LONG AS ALICE IS HAPPY...
HE IS MERELY EMPLOYING A DIFFERENT SUITOR'S TACTIC.
"IF PUSHING DOESN'T WORK, TRY PULLING BACK." A CHILDISH PLOY...
BUT ALAS, OUR SUBORDINATES ARE CHILDISH OAFS.
IS IT WORKING?
GRIN
GRIN
DON'T GET YOUR HOPES UP.
I CAN BE WORRIED WITHOUT BEING IN LOVE.
NOT EVERY FEELING IS LOVE!
THE FEELINGS I HAVE ABOUT PETER...
THEY'RE COMPLETELY DIFFERENT FROM MY FEELINGS FOR BORIS.
PETER WHITE.
HE DRAGGED ME TO THIS WORLD WITHOUT ASKING.
HE NEVER CARES ABOUT MY OPINION.
HE STALKS ME AND CLINGS TO ME...
AND GENERALLY BUGS THE CRAP OUT OF ME.
BUT LIKE ACE, HE'S A PART OF MY LIFE... AND I CAN'T PUSH HIM AWAY COMPLETELY.

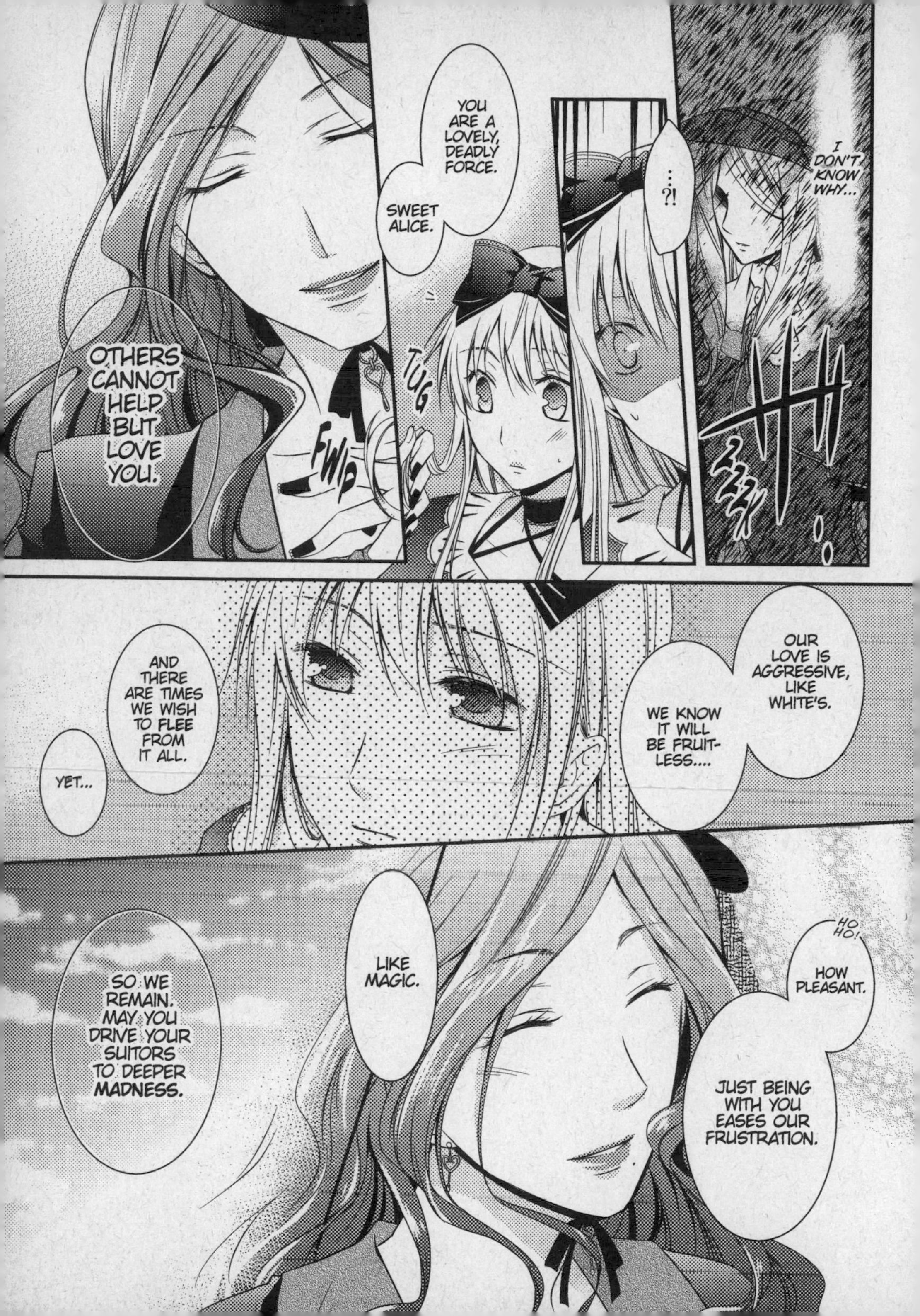
I DON'T KNOW WHY...
...?!
YOU ARE A LOVELY, DEADLY FORCE.
SWEET ALICE.
TUG
FWIP
OTHERS CANNOT HELP BUT LOVE YOU.
OUR LOVE IS AGGRESSIVE, LIKE WHITE'S.
WE KNOW IT WILL BE FRUIT-LESS....
AND THERE ARE TIMES WE WISH TO FLEE FROM IT ALL.
YET...
HO HO!
HOW PLEASANT.
JUST BEING WITH YOU EASES OUR FRUSTRATION.
LIKE MAGIC.
SO WE REMAIN. MAY YOU DRIVE YOUR SUITORS TO DEEPER MADNESS.

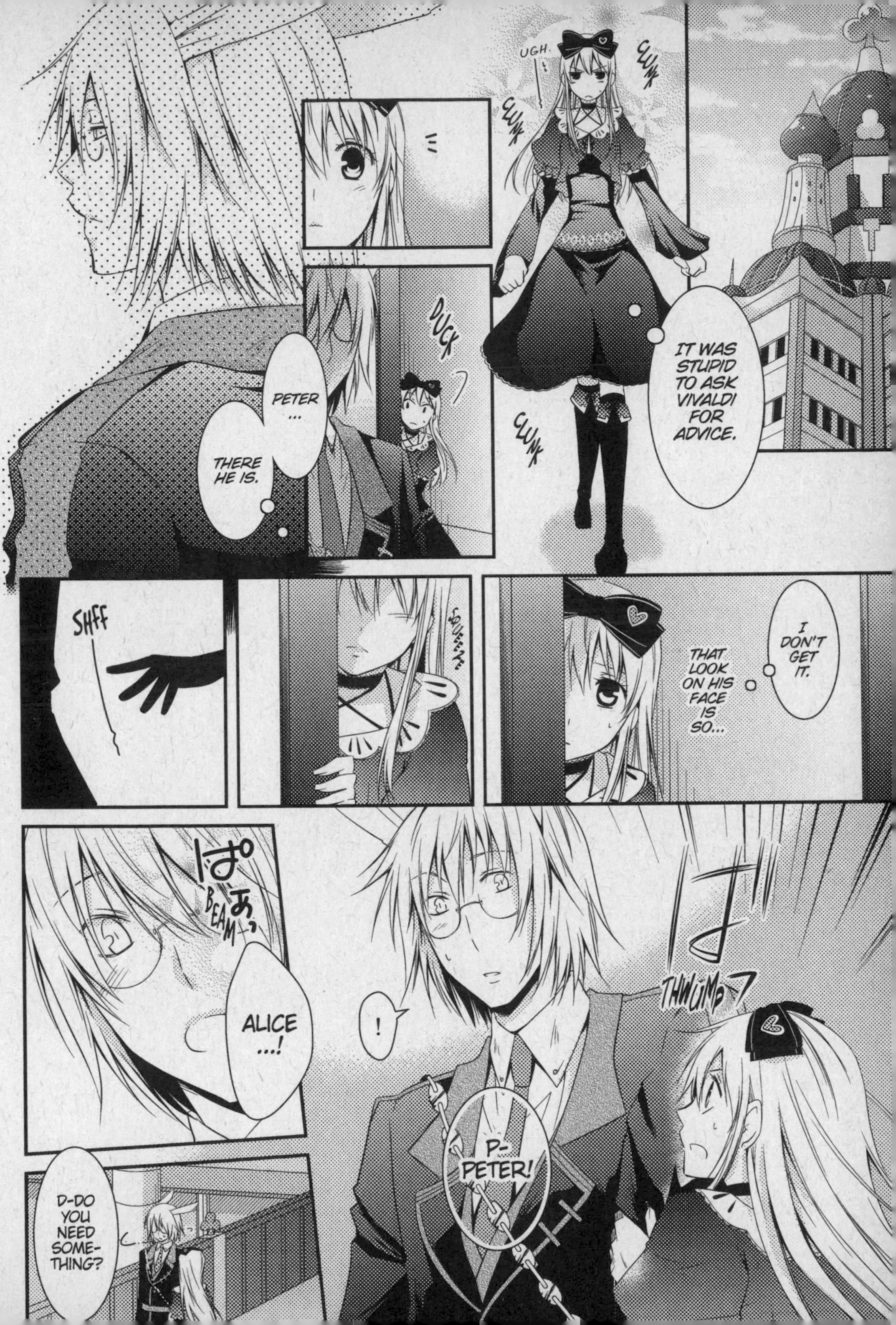

UGH.
CLUNK
CLUNK
CLUNK
IT WAS STUPID TO ASK VIVALDI FOR ADVICE.
DUCK
PETER ...
THERE HE IS.
I DON'T GET IT.
THAT LOOK ON HIS FACE IS SO...
SHFF
THWUMP
!
P-PETER!
BEAM
ALICE ...!
D-DO YOU NEED SOMETHING?

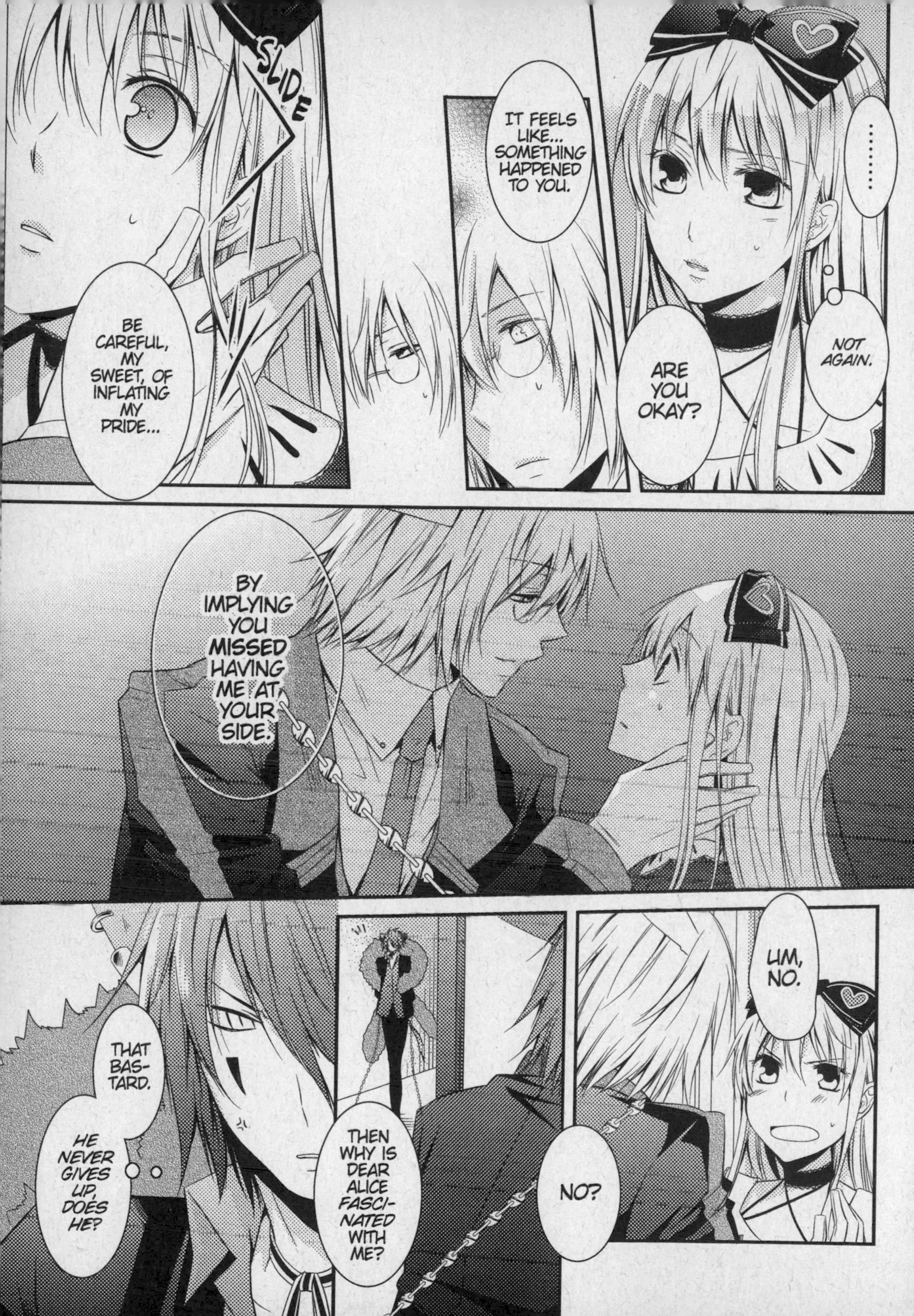
......
NOT AGAIN.
ARE YOU OKAY?
IT FEELS LIKE... SOMETHING HAPPENED TO YOU.
SLIDE
BE CAREFUL, MY SWEET, OF INFLATING MY PRIDE...
BY IMPLYING YOU MISSED HAVING ME AT YOUR SIDE.
UM, NO.
NO?
THEN WHY IS DEAR ALICE FASCINATED WITH ME?
THAT BASTARD.
HE NEVER GIVES UP, DOES HE?

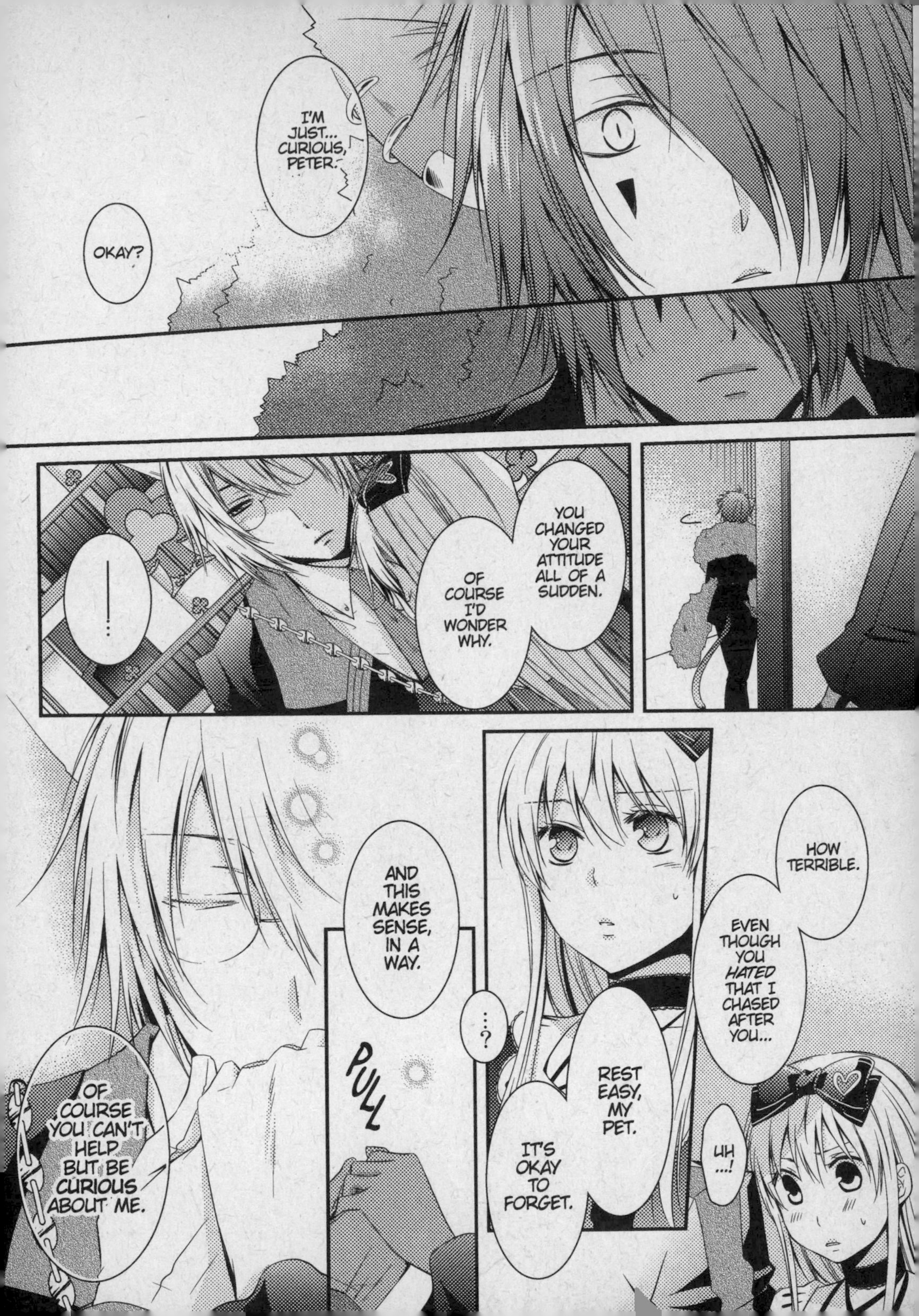
I'M JUST... CURIOUS, PETER.
OKAY?
YOU CHANGED YOUR ATTITUDE ALL OF A SUDDEN.
OF COURSE I'D WONDER WHY.
...!
HOW TERRIBLE.
EVEN THOUGH YOU *HATED* THAT I CHASED AFTER YOU...
UH ...!
...?
AND THIS MAKES SENSE, IN A WAY.
REST EASY, MY PET.
IT'S OKAY TO FORGET.
PULL
OF COURSE YOU CAN'T HELP BUT BE CURIOUS ABOUT ME.

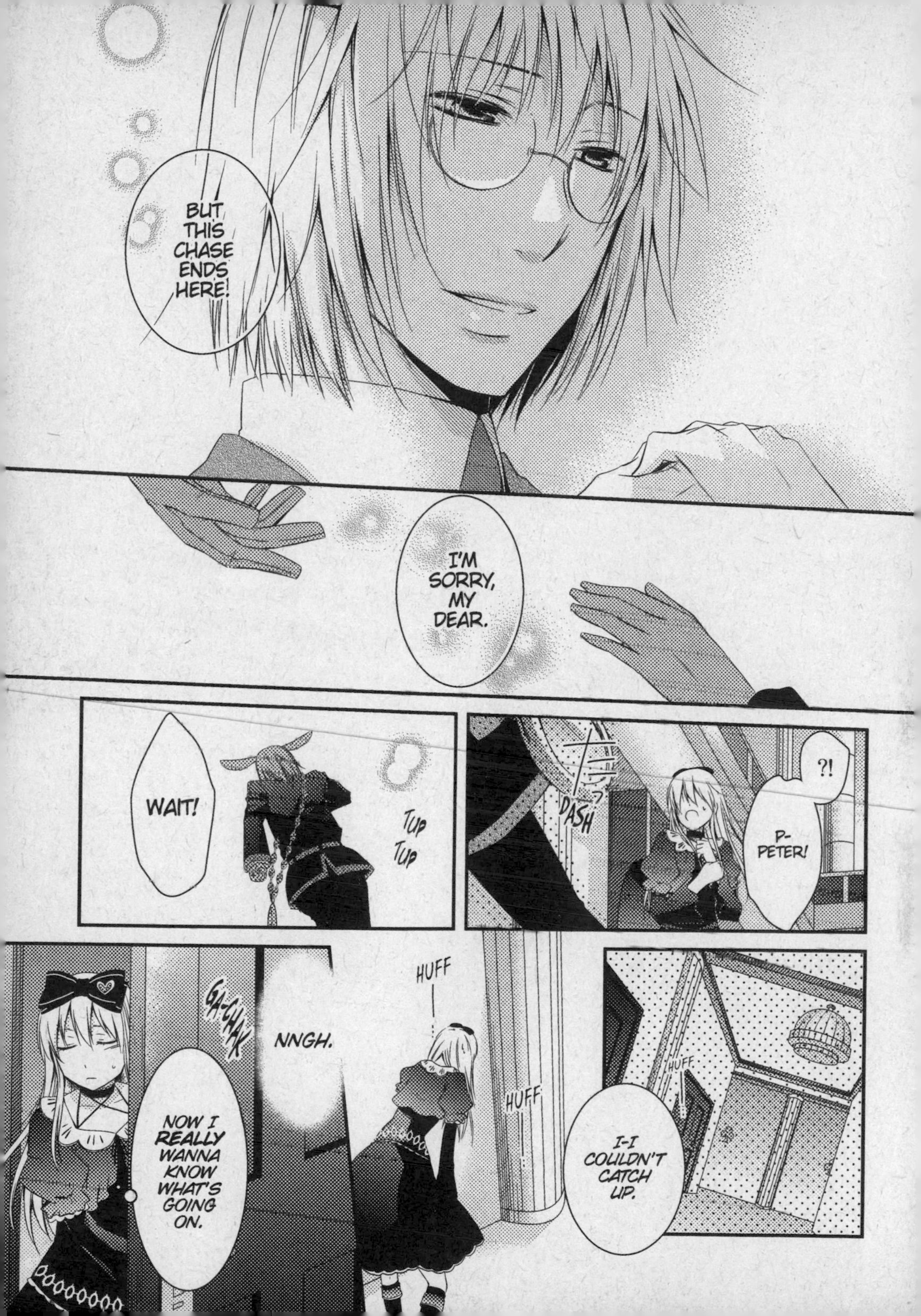

BUT THIS CHASE ENDS HERE!
I'M SORRY, MY DEAR.
?!
P-PETER!
DASH
WAIT!
TUP TUP
HUFF
I-I COULDN'T CATCH UP.
HUFF
HUFF
NNGH.
GA-CHAK
NOW I REALLY WANNA KNOW WHAT'S GOING ON.

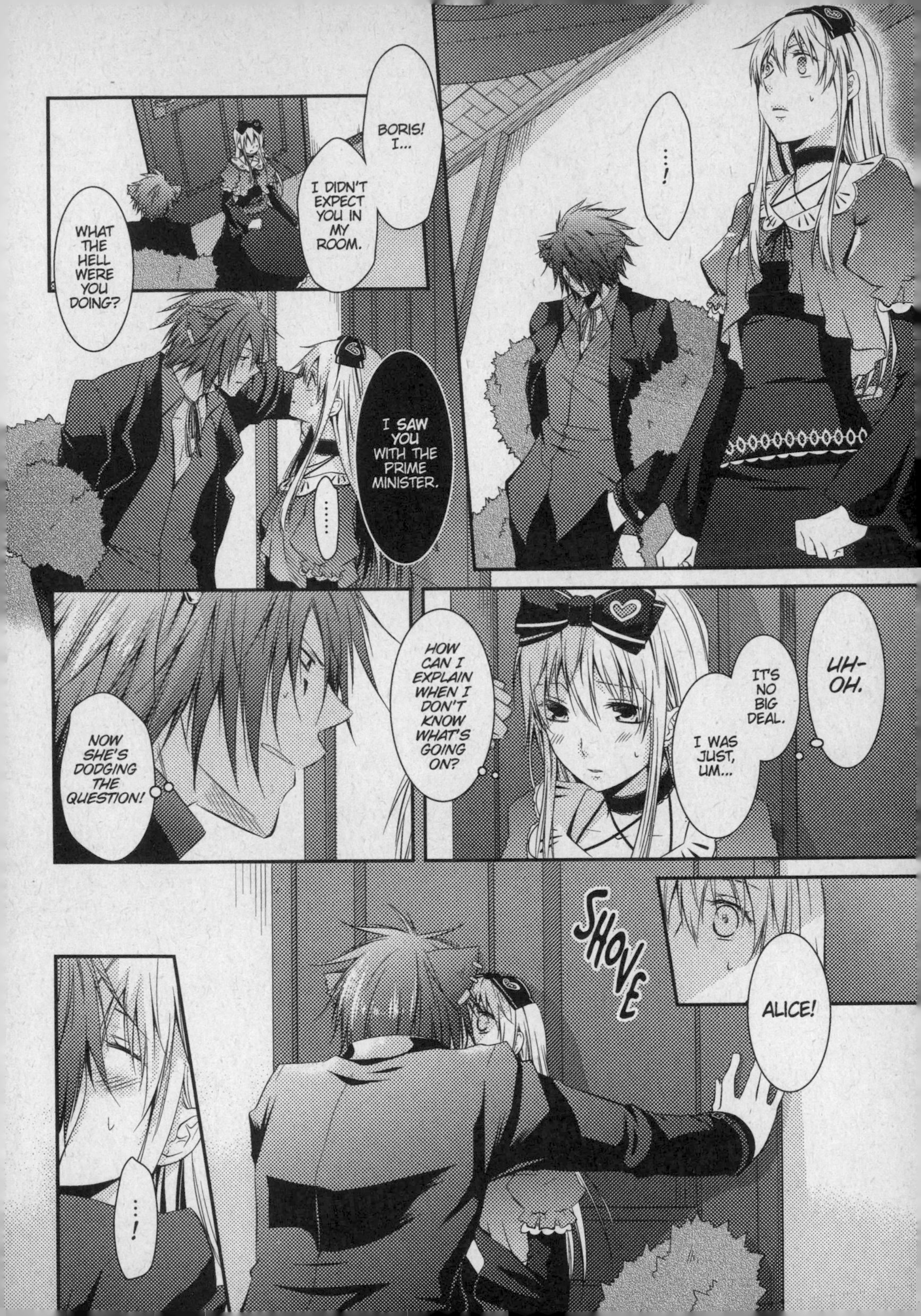

…!
BORIS! I...
I DIDN'T EXPECT YOU IN MY ROOM.
WHAT THE HELL WERE YOU DOING?
I SAW YOU WITH THE PRIME MINISTER.
......
UH-OH.
IT'S NO BIG DEAL.
I WAS JUST, UM...
HOW CAN I EXPLAIN WHEN I DON'T KNOW WHAT'S GOING ON?
NOW SHE'S DODGING THE QUESTION!
ALICE!
SHOVE
…!

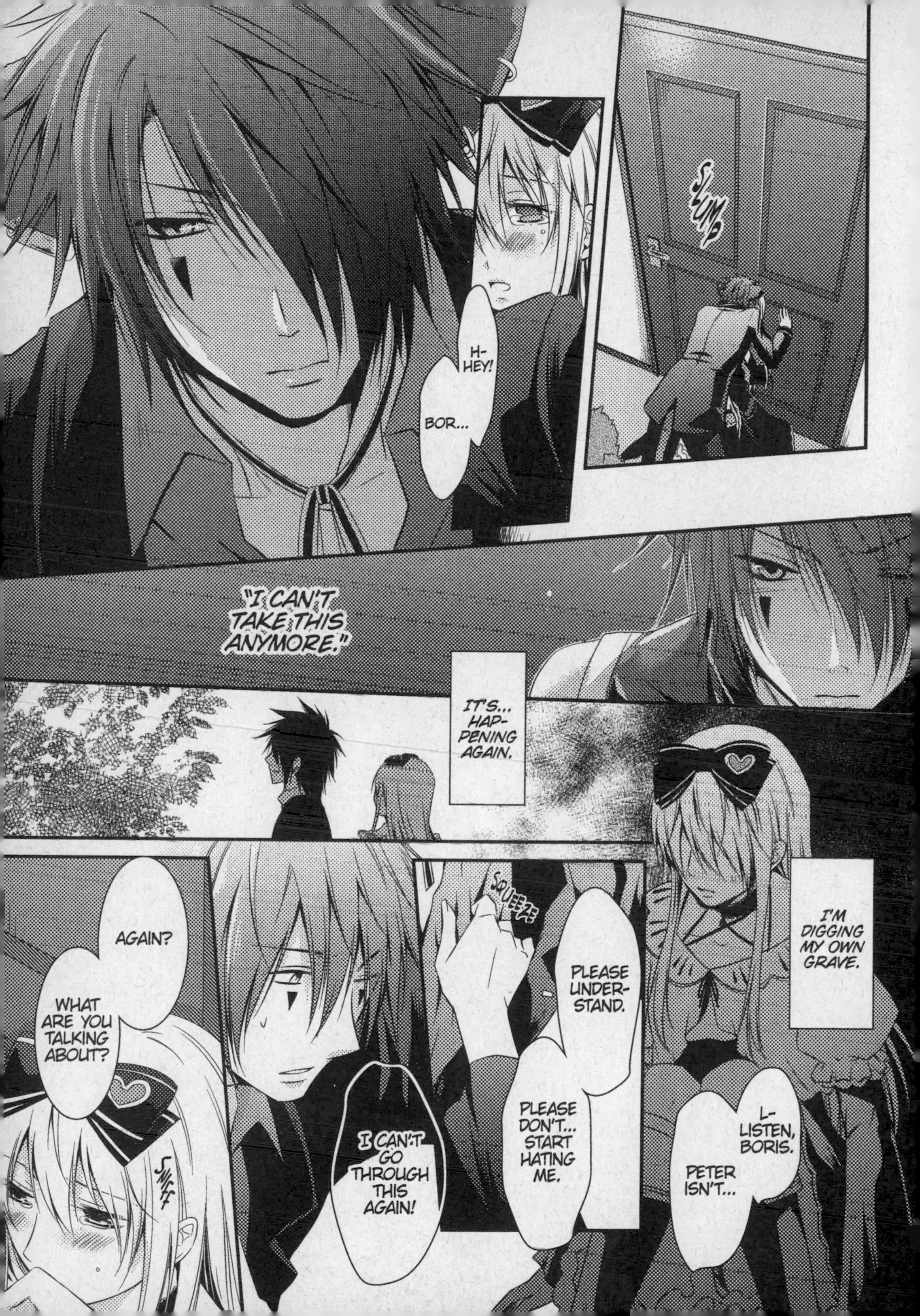
SLUMP
H-HEY!
BOR...
"I CAN'T TAKE THIS ANYMORE."
IT'S... HAPPENING AGAIN.
I'M DIGGING MY OWN GRAVE.
L-LISTEN, BORIS.
PETER ISN'T...
SQUEEZE
PLEASE UNDERSTAND.
PLEASE DON'T... START HATING ME.
I CAN'T GO THROUGH THIS AGAIN!
AGAIN?
WHAT ARE YOU TALKING ABOUT?
SNIFF

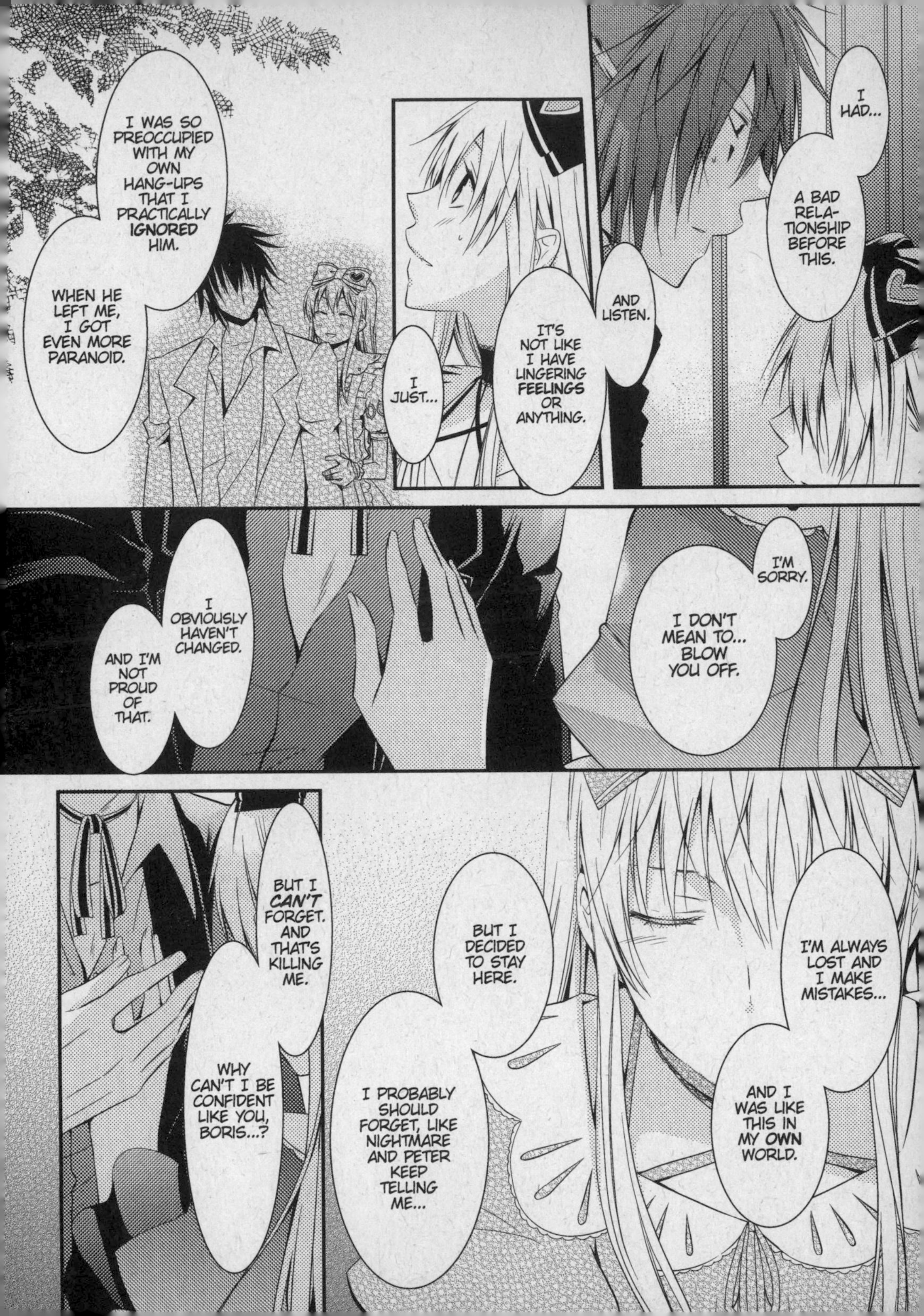
I HAD...
A BAD RELATIONSHIP BEFORE THIS.
AND LISTEN.
IT'S NOT LIKE I HAVE LINGERING FEELINGS OR ANYTHING.
I JUST...
I WAS SO PREOCCUPIED WITH MY OWN HANG-UPS THAT I PRACTICALLY IGNORED HIM.
WHEN HE LEFT ME, I GOT EVEN MORE PARANOID.
I'M SORRY.
I DON'T MEAN TO... BLOW YOU OFF.
I OBVIOUSLY HAVEN'T CHANGED.
AND I'M NOT PROUD OF THAT.
I'M ALWAYS LOST AND I MAKE MISTAKES...
AND I WAS LIKE THIS IN MY OWN WORLD.
BUT I DECIDED TO STAY HERE.
I PROBABLY SHOULD FORGET, LIKE NIGHTMARE AND PETER KEEP TELLING ME...
BUT I CAN'T FORGET. AND THAT'S KILLING ME.
WHY CAN'T I BE CONFIDENT LIKE YOU, BORIS...?

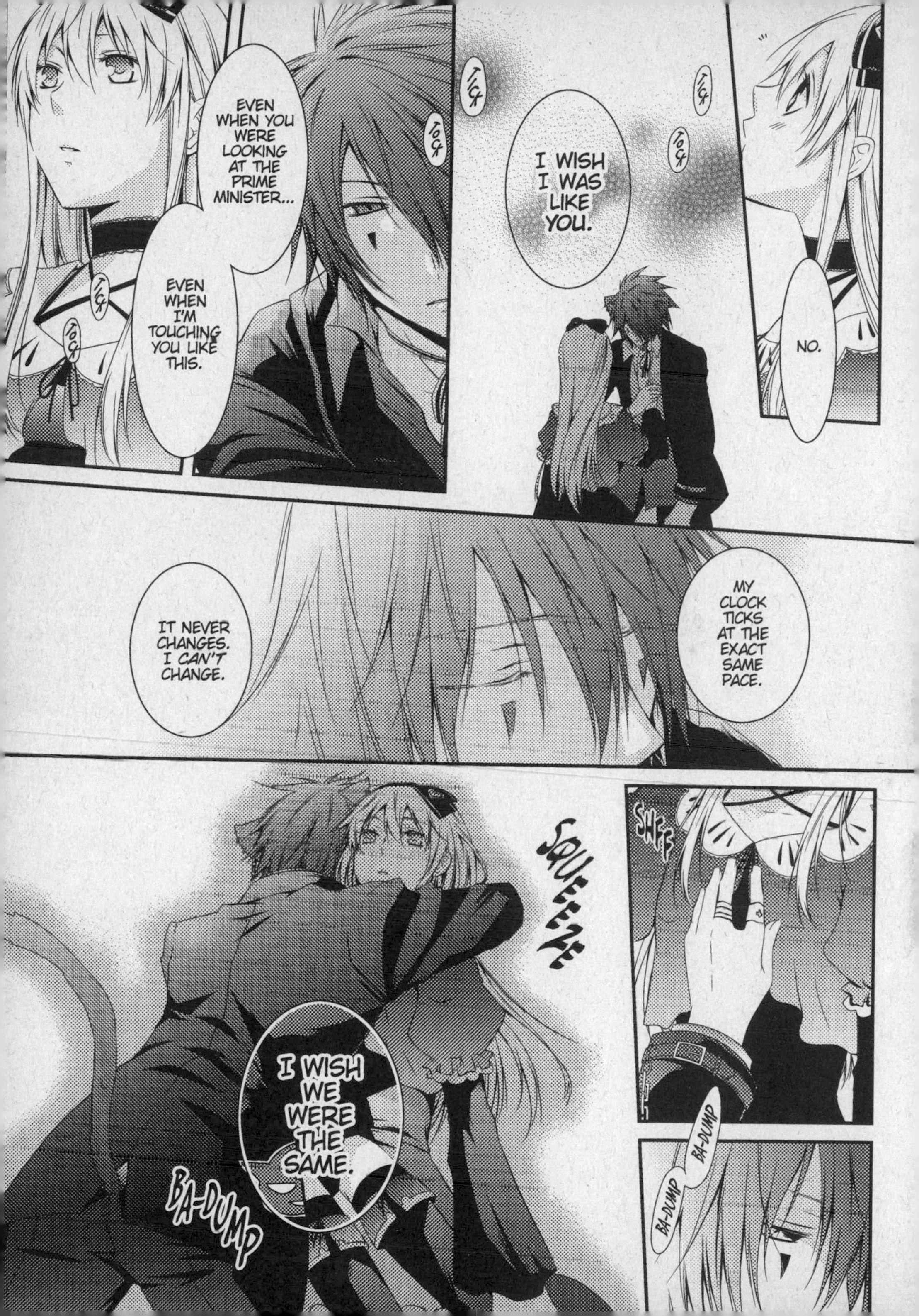
NO.
TICK
TOCK
I WISH I WAS LIKE YOU.
TICK
TOCK
EVEN WHEN YOU WERE LOOKING AT THE PRIME MINISTER...
EVEN WHEN I'M TOUCHING YOU LIKE THIS.
TICK
TOCK
MY CLOCK TICKS AT THE EXACT SAME PACE.
IT NEVER CHANGES. I CAN'T CHANGE.
SHFF
BA-DUMP
BA-DUMP
SQUEEZE
I WISH WE WERE THE SAME.
BA-DUMP

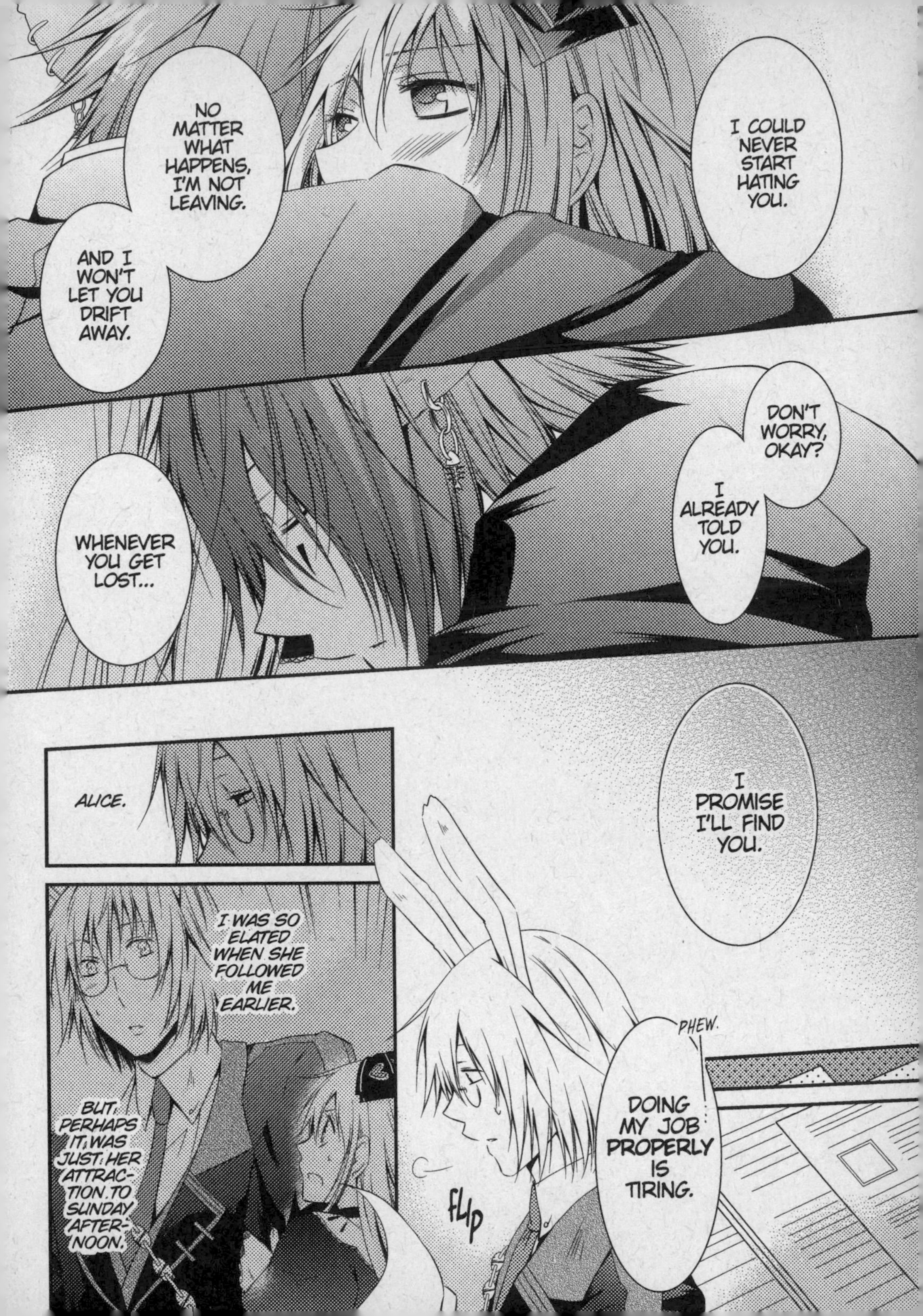
I COULD NEVER START HATING YOU.
NO MATTER WHAT HAPPENS, I'M NOT LEAVING.
AND I WON'T LET YOU DRIFT AWAY.
DON'T WORRY, OKAY?
I ALREADY TOLD YOU.
WHENEVER YOU GET LOST...
I PROMISE I'LL FIND YOU.
PHEW.
DOING MY JOB PROPERLY IS TIRING.
FLIP
ALICE.
I WAS SO ELATED WHEN SHE FOLLOWED ME EARLIER.
BUT PERHAPS IT WAS JUST HER ATTRACTION TO SUNDAY AFTER-NOON.

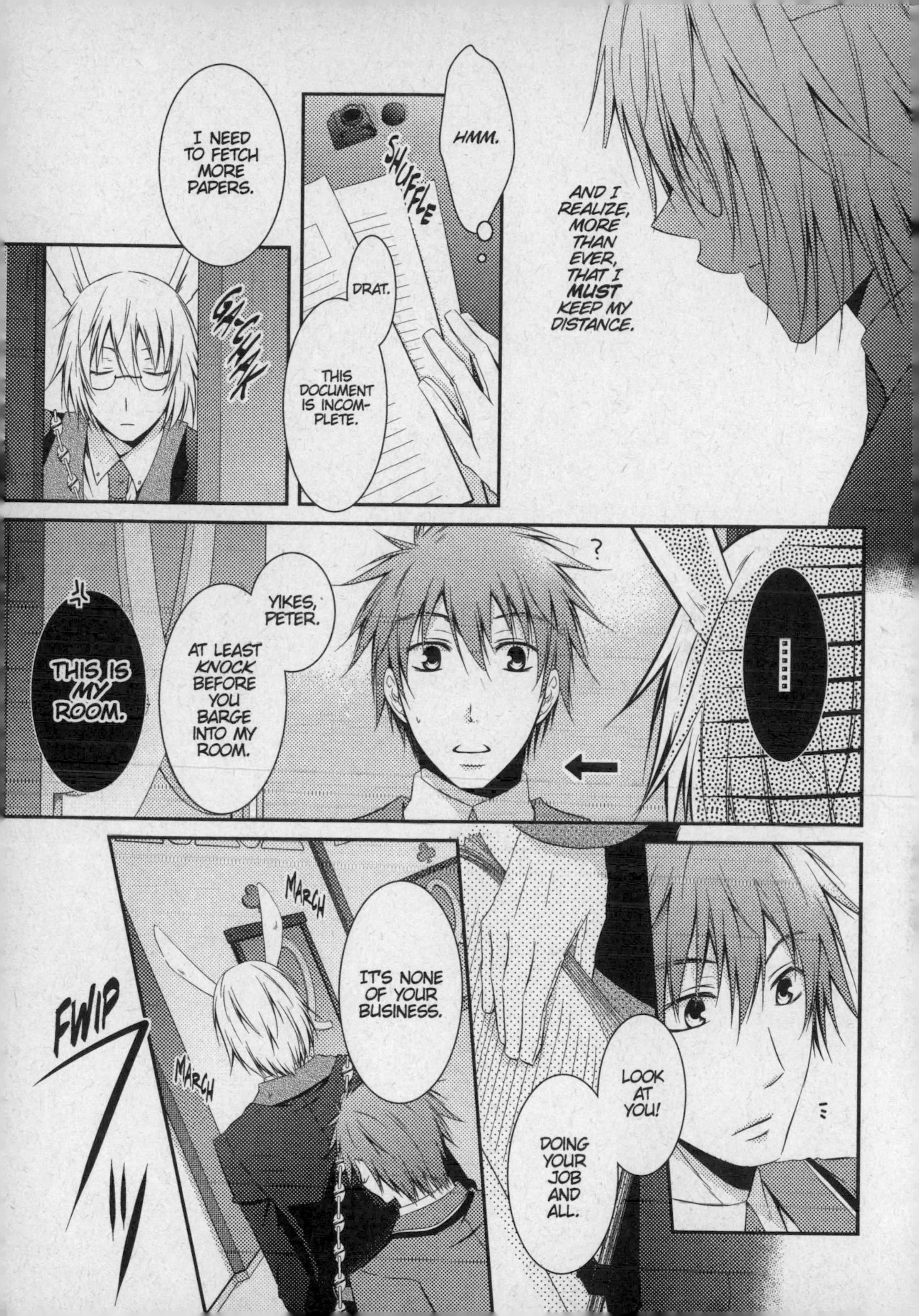
AND I REALIZE, MORE THAN EVER, THAT I MUST KEEP MY DISTANCE.
HMM.
SHUFFLE
DRAT.
THIS DOCUMENT IS INCOMPLETE.
I NEED TO FETCH MORE PAPERS.
GA-CHAK
...
?
YIKES, PETER.
AT LEAST KNOCK BEFORE YOU BARGE INTO MY ROOM.
THIS IS MY ROOM.
LOOK AT YOU!
DOING YOUR JOB AND ALL.
IT'S NONE OF YOUR BUSINESS.
MARCH
MARCH
FWIP

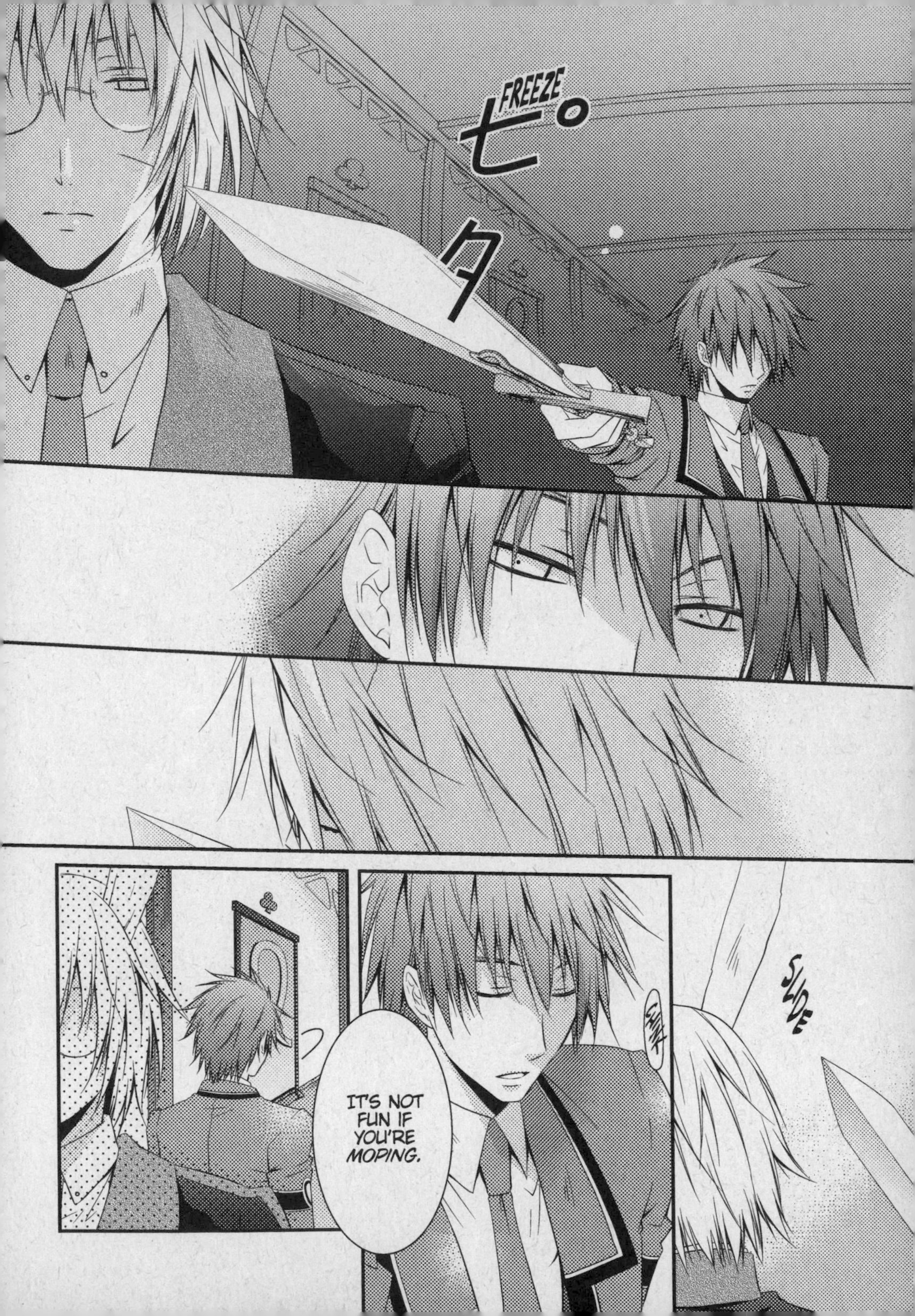
FREEZE
ピタ
SLIDE
CHINK
IT'S NOT FUN IF YOU'RE *MOPING.*

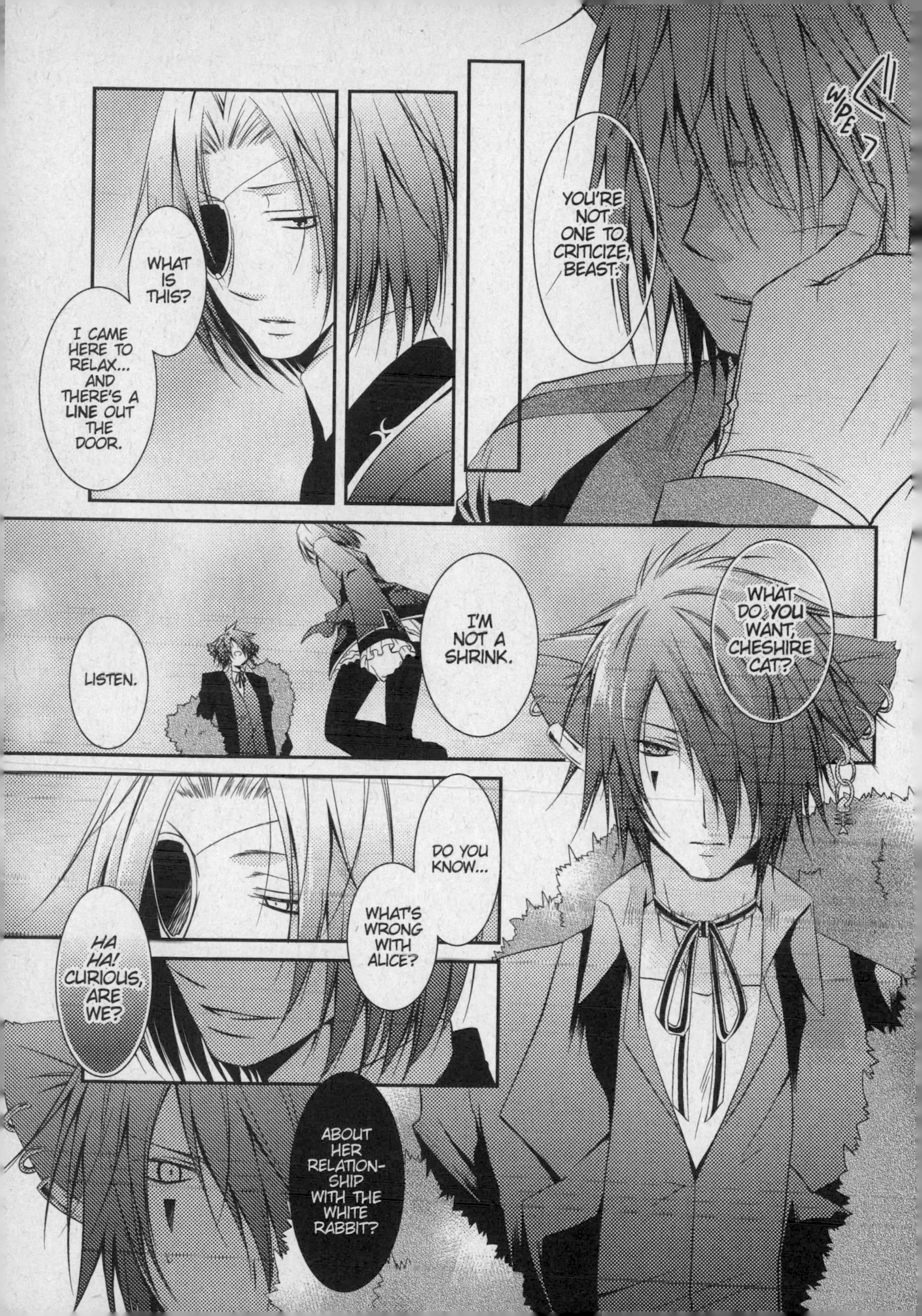
WIPE
YOU'RE NOT ONE TO CRITICIZE, BEAST.
WHAT IS THIS?
I CAME HERE TO RELAX... AND THERE'S A LINE OUT THE DOOR.
WHAT DO YOU WANT, CHESHIRE CAT?
I'M NOT A SHRINK.
LISTEN.
DO YOU KNOW...
WHAT'S WRONG WITH ALICE?
HA HA! CURIOUS, ARE WE?
ABOUT HER RELATIONSHIP WITH THE WHITE RABBIT?

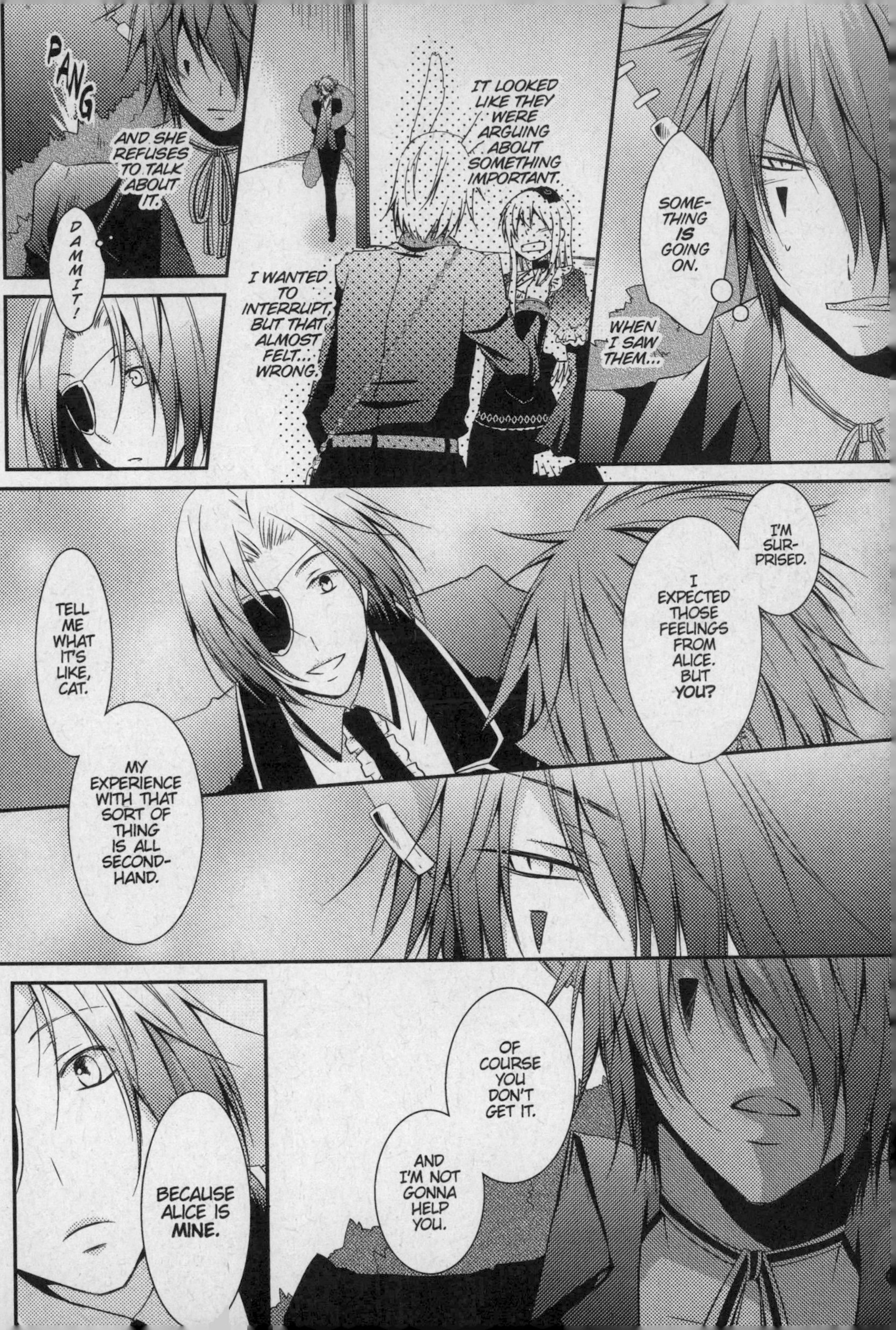
SOMETHING IS GOING ON.
WHEN I SAW THEM...
IT LOOKED LIKE THEY WERE ARGUING ABOUT SOMETHING IMPORTANT.
I WANTED TO INTERRUPT, BUT THAT ALMOST FELT... WRONG.
PANG
AND SHE REFUSES TO TALK ABOUT IT.
DAMMIT!
I'M SURPRISED.
I EXPECTED THOSE FEELINGS FROM ALICE. BUT YOU?
TELL ME WHAT IT'S LIKE, CAT.
MY EXPERIENCE WITH THAT SORT OF THING IS ALL SECOND-HAND.
OF COURSE YOU DON'T GET IT.
AND I'M NOT GONNA HELP YOU.
BECAUSE ALICE IS MINE.

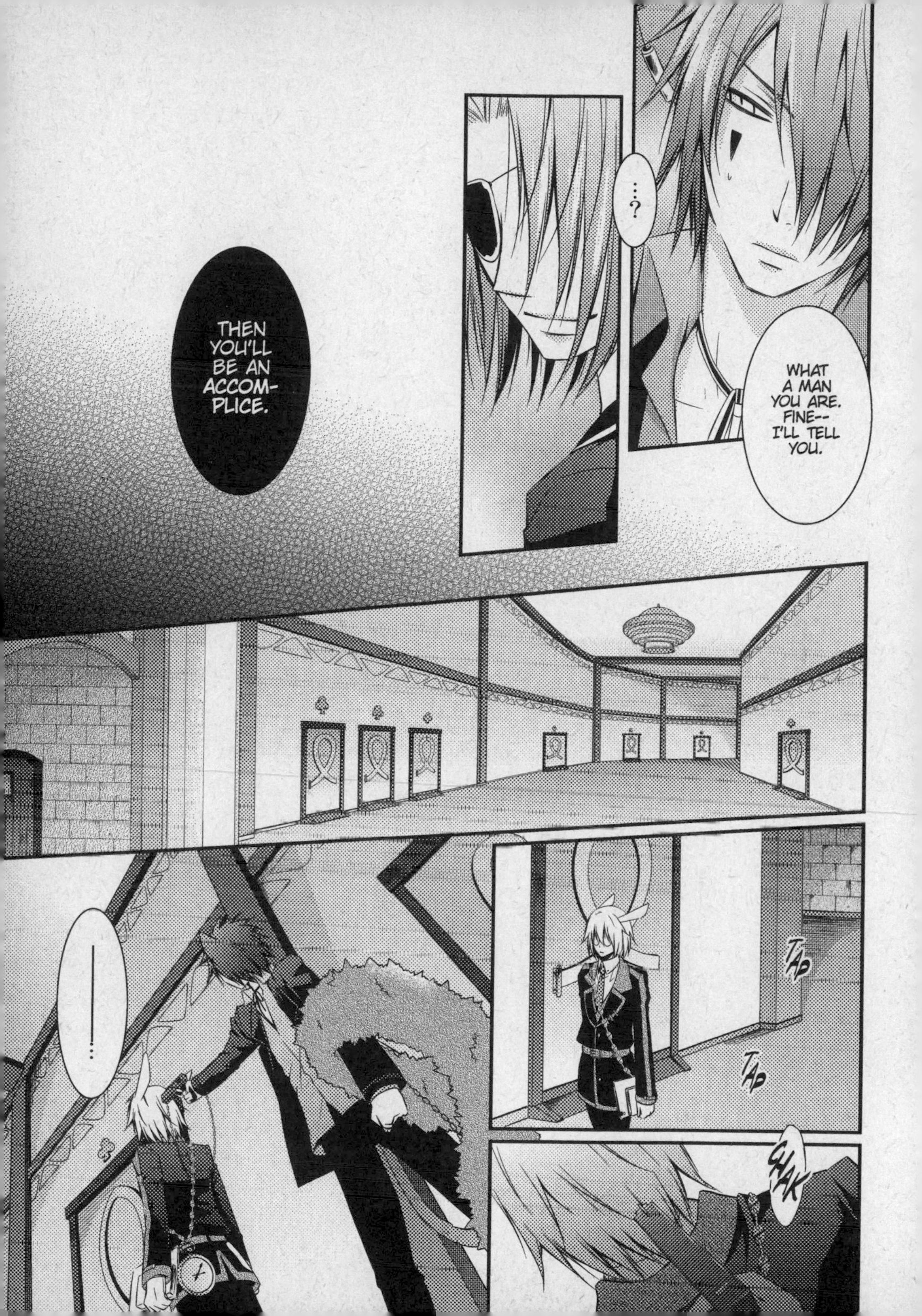

...?
WHAT A MAN YOU ARE. FINE-- I'LL TELL YOU.
THEN YOU'LL BE AN ACCOMPLICE.
TAP
TAP
CHAK
--......

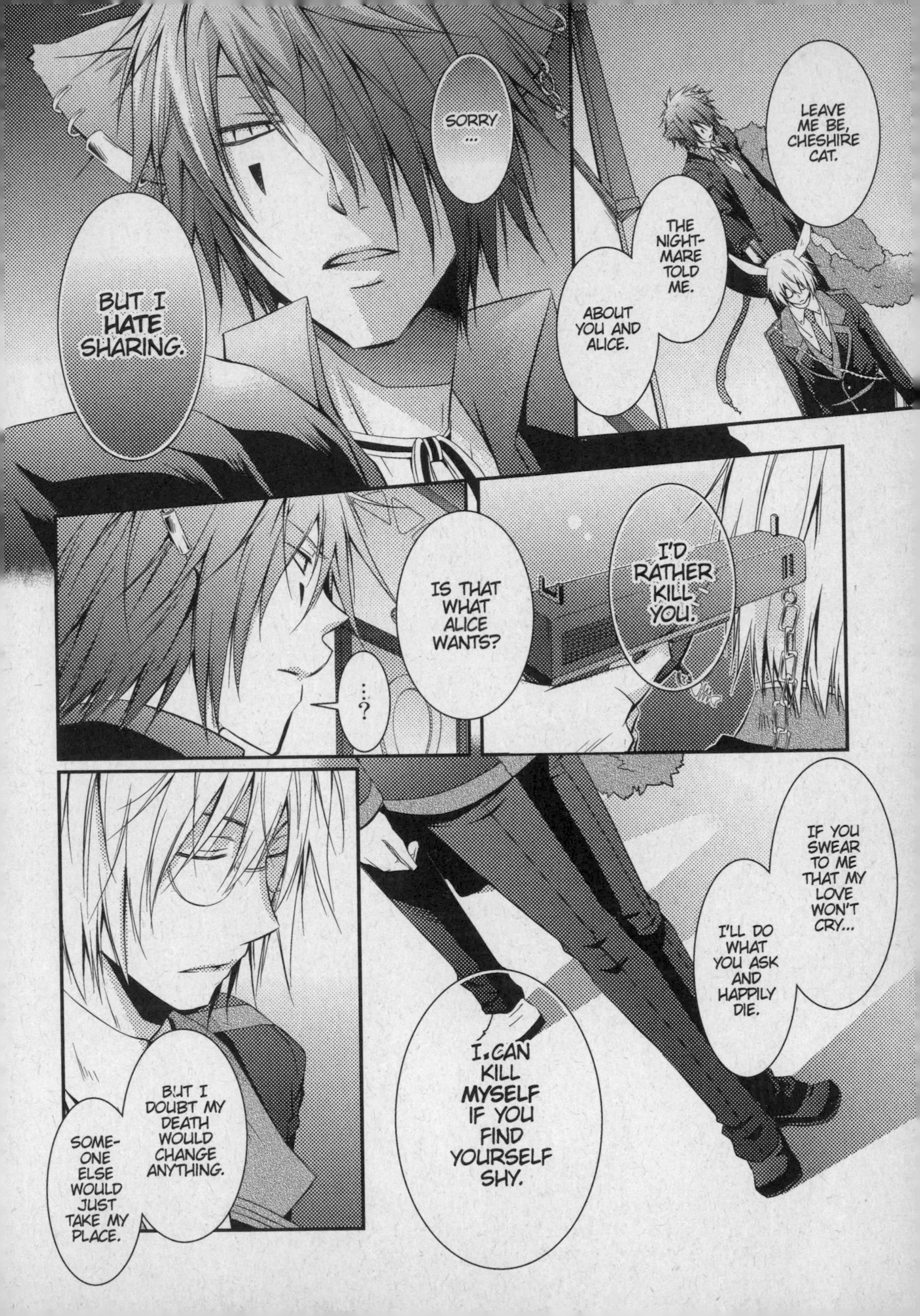
LEAVE ME BE, CHESHIRE CAT.
THE NIGHTMARE TOLD ME.
ABOUT YOU AND ALICE.
SORRY...
BUT I HATE SHARING.
I'D RATHER KILL YOU.
IS THAT WHAT ALICE WANTS?
...?
IF YOU SWEAR TO ME THAT MY LOVE WON'T CRY...
I'LL DO WHAT YOU ASK AND HAPPILY DIE.
I CAN KILL MYSELF IF YOU FIND YOURSELF SHY.
BUT I DOUBT MY DEATH WOULD CHANGE ANYTHING.
SOMEONE ELSE WOULD JUST TAKE MY PLACE.

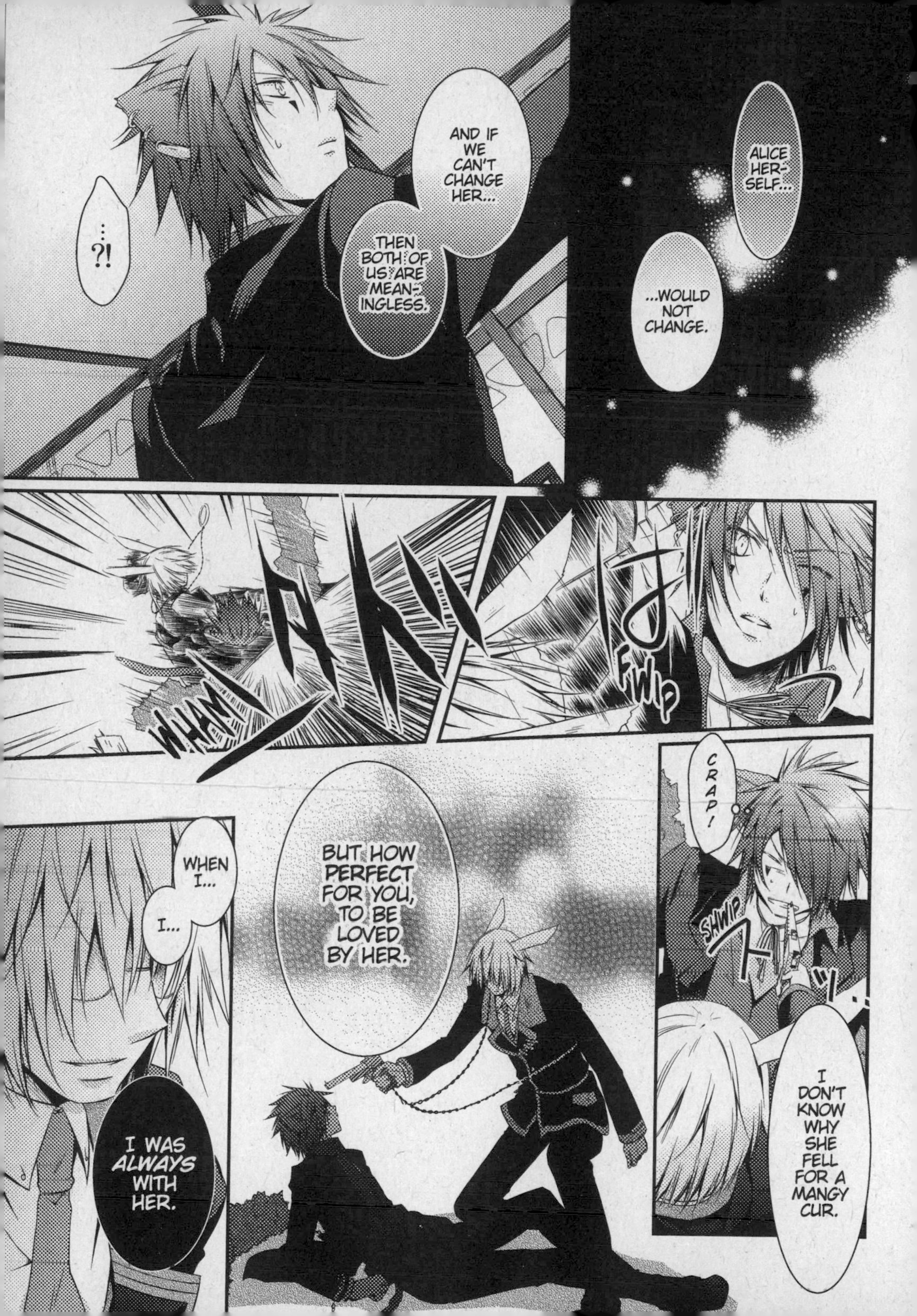
ALICE HER-SELF...
...WOULD NOT CHANGE.
AND IF WE CAN'T CHANGE HER...
THEN BOTH OF US ARE MEAN-INGLESS.
...?!
FWIP
WHAM
CRAP!
SHWIP
I DON'T KNOW WHY SHE FELL FOR A MANGY CUR.
BUT HOW PERFECT FOR YOU, TO BE LOVED BY HER.
WHEN I...
I...
I WAS *ALWAYS* WITH HER.

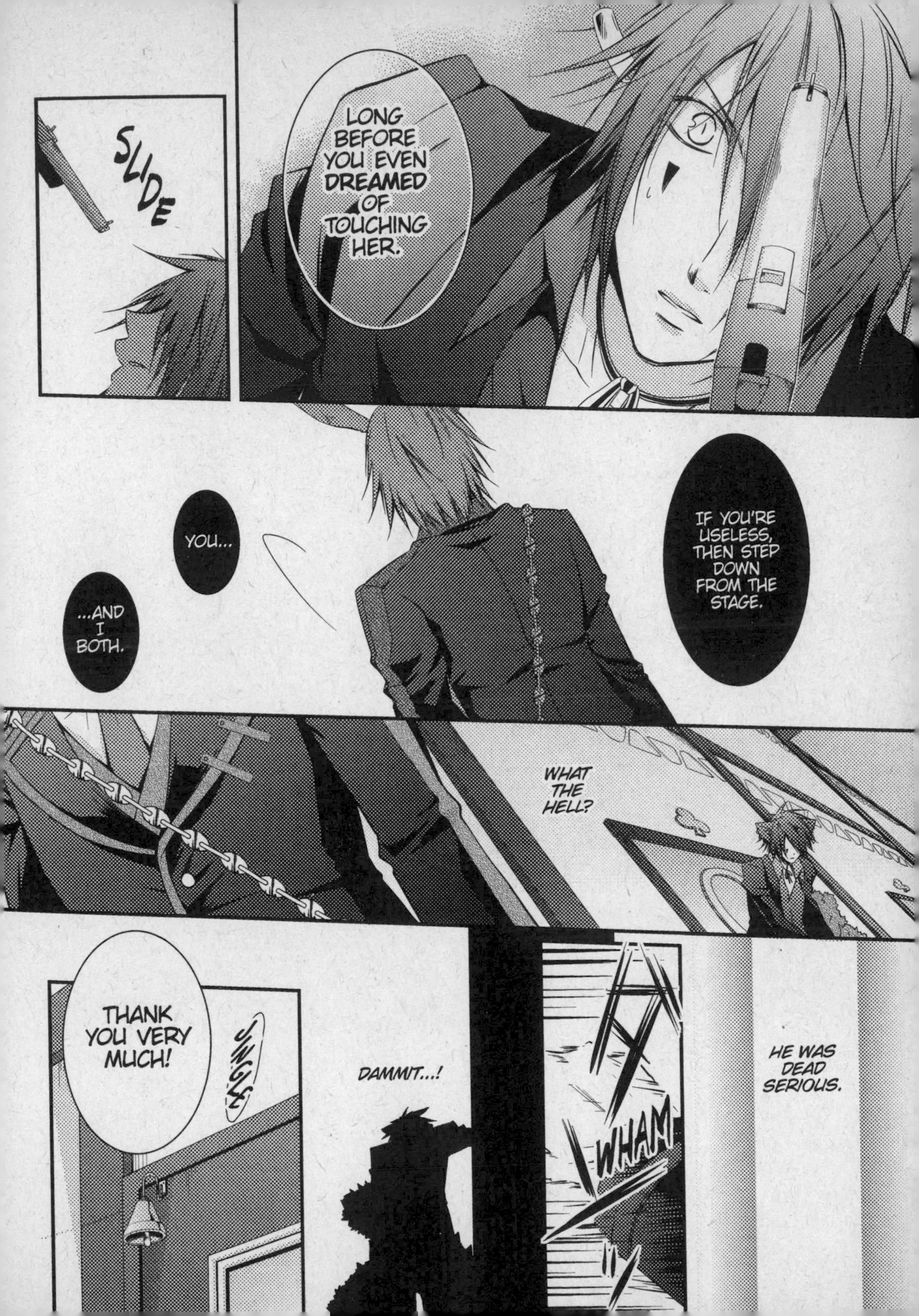
LONG BEFORE YOU EVEN DREAMED OF TOUCHING HER.
SLIDE
IF YOU'RE USELESS, THEN STEP DOWN FROM THE STAGE.
YOU...
...AND I BOTH.
WHAT THE HELL?
HE WAS DEAD SERIOUS.
WHAM
DAMMIT...!
THANK YOU VERY MUCH!
JINGLE

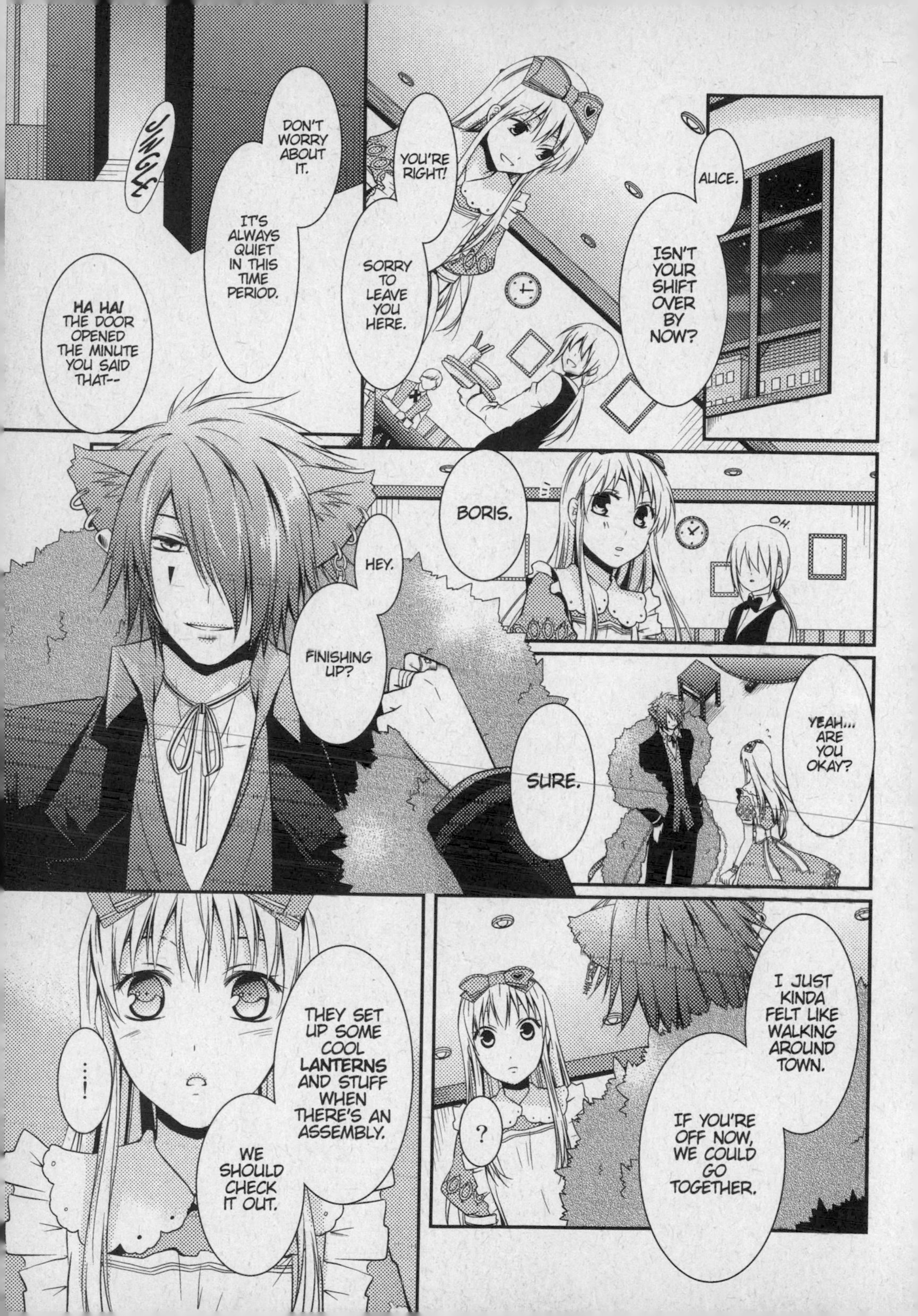
ALICE.
ISN'T YOUR SHIFT OVER BY NOW?
YOU'RE RIGHT!
SORRY TO LEAVE YOU HERE.
DON'T WORRY ABOUT IT.
IT'S ALWAYS QUIET IN THIS TIME PERIOD.
JINGLE
HA HA! THE DOOR OPENED THE MINUTE YOU SAID THAT--
BORIS.
OH.
YEAH... ARE YOU OKAY?
SURE.
HEY.
FINISHING UP?
I JUST KINDA FELT LIKE WALKING AROUND TOWN.
IF YOU'RE OFF NOW, WE COULD GO TOGETHER.
?
THEY SET UP SOME COOL LANTERNS AND STUFF WHEN THERE'S AN ASSEMBLY.
WE SHOULD CHECK IT OUT.
...!

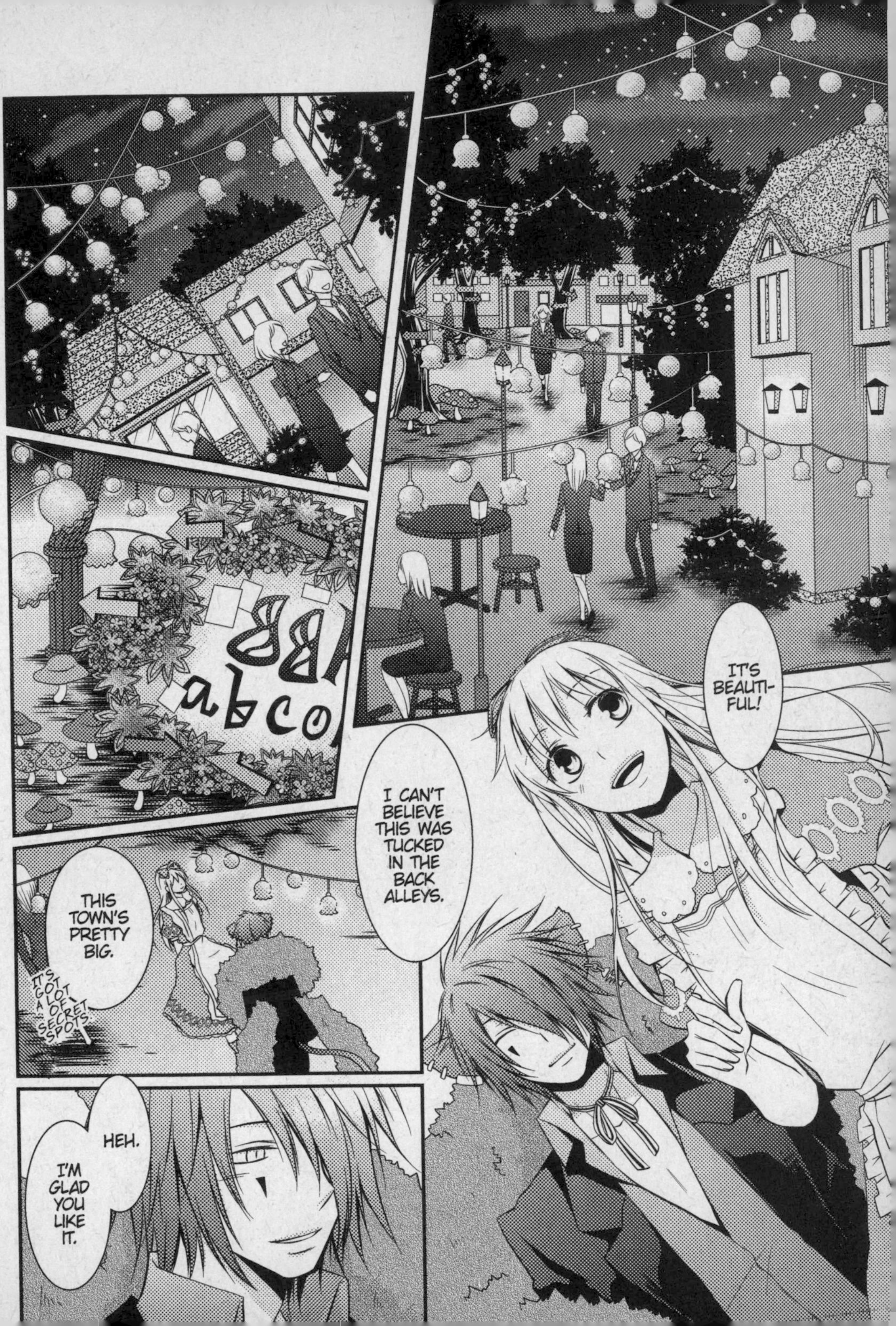
IT'S BEAUTIFUL!
I CAN'T BELIEVE THIS WAS TUCKED IN THE BACK ALLEYS.
THIS TOWN'S PRETTY BIG.
IT'S GOT A LOT OF SECRET SPOTS.
HEH.
I'M GLAD YOU LIKE IT.

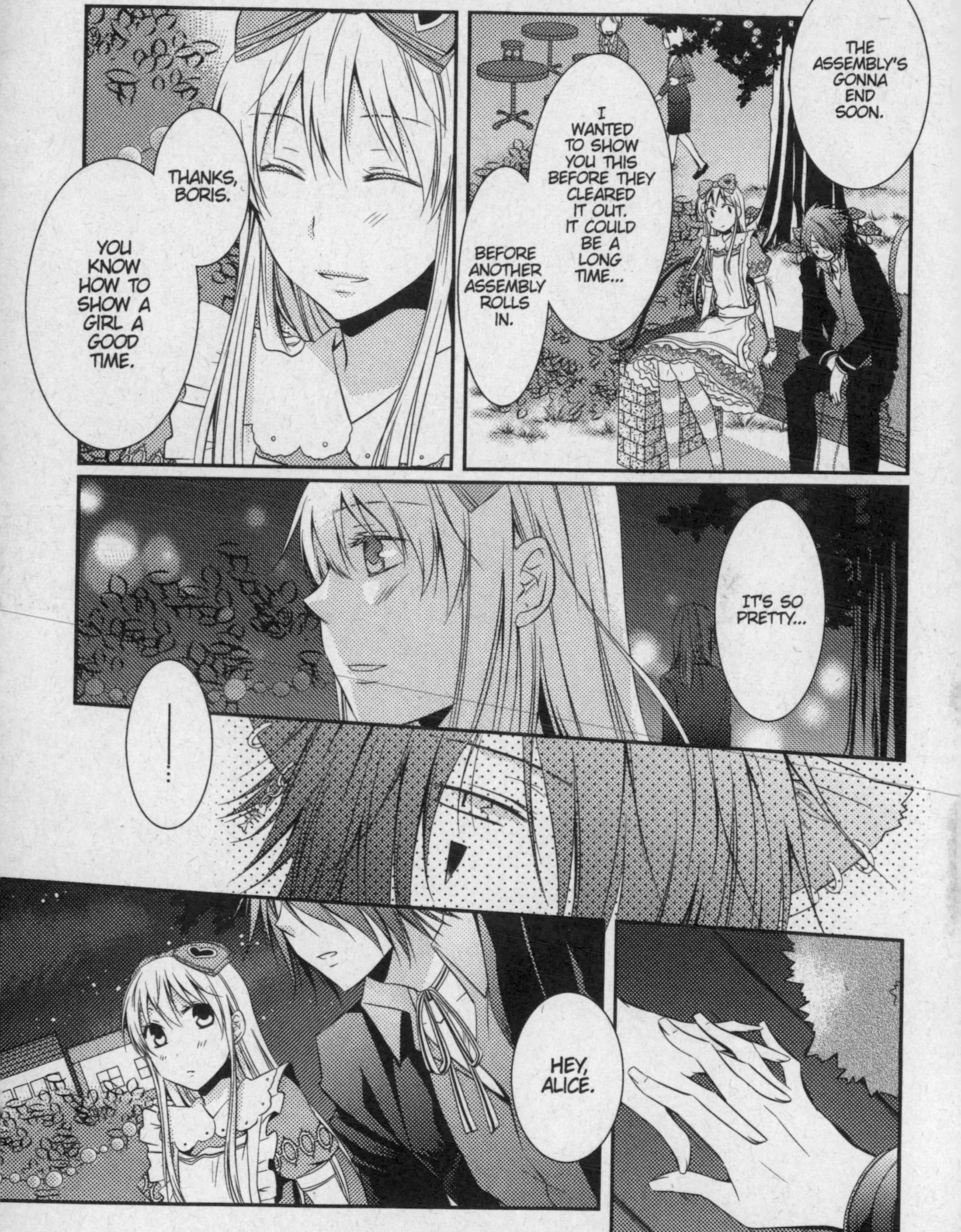
THE ASSEMBLY'S GONNA END SOON.
I WANTED TO SHOW YOU THIS BEFORE THEY CLEARED IT OUT. IT COULD BE A LONG TIME...
BEFORE ANOTHER ASSEMBLY ROLLS IN.
THANKS, BORIS.
YOU KNOW HOW TO SHOW A GIRL A GOOD TIME.
IT'S SO PRETTY...
...!
HEY, ALICE.

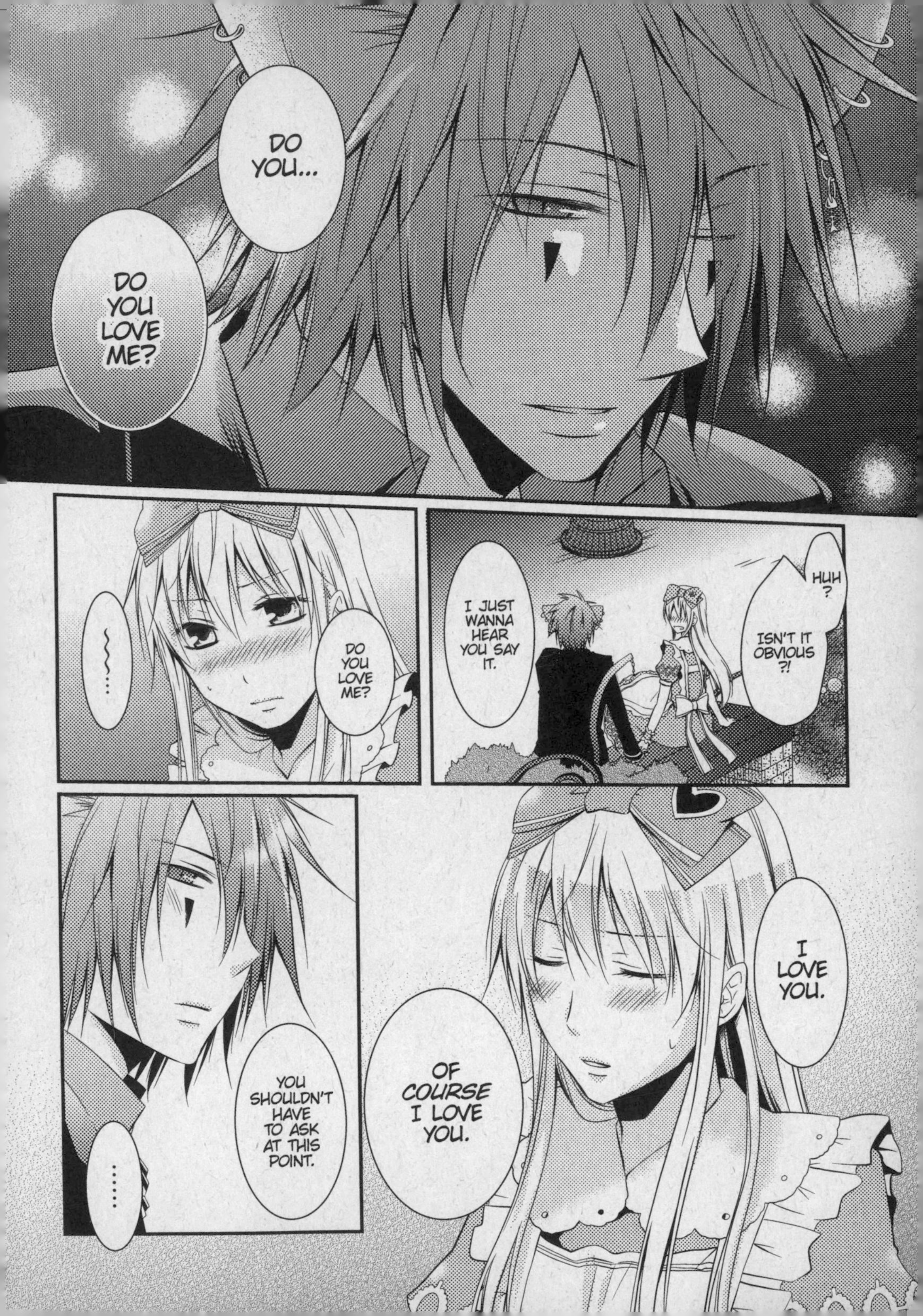
DO YOU...
DO YOU LOVE ME?
HUH?
ISN'T IT OBVIOUS?!
I JUST WANNA HEAR YOU SAY IT.
DO YOU LOVE ME?
~......
I LOVE YOU.
OF COURSE I LOVE YOU.
YOU SHOULDN'T HAVE TO ASK AT THIS POINT.
......

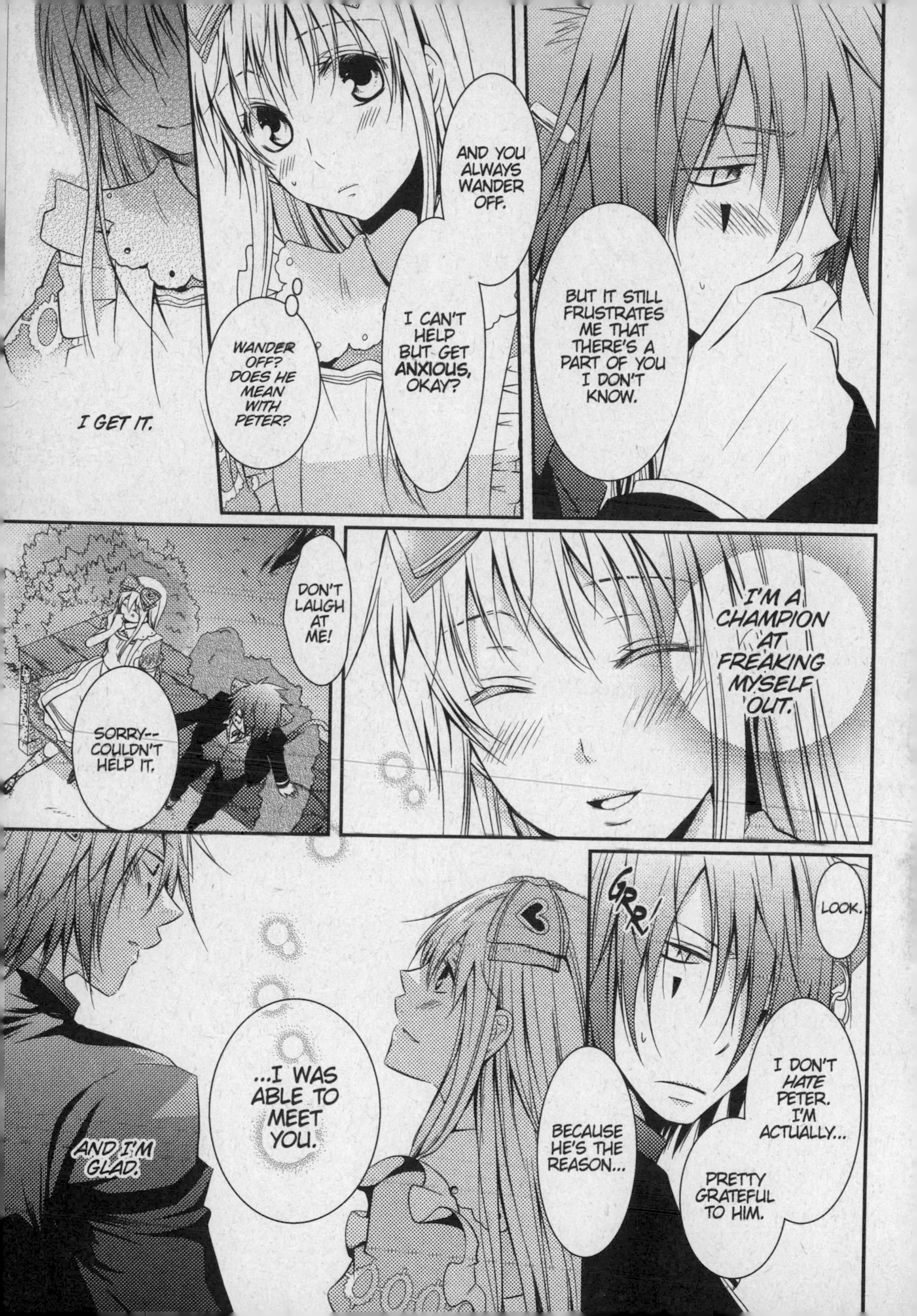
BUT IT STILL FRUSTRATES ME THAT THERE'S A PART OF YOU I DON'T KNOW.
AND YOU ALWAYS WANDER OFF.
I CAN'T HELP BUT GET ANXIOUS, OKAY?
WANDER OFF? DOES HE MEAN WITH PETER?
I GET IT.
I'M A CHAMPION AT FREAKING MYSELF OUT.
DON'T LAUGH AT ME!
SORRY--COULDN'T HELP IT.
LOOK.
GRR
I DON'T HATE PETER. I'M ACTUALLY...
PRETTY GRATEFUL TO HIM.
BECAUSE HE'S THE REASON...
...I WAS ABLE TO MEET YOU.
AND I'M GLAD.

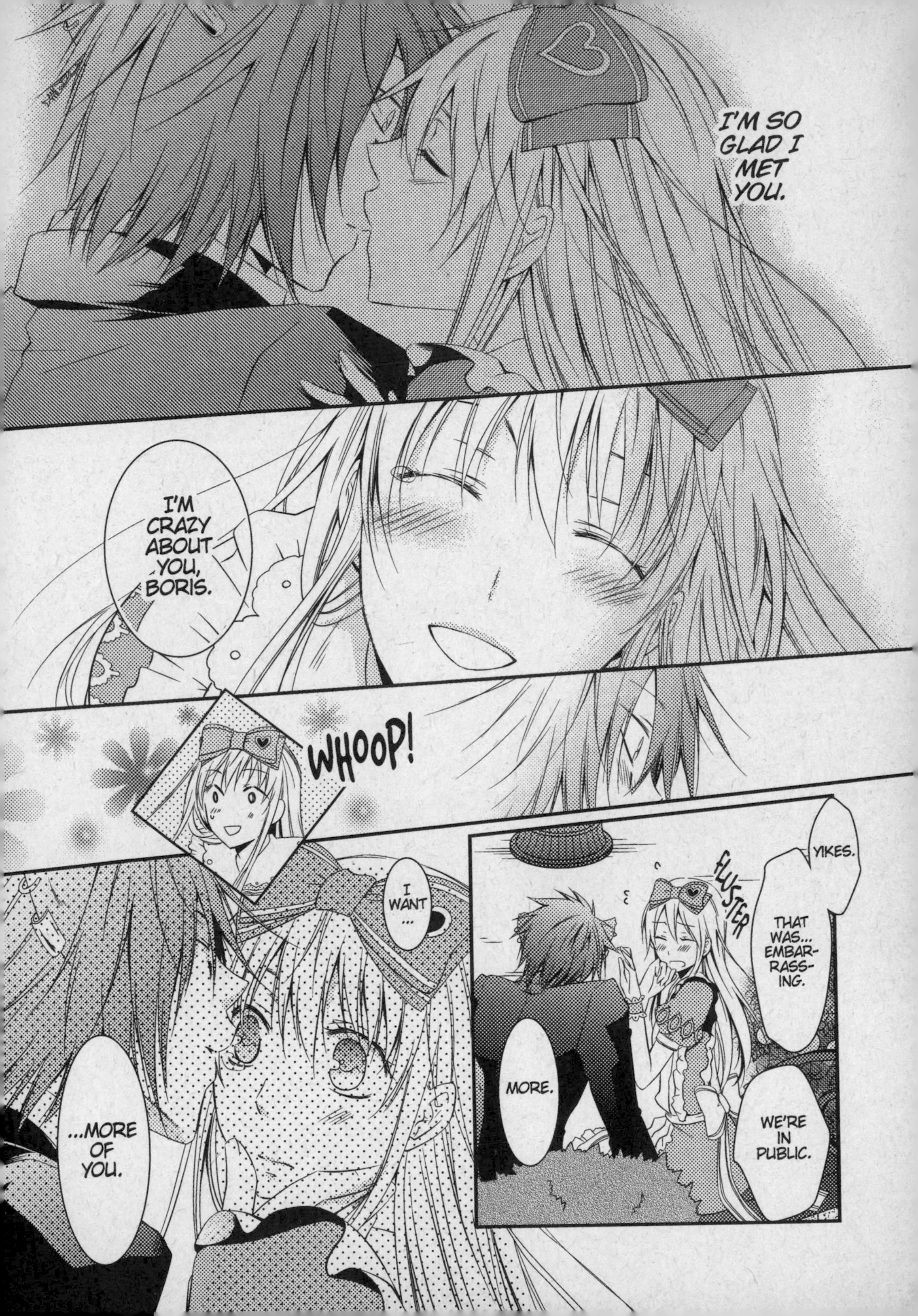
I'M SO GLAD I MET YOU.
I'M CRAZY ABOUT YOU, BORIS.
WHOOP!
YIKES.
FLUSTER
THAT WAS... EMBAR-RASS-ING.
WE'RE IN PUBLIC.
MORE.
I WANT ...
...MORE OF YOU.

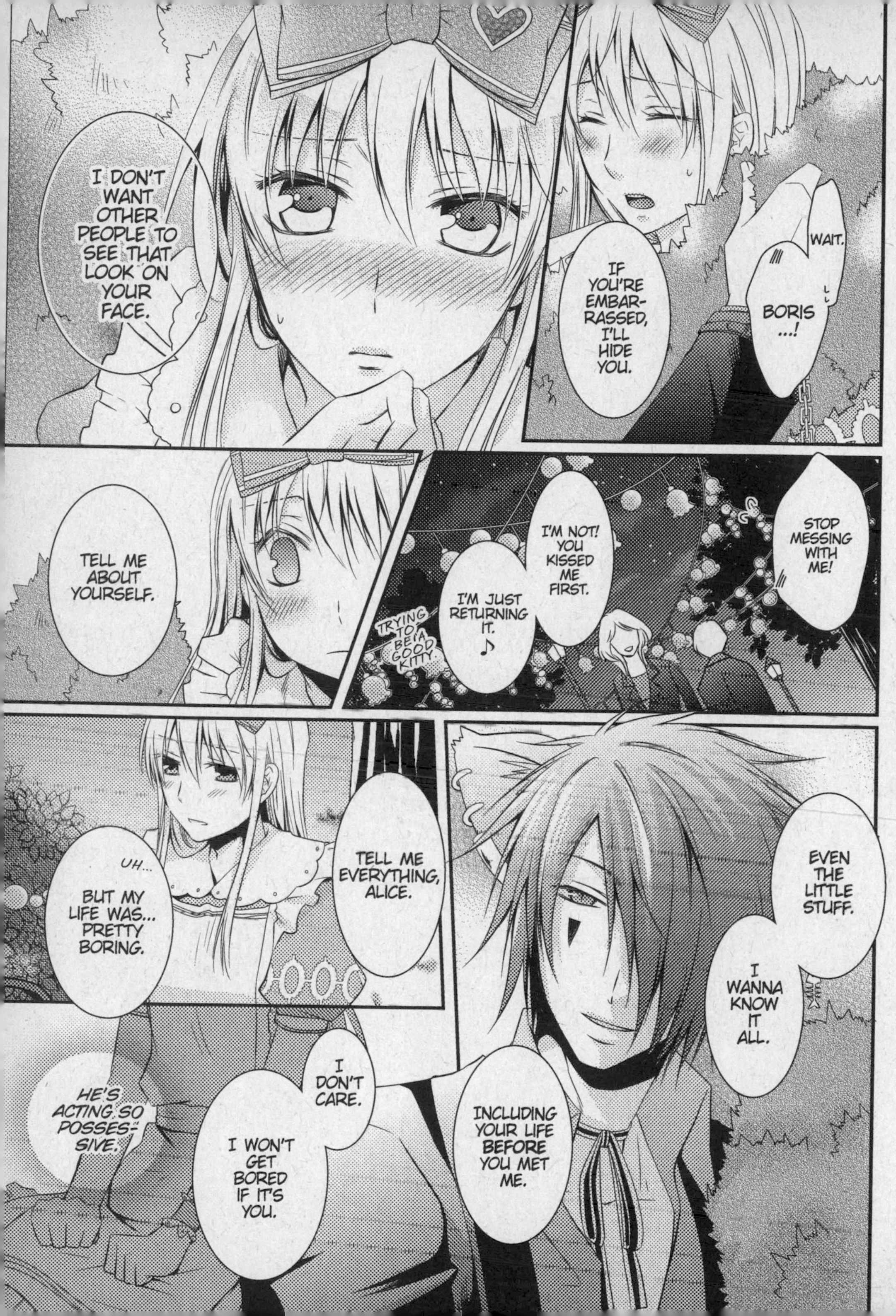
WAIT.
BORIS ...!
IF YOU'RE EMBARRASSED, I'LL HIDE YOU.
I DON'T WANT OTHER PEOPLE TO SEE THAT LOOK ON YOUR FACE.
STOP MESSING WITH ME!
I'M NOT! YOU KISSED ME FIRST.
I'M JUST RETURNING IT. ♪
TRYING TO BE A GOOD KITTY.
TELL ME ABOUT YOURSELF.
EVEN THE LITTLE STUFF.
I WANNA KNOW IT ALL.
INCLUDING YOUR LIFE BEFORE YOU MET ME.
TELL ME EVERYTHING, ALICE.
UH...
BUT MY LIFE WAS... PRETTY BORING.
I DON'T CARE.
I WON'T GET BORED IF IT'S YOU.
HE'S ACTING SO POSSESSIVE.

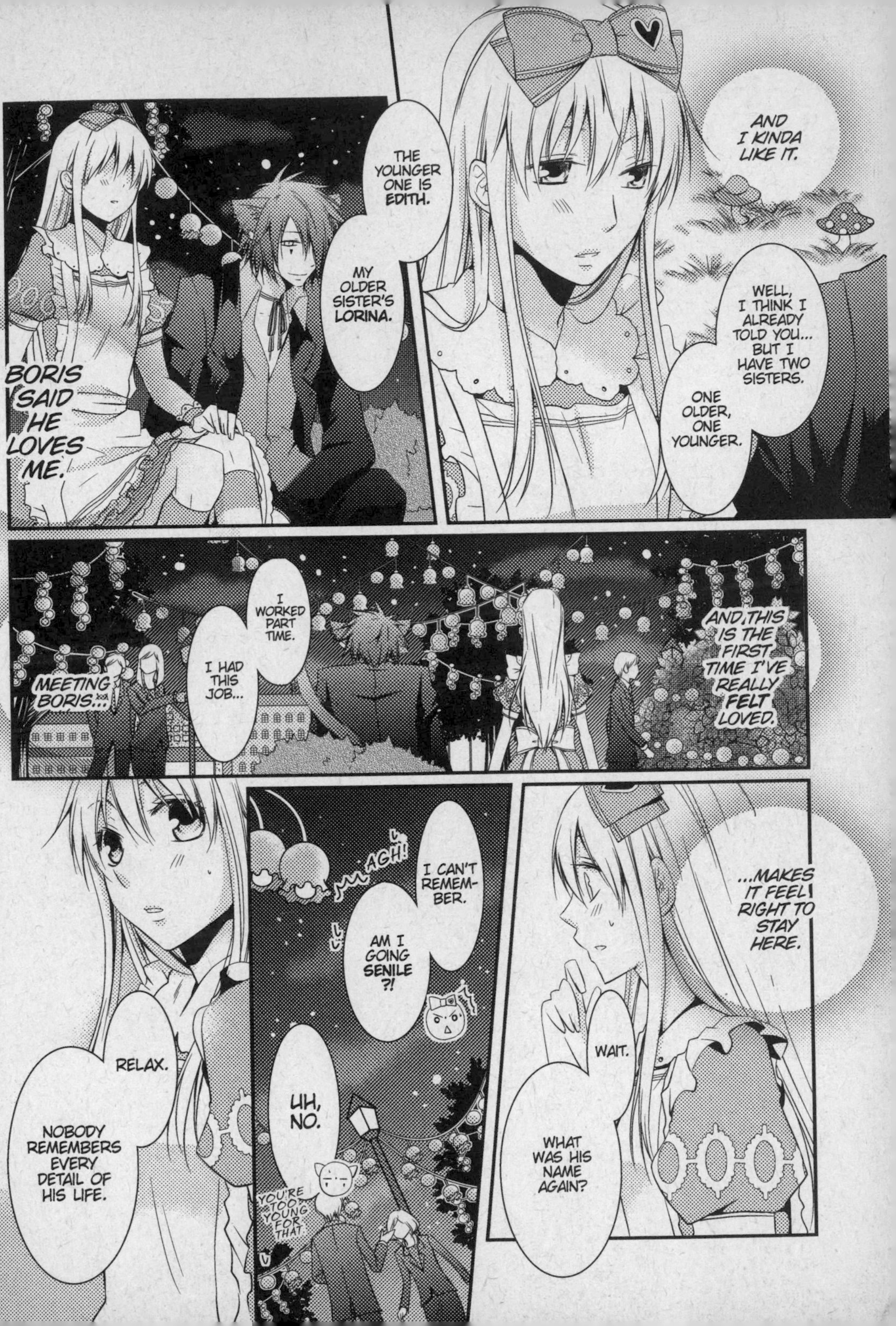
AND I KINDA LIKE IT.
WELL, I THINK I ALREADY TOLD YOU... BUT I HAVE TWO SISTERS.
ONE OLDER, ONE YOUNGER.
THE YOUNGER ONE IS EDITH.
MY OLDER SISTER'S LORINA.
BORIS SAID HE LOVES ME.
AND, THIS IS THE FIRST TIME I'VE REALLY FELT LOVED.
I WORKED PART TIME.
I HAD THIS JOB...
MEETING BORIS...
...MAKES IT FEEL RIGHT TO STAY HERE.
WAIT.
WHAT WAS HIS NAME AGAIN?
I CAN'T REMEMBER.
AGH!
AM I GOING SENILE?!
UH, NO.
YOU'RE TOO YOUNG FOR THAT.
RELAX.
NOBODY REMEMBERS EVERY DETAIL OF HIS LIFE.

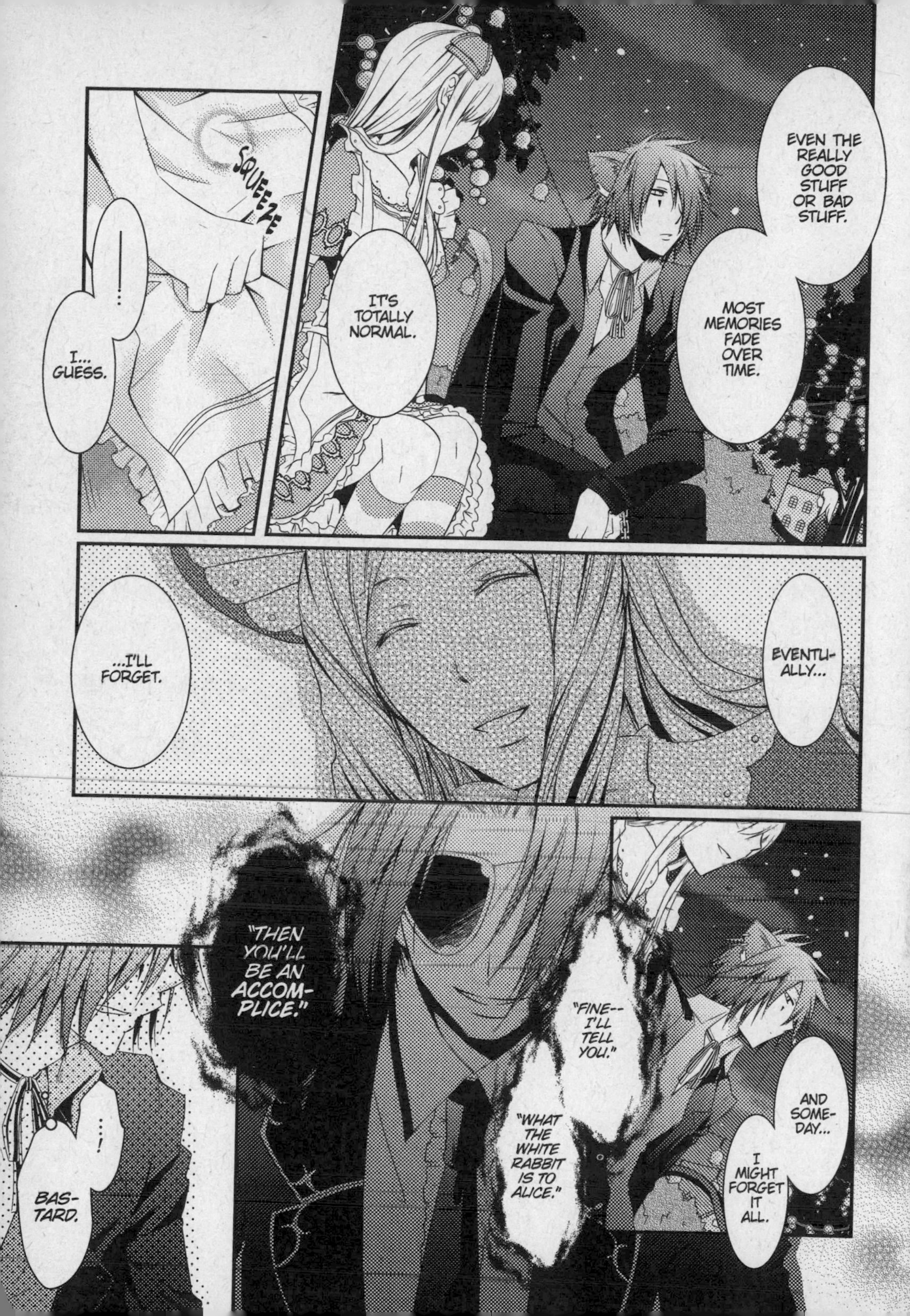

EVEN THE REALLY GOOD STUFF OR BAD STUFF.
MOST MEMORIES FADE OVER TIME.
IT'S TOTALLY NORMAL.
SQUEEZE
...!
I... GUESS.
EVENTU-ALLY...
...I'LL FORGET.
AND SOME-DAY...
I MIGHT FORGET IT ALL.
"THEN YOU'LL BE AN ACCOMPLICE."
"FINE--I'LL TELL YOU."
"WHAT THE WHITE RABBIT IS TO ALICE."
...!
BAS-TARD.

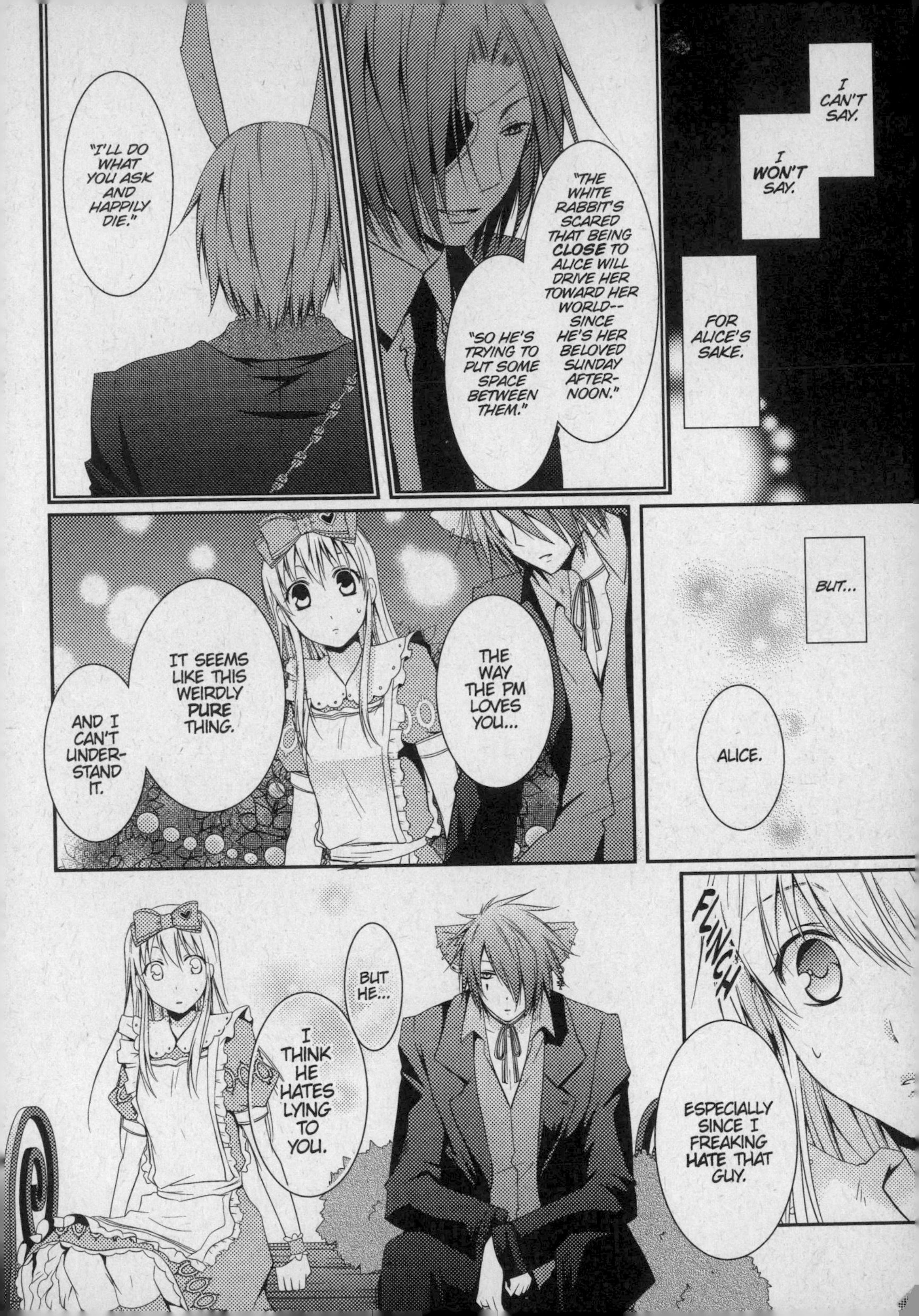
I CAN'T SAY.
I WON'T SAY.
FOR ALICE'S SAKE.
"THE WHITE RABBIT'S SCARED THAT BEING CLOSE TO ALICE WILL DRIVE HER TOWARD HER WORLD-- SINCE HE'S HER BELOVED SUNDAY AFTER-NOON."
"SO HE'S TRYING TO PUT SOME SPACE BETWEEN THEM."
"I'LL DO WHAT YOU ASK AND HAPPILY DIE."
BUT...
ALICE.
THE WAY THE PM LOVES YOU...
IT SEEMS LIKE THIS WEIRDLY PURE THING.
AND I CAN'T UNDER-STAND IT.
FLINCH
ESPECIALLY SINCE I FREAKING HATE THAT GUY.
BUT HE...
I THINK HE HATES LYING TO YOU.

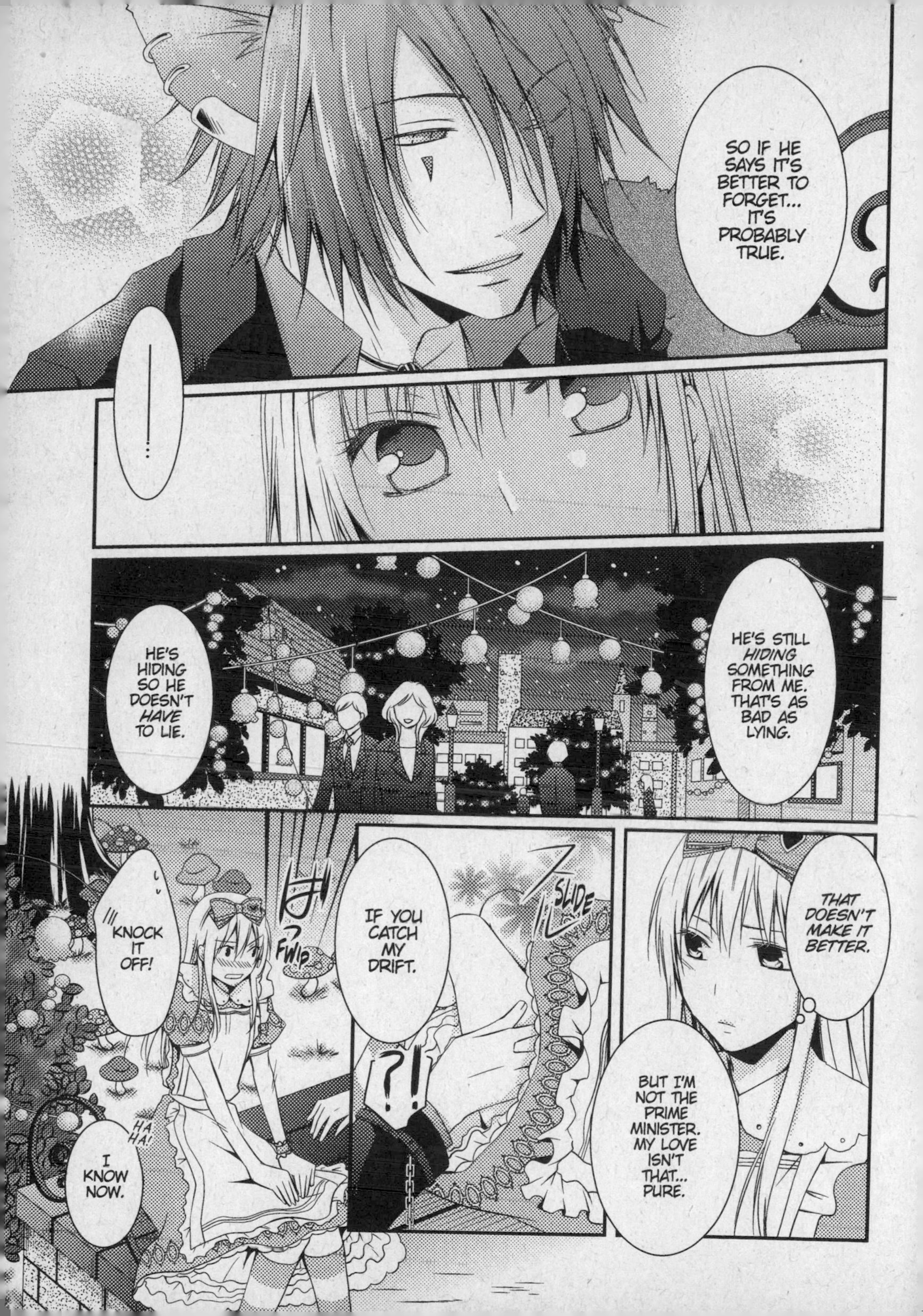
SO IF HE SAYS IT'S BETTER TO FORGET... IT'S PROBABLY TRUE.
......!
HE'S STILL *HIDING* SOMETHING FROM ME. THAT'S AS BAD AS LYING.
HE'S HIDING SO HE DOESN'T *HAVE* TO LIE.
THAT DOESN'T MAKE IT BETTER.
BUT I'M NOT THE PRIME MINISTER. MY LOVE ISN'T THAT... PURE.
SLIDE
IF YOU CATCH MY DRIFT.
?!
FWIP
KNOCK IT OFF!
HA HA!
I KNOW NOW.

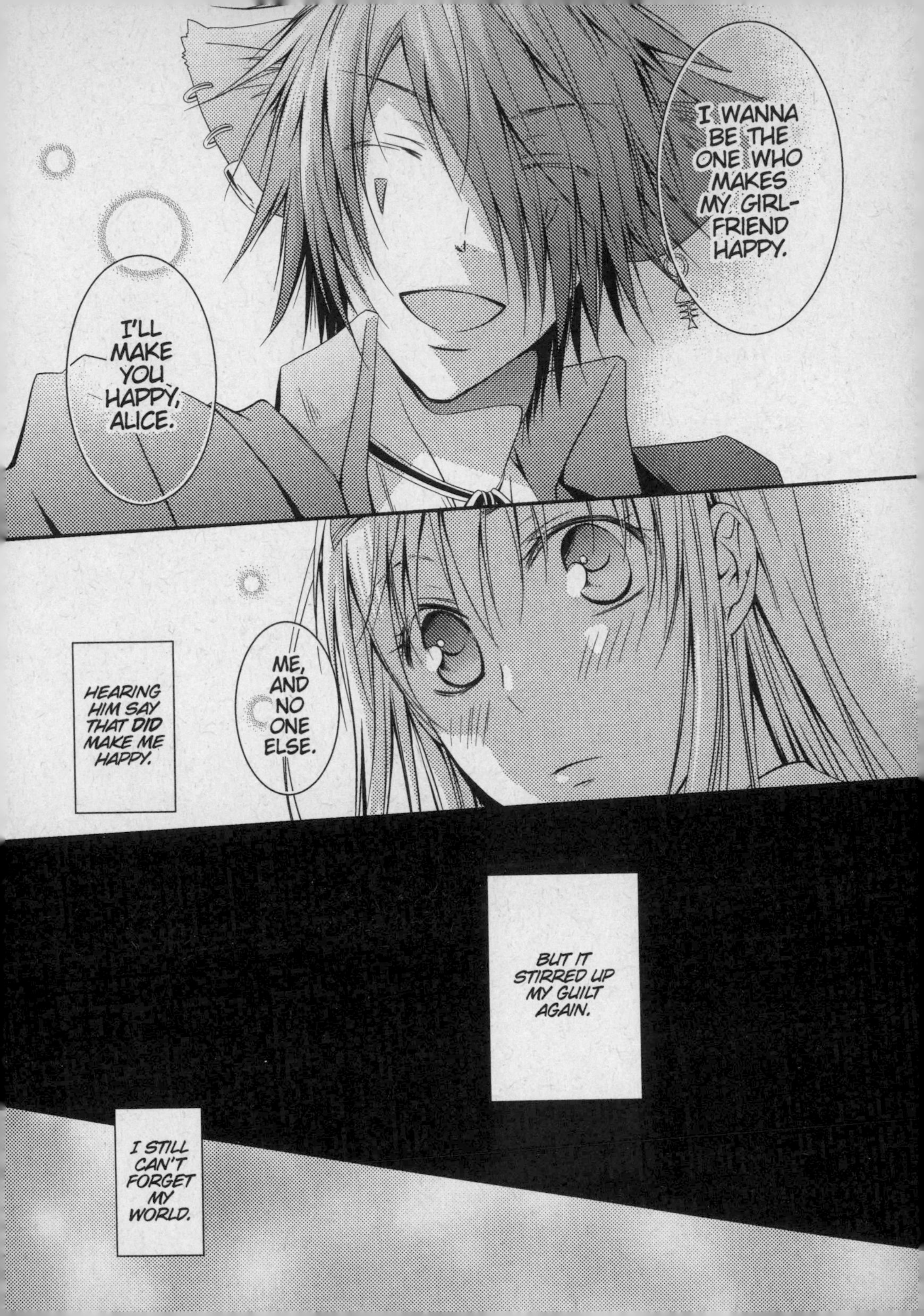
I WANNA BE THE ONE WHO MAKES MY GIRL-FRIEND HAPPY.
I'LL MAKE YOU HAPPY, ALICE.
ME, AND NO ONE ELSE.
HEARING HIM SAY THAT DID MAKE ME HAPPY.
BUT IT STIRRED UP MY GUILT AGAIN.
I STILL CAN'T FORGET MY WORLD.

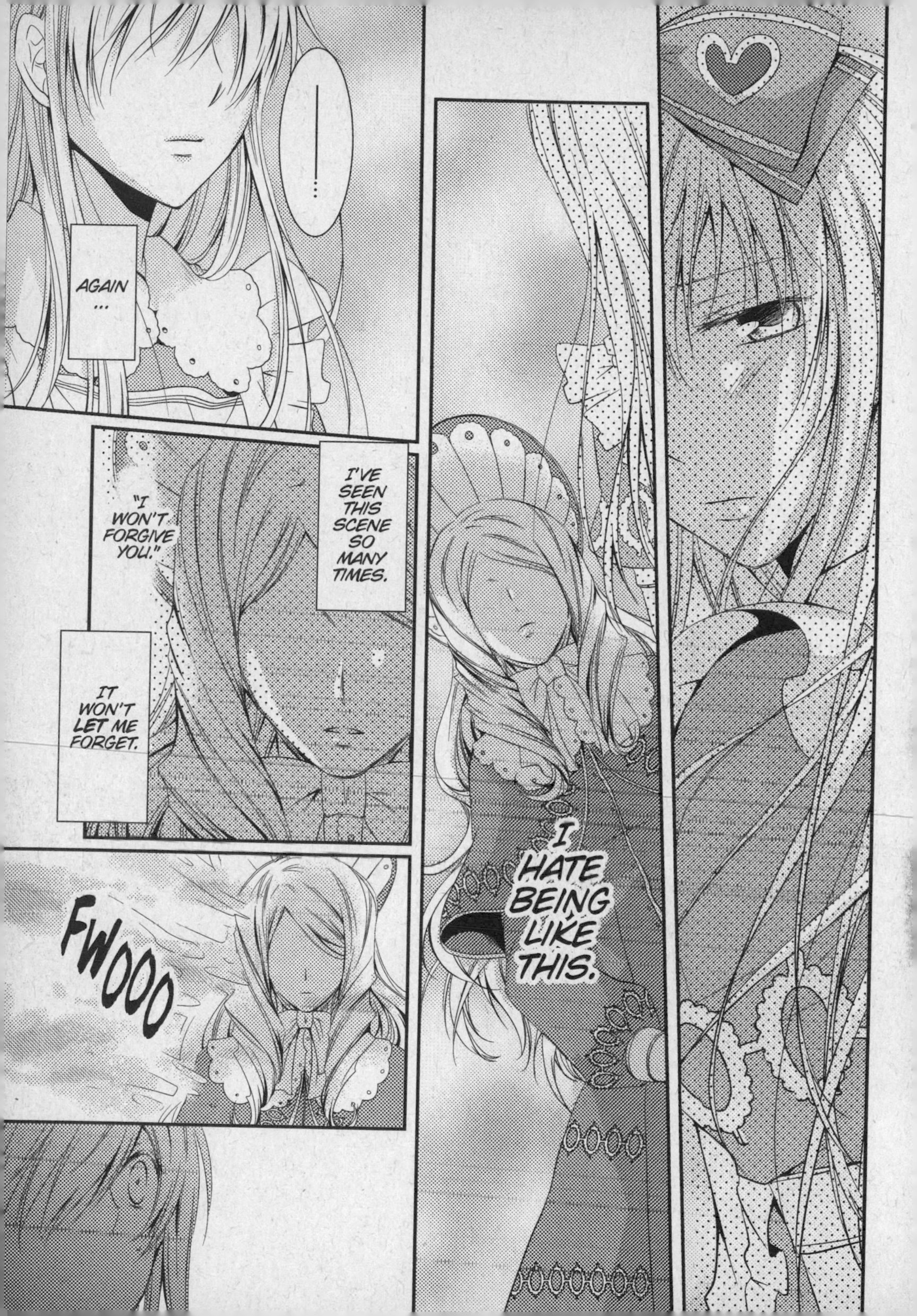
I HATE BEING LIKE THIS.
......
AGAIN ...
I'VE SEEN THIS SCENE SO MANY TIMES.
"I WON'T FORGIVE YOU."
IT WON'T LET ME FORGET.
FWOOO

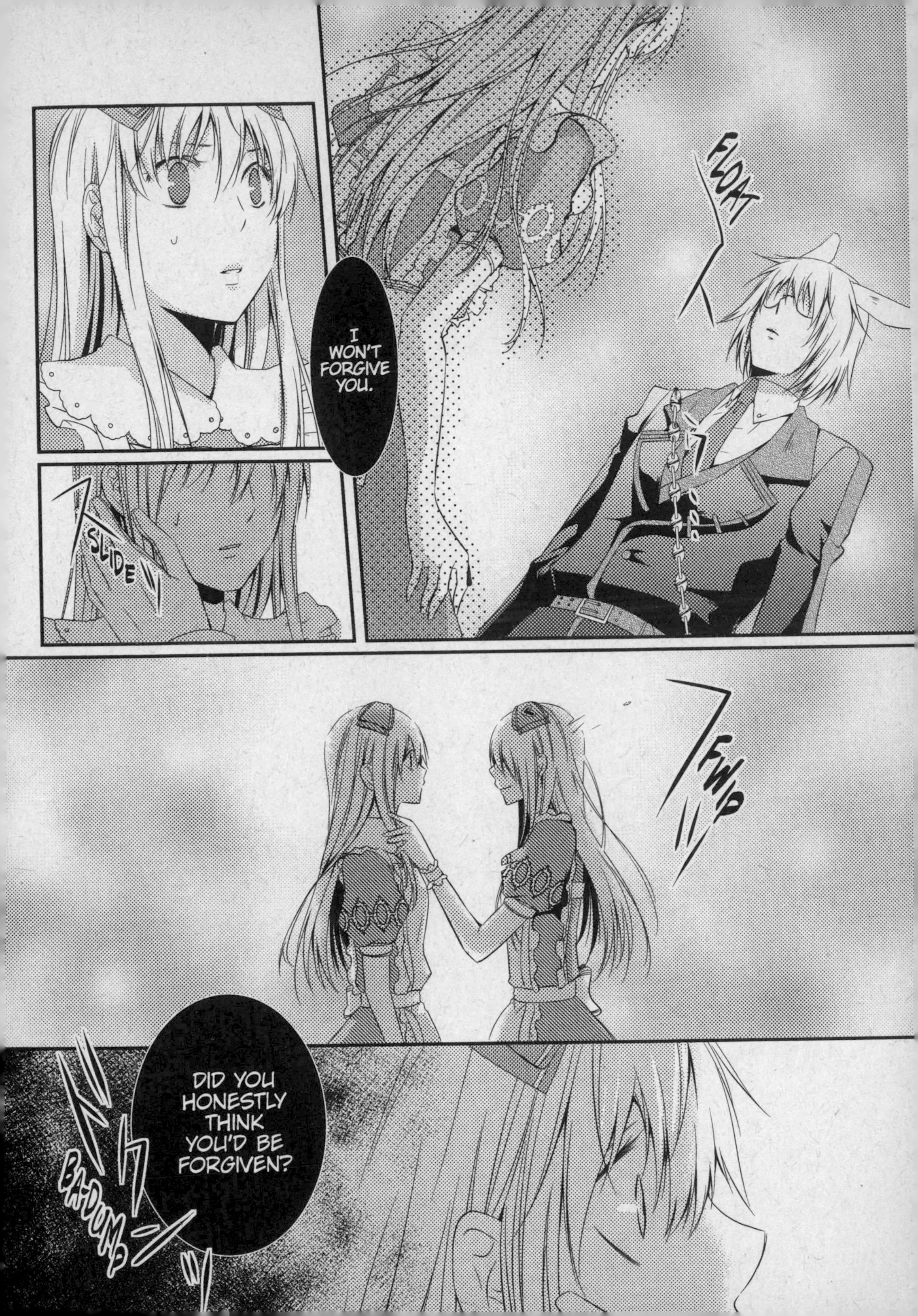
FLOAT
I WON'T FORGIVE YOU.
SLIDE
FWIP
DID YOU HONESTLY THINK YOU'D BE FORGIVEN?
BA-DUMP

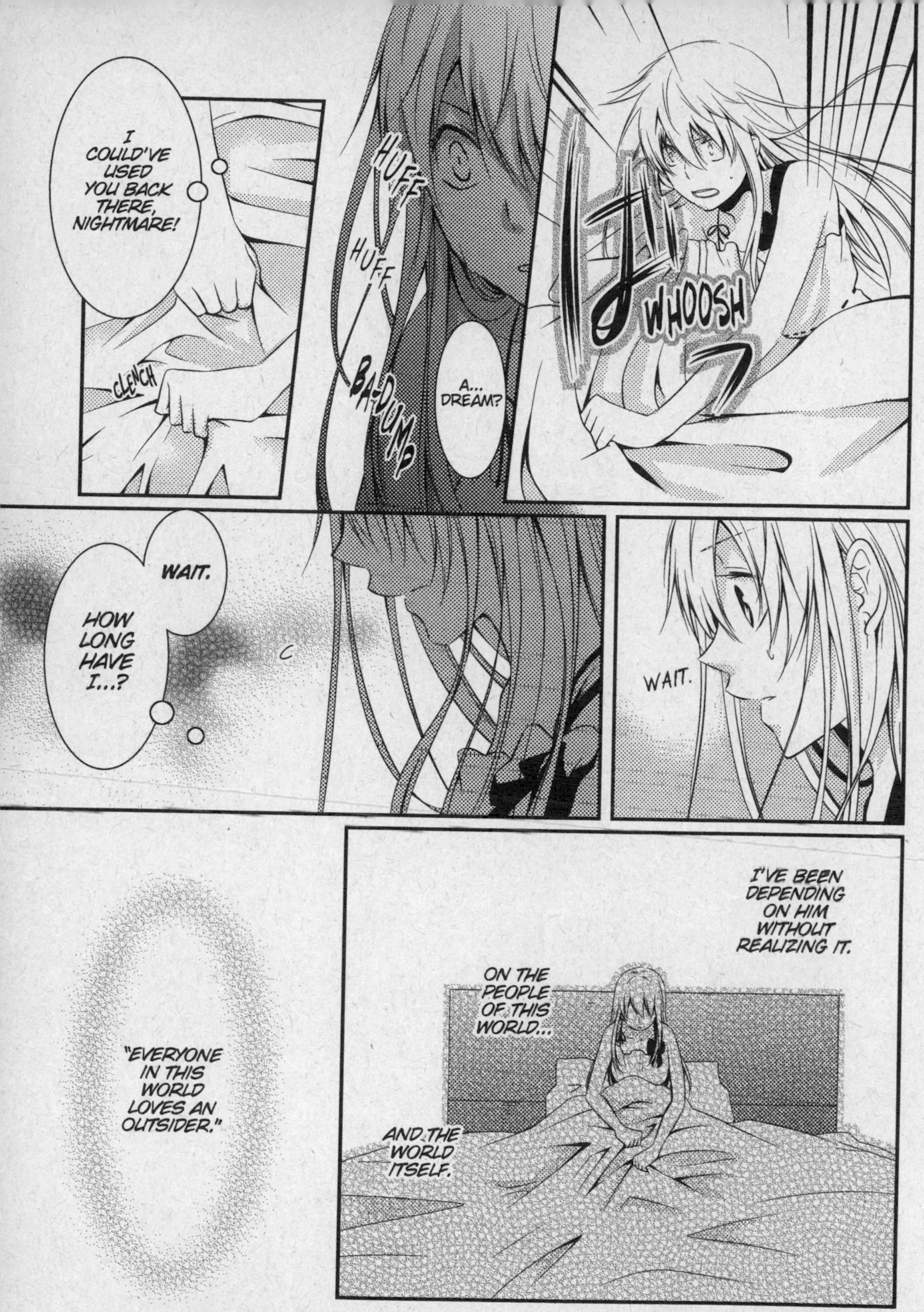
WHOOSH
HUFF
HUFF
BA-DUMP
A... DREAM?
I COULD'VE USED YOU BACK THERE, NIGHTMARE!
CLENCH
WAIT.
WAIT.
HOW LONG HAVE I...?
I'VE BEEN DEPENDING ON HIM WITHOUT REALIZING IT.
ON THE PEOPLE OF THIS WORLD...
AND THE WORLD ITSELF.
"EVERYONE IN THIS WORLD LOVES AN OUTSIDER."

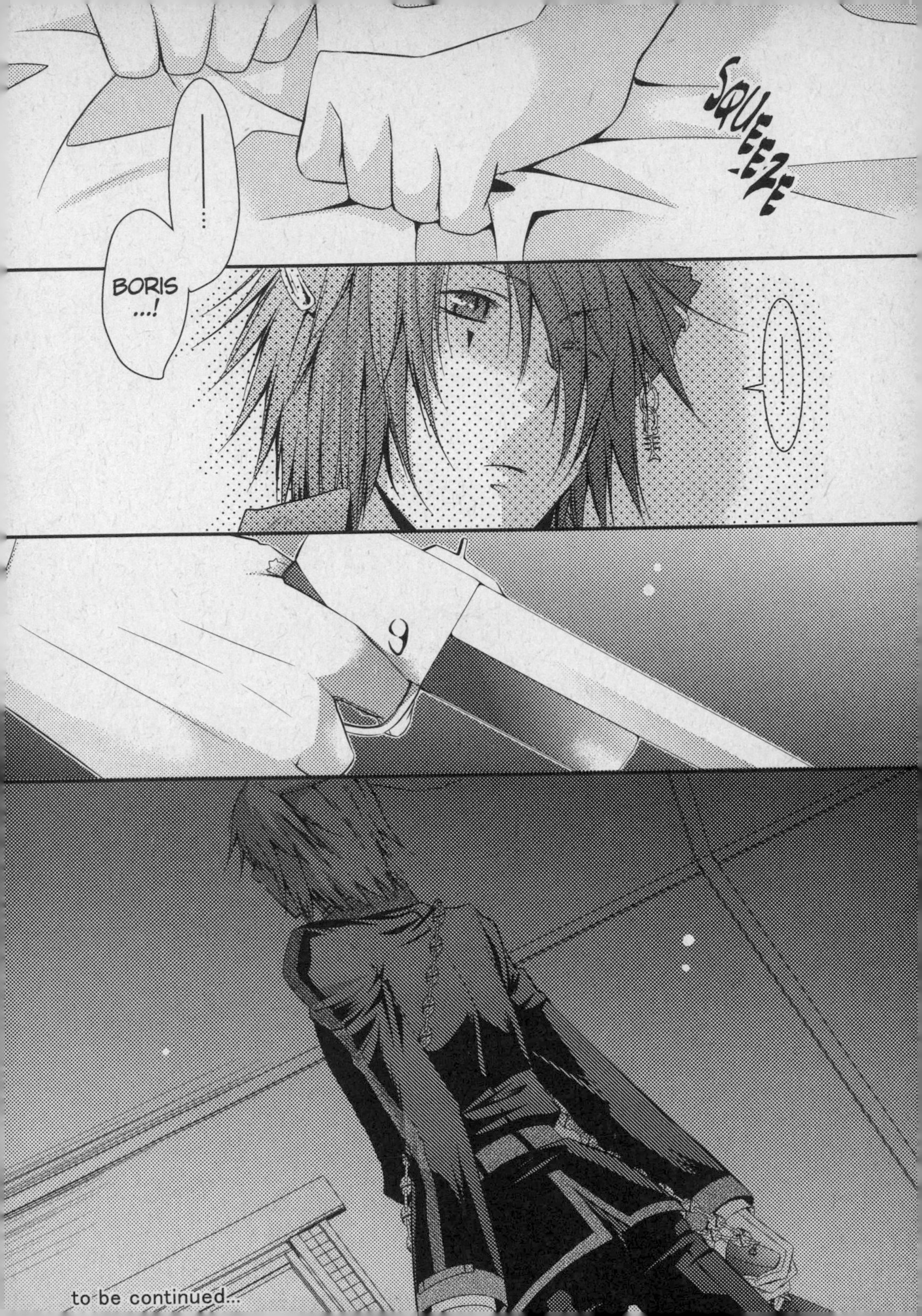
SQUEEZE
BORIS ...!
...!
to be continued...

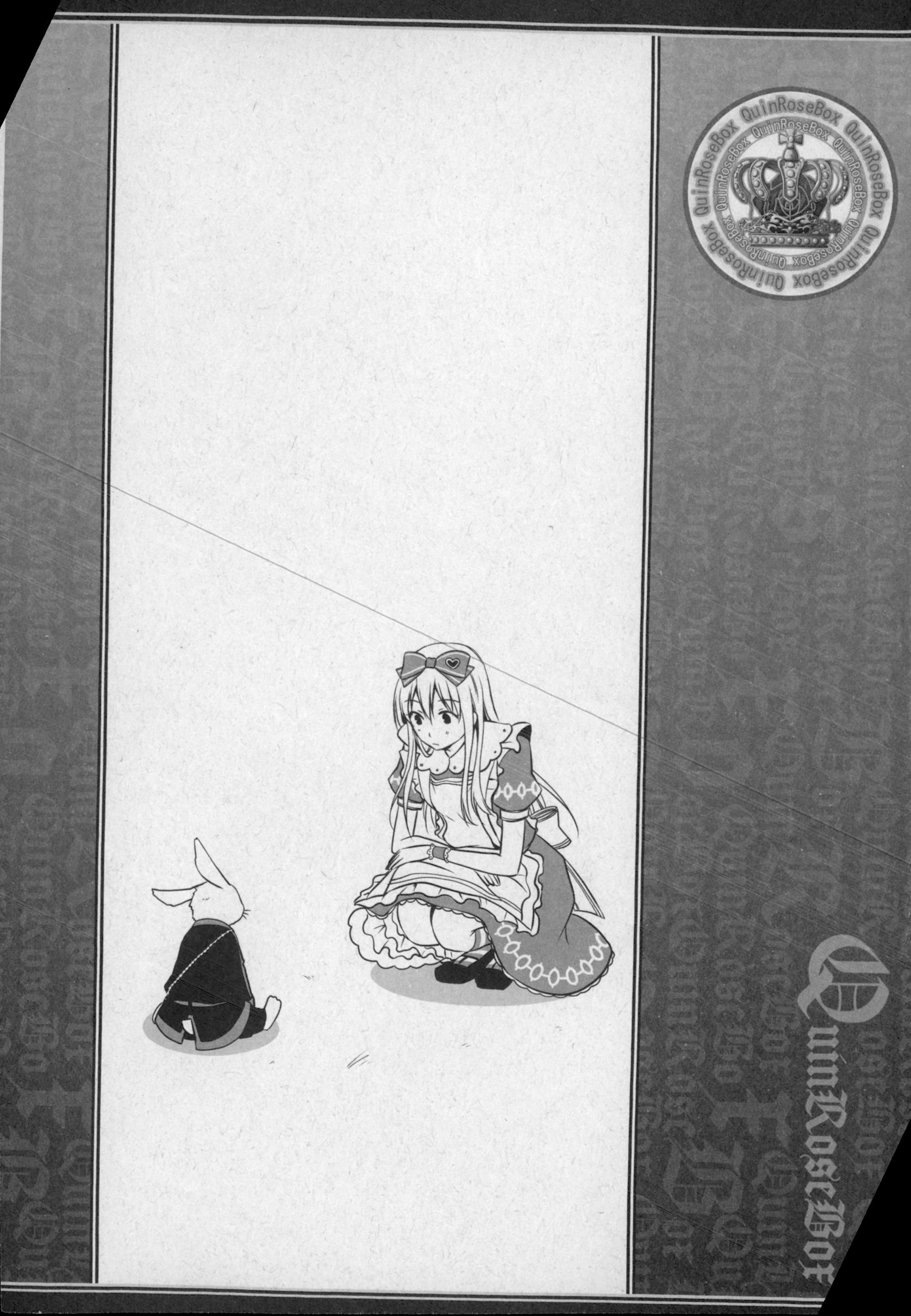
QuinRoseBox

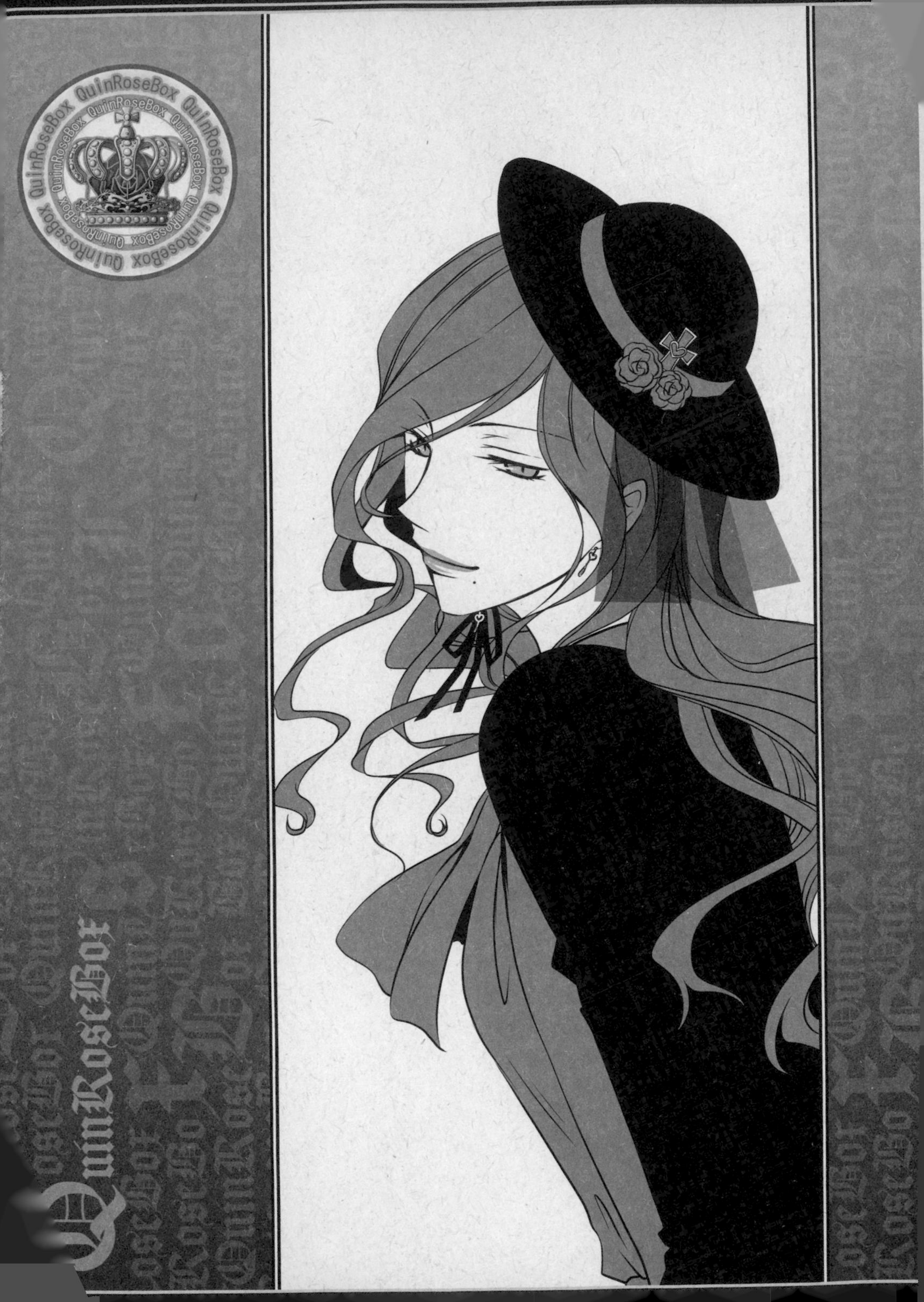
QuinRoseBox

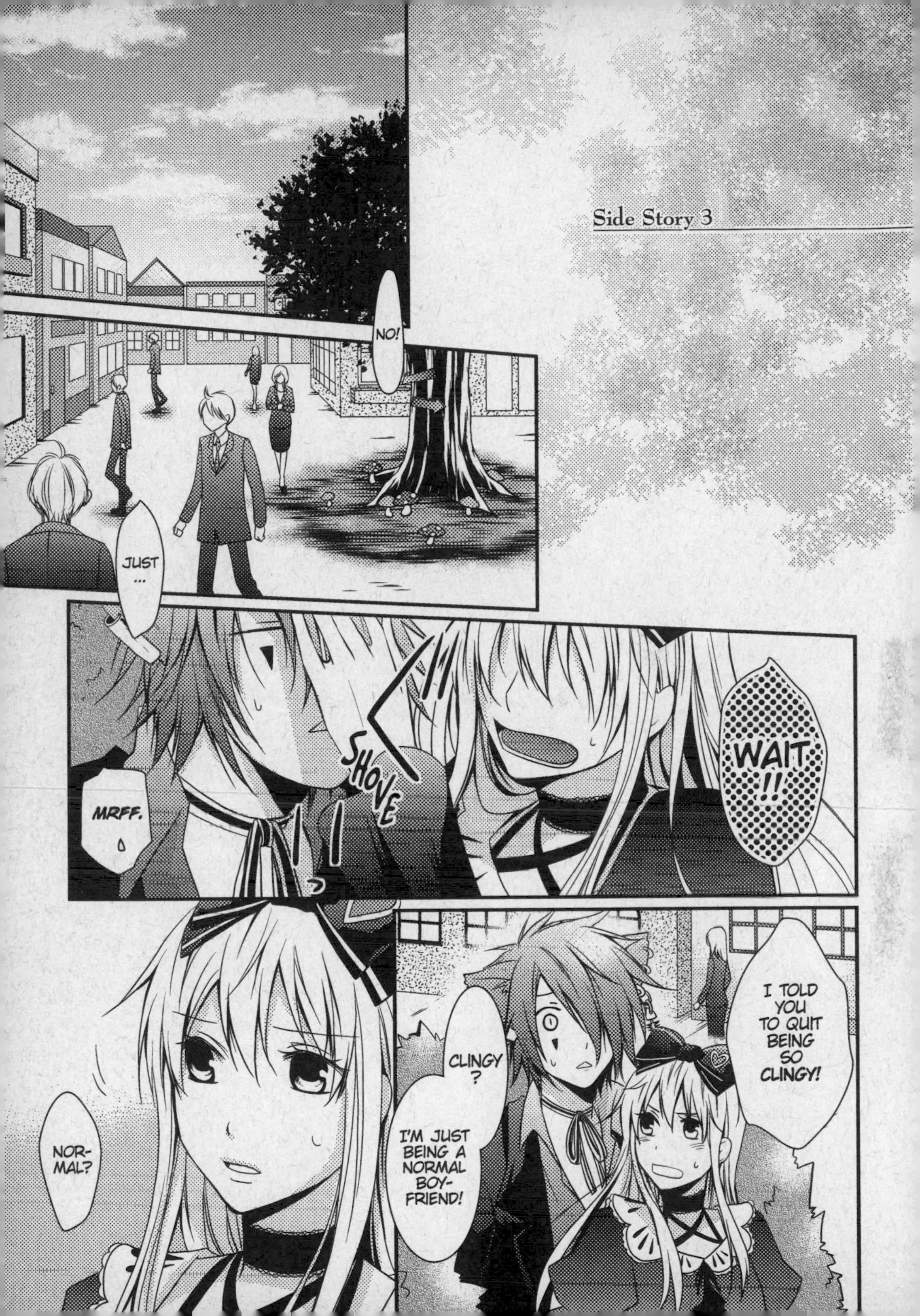
Side Story 3
NO!
JUST ...
WAIT !!
SHOVE
MRFF.
I TOLD YOU TO QUIT BEING SO CLINGY!
CLINGY ?
I'M JUST BEING A NORMAL BOY-FRIEND!
NOR-MAL?

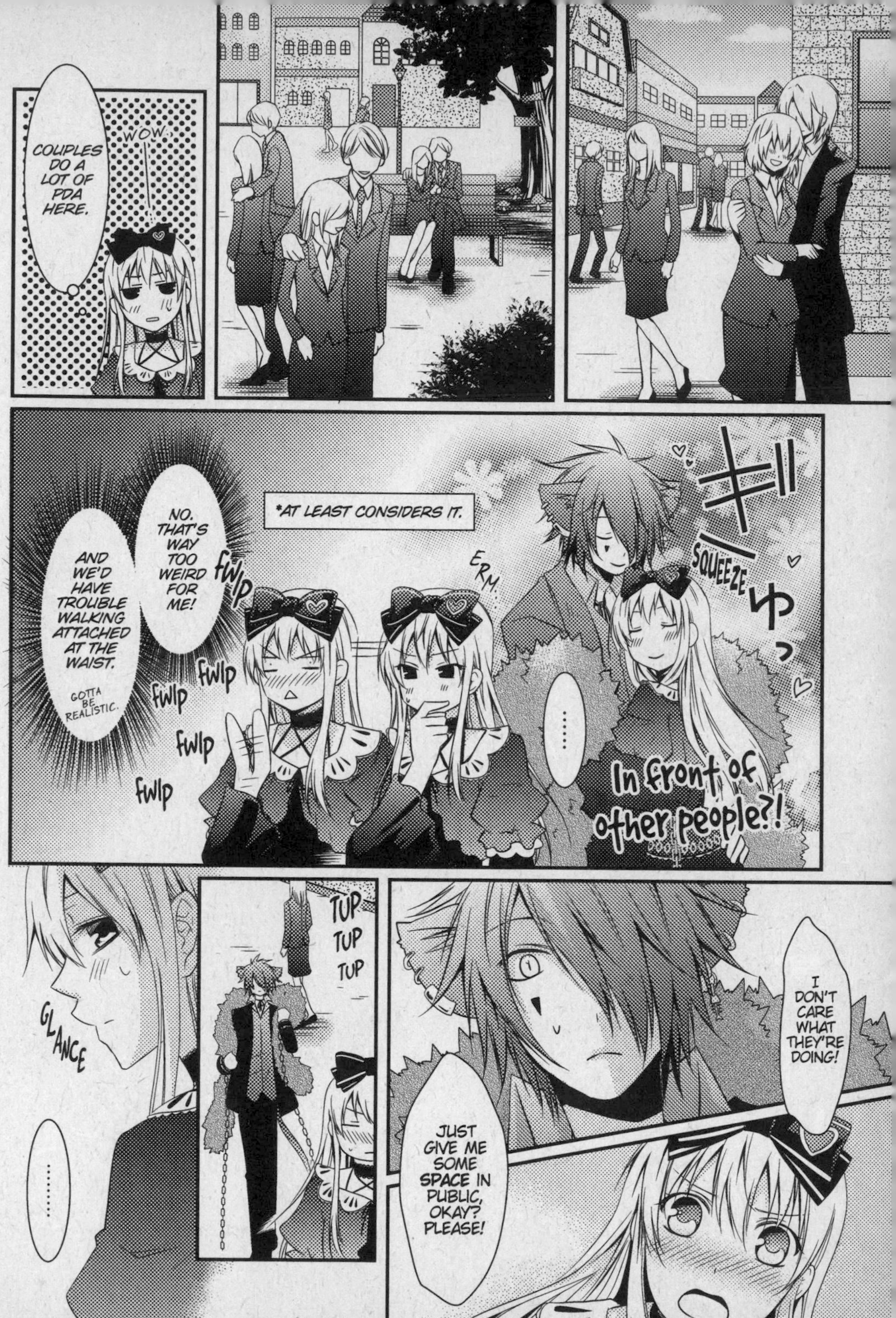
WOW.
COUPLES DO A LOT OF PDA HERE.
SQUEEZE
ゅっ
In front of other people?!
......
ERM.
*AT LEAST CONSIDERS IT.
NO. THAT'S WAY TOO WEIRD FOR ME!
AND WE'D HAVE TROUBLE WALKING ATTACHED AT THE WAIST.
GOTTA BE REALISTIC.
fwlp
fwlp
fwlp
fwlp
fwlp
I DON'T CARE WHAT THEY'RE DOING!
JUST GIVE ME SOME SPACE IN PUBLIC, OKAY? PLEASE!
TUP
TUP
TUP
GLANCE
......

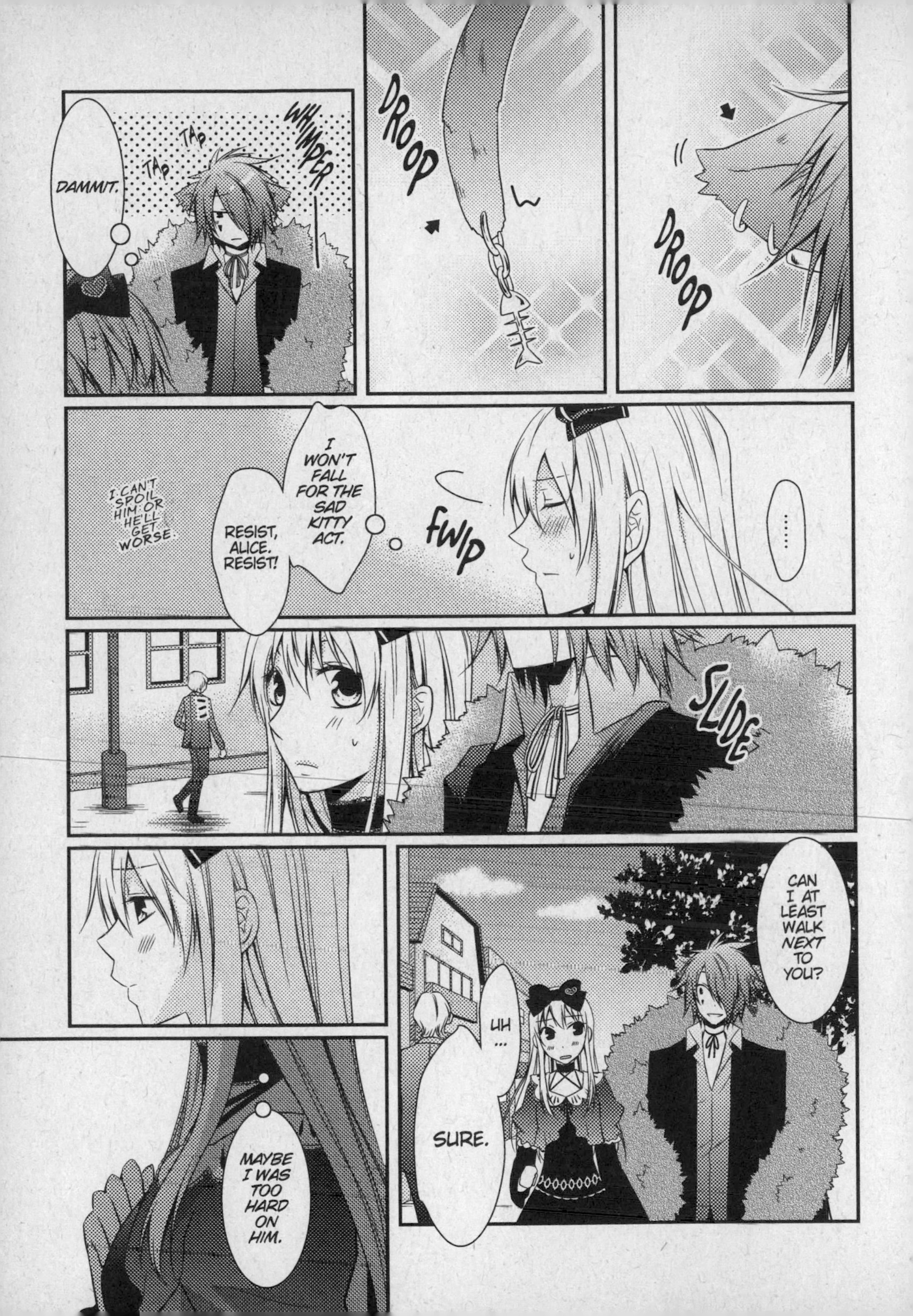
DROOP
DROOP
WHIMPER
TAP TAP
DAMMIT.
.....
FWIP
I WON'T FALL FOR THE SAD KITTY ACT.
RESIST, ALICE. RESIST!
I CAN'T SPOIL HIM OR HE'LL GET WORSE.
SLIDE
CAN I AT LEAST WALK NEXT TO YOU?
UH...
SURE.
MAYBE I WAS TOO HARD ON HIM.

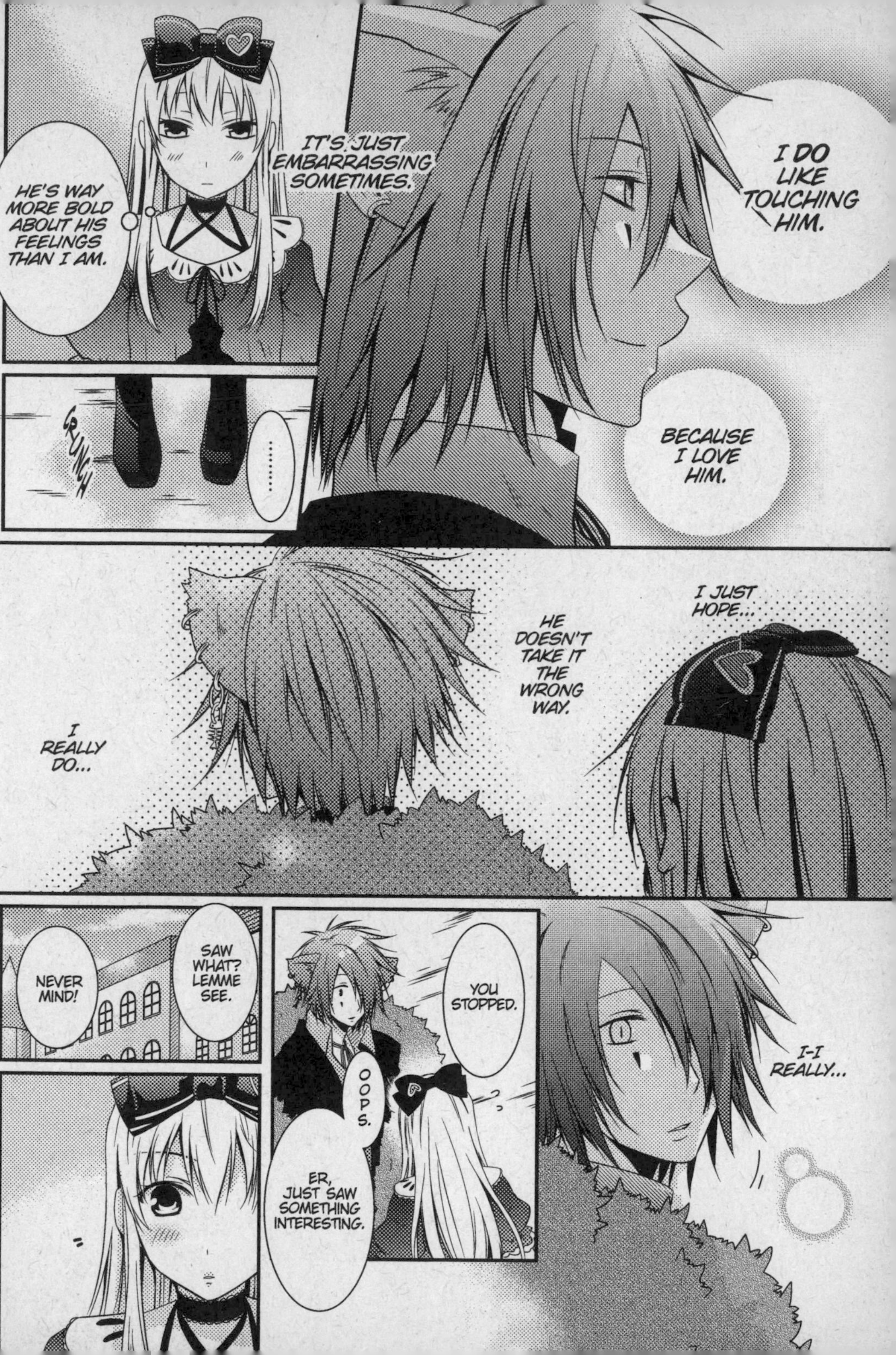
I DO LIKE TOUCHING HIM.
BECAUSE I LOVE HIM.
IT'S JUST EMBARRASSING SOMETIMES.
HE'S WAY MORE BOLD ABOUT HIS FEELINGS THAN I AM.
CRUNCH
......
I JUST HOPE...
HE DOESN'T TAKE IT THE WRONG WAY.
I REALLY DO...
I-I REALLY...
YOU STOPPED.
OOPS.
ER, JUST SAW SOMETHING INTERESTING.
SAW WHAT? LEMME SEE.
NEVER MIND!

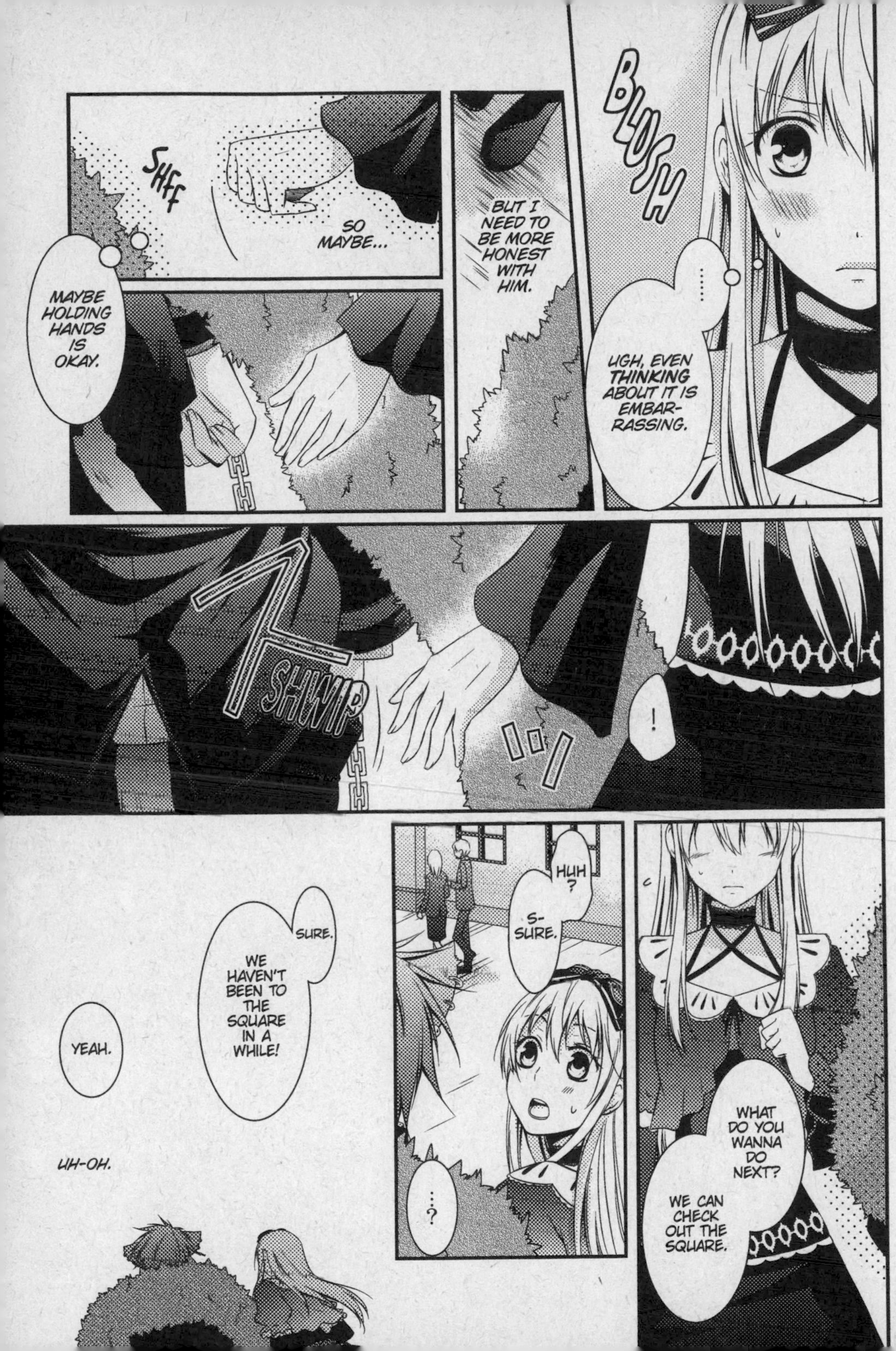
BLUSH
......
UGH, EVEN THINKING ABOUT IT IS EMBARRASSING.
BUT I NEED TO BE MORE HONEST WITH HIM.
SHFF
SO MAYBE...
MAYBE HOLDING HANDS IS OKAY.
!
SHWIP
WHAT DO YOU WANNA DO NEXT?
WE CAN CHECK OUT THE SQUARE.
HUH?
S-SURE.
...?
SURE.
WE HAVEN'T BEEN TO THE SQUARE IN A WHILE!
YEAH.
UH-OH.

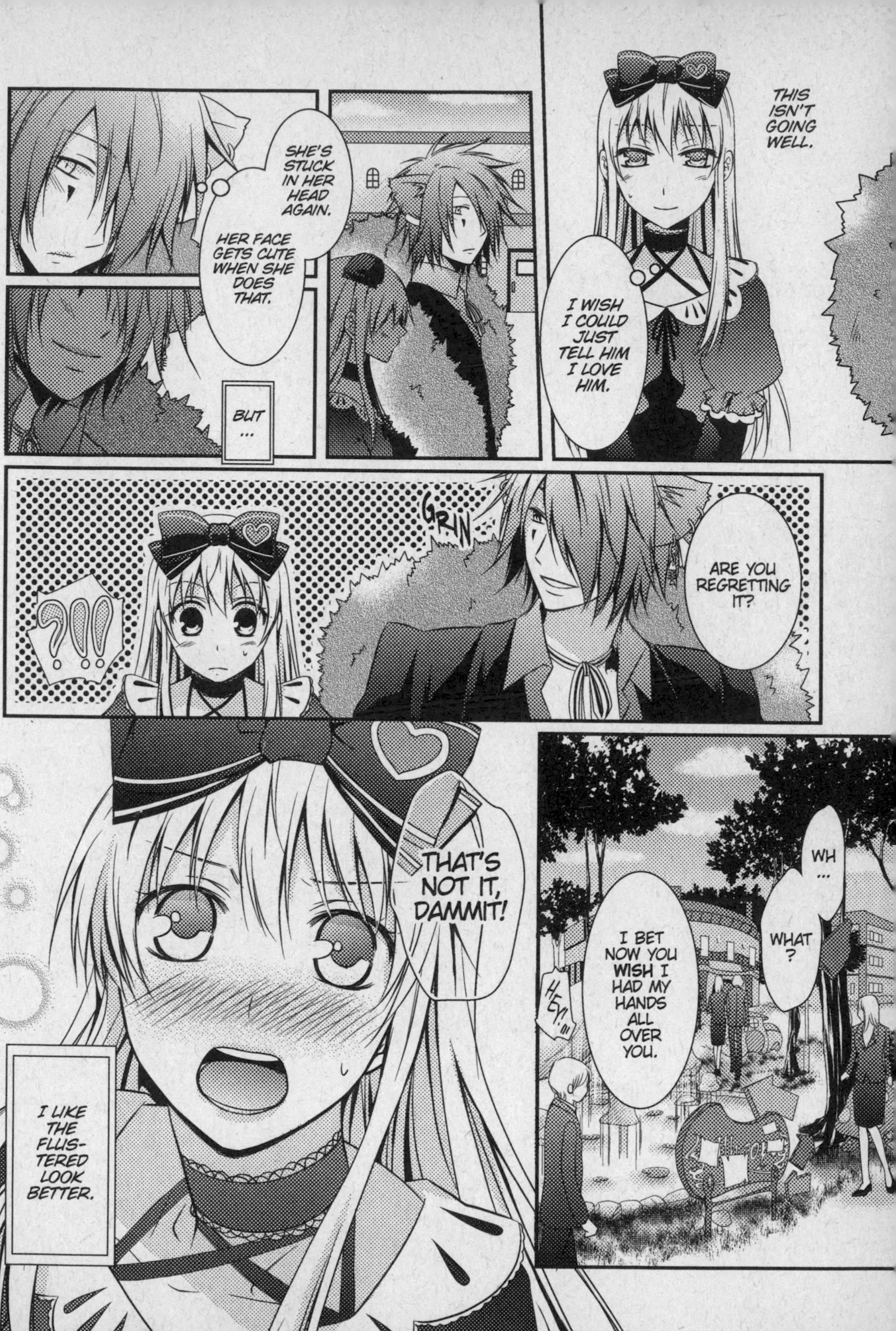
THIS ISN'T GOING WELL.
I WISH I COULD JUST TELL HIM I LOVE HIM.
SHE'S STUCK IN HER HEAD AGAIN.
HER FACE GETS CUTE WHEN SHE DOES THAT.
BUT ...
ARE YOU REGRETTING IT?
GRIN
?!!!
WH ...
WHAT ?
I BET NOW YOU WISH I HAD MY HANDS ALL OVER YOU.
HEY!
THAT'S NOT IT, DAMMIT!
I LIKE THE FLUS-TERED LOOK BETTER.

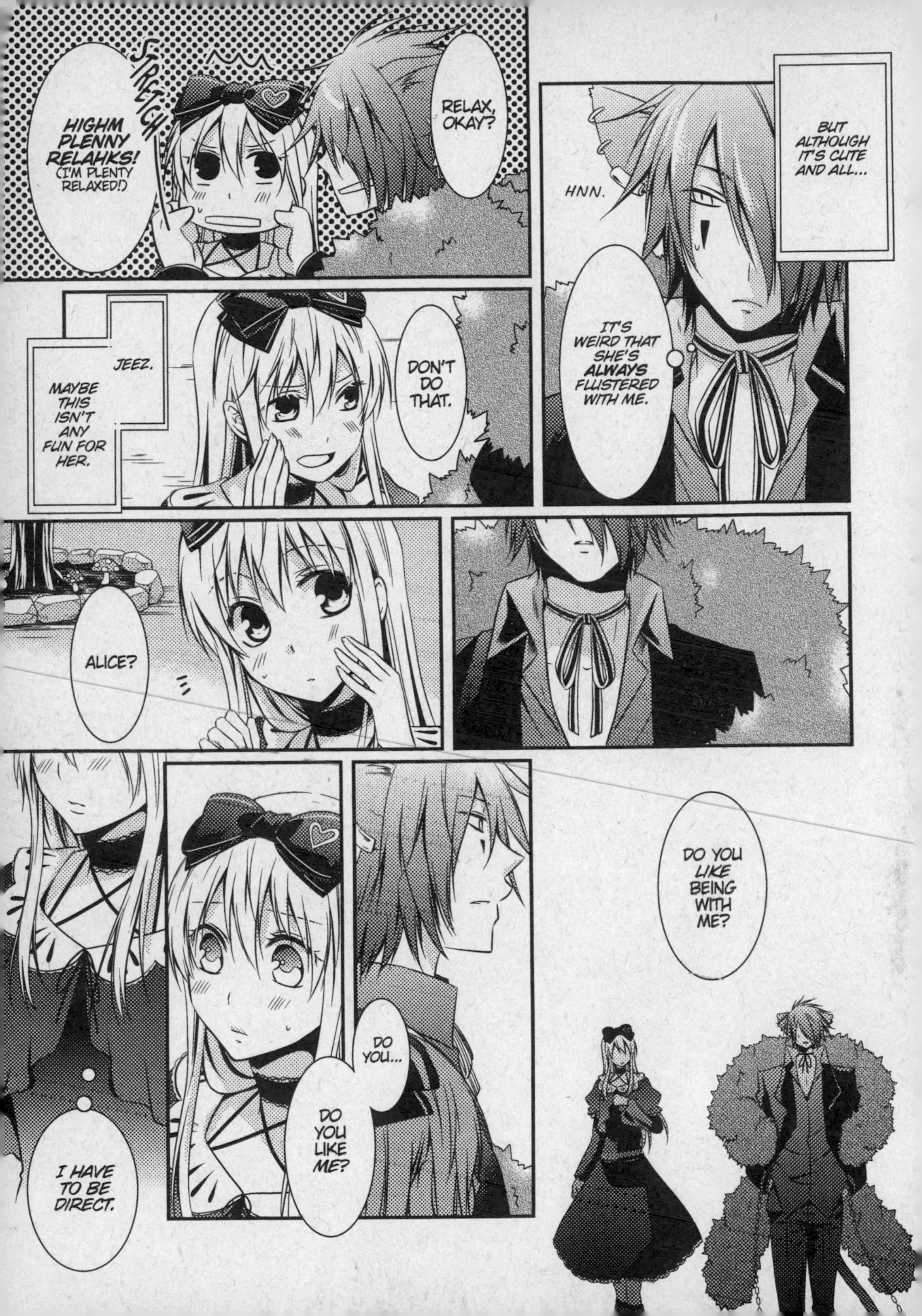
BUT ALTHOUGH IT'S CUTE AND ALL...
HNN.
IT'S WEIRD THAT SHE'S ALWAYS FLUSTERED WITH ME.
RELAX, OKAY?
STRETCH
HIGHM PLENNY RELAHKS! (I'M PLENTY RELAXED!)
DON'T DO THAT.
JEEZ.
MAYBE THIS ISN'T ANY FUN FOR HER.
ALICE?
DO YOU LIKE BEING WITH ME?
DO YOU...
DO YOU LIKE ME?
I HAVE TO BE DIRECT.

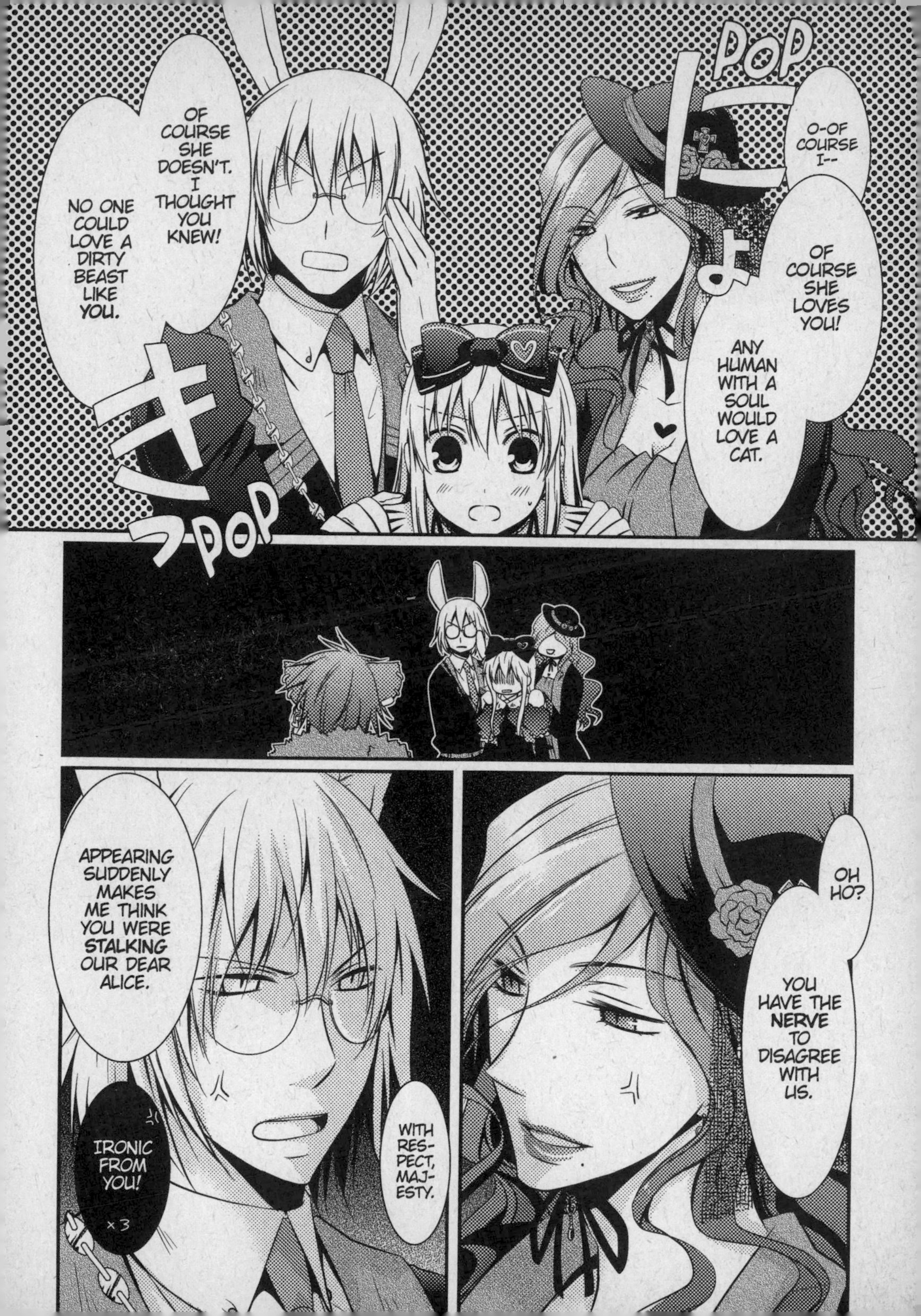
POP
O-OF COURSE I--
OF COURSE SHE LOVES YOU!
ANY HUMAN WITH A SOUL WOULD LOVE A CAT.
OF COURSE SHE DOESN'T. I THOUGHT YOU KNEW!
NO ONE COULD LOVE A DIRTY BEAST LIKE YOU.
POP
OH HO?
YOU HAVE THE NERVE TO DISAGREE WITH US.
APPEARING SUDDENLY MAKES ME THINK YOU WERE STALKING OUR DEAR ALICE.
WITH RES-PECT, MAJ-ESTY.
IRONIC FROM YOU!
×3

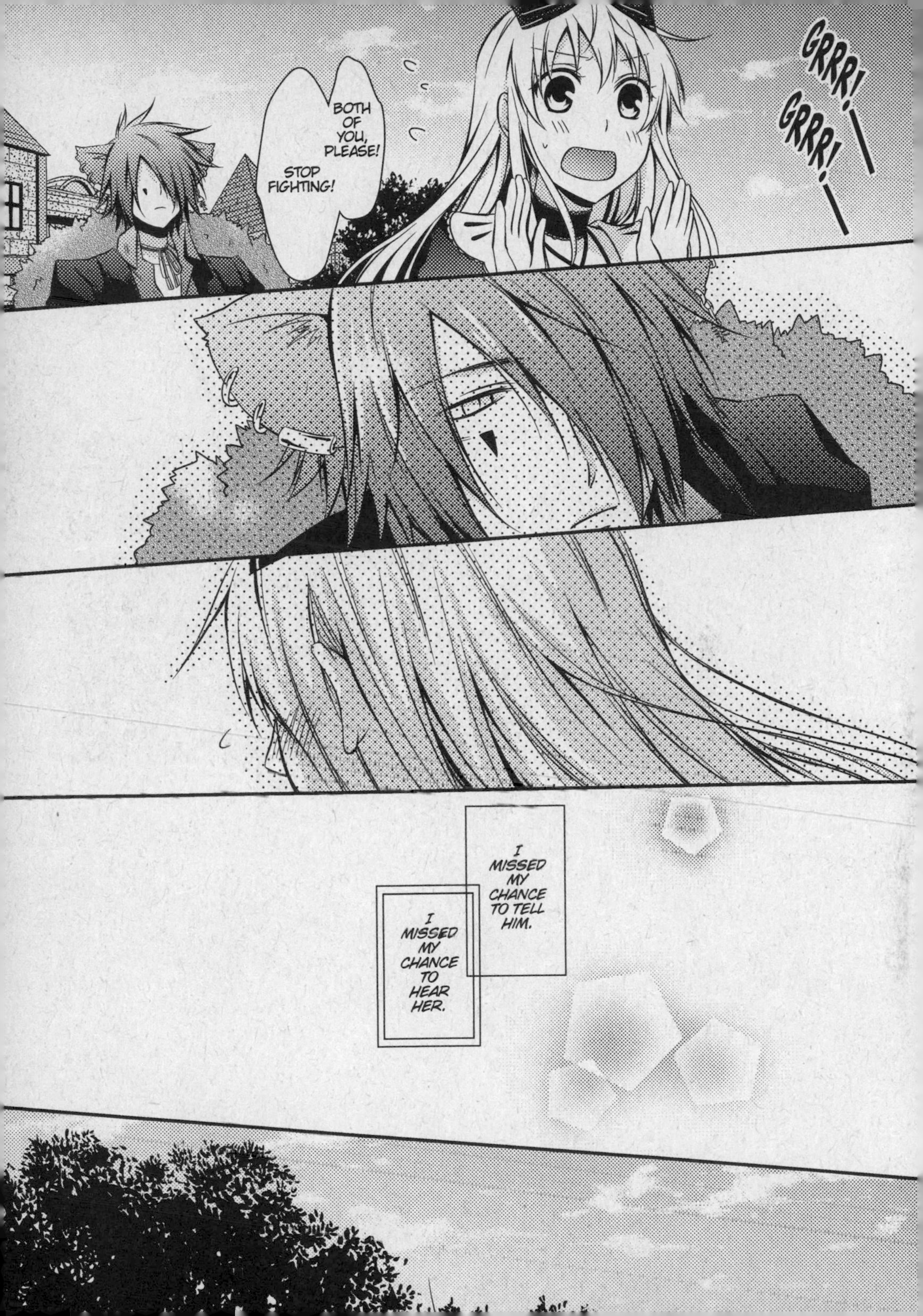
GRRR! GRRR!
BOTH OF YOU, PLEASE!
STOP FIGHTING!
I MISSED MY CHANCE TO TELL HIM.
I MISSED MY CHANCE TO HEAR HER.

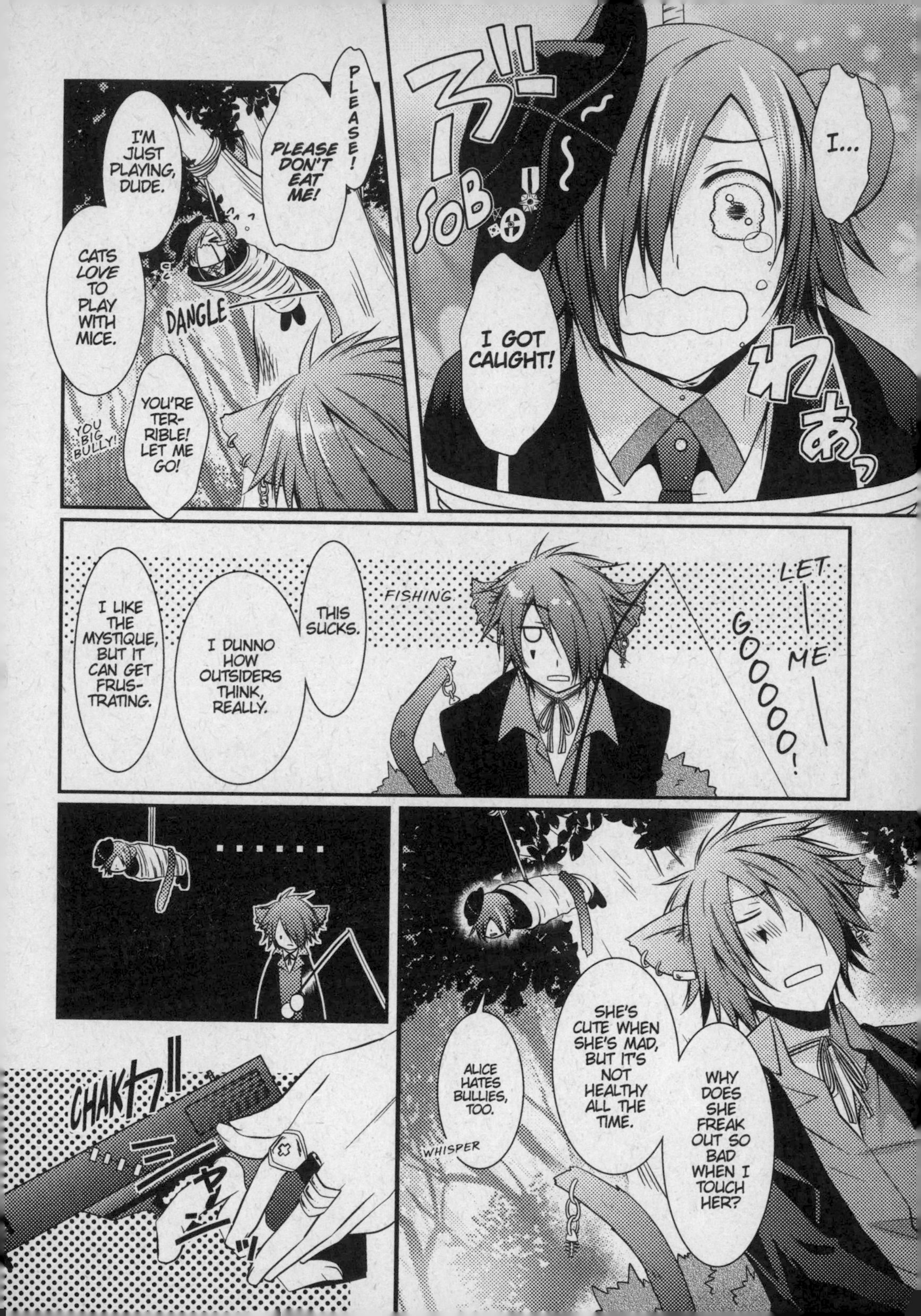
I...
SOB
I GOT CAUGHT!
PLEASE!
PLEASE DON'T EAT ME!
I'M JUST PLAYING, DUDE.
CATS LOVE TO PLAY WITH MICE.
DANGLE
YOU'RE TER-RIBLE! LET ME GO!
YOU BIG BULLY!
LET ME GOOOOOO!
FISHING
THIS SUCKS.
I DUNNO HOW OUTSIDERS THINK, REALLY.
I LIKE THE MYSTIQUE, BUT IT CAN GET FRUS-TRATING.
WHY DOES SHE FREAK OUT SO BAD WHEN I TOUCH HER?
SHE'S CUTE WHEN SHE'S MAD, BUT IT'S NOT HEALTHY ALL THE TIME.
ALICE HATES BULLIES, TOO.
WHISPER
......
CHAK

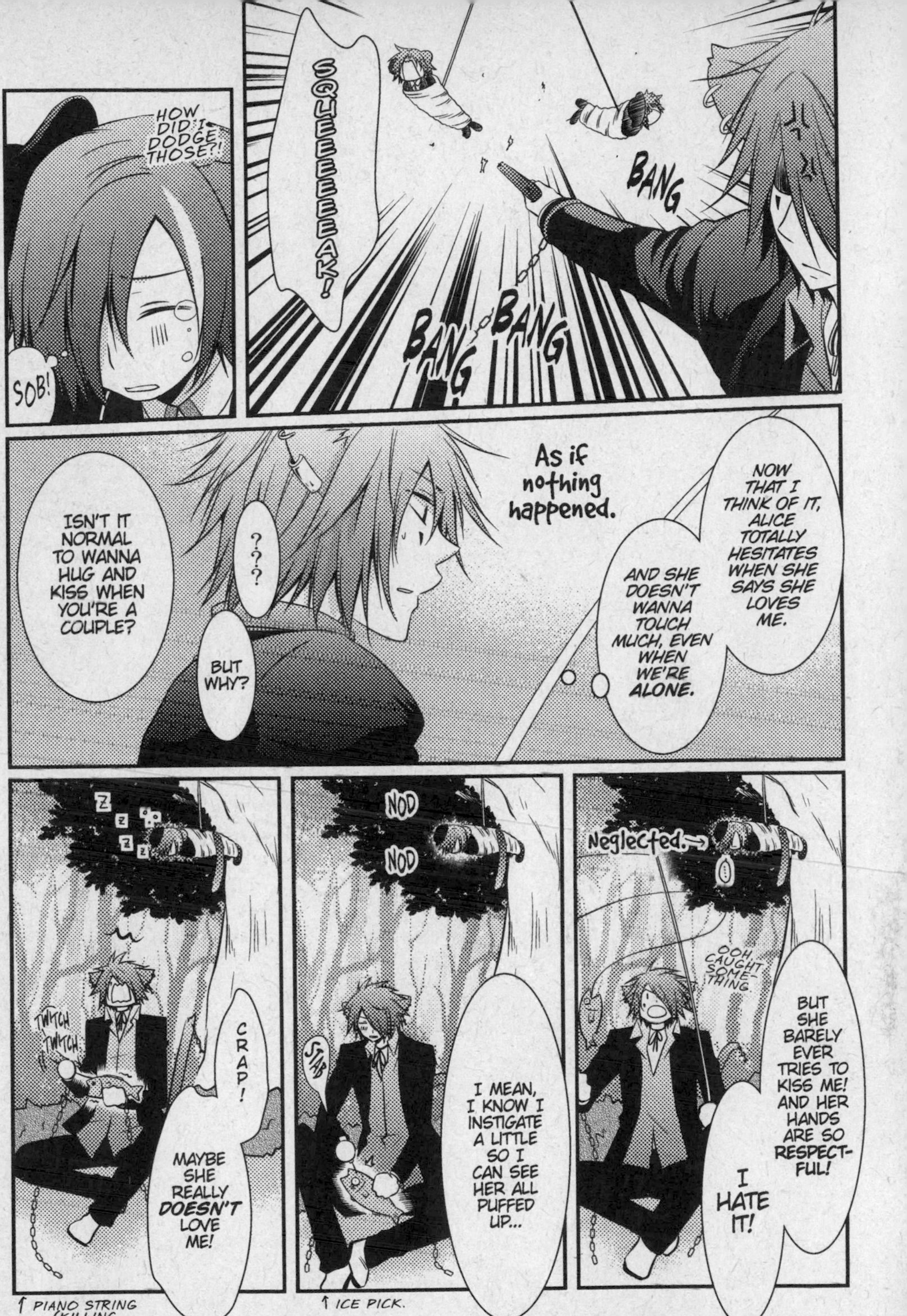
BANG
SQUEEEEEEEAK!
BANG BANG
BANG
HOW DID I DODGE THOSE?!
SOB!
NOW THAT I THINK OF IT, ALICE TOTALLY HESITATES WHEN SHE SAYS SHE LOVES ME.
AND SHE DOESN'T WANNA TOUCH MUCH, EVEN WHEN WE'RE ALONE.
As if nothing happened.
???
BUT WHY?
ISN'T IT NORMAL TO WANNA HUG AND KISS WHEN YOU'RE A COUPLE?
Neglected.
...
OOH CAUGHT SOMETHING.
BUT SHE BARELY EVER TRIES TO KISS ME! AND HER HANDS ARE SO RESPECTFUL!
I HATE IT!
NOD
NOD
STAB
I MEAN, I KNOW I INSTIGATE A LITTLE SO I CAN SEE HER ALL PUFFED UP...
Z Z Z Z
CRAP!
TWITCH TWITCH
MAYBE SHE REALLY DOESN'T LOVE ME!

↑ ICE PICK.

↑ PIANO STRING (KILLING THE NERVE).

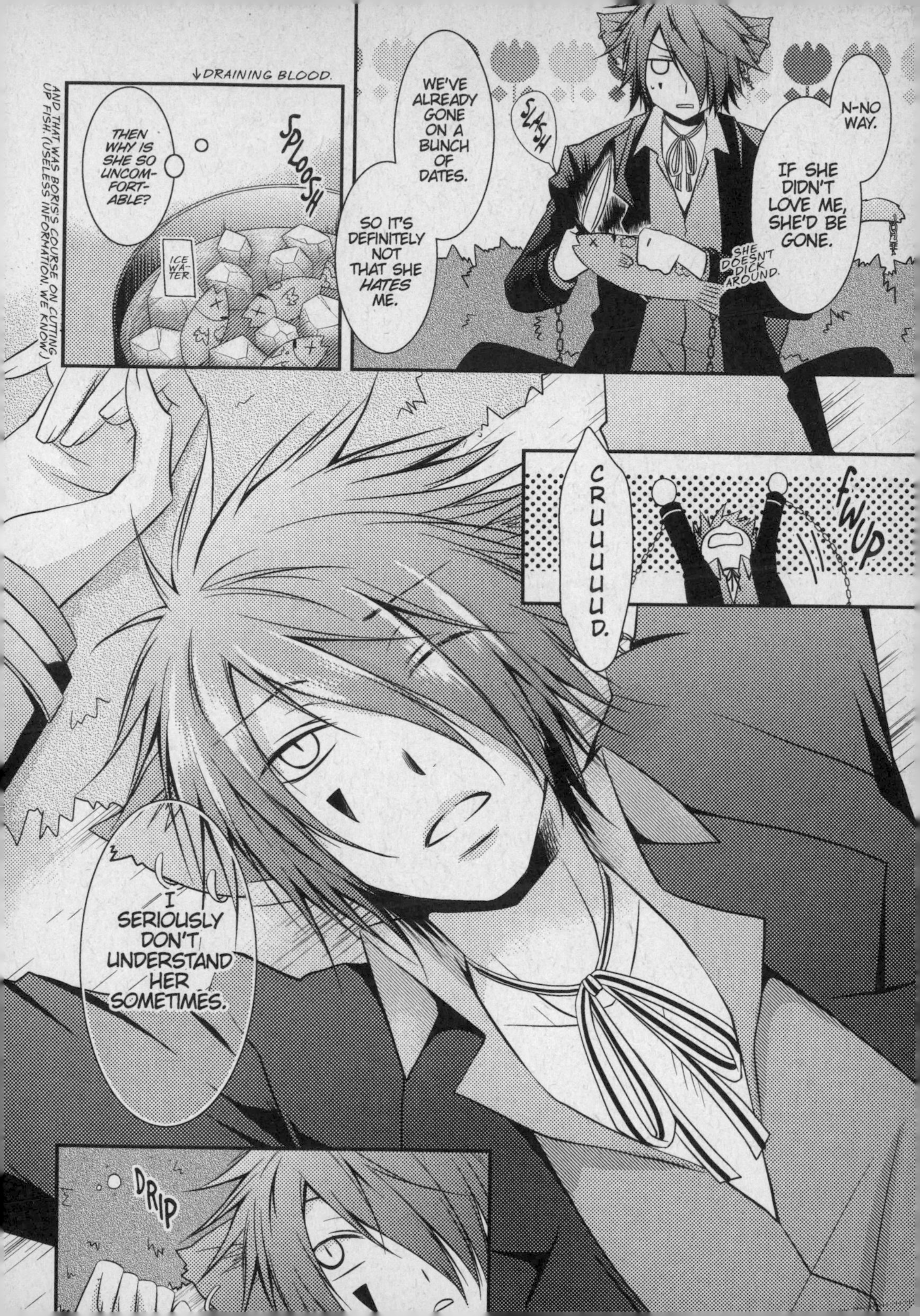
N-NO WAY.
IF SHE DIDN'T LOVE ME, SHE'D BE GONE.
SHE DOESN'T DICK AROUND.
SLASH
WE'VE ALREADY GONE ON A BUNCH OF DATES.
SO IT'S DEFINITELY NOT THAT SHE HATES ME.
↓DRAINING BLOOD.
SPLOOSH
THEN WHY IS SHE SO UNCOMFORTABLE?
ICE WATER.
AND THAT WAS BORIS'S COURSE ON CUTTING UP FISH. (USELESS INFORMATION, WE KNOW.)
CRUUUUUD.
FWUP
I SERIOUSLY DON'T UNDERSTAND HER SOMETIMES.
DRIP

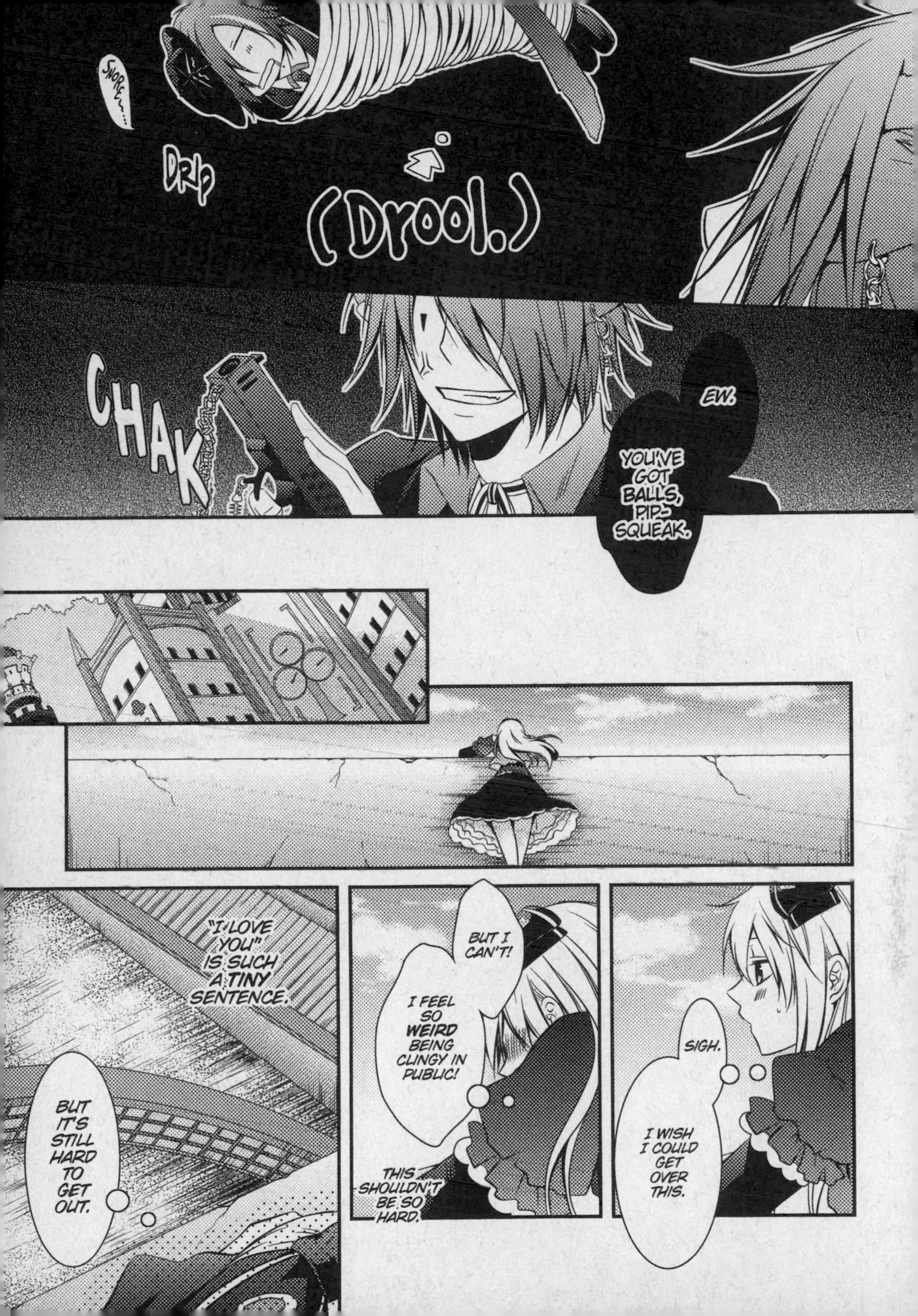
SNORE~...
Drip
(Drool.)
EW.
YOU'VE GOT BALLS, PIP-SQUEAK.
CHAK
SIGH.
I WISH I COULD GET OVER THIS.
BUT I CAN'T!
I FEEL SO WEIRD BEING CLINGY IN PUBLIC!
THIS SHOULDN'T BE SO HARD.
"I LOVE YOU" IS SUCH A TINY SENTENCE.
BUT IT'S STILL HARD TO GET OUT.

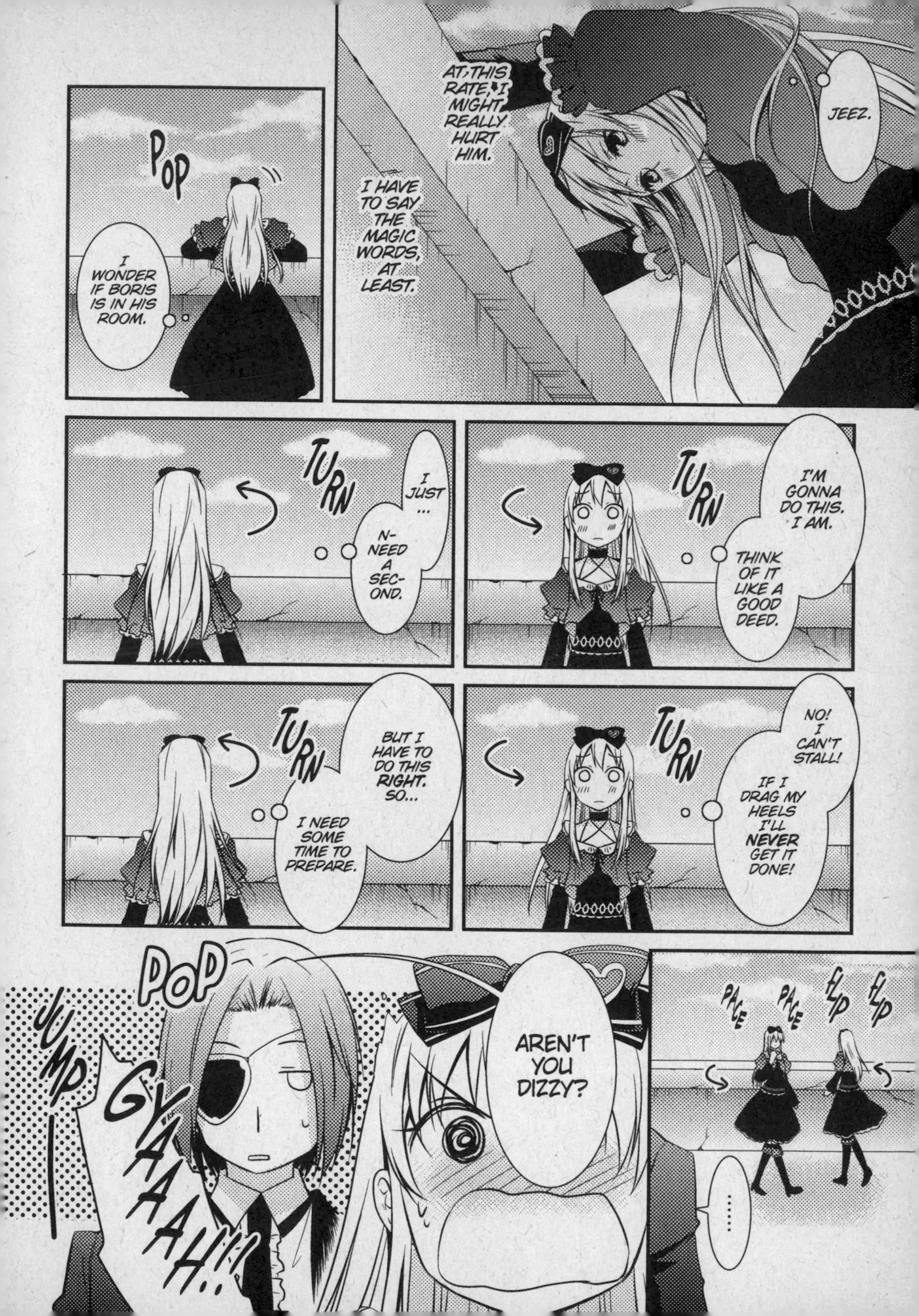
JEEZ.
AT THIS RATE, I MIGHT REALLY HURT HIM.
I HAVE TO SAY THE MAGIC WORDS, AT LEAST.
POP
I WONDER IF BORIS IS IN HIS ROOM.
TURN
I'M GONNA DO THIS. I AM.
THINK OF IT LIKE A GOOD DEED.
TURN
I JUST...
N-NEED A SEC-OND.
TURN
NO! I CAN'T STALL!
IF I DRAG MY HEELS I'LL NEVER GET IT DONE!
TURN
BUT I HAVE TO DO THIS RIGHT. SO...
I NEED SOME TIME TO PREPARE.
PACE
PACE
FLIP
FLIP
......
AREN'T YOU DIZZY?
POP
JUMP
GYAAAAH!!

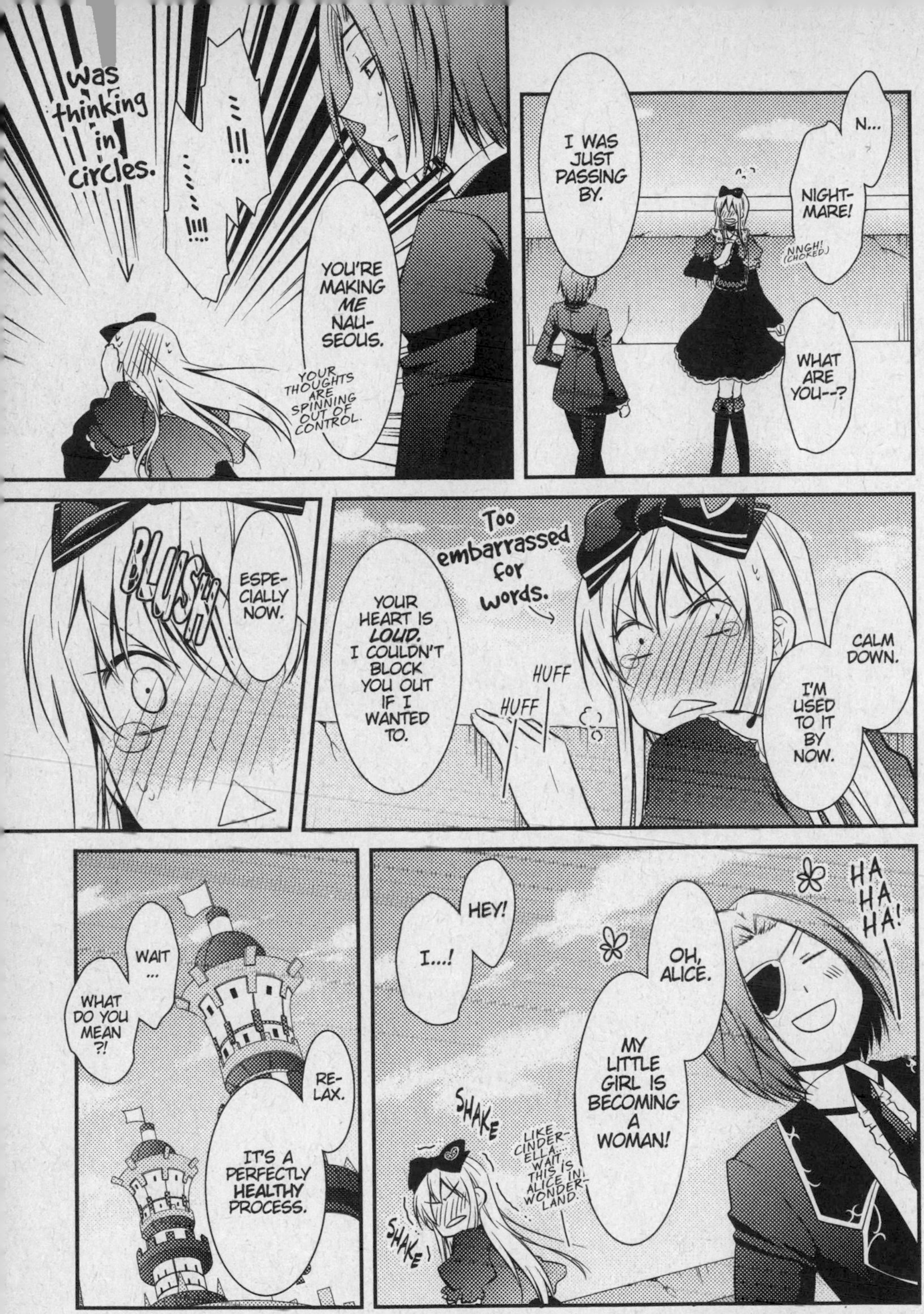
N... NIGHTMARE!
NNGH! (CHOKED)
WHAT ARE YOU--?
I WAS JUST PASSING BY.
YOU'RE MAKING *ME* NAUSEOUS.
YOUR THOUGHTS ARE SPINNING OUT OF CONTROL.
...!!!
...!!!
Was thinking in circles.
CALM DOWN.
I'M USED TO IT BY NOW.
Too embarrassed for words.
HUFF
HUFF
YOUR HEART IS *LOUD.* I COULDN'T BLOCK YOU OUT IF I WANTED TO.
ESPECIALLY NOW.
BLUSH
HA HA HA!
OH, ALICE.
MY LITTLE GIRL IS BECOMING A WOMAN!
HEY!
I...!
LIKE CINDERELLA... WAIT, THIS IS ALICE IN WONDERLAND.
SHAKE
SHAKE
RELAX.
IT'S A PERFECTLY HEALTHY PROCESS.
WAIT... WHAT DO YOU MEAN?!

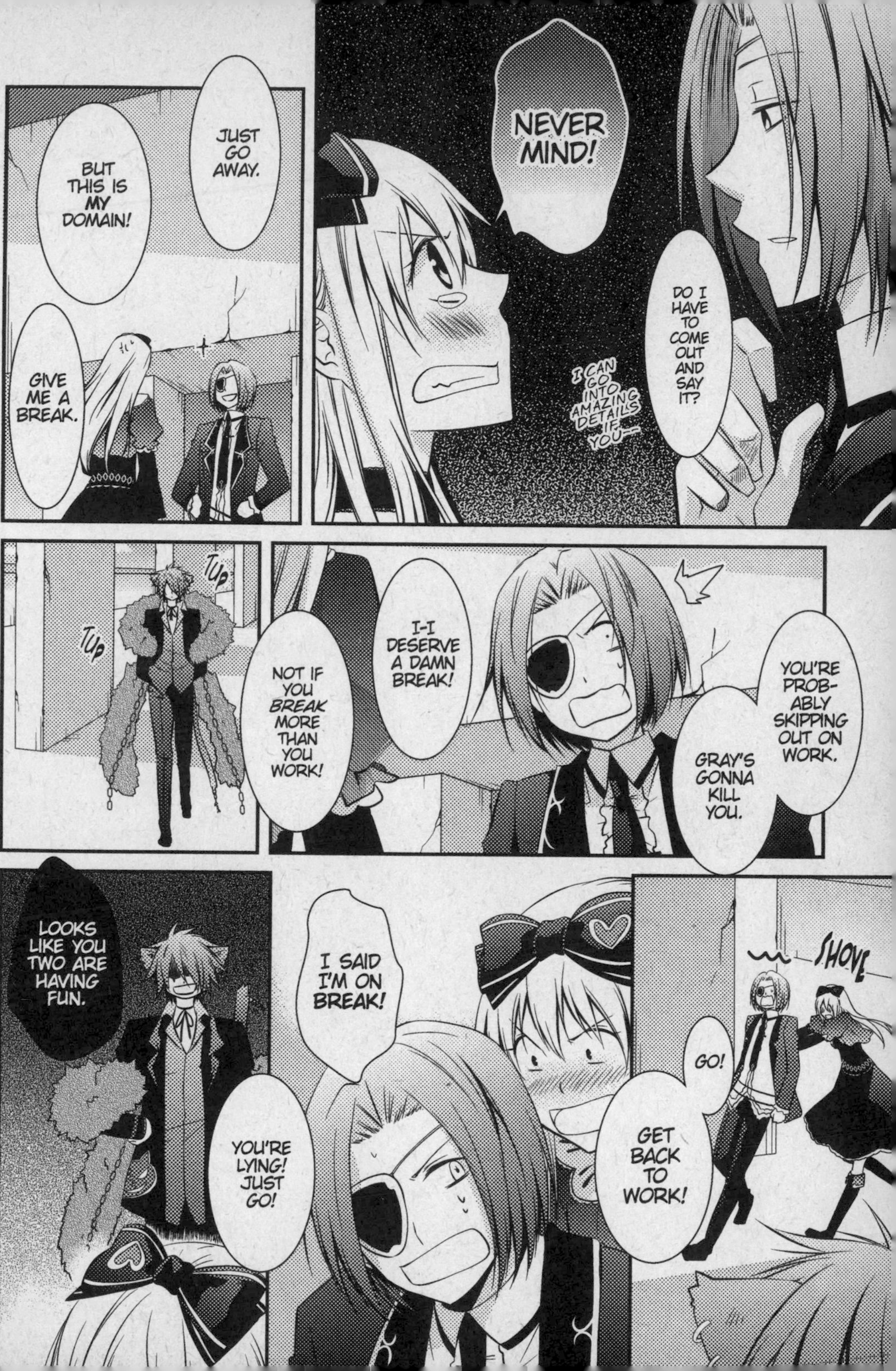
NEVER MIND!
DO I HAVE TO COME OUT AND SAY IT?
I CAN GO INTO AMAZING DETAILS IF YOU—
JUST GO AWAY.
BUT THIS IS MY DOMAIN!
GIVE ME A BREAK.
YOU'RE PROB-ABLY SKIPPING OUT ON WORK.
GRAY'S GONNA KILL YOU.
I-I DESERVE A DAMN BREAK!
NOT IF YOU *BREAK* MORE THAN YOU WORK!
TUP
TUP
SHOVE
GO!
GET BACK TO WORK!
I SAID I'M ON BREAK!
YOU'RE LYING! JUST GO!
LOOKS LIKE YOU TWO ARE HAVING FUN.

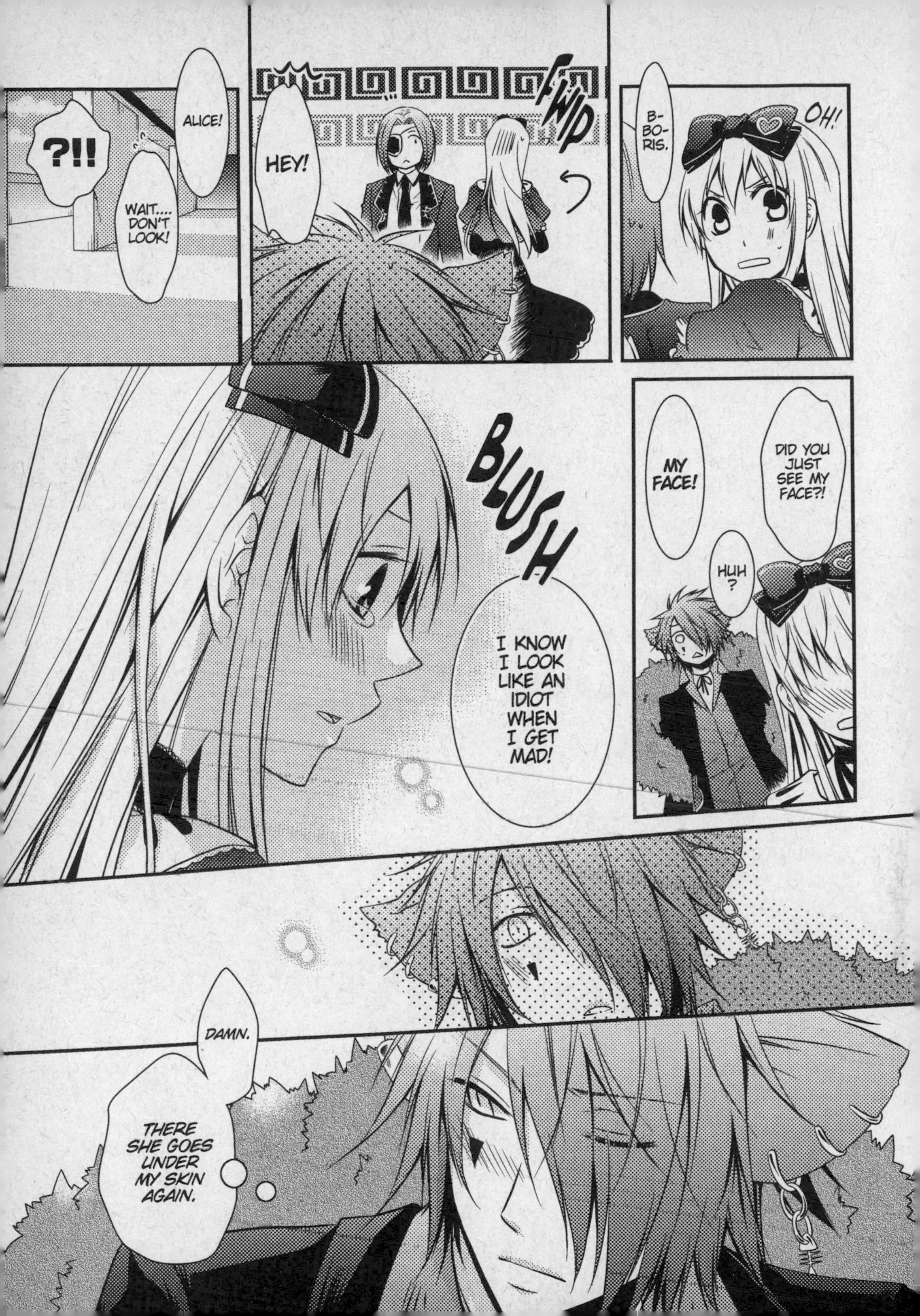
B-BO-RIS.
OH!
FWIP
HEY!
ALICE!
WAIT.... DON'T LOOK!
?!!
DID YOU JUST SEE MY FACE?!
MY FACE!
HUH?
BLUSH
I KNOW I LOOK LIKE AN IDIOT WHEN I GET MAD!
DAMN.
THERE SHE GOES UNDER MY SKIN AGAIN.

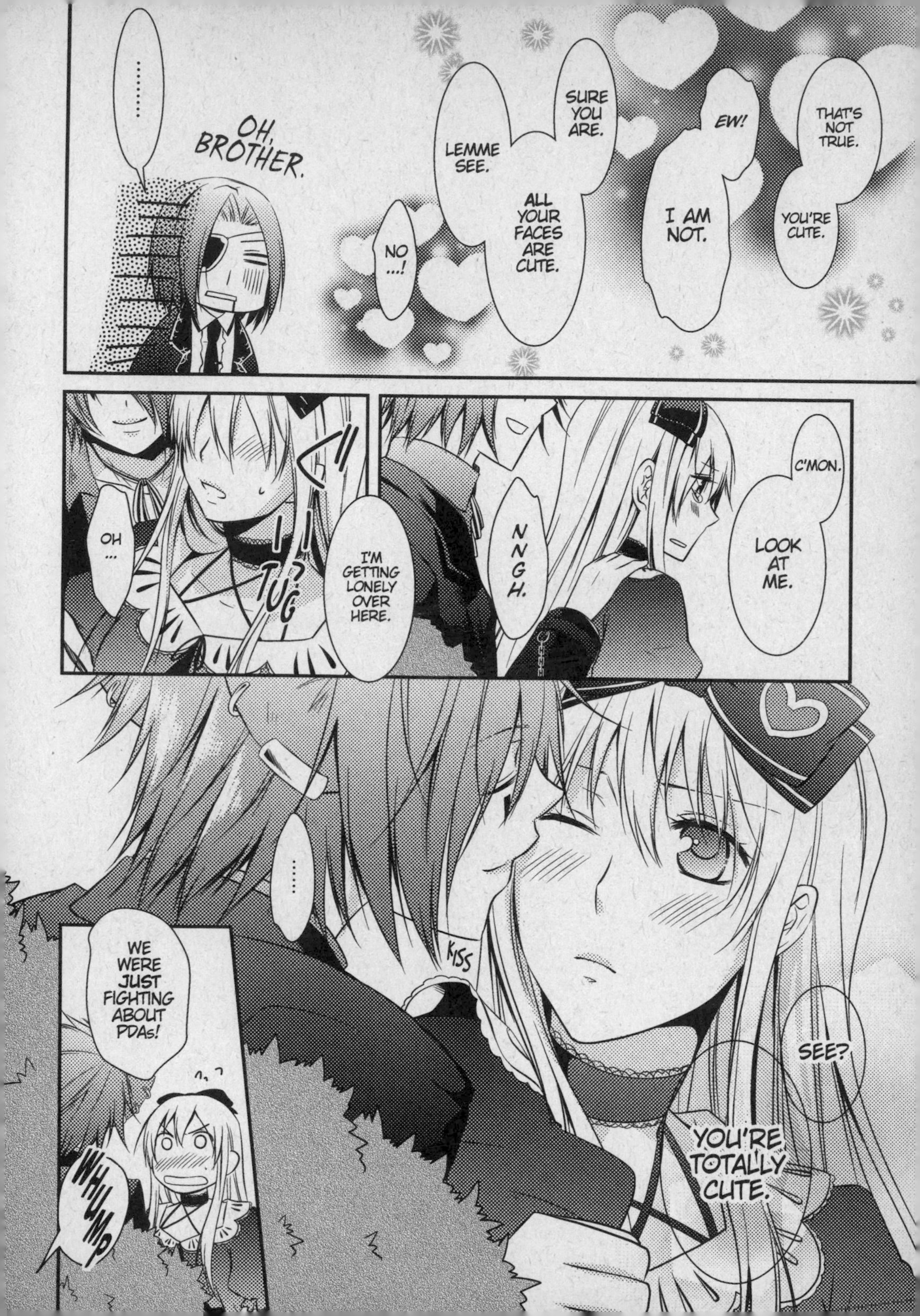
THAT'S NOT TRUE.
YOU'RE CUTE.
EW!
I AM NOT.
SURE YOU ARE.
LEMME SEE.
ALL YOUR FACES ARE CUTE.
NO ...!
OH, BROTHER.
......
C'MON.
LOOK AT ME.
NNGH.
I'M GETTING LONELY OVER HERE.
TUG
OH ...
......
KISS
SEE?
YOU'RE TOTALLY CUTE.
WE WERE JUST FIGHTING ABOUT PDAs!
WHUMP

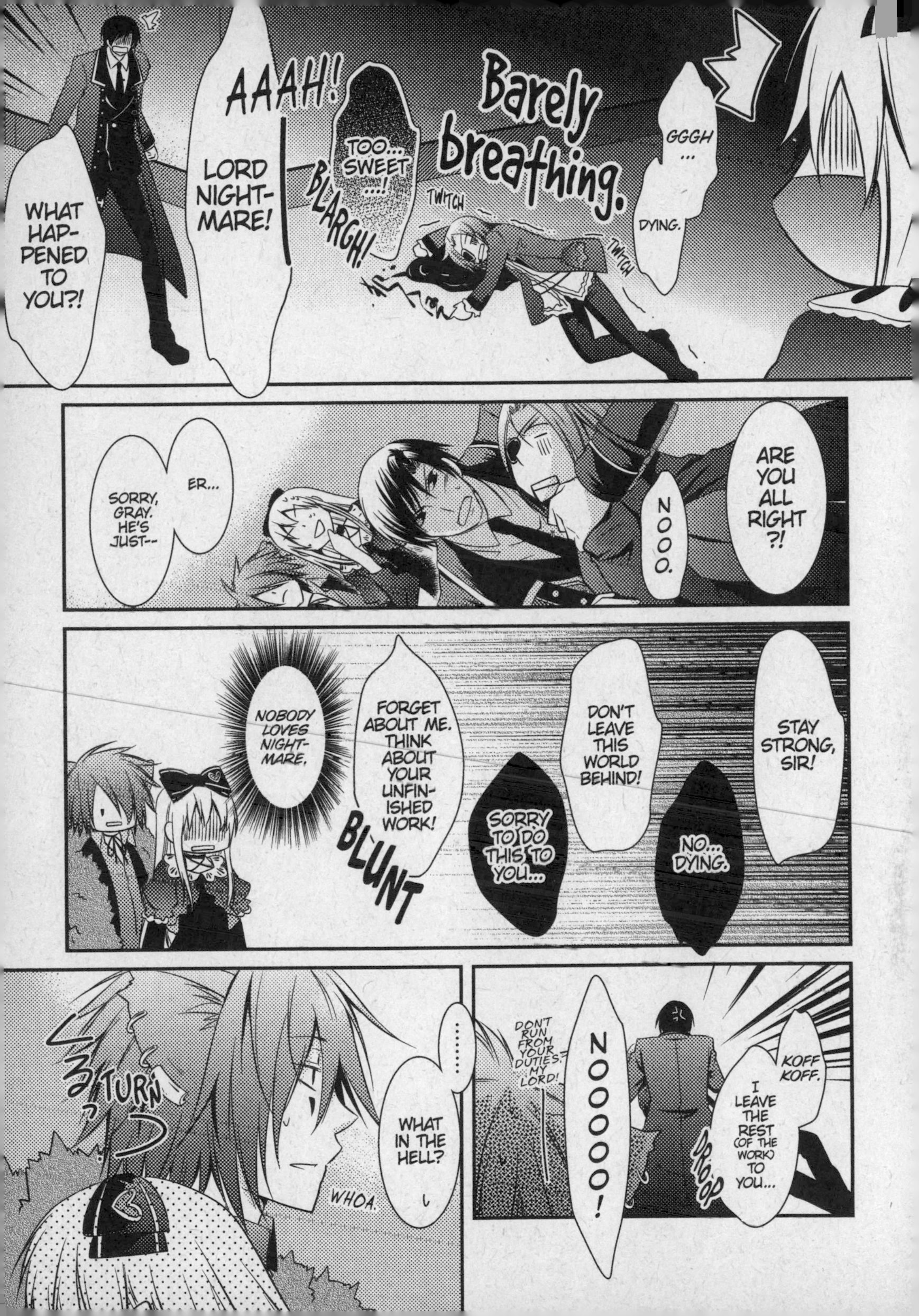
GGGH ...
DYING.
Barely breathing.
TWITCH
TWITCH
TOO... SWEET ...!
BLARGH!
AAAH!
LORD NIGHT-MARE!
WHAT HAP-PENED TO YOU?!
ARE YOU ALL RIGHT ?!
NOOO.
ER...
SORRY, GRAY. HE'S JUST--
STAY STRONG, SIR!
NO... DYING.
DON'T LEAVE THIS WORLD BEHIND!
SORRY TO DO THIS TO YOU...
FORGET ABOUT ME. THINK ABOUT YOUR UNFIN-ISHED WORK!
BLUNT
NOBODY LOVES NIGHT-MARE.
KOFF KOFF.
I LEAVE THE REST (OF THE WORK) TO YOU...
DROOP
NOOOOO!
DON'T RUN FROM YOUR DUTIES, MY LORD!
......
WHAT IN THE HELL?
WHOA.
TURN

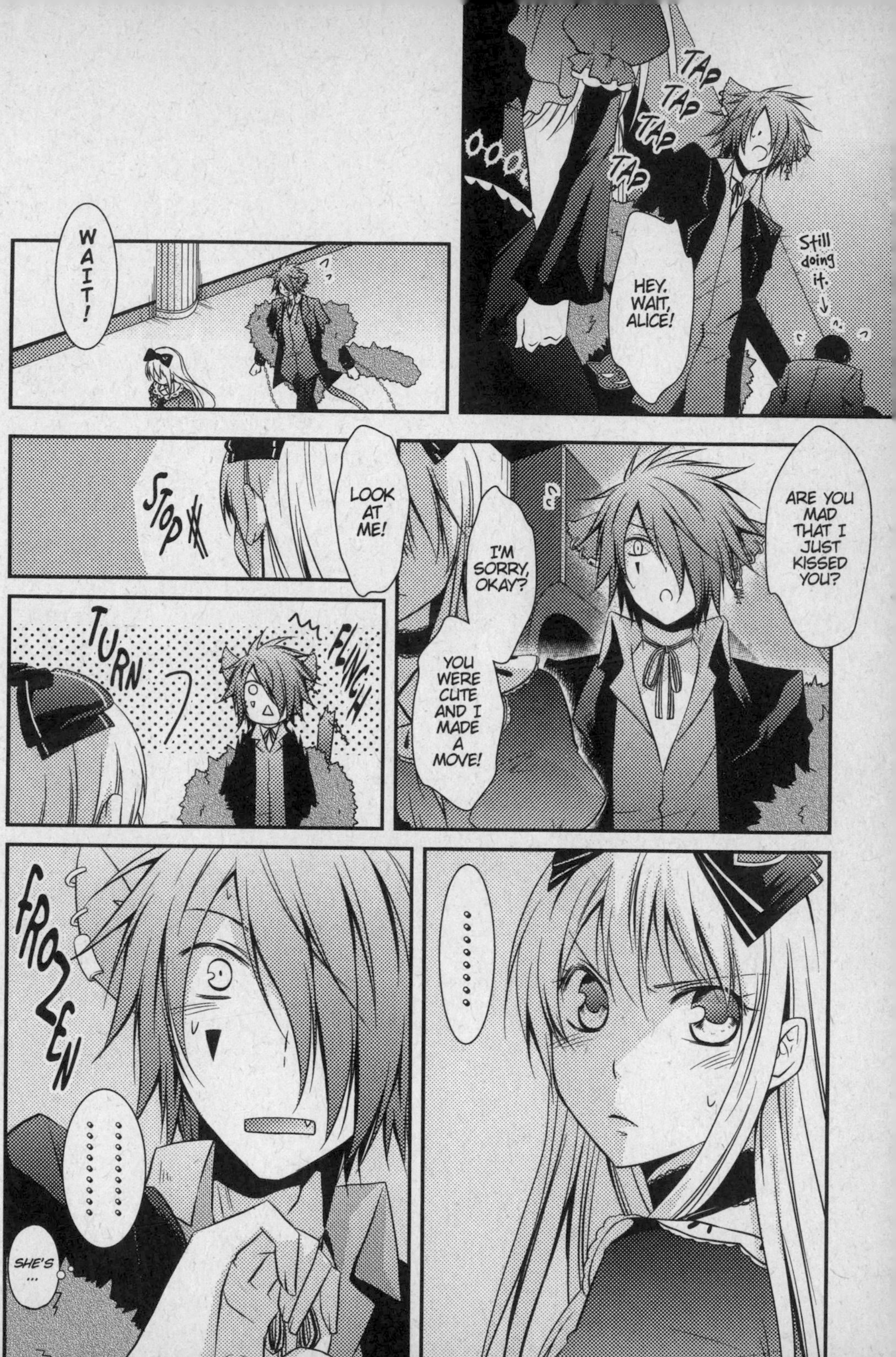

TAP TAP TAP TAP TAP
HEY. WAIT, ALICE!
Still doing it.
WAIT!
ARE YOU MAD THAT I JUST KISSED YOU?
I'M SORRY, OKAY?
YOU WERE CUTE AND I MADE A MOVE!
LOOK AT ME!
STOP
TURN
FLINCH
....
FROZEN
....
SHE'S...

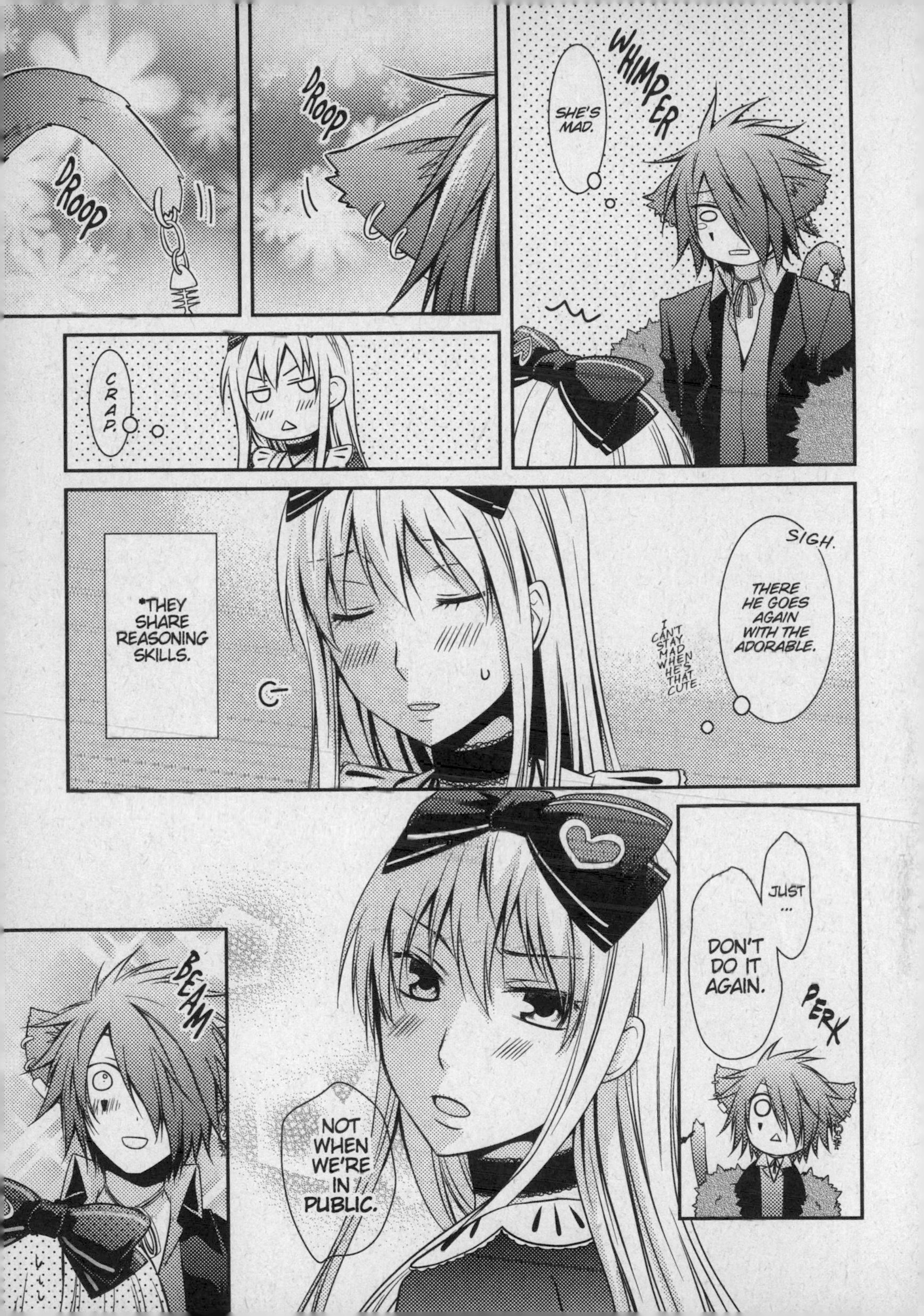
WHIMPER
SHE'S MAD.
DROOP
DROOP
CRAP.
SIGH.
THERE HE GOES AGAIN WITH THE ADORABLE.
I CAN'T STAY MAD WHEN HE'S THAT CUTE.
*THEY SHARE REASONING SKILLS.
JUST...
DON'T DO IT AGAIN.
PERK
NOT WHEN WE'RE IN PUBLIC.
BEAM

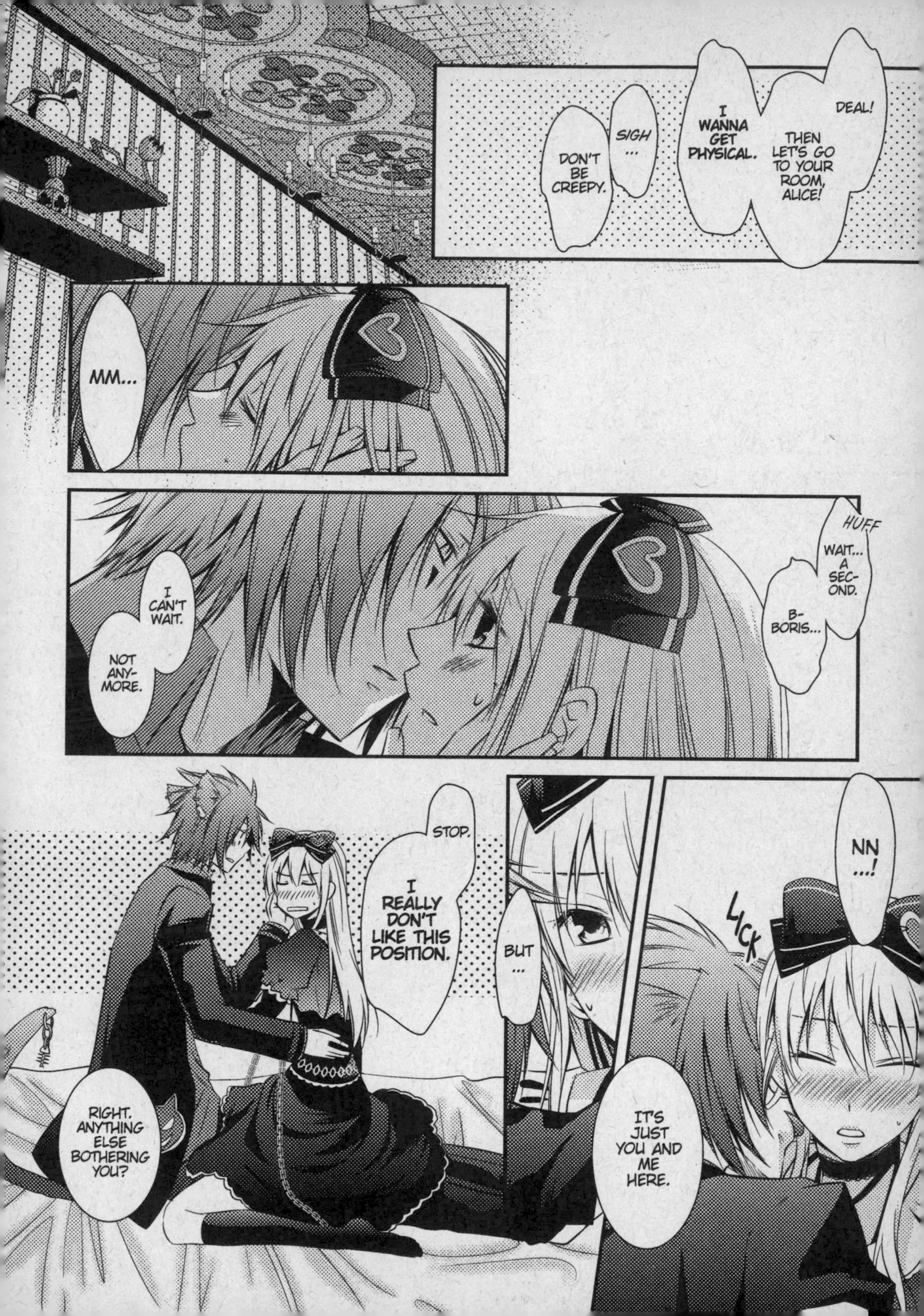
DEAL!
THEN LET'S GO TO YOUR ROOM, ALICE!
I WANNA GET PHYSICAL.
SIGH ...
DON'T BE CREEPY.
MM...
HUFF
WAIT... A SEC-OND.
B-BORIS...
I CAN'T WAIT.
NOT ANY-MORE.
NN ...!
LICK
IT'S JUST YOU AND ME HERE.
BUT ...
STOP.
I REALLY DON'T LIKE THIS POSITION.
RIGHT. ANYTHING ELSE BOTHERING YOU?

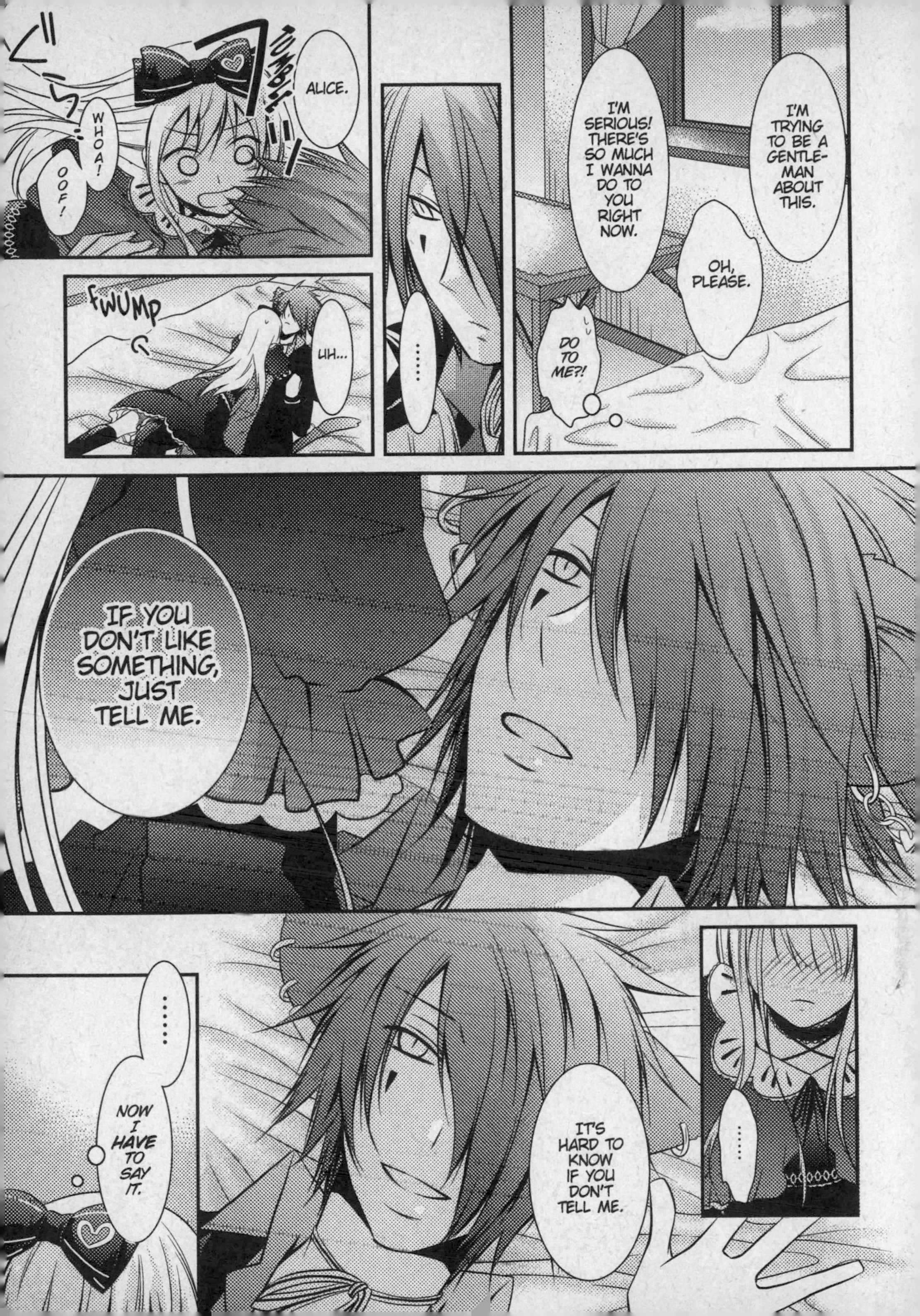
I'M TRYING TO BE A GENTLEMAN ABOUT THIS.
I'M SERIOUS! THERE'S SO MUCH I WANNA DO TO YOU RIGHT NOW.
OH, PLEASE.
DO TO ME?!
......
ALICE.
TUMBLE
WHOA!
OOF!
UH...
FWUMP
IF YOU DON'T LIKE SOMETHING, JUST TELL ME.
......
IT'S HARD TO KNOW IF YOU DON'T TELL ME.
NOW I HAVE TO SAY IT.
......

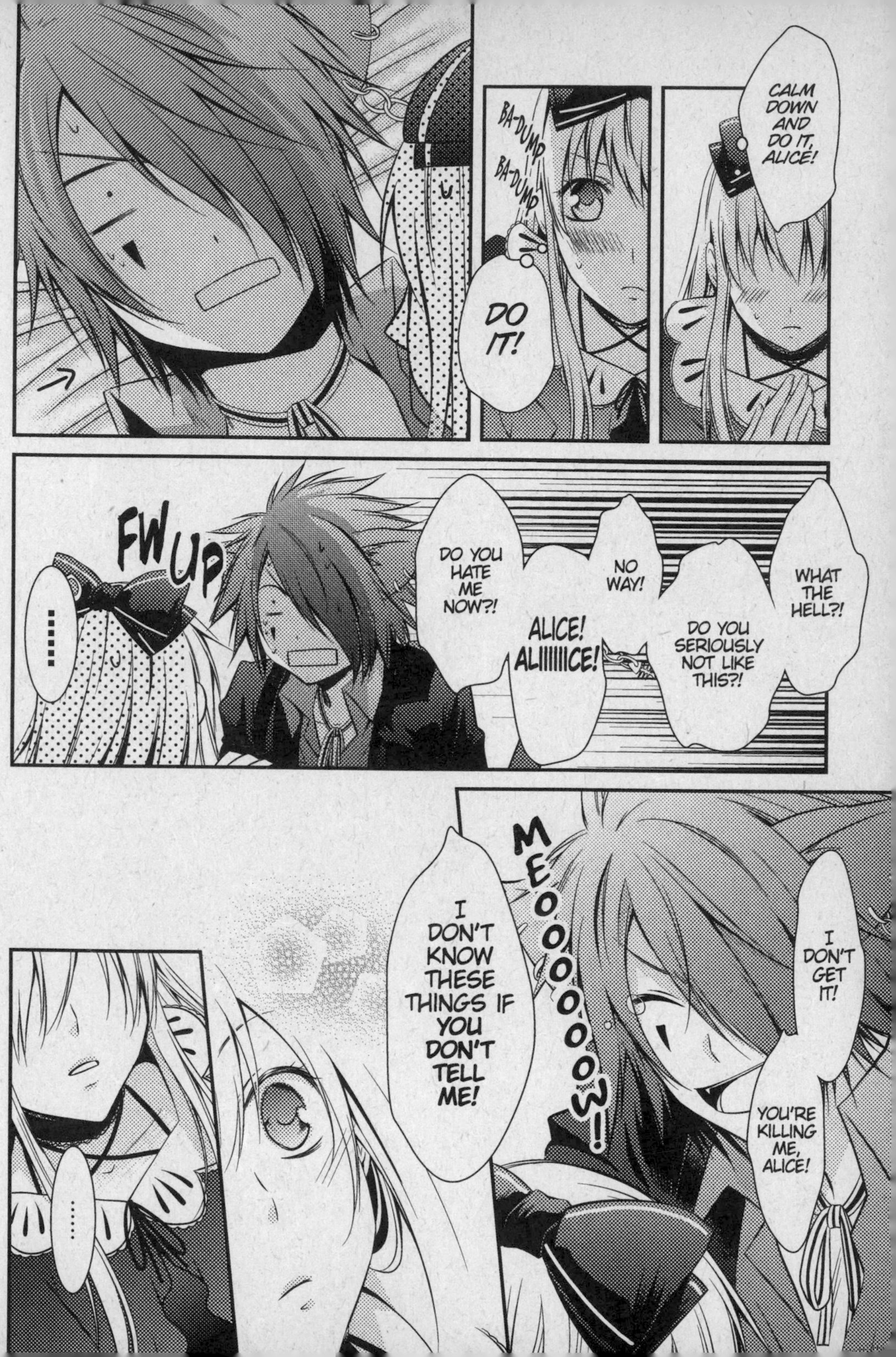
CALM DOWN AND DO IT, ALICE!
BA-DUMP BA-DUMP
DO IT!
WHAT THE HELL?!
DO YOU SERIOUSLY NOT LIKE THIS?!
NO WAY!
ALICE! ALIIIIIICE!
DO YOU HATE ME NOW?!
FWUP
......
I DON'T GET IT!
YOU'RE KILLING ME, ALICE!
MEOOOOOOOW!
I DON'T KNOW THESE THINGS IF YOU DON'T TELL ME!
......

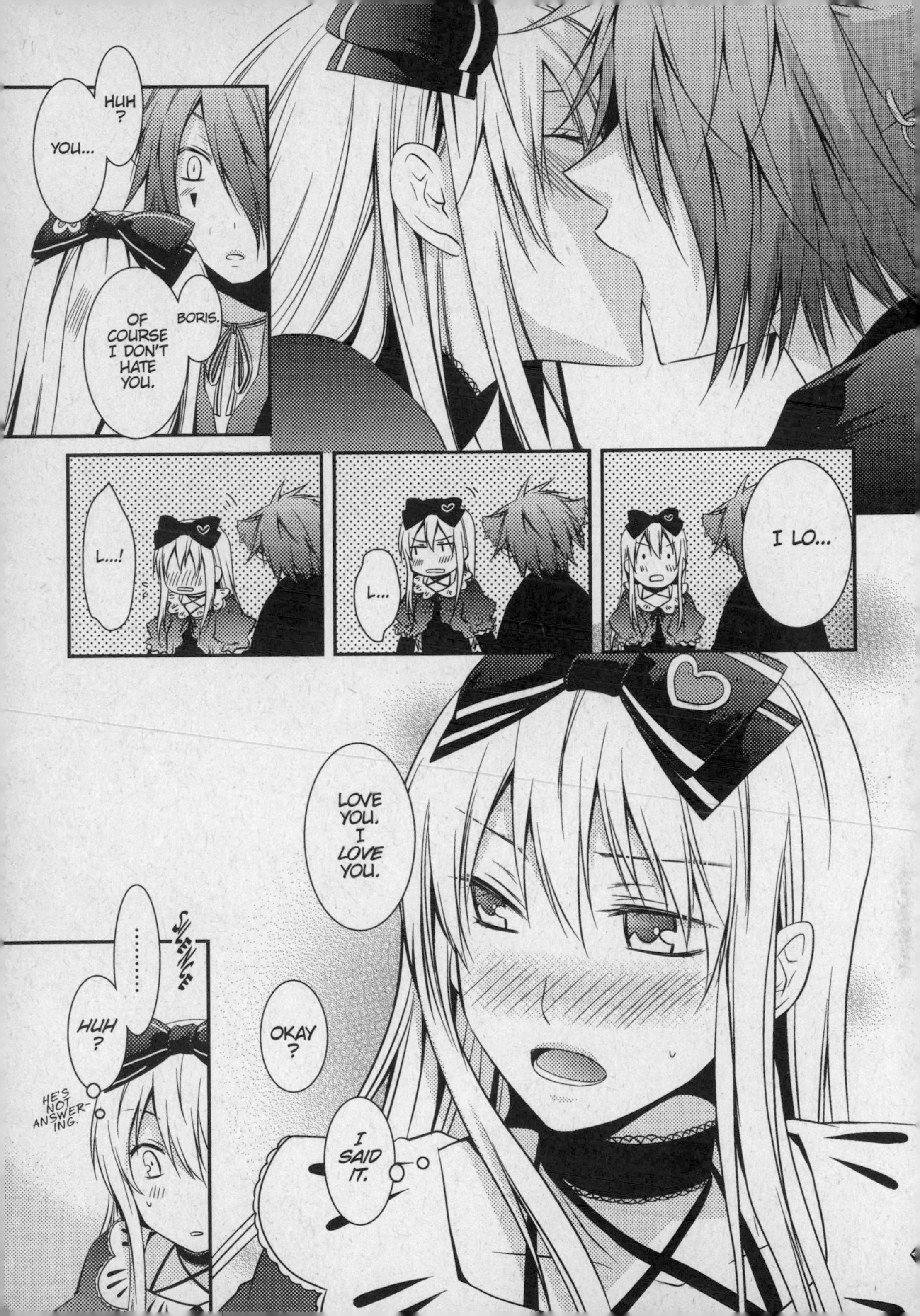
HUH? YOU...
BORIS. OF COURSE I DON'T HATE YOU.
I LO...
L...
L...!
LOVE YOU. I LOVE YOU.
OKAY?
I SAID IT.
......
SILENCE
HUH?
HE'S NOT ANSWERING.

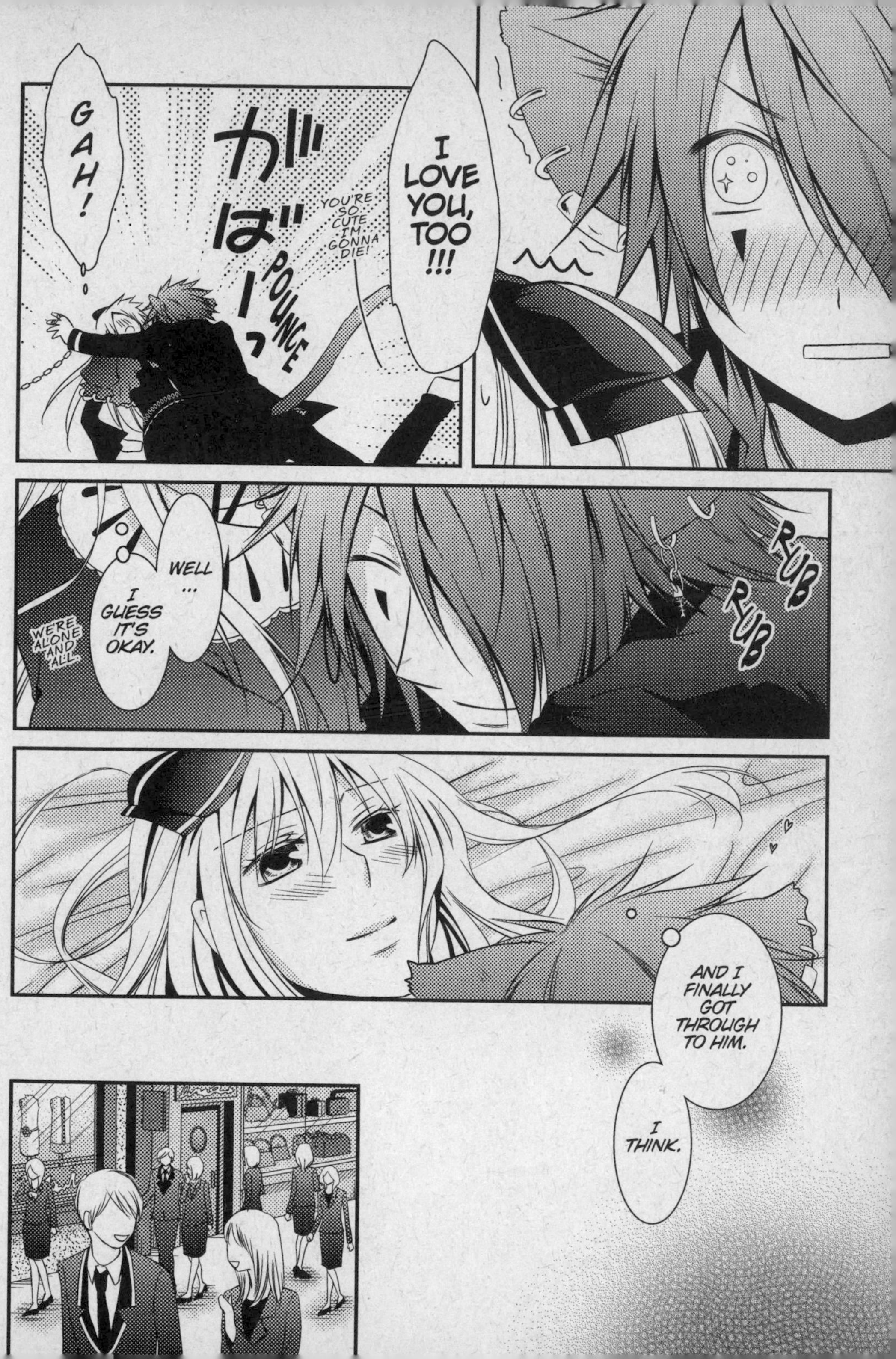
I LOVE YOU, TOO !!!
がばーっ
POUNCE
YOU'RE SO CUTE I'M GONNA DIE!
GAH!
RUB RUB
WELL ...
I GUESS IT'S OKAY.
WE'RE ALONE AND ALL.
AND I FINALLY GOT THROUGH TO HIM.
I THINK.

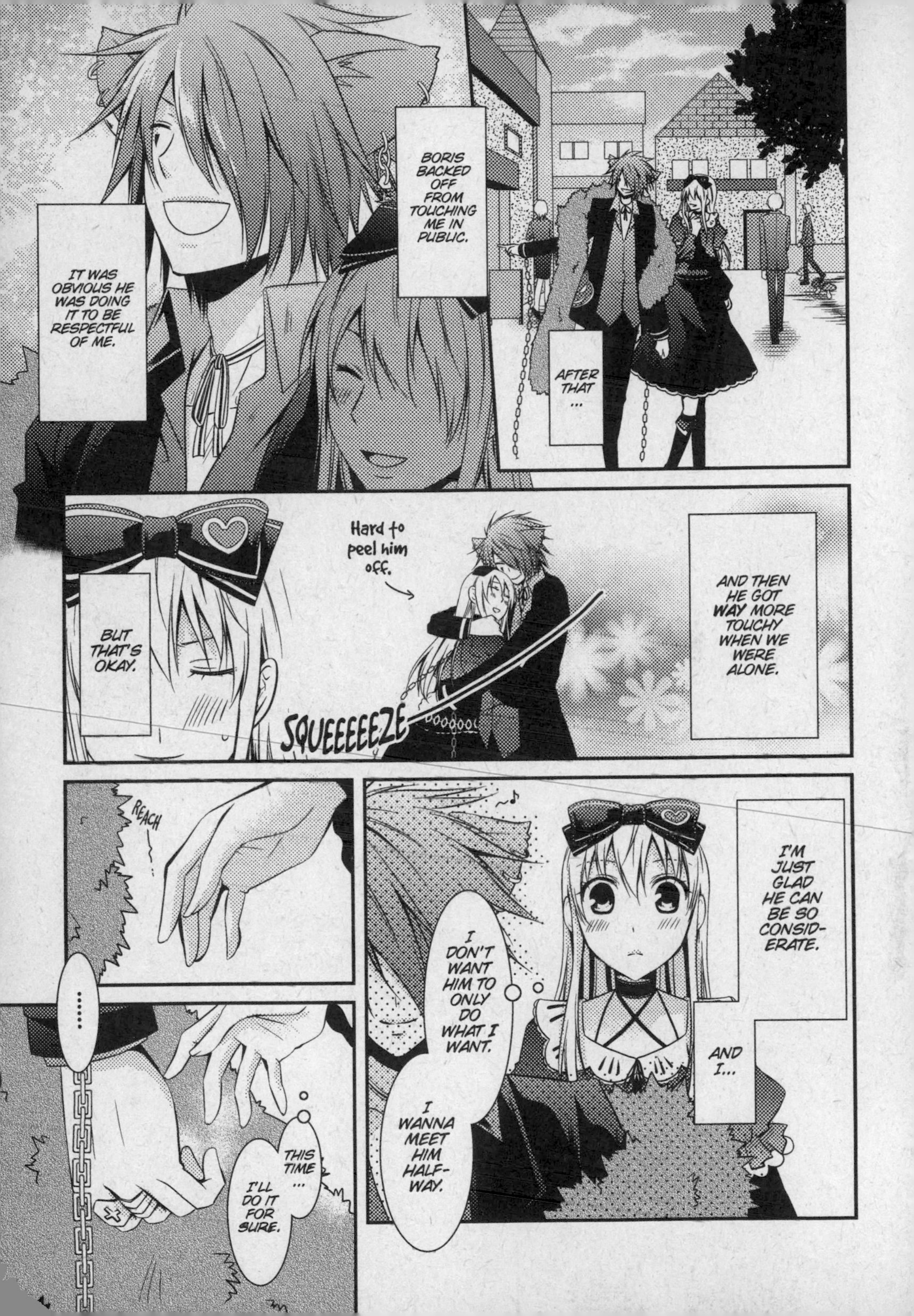
AFTER THAT...
BORIS BACKED OFF FROM TOUCHING ME IN PUBLIC.
IT WAS OBVIOUS HE WAS DOING IT TO BE RESPECTFUL OF ME.
AND THEN HE GOT WAY MORE TOUCHY WHEN WE WERE ALONE.
Hard to peel him off.
SQUEEEEEZE
BUT THAT'S OKAY.
I'M JUST GLAD HE CAN BE SO CONSID-ERATE.
AND I...
I DON'T WANT HIM TO ONLY DO WHAT I WANT.
I WANNA MEET HIM HALF-WAY.
REACH
......
THIS TIME...
I'LL DO IT FOR SURE.

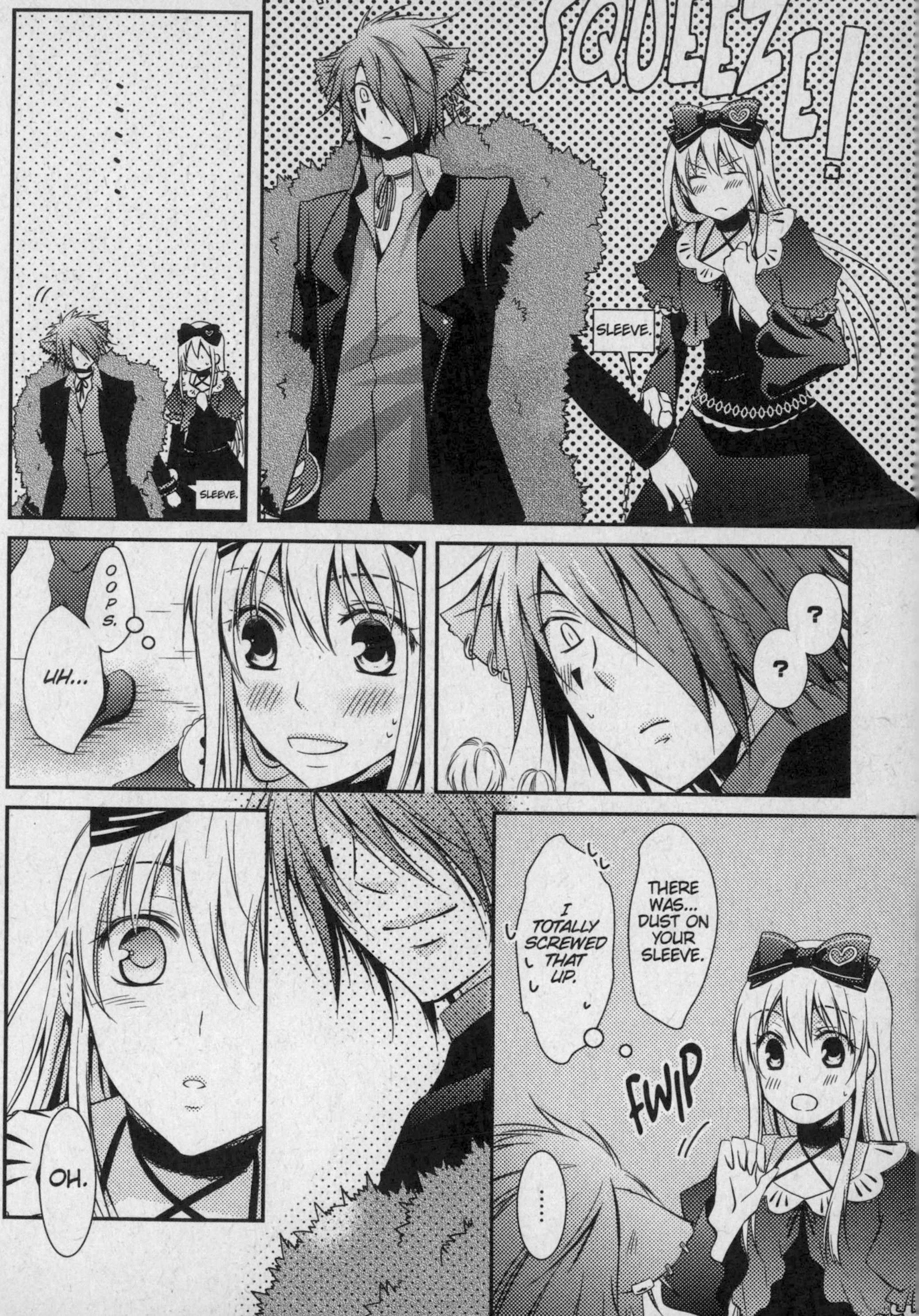
SQUEEZE!
SLEEVE.
......
SLEEVE.
?
?
OOPS.
UH...
THERE WAS... DUST ON YOUR SLEEVE.
I TOTALLY SCREWED THAT UP.
FWIP
....
OH.

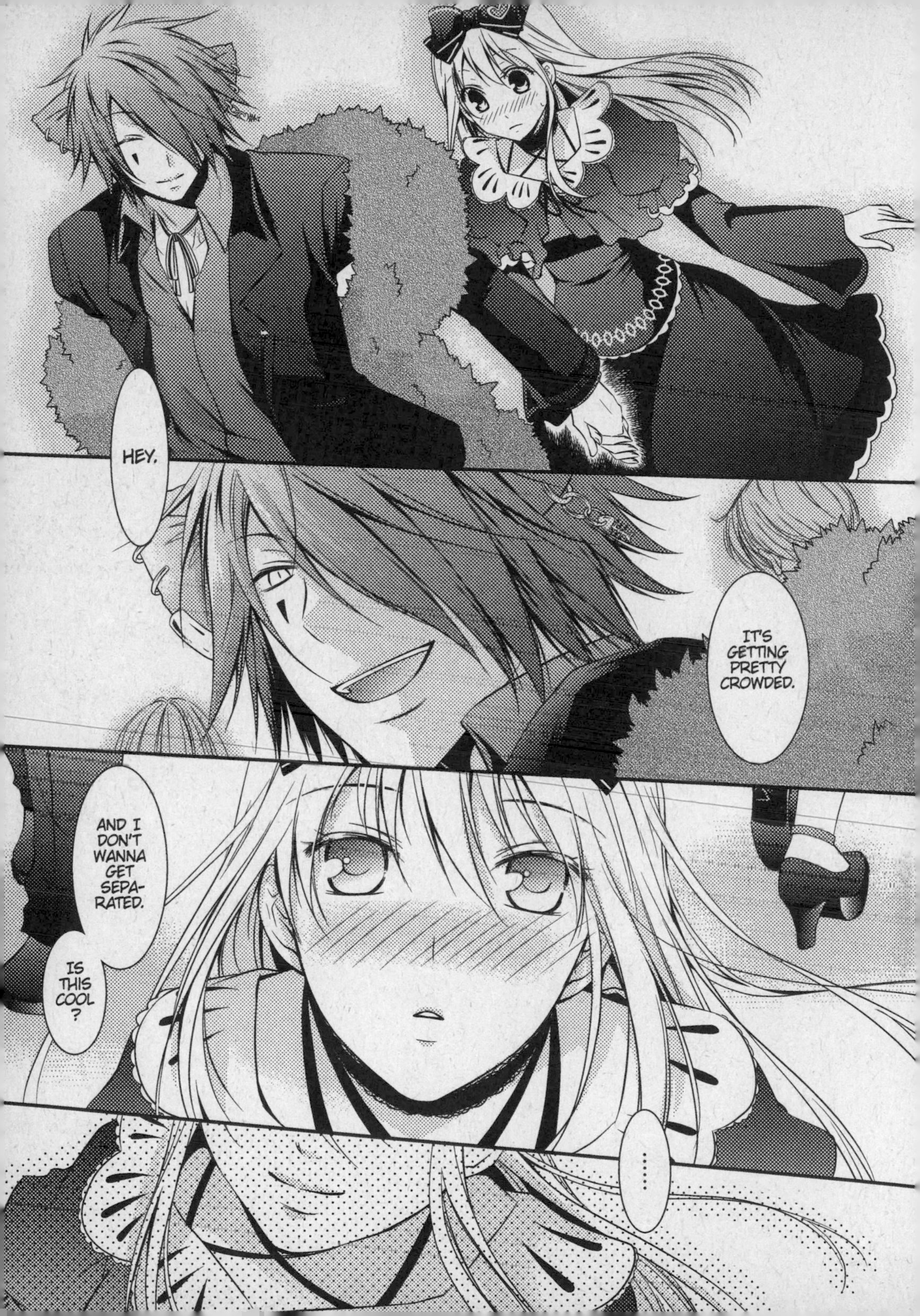
HEY.
IT'S GETTING PRETTY CROWDED.
AND I DON'T WANNA GET SEPA-RATED.
IS THIS COOL?
......

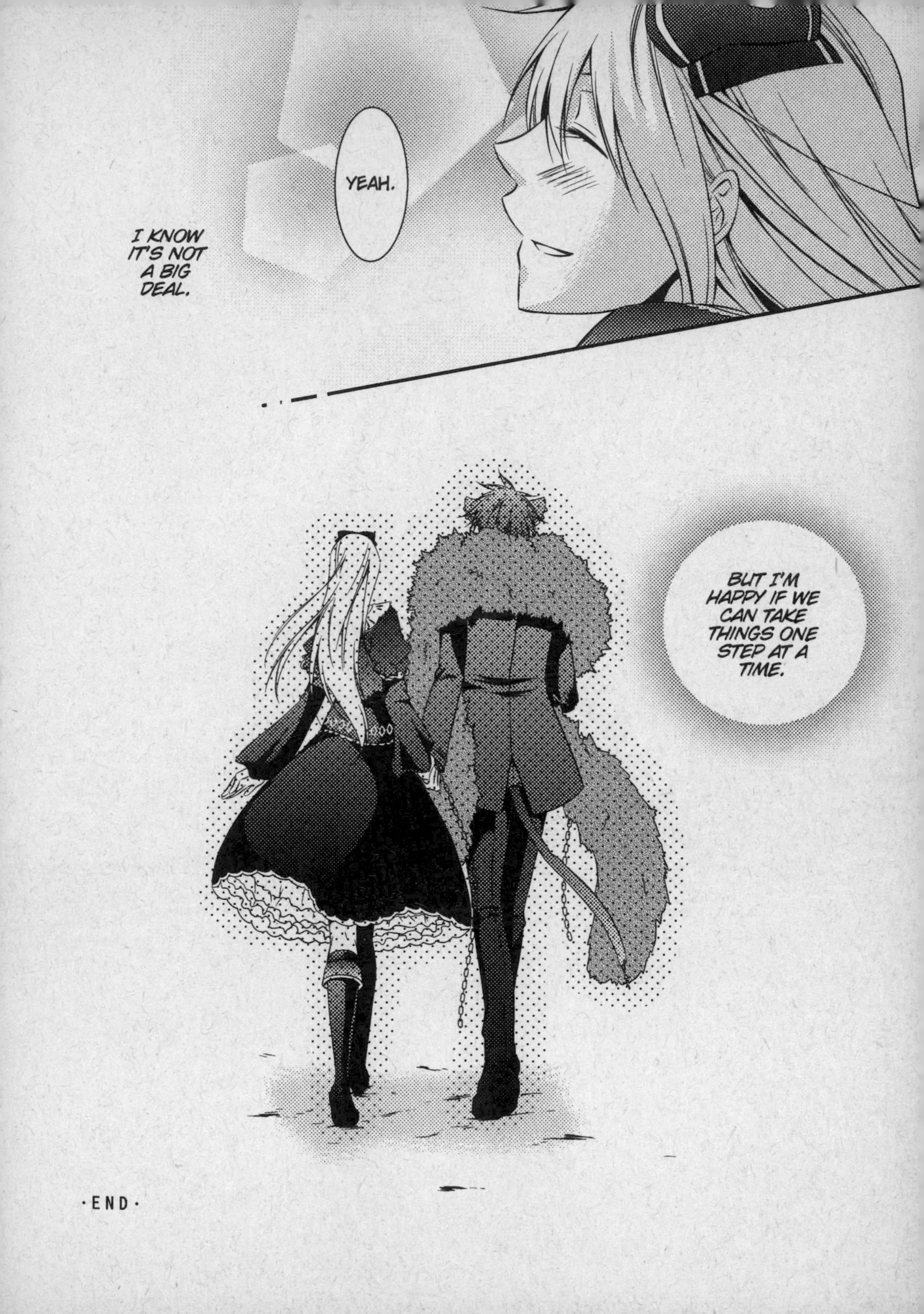
YEAH.
I KNOW IT'S NOT A BIG DEAL.
BUT I'M HAPPY IF WE CAN TAKE THINGS ONE STEP AT A TIME.
·END·

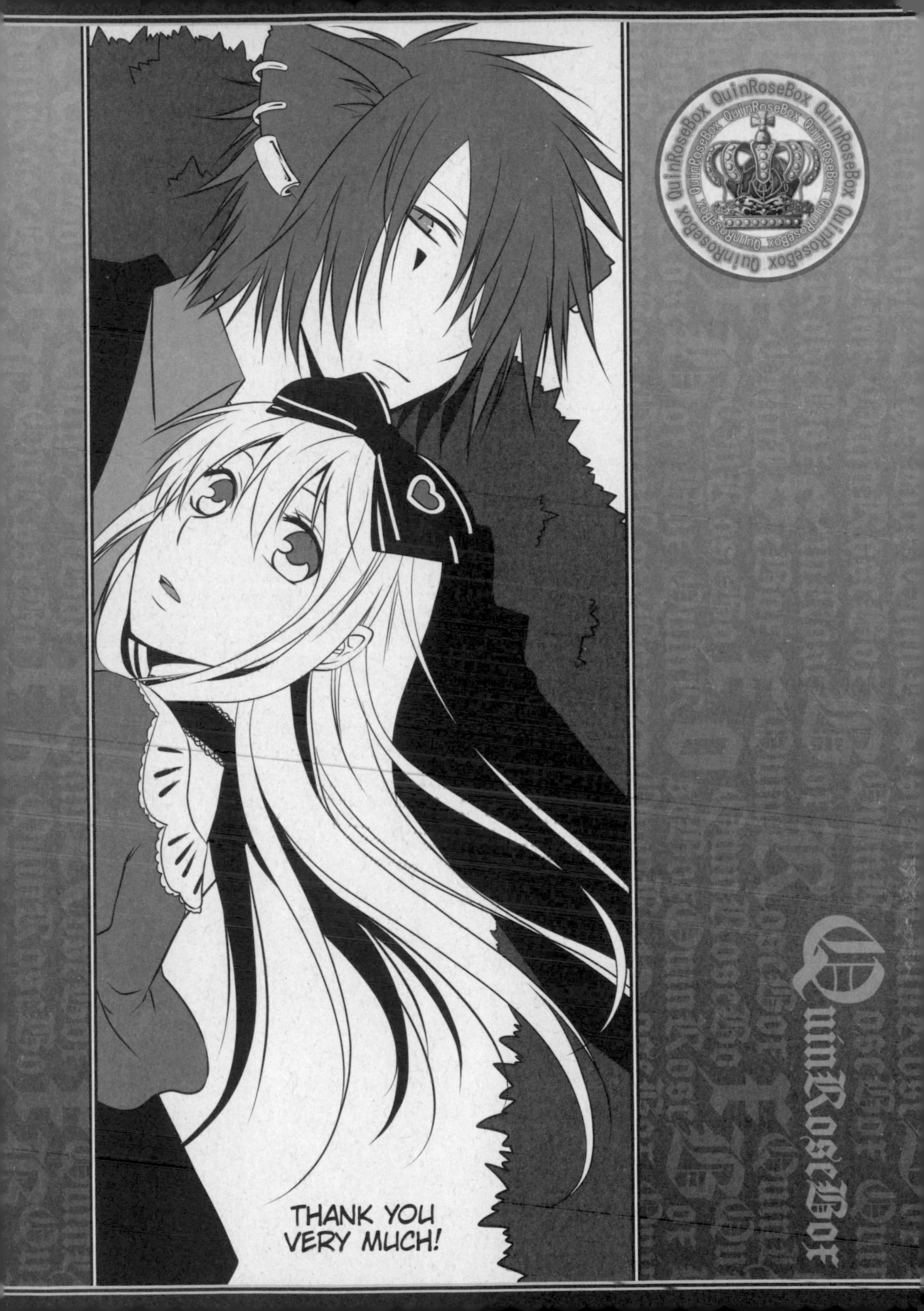
THANK YOU VERY MUCH!

CHESHIRE CAT WALTZ VOL. 3 - POST-MORTEM

*NEAR THE END OF THE SIDE STORY.

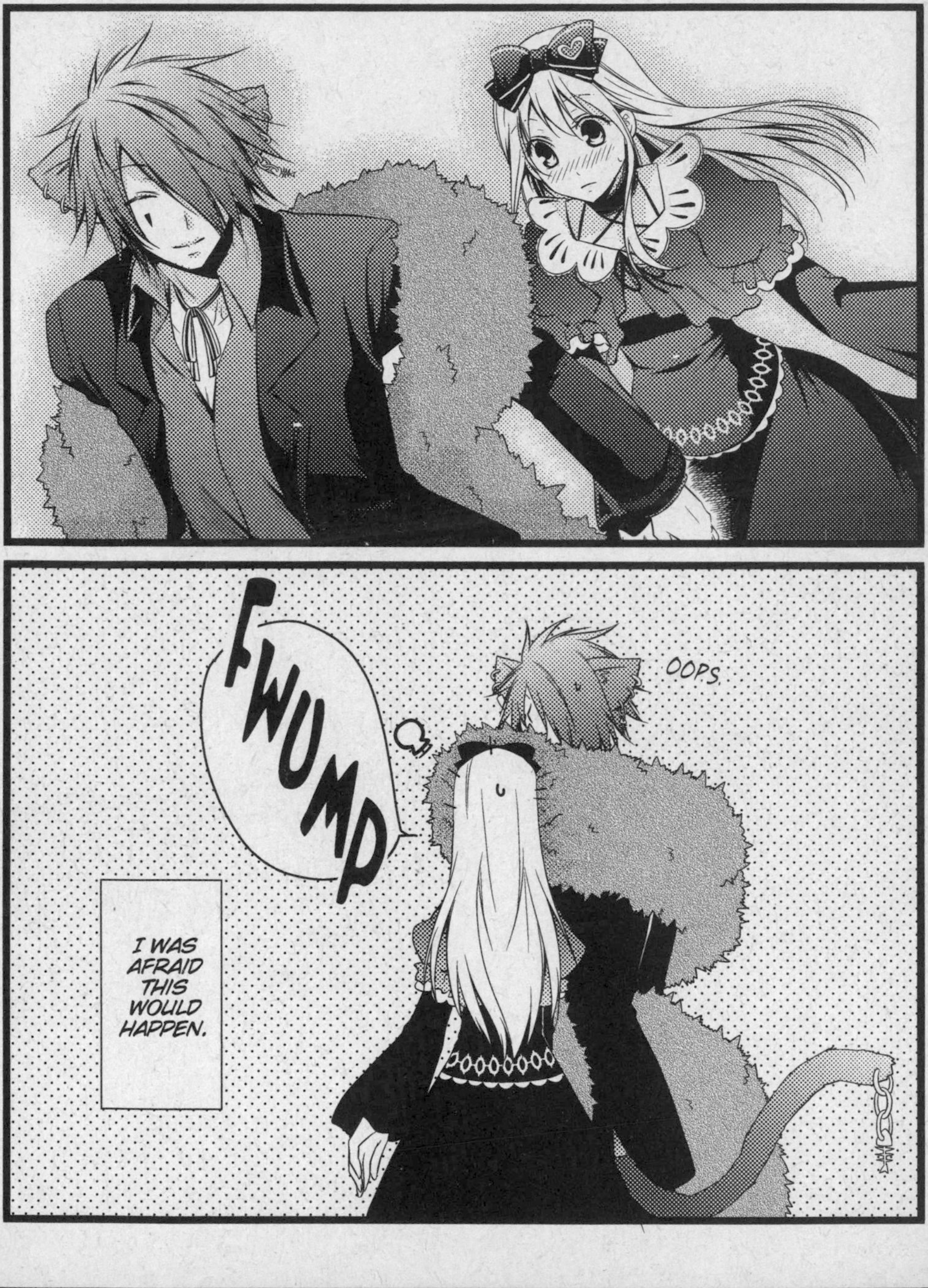
OOPS.
FWUMP
I WAS AFRAID THIS WOULD HAPPEN.

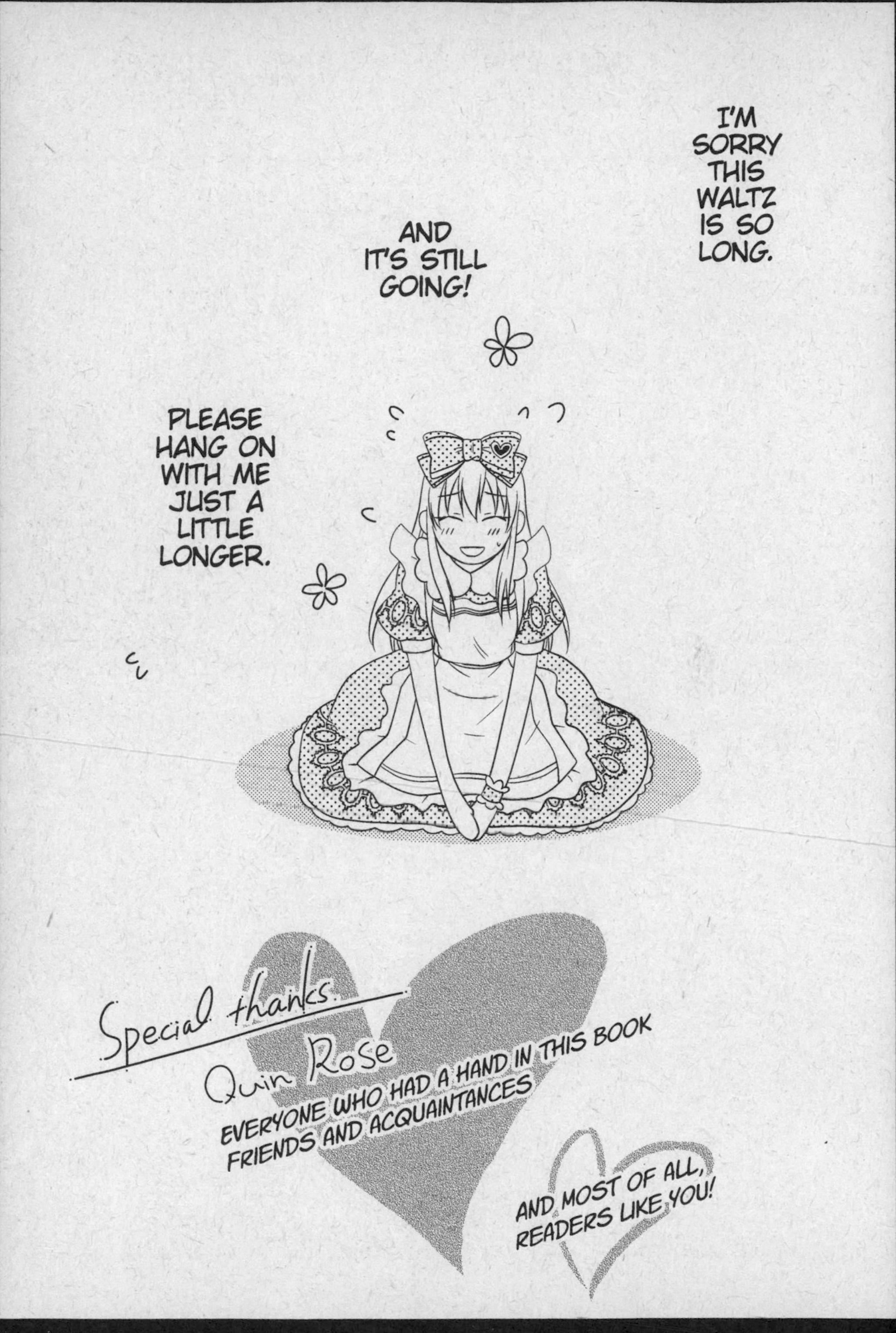
I'M SORRY THIS WALTZ IS SO LONG.
AND IT'S STILL GOING!
PLEASE HANG ON WITH ME JUST A LITTLE LONGER.
Special thanks.
Quin Rose
EVERYONE WHO HAD A HAND IN THIS BOOK
FRIENDS AND ACQUAINTANCES
AND MOST OF ALL, READERS LIKE YOU!

COMING SOON

FEBRUARY 2013

Alice in the Country of Joker:
Circus and Liar's Game Vol. 1

MARCH 2013

Alice in the Country of Clover:
Cheshire Cat Waltz Vol. 4

APRIL 2013

Crimson Empire Vol. 1

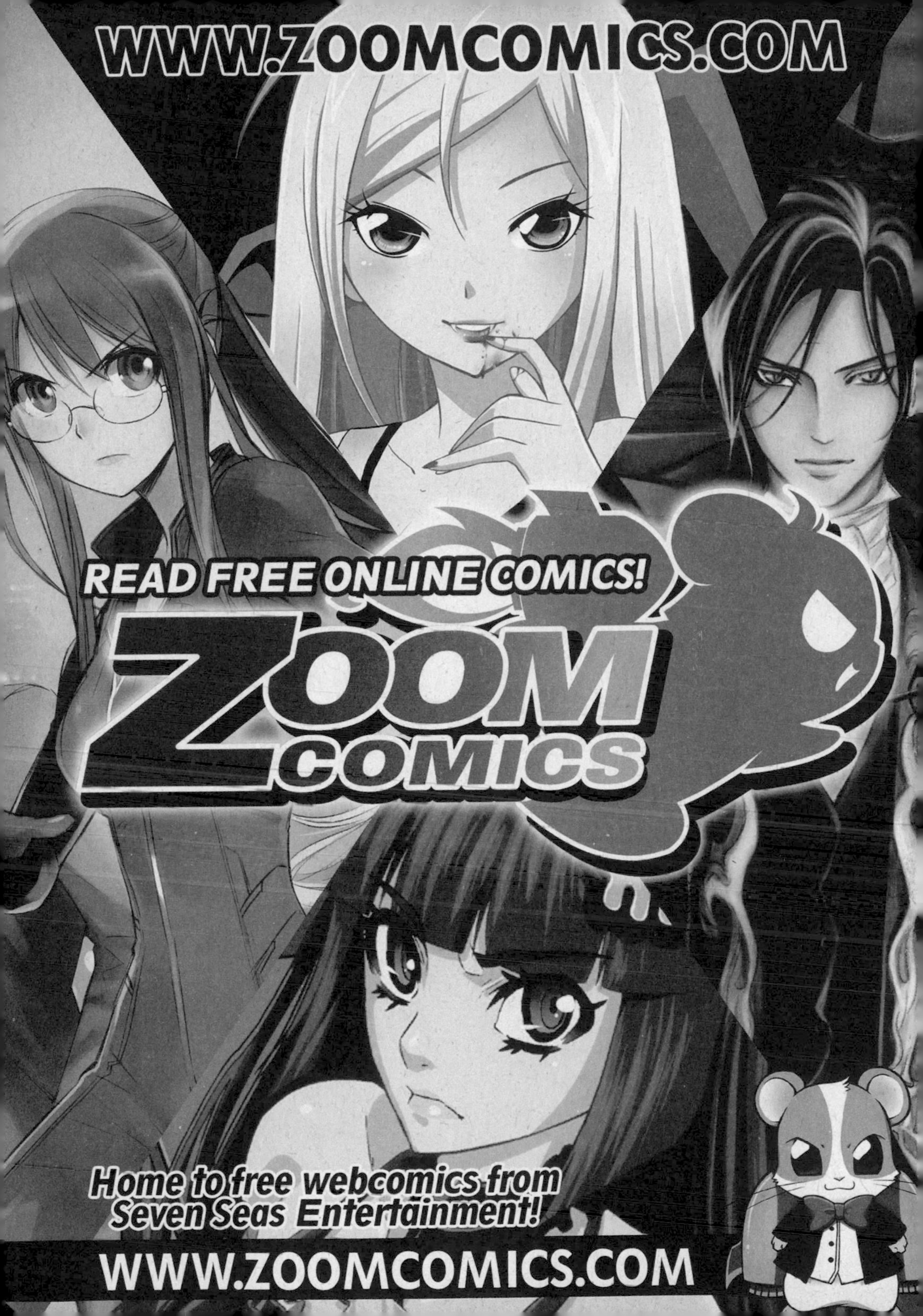
WWW.ZOOMCOMICS.COM
READ FREE ONLINE COMICS!
ZOOM COMICS
Home to free webcomics from Seven Seas Entertainment!
WWW.ZOOMCOMICS.COM

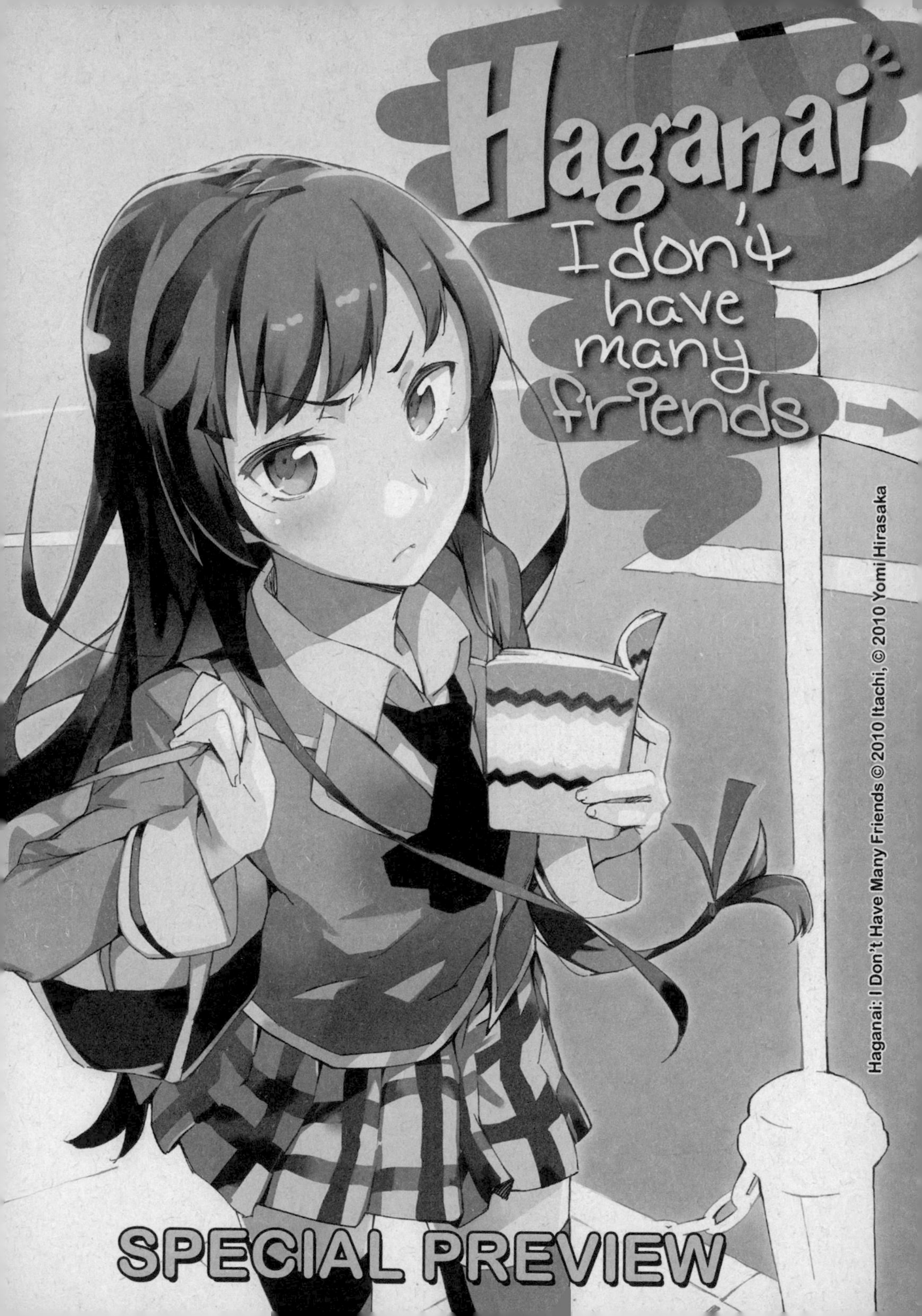
Haganai
I don't have many friends
SPECIAL PREVIEW

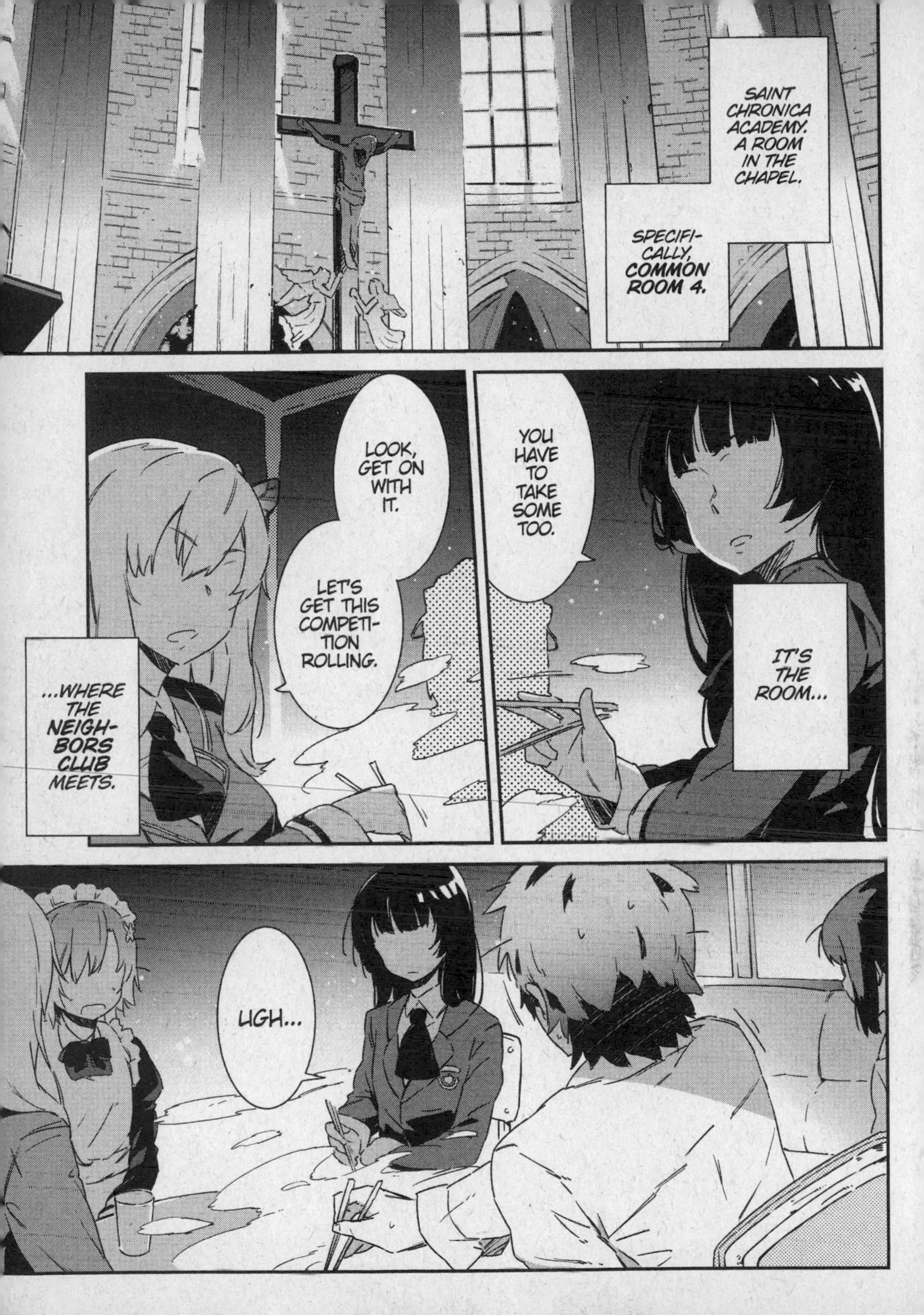
SAINT CHRONICA ACADEMY. A ROOM IN THE CHAPEL.
SPECIFI-CALLY, COMMON ROOM 4.
YOU HAVE TO TAKE SOME TOO.
IT'S THE ROOM...
LOOK, GET ON WITH IT.
LET'S GET THIS COMPETI-TION ROLLING.
...WHERE THE NEIGH-BORS CLUB MEETS.
UGH...

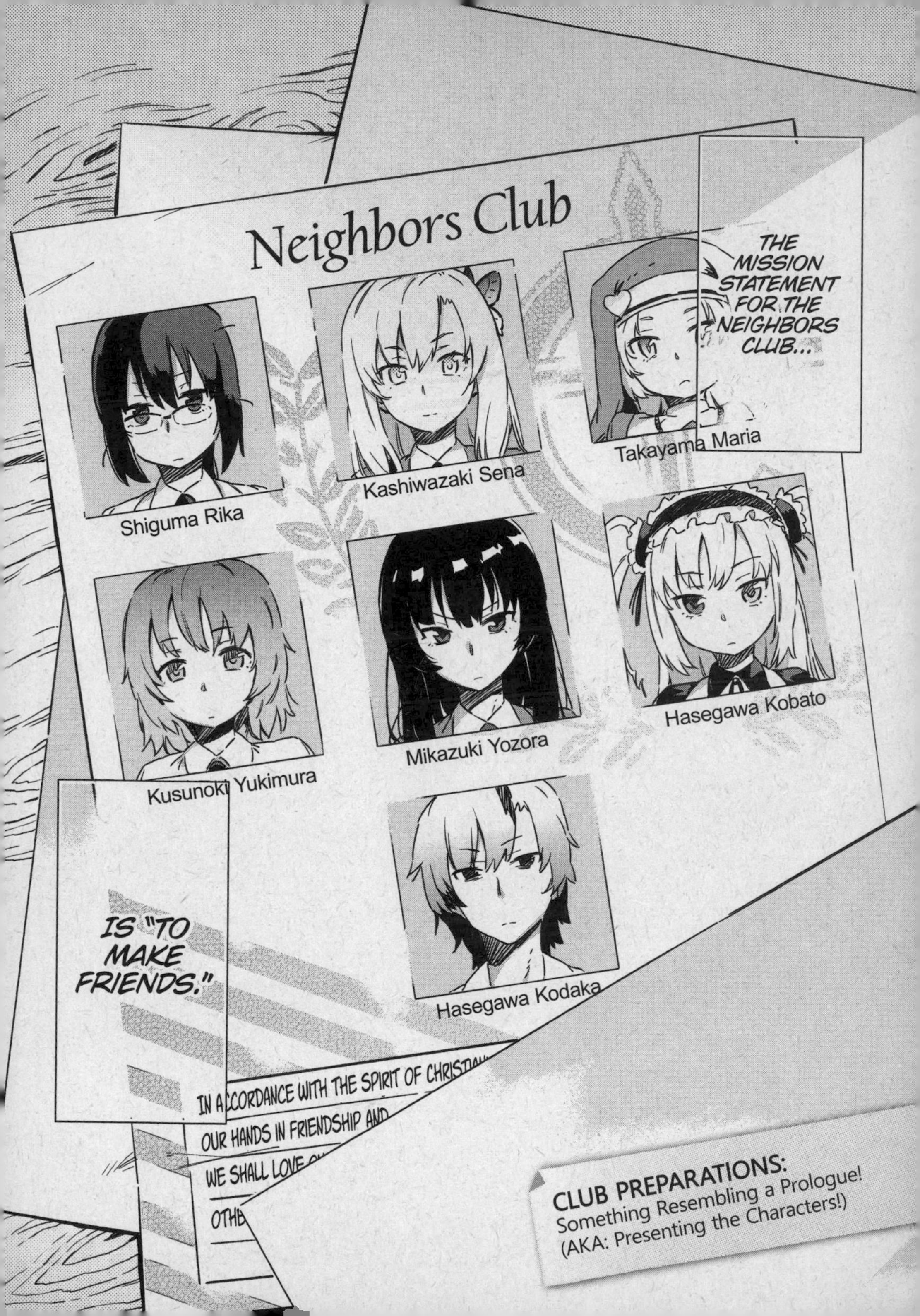
Neighbors Club
THE MISSION STATEMENT FOR THE NEIGHBORS CLUB...
Takayama Maria
Kashiwazaki Sena
Shiguma Rika
Hasegawa Kobato
Mikazuki Yozora
Kusunoki Yukimura
Hasegawa Kodaka
IS "TO MAKE FRIENDS."
IN ACCORDANCE WITH THE SPIRIT OF CHRISTIA
OUR HANDS IN FRIENDSHIP AND
WE SHALL LOVE O
OTHE
CLUB PREPARATIONS:
Something Resembling a Prologue!
(AKA: Presenting the Characters!)

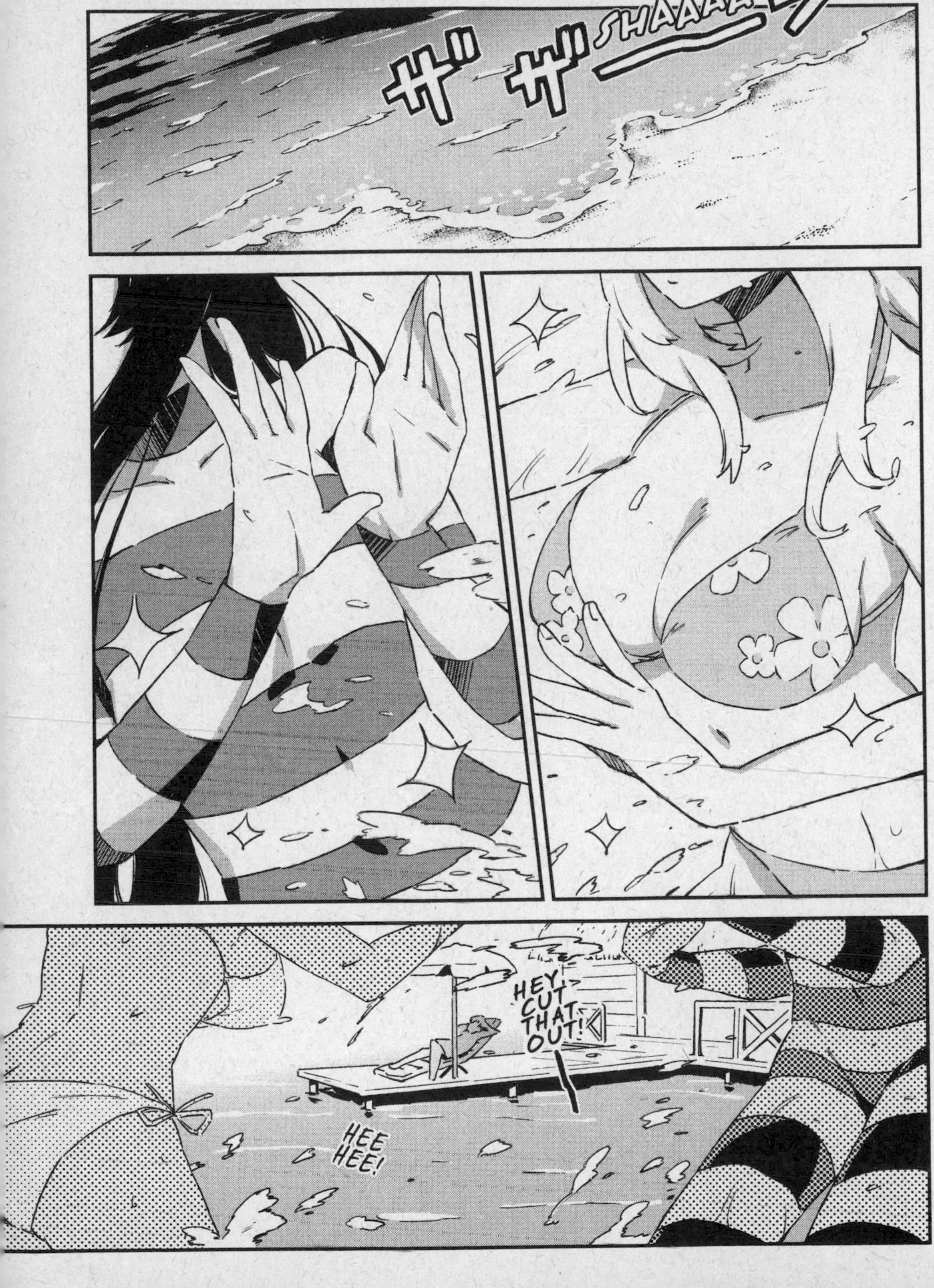
ザザ
SHAAAA—!
HEY CUT THAT OUT!
HEE HEE!

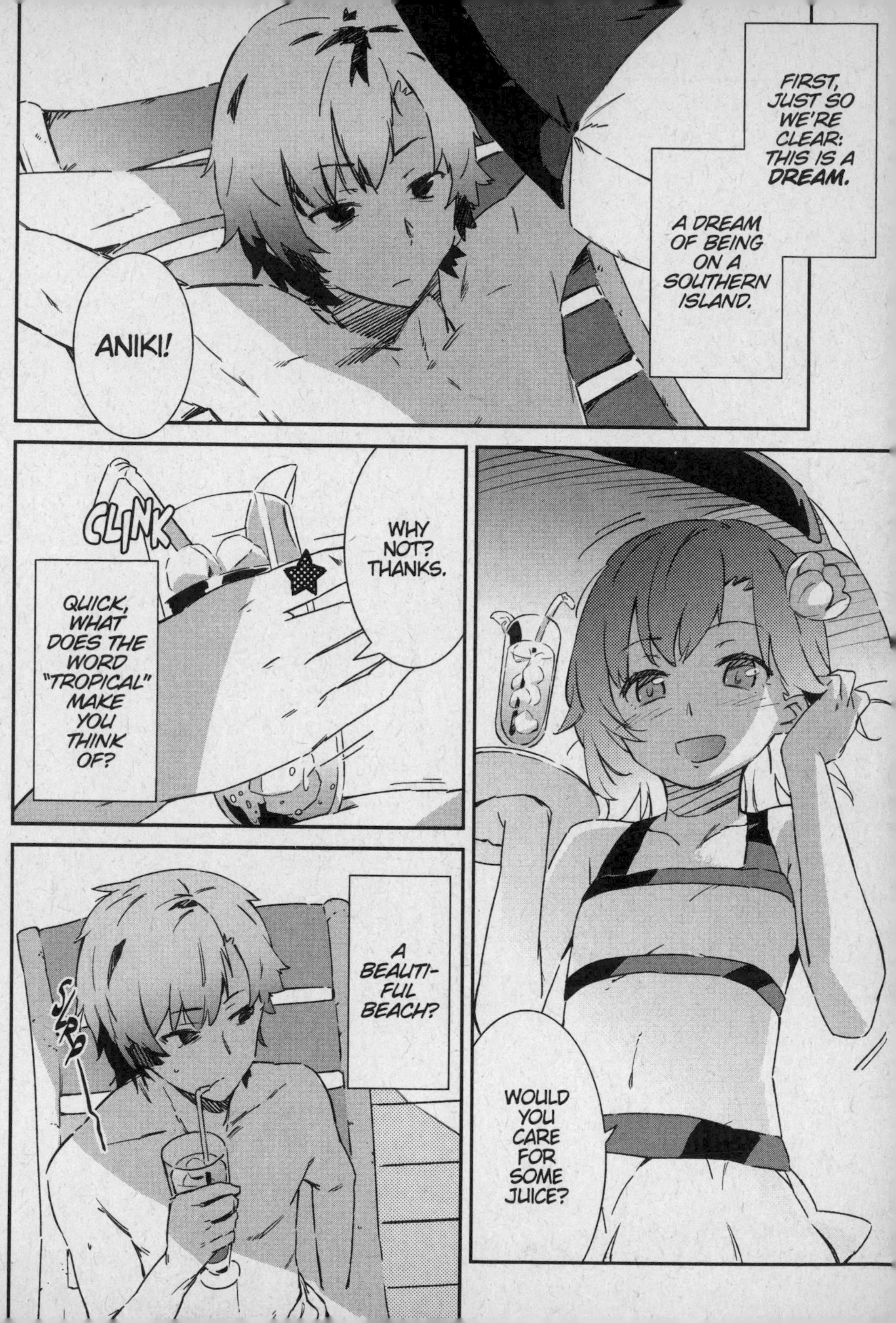
FIRST, JUST SO WE'RE CLEAR: THIS IS A **DREAM.**
A DREAM OF BEING ON A SOUTHERN ISLAND.
ANIKI!
WOULD YOU CARE FOR SOME JUICE?
WHY NOT? THANKS.
CLINK
QUICK, WHAT DOES THE WORD "TROPICAL" MAKE YOU THINK OF?
A BEAUTIFUL BEACH?
SLRP

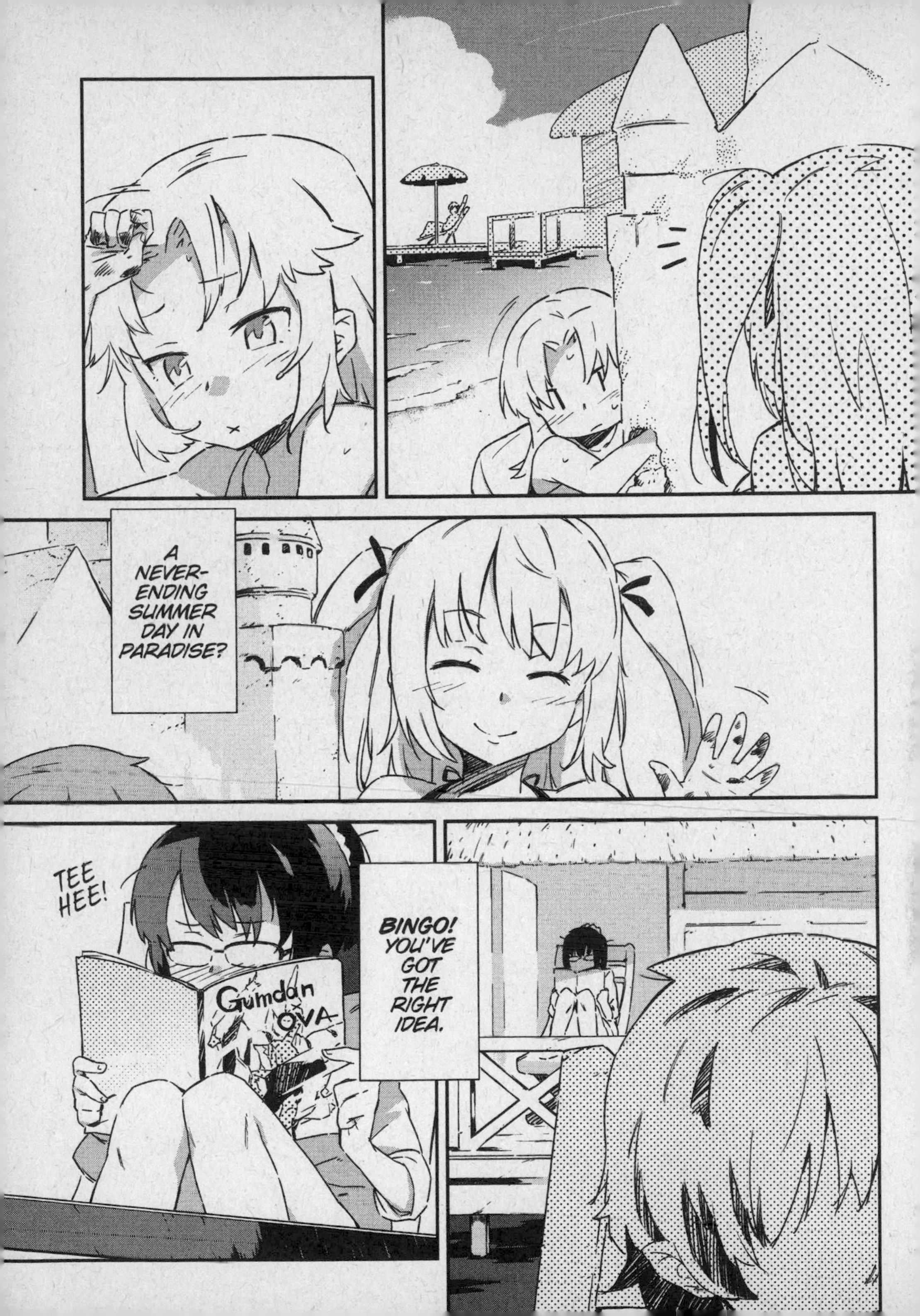
A NEVER-ENDING SUMMER DAY IN PARADISE?
BINGO! YOU'VE GOT THE RIGHT IDEA.
TEE HEE!
Gumdan OVA

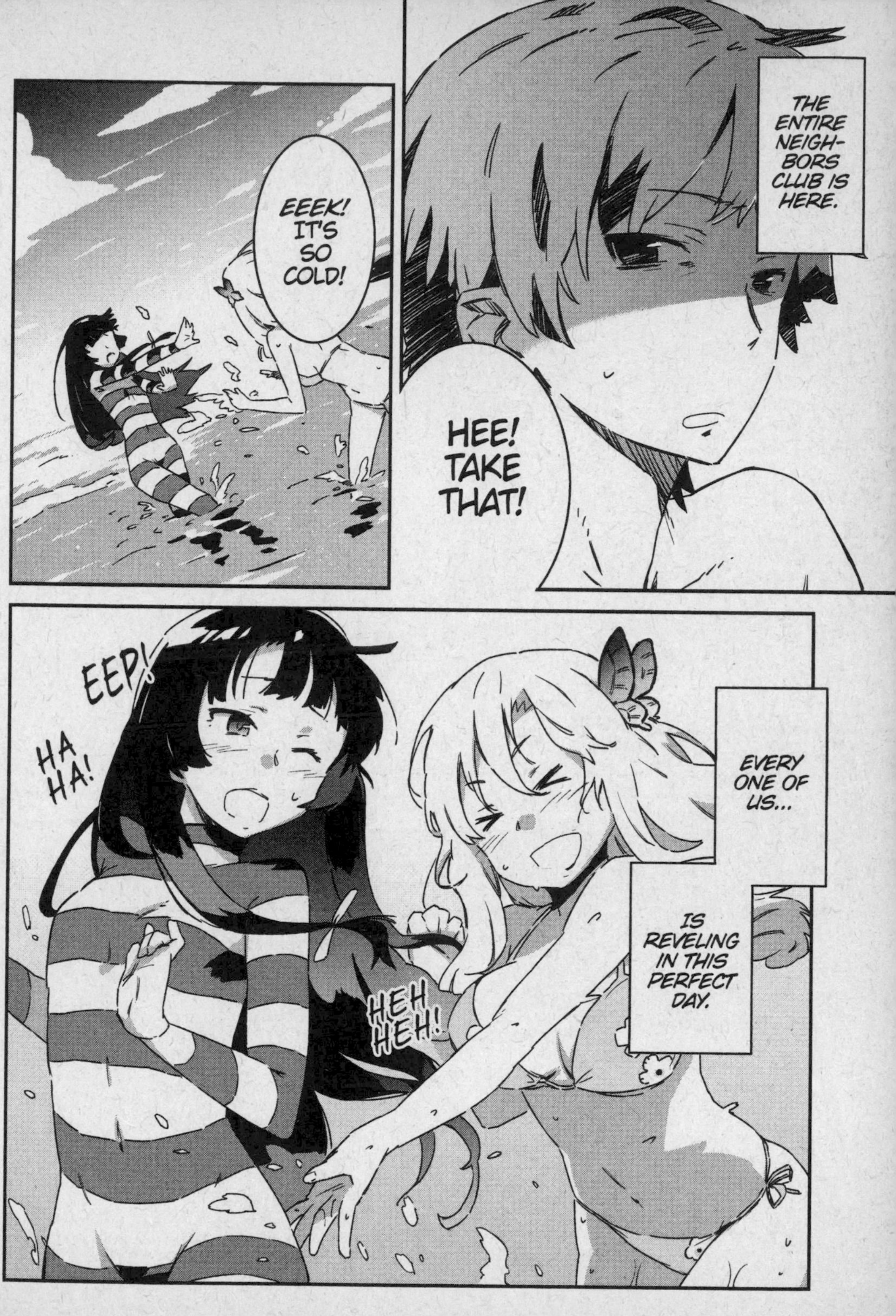
THE ENTIRE NEIGHBORS CLUB IS HERE.
HEE! TAKE THAT!
EEEK! IT'S SO COLD!
EVERY ONE OF US...
IS REVELING IN THIS PERFECT DAY.
EEP!
HA HA!
HEH HEH!

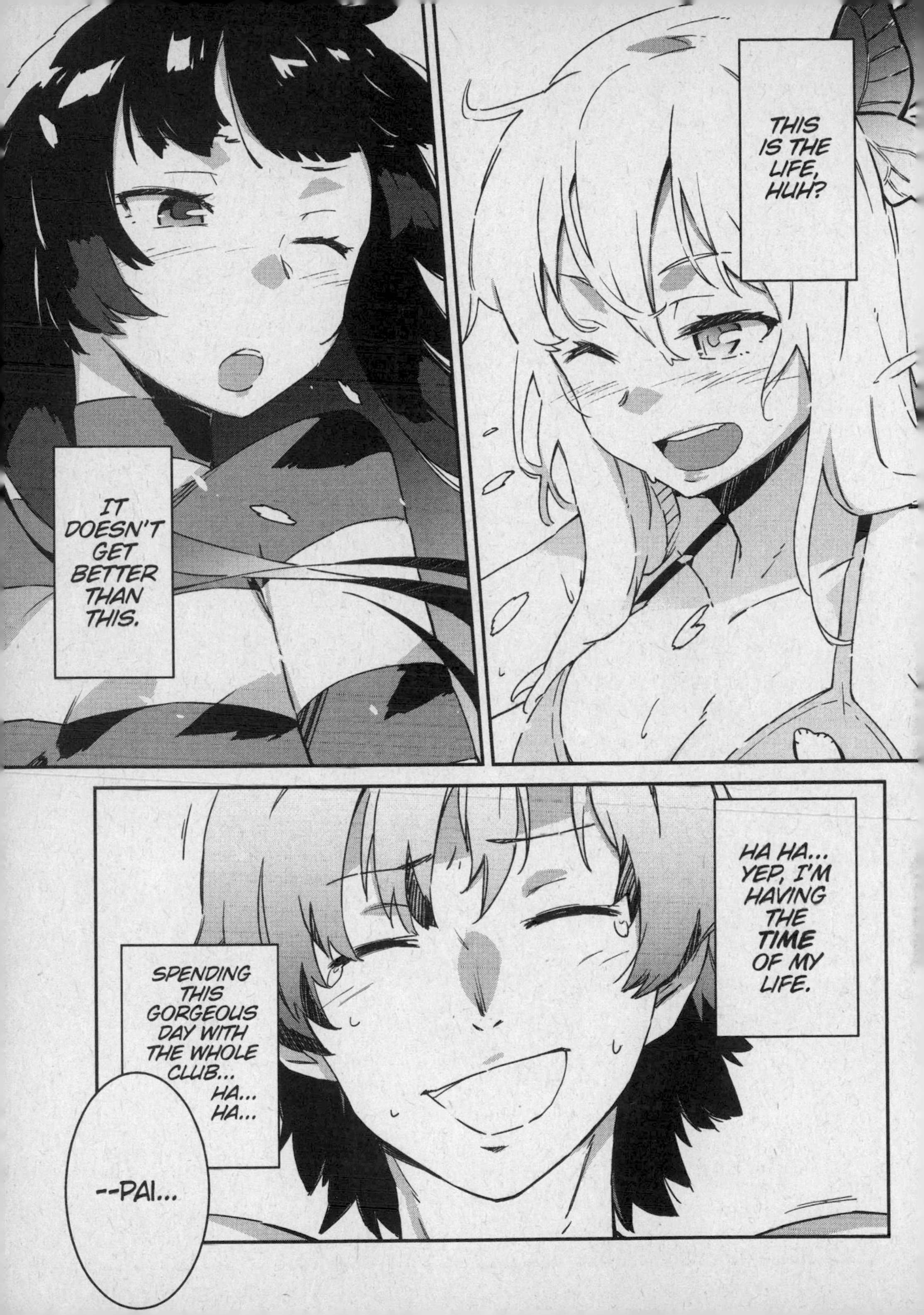
THIS IS THE LIFE, HUH?
IT DOESN'T GET BETTER THAN THIS.
HA HA... YEP, I'M HAVING THE TIME OF MY LIFE.
SPENDING THIS GORGEOUS DAY WITH THE WHOLE CLUB... HA... HA...
--PAI...

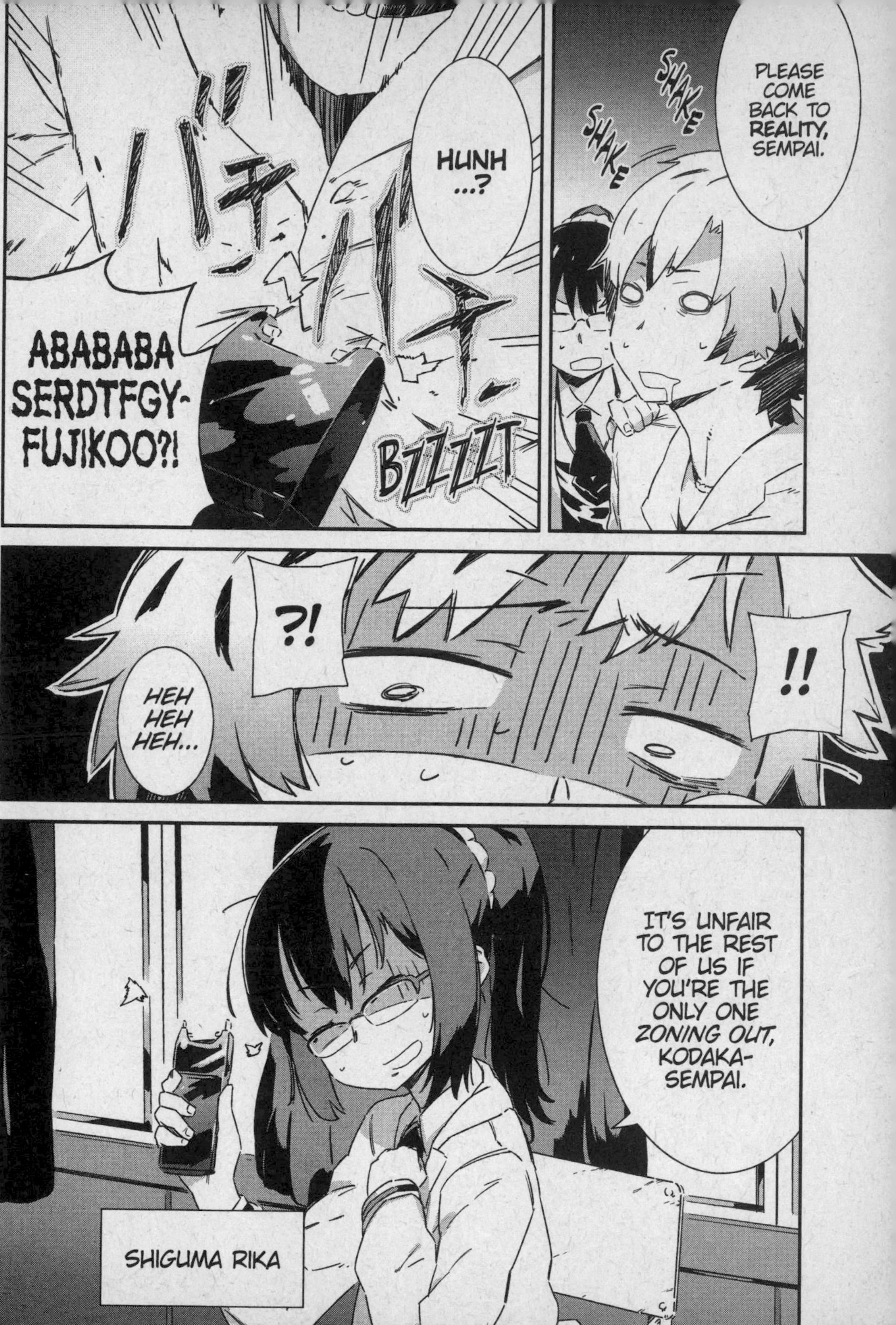
SHAKE
SHAKE
PLEASE COME BACK TO REALITY, SEMPAI.
HUNH ...?
ABABABA SERDTFGY-FUJIKOO?!
BZZZZT
!!
?!
HEH HEH HEH...
IT'S UNFAIR TO THE REST OF US IF YOU'RE THE ONLY ONE ZONING OUT, KODAKA-SEMPAI.
SHIGUMA RIKA

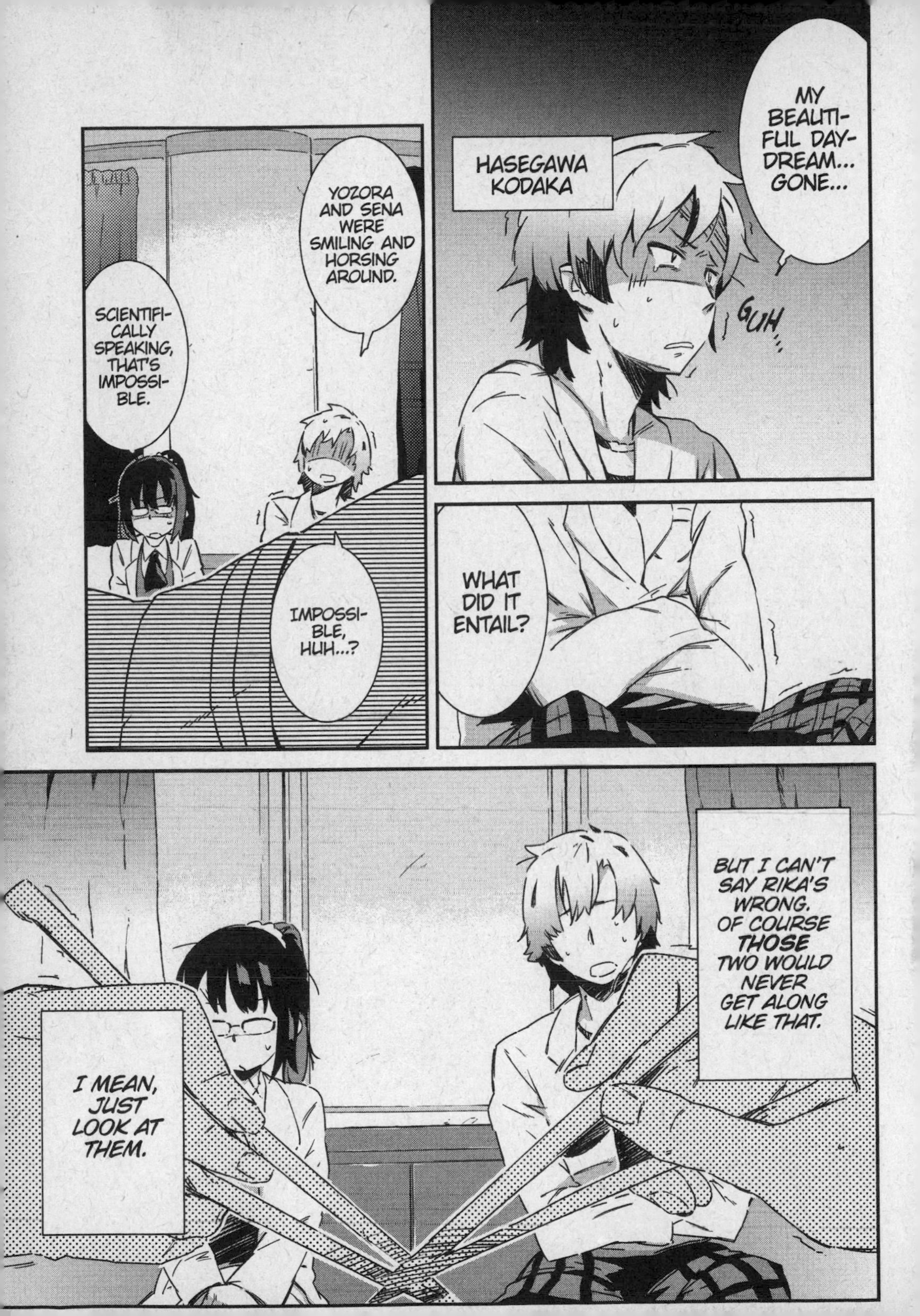
MY BEAUTIFUL DAYDREAM... GONE...
HASEGAWA KODAKA
GUH...
WHAT DID IT ENTAIL?
YOZORA AND SENA WERE SMILING AND HORSING AROUND.
SCIENTIFICALLY SPEAKING, THAT'S IMPOSSIBLE.
IMPOSSIBLE, HUH...?
BUT I CAN'T SAY RIKA'S WRONG. OF COURSE THOSE TWO WOULD NEVER GET ALONG LIKE THAT.
I MEAN, JUST LOOK AT THEM.

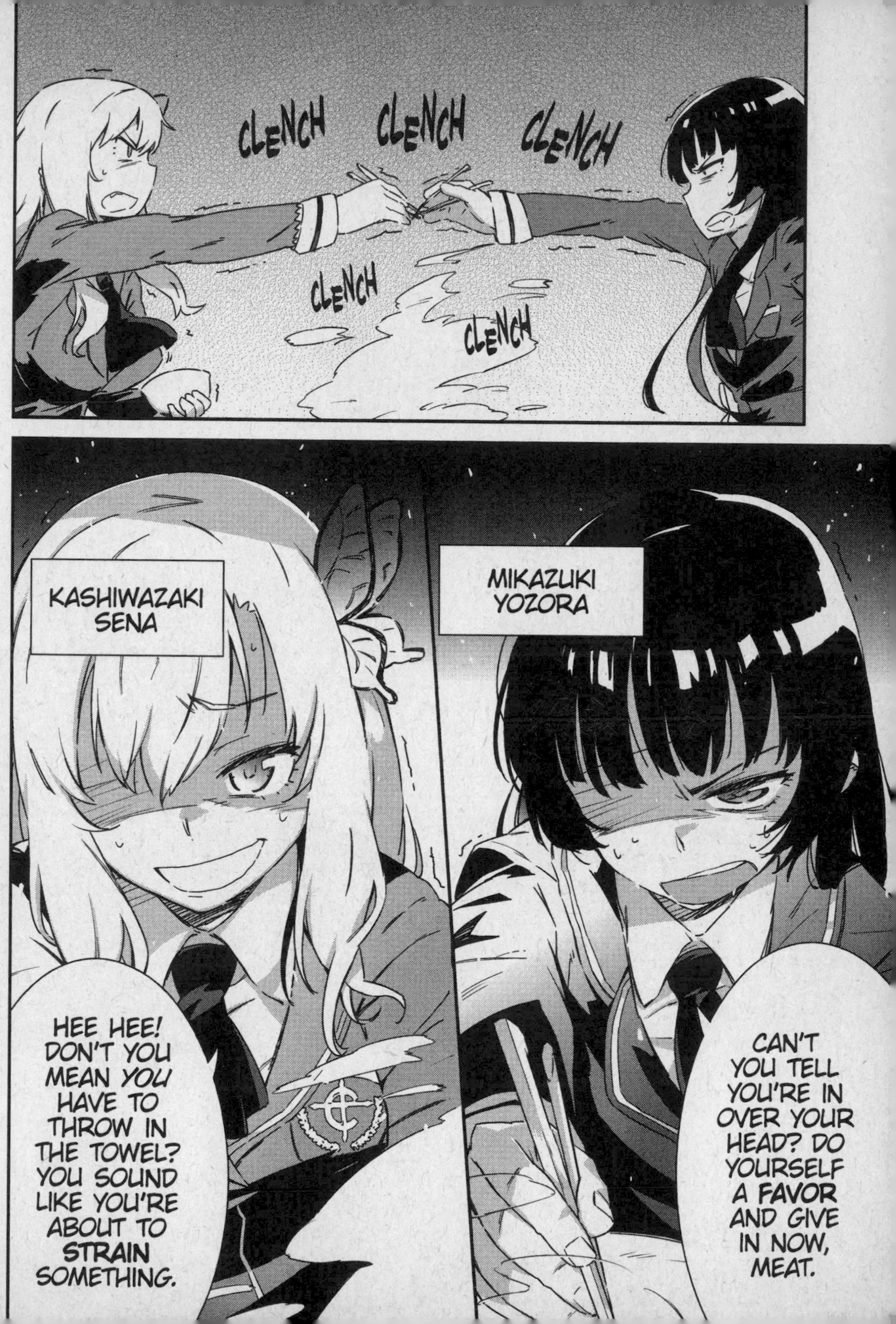
CLENCH
CLENCH
CLENCH
CLENCH
CLENCH
MIKAZUKI YOZORA
CAN'T YOU TELL YOU'RE IN OVER YOUR HEAD? DO YOURSELF A **FAVOR** AND GIVE IN NOW, MEAT.
KASHIWAZAKI SENA
HEE HEE! DON'T YOU MEAN *YOU* HAVE TO THROW IN THE TOWEL? YOU SOUND LIKE YOU'RE ABOUT TO **STRAIN** SOMETHING.

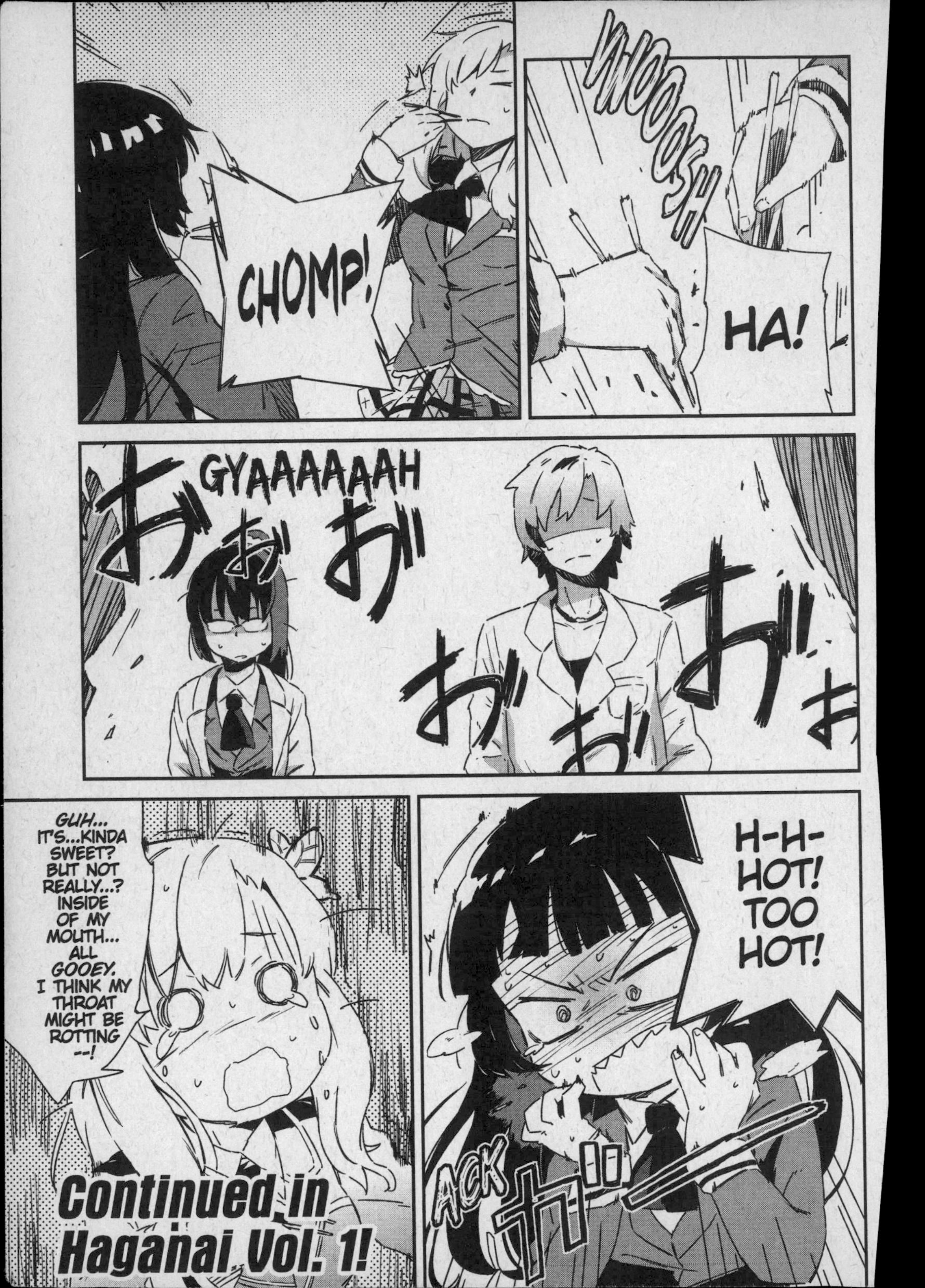
WHOOOSH
HA!
CHOMP!
GYAAAAAAH
H-H-HOT! TOO HOT!
ACK
GUH... IT'S...KINDA SWEET? BUT NOT REALLY...? INSIDE OF MY MOUTH... ALL GOOEY. I THINK MY THROAT MIGHT BE ROTTING--!
Continued in Haganai Vol. 1!